Company Directors' Responsibilities to Creditors

Company directors have certain responsibilities to creditors of their companies. In particular, they should avoid fraudulent and wrongful trading and should consider, as part of their duties to their companies, the interests of creditors when their companies might be, or are, in financial difficulty.

The work is precipitated by the lack of coherence in the consideration of wrongful trading and the recent delivery of important cases on fraudulent trading. Also, this timely work is the first to examine comprehensively directors' responsibilities to creditors in times of financial strife, as well as addressing when these responsibilities arise, and what directors should have to do to ensure that they comply with their obligations.

Keay explores the relevant issues from doctrinal, normative and comparative perspectives, seeking to address the question as to when directors are liable for wrongful trading, fraudulent trading or breach of their duties to creditors and whether directors should be held responsible for wrongful trading and failing to consider the interests of creditors. Besides the relevant UK legislation and case law, legislation and case law from several Commonwealth countries, and especially Australia and Canada, as well as Ireland and the United States are examined and compared, and reforms which take into account the aims and rationale of the relevant legislation as well as creditors' interests are proposed and assessed. Importantly, as far as directors' duties to creditors are concerned, new approaches for courts which would make the nature of the responsibility and its timing more precise are suggested.

Andrew Keay is Professor of Corporate and Commercial Law in the School of Law's Centre for Business Law and Practice at the University of Leeds, where he specialises in teaching Corporate Law and Insolvency Law. He is the Commonwealth editor of *Gore Browne on Companies* and he is a member of the editorial boards of several journals. He has authored a number of books, including *McPherson's Law of Company Liquidation*, 2001, *Insolvency Law: Corporate and Personal*, 2003, *Insolvency Legislation: Annotations and Commentary*, 2005 (the latter two co-authored).

Company Directors' Responsibilities to Creditors

Andrew Keay

Routledge·Cavendish
Taylor & Francis Group
LONDON AND NEW YORK

First published 2007
by Routledge-Cavendish
2 Park Square, Milton Park, Abingdon, Oxon OX14 4RN, UK

Simultaneously published in the USA and Canada
by Routledge-Cavendish
270 Madison Ave, New York, NY 10016

*Routledge-Cavendish is an imprint of the Taylor & Francis Group, an
informa business*

© 2007 Andrew Keay

Typeset in Times by
RefineCatch Limited, Bungay, Suffolk
Printed and bound in Great Britain by
TJ International, Padstow, Cornwall

British Library Cataloguing in Publication Data
A catalogue record for this book is available from the British Library

Library of Congress Cataloging in Publication Data
Keay, Andrew R.
   Company directors' responsibilities to creditors / Andrew Keay.
     p. cm.
   Includes index.
   ISBN 1–84568–008–1 (pbk.)—ISBN 1–84568–075–8 (hardback)
1. Directors of Corporations—Legal status, laws, etc.—United
States. 2. Corporations—Finance—Law and legislation—United
States. 3. Securities fraud—United States. 4. Debtor and creditor—
United States.   I. Title.
   KF1423.K43 2006
   346.73′06642—dc22

                                    2006019776

ISBN 10: 1–84568–008–1 (pbk)
ISBN 10: 1–84568–075–8 (hbk)

ISBN 13: 978–1–84568–008–4 (pbk)
ISBN 13: 978–1–84568–075–6 (hbk)

Contents

vi *Contents*

PART D
A duty to consider the interests of creditors 151

x   *Contents*

Preface

The focus of the corporate governance debate, certainly in the UK, has been on the accountability of directors to shareholders and employees. But other persons involved in companies must not be forgotten. This book concerns itself with directors and the interests of creditors. If one wanted to be very technical, one could say that there are, indirectly, a number of responsibilities that directors of companies owe to their companies' creditors. I mention some of these in Chapter 1. Most of them are clear and warrant little attention. But the focus of this book is on those responsibilities that are not precise and which are worthy of not only a doctrinal examination, but also a theoretical examination. Essentially, the book addresses three responsibilities that directors have to their companies' creditors. These are: not to engage in fraudulent trading; not to engage in wrongful trading; and a duty to consider the interests of the creditors in certain circumstances.

The doctrinal aspects of these responsibilities are not without a significant lack of clarity. But also, there is some substantial theoretical debate concerning whether these responsibilities should in fact be imposed on directors at all. First, the book endeavours to provide an exposition of the law relating to these responsibilities as well as engaging in some analysis of problem issues and making suggestions for reform. Second, the book seeks to identify the theoretical arguments that may be propounded in favour and against the existence of these responsibilities. Third, the book includes some comparative discussion, using, primarily, common law jurisdictions as relevant comparators. Because of limits on length I have not been able to engage in detailed comparative discussions, but nevertheless it might be that academics and lawyers in other jurisdictions, particularly Ireland, Australia, the United States, Canada and New Zealand, might find aspects of the book to be interesting and also relevant to issues pertaining to their respective jurisdictions.

It is hoped that the work provides a rounded examination of the responsibilities owed by directors. I have sought to discuss the doctrinal and theoretical issues in separate parts of the book for ease of exposition and to make sure that the reader understands and can distinguish what the law appears to be at the present and what it arguably should be from a normative perspective. In places it is difficult (and inappropriate) to separate doctrinal and theoretical discussion, and there will, on occasions, be overlaps. I have endeavoured to limit repetition of arguments. The comparative discussion is scattered throughout the book and included in appropriate places.

I wish to pay tribute to some interesting and incisive works written in the late 1980s and early 1990s by several writers that have been particularly helpful to me in developing, as well as challenging, some of my thinking on directors' duties to creditors contained in this book. In particular I acknowledge the writings of Len Sealy and Vanessa Finch, which have been especially thought-provoking. The relevant works of these commentators and others who have written important contributions are cited in several chapters and in particular in Chapters 11–13.

I wish to thank a number of people and organisations. First, the School of Law at the University of Leeds for granting me some study leave to permit me to work on this book. Second, I thank the Arts and Humanities Research Council (AHRC) for awarding me a Research Leave Grant that also enabled me to complete the research for, and the writing of, this book. I should also acknowledge the work of those anonymous persons who acted as reviewers for the AHRC, for such work often goes unnoticed and without appropriate recognition. Without the support of the School of Law and the AHRC this book would have taken much longer to see light of day.

Third, I am also thankful for helpful and provocative comments provided by anonymous referees relating to the following articles that I have had published: 'The director's duty to take into account the interests of company creditors: when is it triggered?' (2001) 25 *Melbourne University Law Review* 315; 'Directors' duties to creditors: contractarian concerns relating to efficiency and over-protection of creditors' (2003) 66 MLR 665; 'A theoretical analysis of the director's duty to consider creditor interests: the Progressive School's approach' (2004) 4 *Journal of Corporate Law Studies* 87; and 'Formulating a framework for directors' duties to creditors: an entity maximisation approach' (2005) 64 *Cambridge Law Journal* 614. Large parts of these articles, with some updated thinking on my part, are included in the book. Of course, I alone am responsible for any errors.

Fourth, I thank Michael Murray, my co-author in the article, 'Making company directors liable: a comparative analysis of wrongful trading in the United Kingdom and insolvent trading in Australia' (2005) 14 *International Insolvency Review* 27, for allowing me to draw upon material in that article. Fifth, I thank Louis Doyle, my co-author on the book, *Insolvency Legislation: Annotations and Commentary*, for allowing me to use material written in relation to ss 213, 214 and 215 and included in that book. Sixth, I am most thankful to several publishers for allowing me to draw upon material that I have had published by them in articles and books. I acknowledge that I use, with the permission of the named publishers, material from the following:

'Fraudulent trading: the intent to defraud element' (2006) 35 *Common Law World Review* 121–134 (Vathek Publishing);

Insolvency Legislation: Annotations and Commentary, 2005 (Jordan Publishing);

'Making company directors liable: a comparative analysis of wrongful trading in the United Kingdom and insolvent trading in Australia' (2005) 14 *International Insolvency Review* 27 (John Wiley and Sons);

'Do recent Canadian developments require a re-think in the United Kingdom on the issue of directors' duties to consider creditor interests?' (2005) 18 *Insolvency Intelligence* 65–68 (Sweet & Maxwell);

'Wrongful trading and the liability of company directors: a theoretical perspective' (2005) 25 *Legal Studies* 431 (Society of Legal Scholars);

'Formulating a framework for directors' duties to creditors: an entity maximisation approach' (2005) 64 *Cambridge Law Journal* 614 (Cambridge University Press);

'A theoretical analysis of the director's duty to consider creditor interests: the Progressive School's approach' (2004) 4 *Journal of Corporate Law Studies* 307 (Hart Publishing);

'Another way of skinning the cat: enforcing directors' duties to creditors' (2004) 17 *Insolvency Intelligence* 1 (Sweet & Maxwell);

'Directors' duties to creditors: contractarian concerns relating to efficiency and over-protection of creditors' (2003) 66 *Modern Law Review* 665 (Blackwell Publishing);

'Directors taking into account creditor interests' (2003) 24 *Company Lawyer* 300 (Sweet & Maxwell);

'The duty of directors to take into account creditors' interests: has it any role to play?' [2002] *Journal of Business Law* 379 (Sweet & Maxwell);

'The director's duty to take into account the interests of company creditors: when is it triggered?' (2001) 25 *Melbourne University Law Review* 315 (Melbourne University Law Review Association Inc 2001);

McPherson's Law of Company Liquidation, 2001, parts of Chapters 11 and 16 (Sweet & Maxwell).

Seventh, I would like to thank Daniel Attenborough, my research assistant in the School of Law at the University of Leeds, for his assistance in researching comparative aspects of material relating to fraudulent and wrongful trading.

Finally, as always, I thank my wife, Rhonda, for her patience and support at all times, but particularly when it comes to my research and writing.

I have endeavoured to state the law as it is available to me as at 1 April 2006 although I have made some mention of changes to the Company Law Reform Bill 2005 effected after that date.

Andrew Keay
Leeds

Table of Cases

Table of Legislation

Table of Statutory Instruments

Table of International Legislation

Part A
Introduction

1 Background to directors' responsibilities

Introduction

Directors of companies occupy important and critical roles in the lives and affairs of their companies. In fulfilling this function, multifarious responsibilities are imposed on directors. It is not intended to discuss the work and roles of directors, as this is accomplished in many standard texts; what this book seeks to do is to examine a specific aspect of the role of directors, namely their responsibilities to the creditors of their companies. We might talk, in a loose sense, of duties to creditors, but the word, 'duty' is, as Professor Len Sealy has pointed out, a slippery word.[1] It is trite law that directors owe duties to their companies as a whole, and these include duties that are known as 'fiduciary duties'. These are duties of loyalty and good faith (*Bristol and West Building Society v Mothew* [1998] 1 Ch 1; [1996] 4 All ER 698, CA), and they are not generally owed to any individual members of the company, or other persons, and this includes creditors (*Percival v Wright* [1902] 2 Ch 421; *Multinational Gas and Petrochemical Co v Multinational Gas and Petrochemical Services Ltd* [1983] Ch 258; *Peskin v Anderson* [2000] BCC 1110 (and affirmed on appeal by the Court of Appeal [2001] BCC 874)).[2] The legislature has provided that directors must do certain things during their tenure, and some of these obligations can, in general terms, be regarded as being owed to creditors, either directly or indirectly. I will mention some of these shortly, but it is important at this point to state that the focus of the book is on legislation and case law that has imposed responsibilities on directors as far as creditors of their companies are concerned. The responsibilities that we are talking about are not precise, and, as a consequence, the case law that has developed tends

---

1   Sealy, L S, 'Directors' wider responsibilities – problems conceptual practical and procedural' (1987) 13 *Monash University Law Review* 164 at 175.
2   For the USA see, for example, *Nuclear Corporation of America v Hale* 355 F Supp 193 (1973) (ND); *Revlon Inc v MacAndrews and Forbes Holdings Inc* 506 A 2d 173, 179 (1986) (DE). Also see the comments of the Jenkins Committee, Cmnd 1749 (1962), para 89.

to be indefinite in many aspects, causing uncertainty. The lack of certainty and precision are at the forefront of the issues that we will consider during the course of the book. Besides assessing the positive law on the responsibilities, the book also considers them from a normative perspective and asks whether directors should in fact be subject to such responsibilities.

It is important for us to identify the people about whom we are talking in this book. Two groups are critical, namely the directors and the creditors. The latter will be discussed in Chapter 2. We will now take a look at directors.

Directors – who are they?

General

As stated above, it is not intended to indulge in an examination of the roles and work of directors, save in limited terms, as standard company law texts provide discussions of these matters, but it is appropriate that we say some things about the directors. Principally, we are concerned about noting who they are in legal terms. Before doing so, we should note that the role of a director is an important one in commercial life, and it has been estimated that there are about two million persons acting as directors.[3]

While all companies are required by law to have at least one director (Companies Act 1985, s 282), what they actually do will depend on the constitution of the company. After saying that, the directors of the company are usually empowered to manage the business of their company,[4] but are, unless the articles of association state to the contrary, to follow any directions given by the members at a general meeting. In any event, common law, the Companies Act 1985, subordinate companies legislation and even some non-companies legislation dictate that directors fulfil certain duties and functions.

The Companies Act 1985 does not provide a detailed definition of who directors are, rather it provides, in s 741, that 'director' includes any person occupying the position of director, by whatever name called. So, it is not necessarily critical before a person is to be regarded as a director for the purposes of company law, that he or she is called 'a director'; what is critical is whether a person occupies the position of director. Unfortunately, there is no legislative interpretation of 'occupying the position of a director'.

In becoming directors, persons should realise the important duties that they owe, the extensive powers they wield and the substantial obligations

---

3   De Lacy, J, 'The concept of a company director: time for a new expanded and unified concept', [2006] JBL 267 at 268.
4   The Companies (Tables A-F) Regulations 1985, Table A, reg 70.

and responsibilities with which they must comply (*Re Westmid Packing Service Ltd* [1998] 2 All ER 124 at 130–131). A critical point is that notwithstanding the extent of a director's obligations, a director is not usually personally liable for the liabilities of his or her company because of the fact that a director's company is a separate legal entity (*Salomon v Salomon and Co Ltd* [1897] AC 22). However, as we will see in this book, directors might be made liable for company liabilities in certain circumstances.

In practice, directors can be divided into either executive directors or non-executive directors, although one does not find these designations mentioned in the Companies Act 1985. The former type of director are employed full-time by the company, and in some companies they might be appointed to specific posts, such as finance director or sales director. In contrast, non-executive directors are not engaged on a full-time basis. They are appointed to provide expertise and experience for the board and are usually paid annual retainers and expenses for giving their advice and attending board meetings. While non-executive directors are not required to engage in as much work as executives, the companies legislation does not distinguish between executive and non-executive directors when imposing duties and obligations on directors, although more will usually be expected of executive directors because of the nature of their full-time role. Effectively, there are three main kinds of director:

(a) *de jure*;
(b) *de facto*;
(c) shadow.

Before discussing these kinds of director, it should be pointed out that there are yet other kinds of director. First, companies might have nominee directors, who are *de jure* directors owing their appointment due to some third person, often a member or members of the company who hold a strong position in relation to company affairs. Second, an alternate director is a person who only acts temporarily on behalf of a director who has nominated the alternative to act for him or her on the board when the director is absent, perhaps because of illness or other pressing commitments. This arrangement must be permitted by the articles of association.

De jure *directors*

These directors are those who have been formally appointed by their consent, and according to the company's articles.[5] Such appointments will appear on the company records held by the Registrar of Companies.

---

5   For instance, see Table A, reg 78.

De facto *directors*

There is no legislative provision that defines the term, '*de facto* director', but it has been used for a long time (*Re Kaytech International plc* [1999] 2 BCLC 351, CA), and covers a person who is held out as a director by the company and claims to be one and acts as a director, while yet never being appointed as such according to law. As one would expect, usually the name of a person alleged to be a *de facto* director is not to be found on the company's records held by the Registrar of Companies. A *de facto* director is a person who assumes the functions and status of a director (*Re Kaytech International*). A person will only be held to be a *de facto* director if it can be established that he or she carried out director-like functions, and they are functions that could only be discharged by a director (*Secretary of State for Trade and Industry v Becker* [2003] 1 BCLC 555). There is no single decisive test that establishes whether a person is or is not a *de facto* director. Courts have to take into account all relevant factors, including :

(a) whether there was a holding out of the person as a director;
(b) whether the person used the title;
(c) whether the person had proper information on which to base decisions; and
(d) whether the person had to make major decisions (*Secretary of State for Trade and Industry v Tjolle* [1998] 1 BCLC 333, CA).

But none of these factors are necessarily decisive on their own (*Tjolle*), and even where a person uses the title of 'director' a court might not hold that the person is a *de facto* director (*Tjolle*). In the Australian case of *Deputy Commissioner of Taxation v Solomon* (2003) 199 ALR 325, two persons who had resigned as directors of a company were held to be *de facto* directors because they were involved in the main activity of the company, performed top-level management functions, acted for the company in important matters, and outsiders perceived that they were directors. Specifically, one of the persons had daily contact with directors, had the right to approve an asset sale, and was actively involved in the preparation of projections of cash flows. The other person was involved in negotiations with directors and third parties in relation to possible capital injections into the company, sought professional advice for the company and also was actively involved in the preparation of projections of cash flow.

  A person does not have to believe that he or she is a director, before being regarded as a *de facto* director (*Re Kaytech International*). Also, a person does not have to be actually referred to as a director, for according to s 741(1) a director includes anyone occupying the position of director 'by whatever name called'. Consequently, the law is concerned with the substantive nature of what the person does in the life of the company, rather than with how he or she is referred to. Interestingly, a person was not held to be a *de facto* director, despite the fact that the titles of 'deputy managing director' and 'chief executive' were used to describe her (*Tjolle*), but it has been said that the use of 'director' to refer to a person is significant in going towards a view that a person is a *de facto* director (*Secretary of State for Trade and Industry v Jones* [1999] BCC 336 at 349).

A person can be designated as a *de facto* director where the company has sought to appoint the person as a *de jure* director, but there is a defect in the appointment.

Shadow directors

While the definition in s 741(1) of the Companies Act 1985 only encompasses *de jure* and *de facto* directors, there is one other kind of director who is recognised by the law – the shadow director. This kind of director is recognised in s 741(2). It provides that a shadow director means 'a person in accordance with whose directions or instructions the directors of the company are accustomed to act'. The subsection then states that persons are not deemed to be shadow directors just because the directors act on their advice, in situations where the advice is given in a person's professional capacity. Ordinarily, this will exclude as shadow directors people such as lawyers, accountants and auditors. But, while professional advisers are not considered to be shadow directors, they might act in such a way that they cross the line and move from advising to instructing. A company could be held to be a shadow director (*Re a Company No 005009 of 1987* (1988) 4 BCC 424), but if a company is deemed to be a shadow director, it does not mean that the directors of that shadow will be regarded as shadows themselves, simply because they are members of the board of the shadow (*Re Hydrodan (Corby) Ltd* [1994] BCC 161 at 164).

In determining whether a person is a shadow director, courts will look at the communications between the alleged shadow and the board, and ascertain, from an objective perspective, whether those communications might be able to be regarded as directions or instructions. In this regard the outcome of the communication is the important element on which to focus (*Secretary of State for Trade and Industry v Deverell* [2001] Ch 340; [2000] 2 WLR 907; [2000] 2 BCLC 133, CA). There is no need to establish the fact that the giver of instructions expected them to be followed (*Deverell*). If the board is able to be characterised as subservient to a particular person, that indicates shadow directorship on the part of that person, but it is not necessary to establish subservience before one can deem a person to be a shadow director (*Deverell*). It is necessary to establish that the directors acted on more than one occasion on the instructions or directions of a person for him or her to be regarded as a shadow, but there is no need to prove that the directors either constantly took instructions during the life of the company or even for a significant period of time (*Secretary of State for Trade and Industry v Becker* [2002] EWHC 2200; [2003] 1 BCLC 555).

While a bank will not usually be regarded as a shadow director, the possibility of this being proven has been raised (*Re a Company (No 005009 of 1987*) (1988) 4 BCC 424). But banks will not be categorised as shadow directors when they merely lay down terms for continuing to provide credit for the business of a company, as these cannot be taken as instructions, for the company is at liberty to take or leave the terms (*Re PFTZM Ltd* [1995] BCC 280 at 292).

Dr Riz Mokal has made the point that if a director delegates his or her decision-making power to a person (X) lower in the chain of command and the director is accustomed to acting on the instructions of X, then X may be regarded as a shadow director and liable under certain provisions.[6]

Distinguishing between **de facto** *and shadow directors*

It is important that one distinguishes between a shadow and a *de facto* director, as the terms do not overlap (*Hydrodan* at 163). A *de facto* director claims, and purports, to act for the company as a director and is held out as such by the company even though he or she has never been appointed properly. To prove that a person was a *de facto* director, it is necessary 'to plead and prove that he undertook functions in relation to the company which could properly be discharged only by a director' (*Hydrodan* at 163), and it is not sufficient that it is proved that the person was involved in the company's management. In contrast, a shadow does not make a claim to act for the company as a director; on the contrary he or she usually maintains that he or she is not a director. Shadows tend to act behind the scenes (although this is not necessary) and hide behind the *de jure* directors of the company, perhaps 'pulling the strings' (*Re PFTZM Ltd* at 290), while the activity of *de facto* directors may well be more obvious (*Hydrodan* at 163).

Responsibilities and obligations

As mentioned above, directors owe what can be called, in the broad sense, obligations to creditors. Most of these obligations can be listed and little else need be said about them, as they are either clear-cut or are uninteresting, or both. Many of these only provide very indirect obligations to creditors. They flow from the idea that while companies are formed for the benefit of the shareholders, this is done subject to safeguards for the benefit of creditors.[7] Most of the obligations placed on directors are designed to prevent the expropriation of creditor wealth and to protect creditors' legitimate expectations when providing credit to a company.[8]

---

6   *Corporate Insolvency: Theory and Application*, 2005, Oxford: Oxford University Press, p 266.
7   Company Law Review, *Modernising Company Law: The Strategic Framework*, London, DTI, 1999, at para 5.1.4.
8   This latter issue is taken up and discussed in Chapter 19.

This book is primarily concerned with the responsibilities that are owed by directors under the civil law, although in Part B there is some discussion of the criminal action that can be taken pursuant to s 458 of the Companies Act 1985 where directors (and others) have engaged in fraudulent trading.[9]

Directors are liable under several provisions if they engage in certain activities which could well affect creditors. The ensuing discussion does not purport to be exhaustive, but mentions some instances of directors' obligations to creditors. We must note initially that the share capital provisions of the Companies Act 1985 'protect corporate creditors from the abuse of limited liability by shareholders',[10] and so there are limits placed on a company's dealings in relation to its corporate share capital. First, companies are not permitted to give financial assistance in the purchase of their shares (ss 151, 152). Furthermore, directors of private companies, for whom the proscriptions in s 151 are relaxed, are obliged to publicise any resolution that provides for the payment from capital for the purchase of the company's own shares (ss 173, 174) and creditors may object (s 176). Likewise, the law obliges directors not to repay any paid-up capital to the shareholders except by means of an authorised reduction of capital, and this might be regarded as an indirect duty owed by directors to creditors (*Re Horsley & Weight Ltd* [1982] 1 Ch 442, 454; [1982] 3 All ER 1045, 1055, CA). Directors are to ensure that they do not engage in making an unlawful reduction of capital, and, as Buckley LJ stated in *Re Horsley & Weight Ltd*, this might be regarded as an indirect duty to creditors, but his Lordship preferred to see this as a duty to the company (at 454). Any reduction of company capital will, of course, impact on the company's ability to repay creditors in the event of insolvency. The principle is that companies should maintain their capital as a fund from which the creditors can claim what they are owed. So, before reducing capital, it is necessary for a company to secure the approval of the court (s 135). Second, and allied to what has just been discussed, the Companies Act prohibits the payment of dividends to shareholders from capital – they must only be paid out of profits (s 263). Third, when raising capital, a company is not entitled to issue shares at a discount in relation to their par value (s 100).

Another obligation, although not relating to share capital, is that under s 349 of the Companies Act 1985 directors must ensure that the company's name is mentioned in legible characters on certain documents, such as letters, bills of exchange, promissory notes, endorsements, cheques or orders for money or goods. A recent case where directors were held liable under this provision is *Fiorentino Comm Guiseppe Srl v Farnesi* [2005] BCC 771. A third obligation relates to the fact that directors must ensure that their company

---

9 For a discussion of responsibilities under the criminal law, see Scanlan, G, 'The criminal liabilities of directors to the creditors of the company' (2003) 24 Co Law 234.

10 Armour, J, 'Share Capital and Creditor Protection: Efficient Rules for a Modern Company Law' (2000) 63 MLR 355 at 355.

does not breach s 117 of the Companies Act 1985 by doing business or exercising borrowing powers where the Registrar of Companies has not issued a certificate. If the company enters into a contract in breach of the section and fails to discharge its obligations within 21 days of being called upon to do so, the directors are liable to indemnify the other party to the transaction in respect of any loss or damage (s 117(8)).

Fourth, there are indirect obligations to creditors which involve directors ensuring that company property is not disposed of in certain situations. During the life of the company, directors should not enter into transactions that might be classified as transactions defrauding creditors under s 423 of the Insolvency Act 1986.[11] This usually involves putting assets out of the reach of creditors. Directors might be regarded as having an obligation to the general body of their company's creditors, when their company is insolvent, not to prefer one or more creditors by paying them and not paying others (Insolvency Act 1986, s 239), on the basis that any distribution of funds should be according to the statutory scheme set out in the Insolvency Act 1986. Directors are also under an obligation not to enter into a transfer if that would lead to the insolvency of the company and the payment is regarded as a preference. If a director does pay a preference then he or she might be held liable for a breach of duty or trust covered by s 212 of the Insolvency Act (the misfeasance section). Usually, in practice a director will only be the subject of an action if the person who was the recipient of the preference is impecunious or not able to be traced. Of course, the company might not end up in administration or liquidation, or such payments might not be deemed to constitute preferences. The fact of the matter is that until a company enters administration or liquidation and an administrator or liquidator successfully claims in court that a preference was given, it is not possible to say that the directors had an obligation and that obligation was not honoured. Therefore, it is highly debatable whether one can say that this is a responsibility owed to creditors. One can say that directors should be careful in paying only one or some of their company's accounts when their company is insolvent and likely to enter liquidation.

Again, if their company is insolvent, directors are not to engage in transactions which are able to be classified as transactions at an undervalue. The same applies if the transaction will lead to the insolvency of the company. Transactions at an undervalue are explained in s 238 of the Insolvency Act. They are transactions that have left the company short of funds or property, because the company has either made gifts to others or received consideration of a value that is significantly less than that which was given by the company. Again action will only be taken against directors where the

---

11 For more detailed discussion of this field, see Miller, G, 'Transactions prejudicing creditors' [1998] Conv 362; Parry, R, *Transaction Avoidance in Insolvencies*, 2001, Oxford: Oxford University Press, Ch 10; Keay, A, *McPherson's Law of Company Liquidation*, 2001, London: Sweet and Maxwell, pp 612–621.

company enters administration or liquidation. Finally, I should mention the fact that directors of a company that has gone into insolvent liquidation are not permitted, because of s 216 of the Insolvency Act 1986, to re-use the company's name, save in limited circumstances.[12] This proscription is designed to protect creditors.

There are, of course, obligations that companies have to their creditors, but we are concerned in this book with the personal responsibilities of the directors of companies, and not their responsibilities when acting for the company. For instance, under the Late Payment of Commercial Debts (Interest) Act 1998, companies must not, as must not any recipient of goods or services, delay the payment of the supplier. The directors have the responsibility to ensure timely payment, but this responsibility is merely humanising the responsibility of the company.

Having set out some of the important obligations that directors have to creditors, we now note the responsibilities that are at the heart of this book. Two are set in negative terms, and they are that directors have the responsibility not to engage either in fraudulent trading or wrongful trading. Directors also have the positive obligation, at certain times in the life of their company, to have consideration for the interests of creditors of their company (often referred to as 'duties to creditors'). In relation to this last obligation, I should note, as the words in parenthesis indicate, that I and many commentators refer to this as a duty to creditors. Whether this is strictly correct or not is a matter of debate that is discussed in various places in Chapters 11–19, with particular emphasis on the subject in Chapter 15.

As mentioned already, it is generally against company law principles for directors to be liable personally to creditors of their companies. The classic case of *Salomon v Salomon and Co Ltd*, of course, laid down the inveterate principle that a company was a separate entity at law and, hence, that the company's directors and shareholders were not liable for the debts of the company. There has, generally speaking, been a reluctance on the part of judges to impose personal liability on directors as it tends to undermine the doctrine of separate legal entity, namely the company entity is separate from its directors and shareholders. The consequence of this doctrine is, of course, that the directors (and the members) are not liable for the debts and liabilities of the company. Creditors will contract with the company and not the directors. But there are social and economic reasons why, in certain cases, directors are made responsible by the legislature or the courts for what they do on behalf of their companies. The problem with permitting directors to get off scot-free if their company is unable to discharge wholly or in part its

---

12 This means that at the time of entering liquidation, the company's assets are insufficient for the payment of its debts and other liabilities and the expense of winding up: s 216(7). For a concise and recent discussion of this, see Carter, T, 'The phoenix syndrome – the personal liability of directors' (2006) 19 *Insolvency Intelligence* 38.

liabilities, is that directors might act cavalierly or even improperly in managing the affairs of the company. The doctrines of limited liability and separate legal personality are often 'easily manipulated'.[13] As Cooke J of the New Zealand Court of Appeal stated in *Nicholson v Permakraft (NZ) Ltd* (1985) 3 ACLC 453 at 459:

> [Limited liability] is a privilege healthy as tending to the expansion of opportunities and commerce, but it is open to abuse. Irresponsible structural engineering – involving the creating, dissolving and transforming of incorporated companies to the prejudice of creditors – is a mischief to which the courts should be alive.

The lay-out of the book

Including this part, Part A, which is introductory in nature, the book consists of five parts. Fraudulent trading is discussed in Part B, wrongful trading in Part C and duties to creditors in Part D. Part E then considers theoretical arguments pertaining to whether these responsibilities should in fact exist, or whether directors are being unfairly dealt with and it also considers whether it is possible, and if not whether it should be, for creditors of companies to opt out of being the potential recipient of benefits of these responsibilities if directors fail to adhere to them. At the end of the book, Chapter 22 provides some conclusions and reflections. While the focus of the book is on the fraudulent and wrongful trading provisions applying in the UK, and the common law that has developed in the UK concerning the responsibility of directors to take into account creditor interests, reference will be made to the legislation and common law operating in other common law jurisdictions, and particularly Ireland, Australia, Canada, the United States and New Zealand, and to a lesser extent Singapore, South Africa and Hong Kong. In addition, and where appropriate, there will be some discussion of the law in some European jurisdictions.

---

13 Glasbeek, H J, 'More direct director responsibility: much ado about . . . what?' [1985] *Canadian Business Law Journal* 416 at 422.

2 Creditors – who are they?

The book is concerned with the responsibilities owed to creditors. It is necessary to be more specific about whom we are talking. The term 'creditors' encompasses a broad group and there are many different kinds of creditor. This chapter seeks to examine the nature of a creditor and about whom we are talking, identifying various types of creditor and what rights they enjoy. The discussion is necessarily brief and introductory as the book's focus is not on defining creditors, but on examining the responsibilities that directors owe to such persons. There are other chapters, primarily Chapters 19 and 20, that focus on problems confronting, and rights enjoyed by, various kinds of creditor.

Who is a creditor?

Essentially, and in broad terms, a creditor is someone who is owed a debt by a debtor,[1] or someone who is owed money by another.[2] Who is a creditor will often depend on the circumstances in which one is asking the question. Of course, the term might be given a specialist meaning in appropriate circumstances, especially in legislation.

As indicated above, a creditor is owed a debt. 'Debt' is a broad term. It can be regarded as wider than what is generally regarded as a debt, namely money owed for money lent or goods supplied or services rendered. According to r 13.12 of the Insolvency Rules 1986, which defines 'debt' for the purposes of the liquidation of companies, it is a term which includes any debt or liability that is present or future, whether it is certain or contingent or whether its amount is fixed or liquidated, or is able to be ascertained by fixed rules or as a matter of opinion. Further, it would include liabilities involving the liability to pay money or money's worth, including any liability under an enactment, any liability for breach of trust, any liability in

1   See Martin, E A (ed), 'Creditor' *The Oxford Dictionary of Law*, 2003, Oxford: Oxford University Press, p 127.
2   Hardy Ivamy, E, *Mozley & Whiteley's Law Dictionary*, 1990, London: Butterworths, p 119.

contract, tort or bailment, and any liability arising out of any obligation to make restitution.

There are three particular kinds of debts that are worth mentioning.

Contingent debts

In *Re William Hockley Ltd* [1962] 1 WLR 555 Pennycuick J said that a 'contingent creditor' is taken to be 'a person towards whom, under an existing obligation, the company [debtor] may or will become subject to a present liability on the happening of some future event or at some future date' (at 558). This is broadly in accord with the statement of Lord Reid on the subject in *Re Sutherland Dec'd* [1963] AC 235; [1961] 3 WLR 1062, that a contingent liability was 'a liability which, by reason of something done by the person bound, would necessarily arise or come into being upon an event or events which might or might not happen' (at 249; 1069). A prime example of contingent liability is the liability of a surety as a result of the failure of the principal debtor to pay what is owed.

Prospective debts

A person or company who owes a prospective debt has been described as one who is indebted in a sum of money not immediately payable,[3] and one who is owed a debt which will certainly become due in the future, either on some determined date or some date which will be determined by reference to future events (*Stonegate Securities Ltd v Gregory* [1980] 1 Ch 576 at 579). The nature of a prospective creditor presumes that that there is an existing obligation. An example of a prospective creditor is a person who has a claim, unable to be disputed, for unliquidated damages which remains to be quantified and will lead to a debt for more than a nominal amount (*Re Dollar Land Holdings Ltd* [1994] BCLC 404).

Future debts

These are similar to contingent debts in that both future and contingent creditors will look to the future before the debts owed become payable. However, while contingent creditors are not certain that a debt will be payable, future creditors are. There seems little, if any, difference between prospective and future debts.

---

3   Wright, R, and Buchanan, R, *Palmer's Company Precedents, Part 2: Winding-Up Forms and Practice*, 17th edn, 1960, London: Stevens and Sons Ltd, p 41.

Kinds of creditor

Any company might have all or any of the following creditors: secured creditors; suppliers with a retention of title clause in the supply contracts; trade creditors; suppliers under long-term contracts; lessors; holders of unexpired intellectual property licences; employees; Inland Revenue Commissioners and HM Customs; tort victims with claims; and customers who have paid deposits for goods or services to be supplied by the company. Some of these creditors, and their problems in recouping what is owed to them by companies in financial difficulty, are discussed in Chapter 19.

Consensual creditors

These are creditors who have voluntarily extended credit to a company pursuant to some form of agreement. The category can be divided into secured and unsecured creditors.

Secured creditors

Such creditors (of companies) are granted proprietary rights over a company's asset(s), enabling them to exert some action over the asset(s) if necessary. This will usually be where the company fails to meet its repayment schedule or the company enters some form of insolvency regime, such as liquidation. For the most part, secured creditors are not going to be overly concerned about the responsibilities that are examined in this book. They will monitor the company and, more specifically, the assets over which they have security, to ensure that the assets will realise funds that will adequately cover what is owed. 'Security' as a concept is discussed later in the chapter.[4]

Unsecured creditors

This category contains the vast majority of creditors. These creditors have been said to 'receive a raw deal' (*Borden (UK) Ltd v Scottish Timber Products Ltd* [1981] Ch 25 at 42 per Templeman LJ), a view expressed in several judicial observations, such as in *Business Computers v Anglo-African Leasing* [1977] 1 WLR 578 at 580. Such creditors have to rely primarily on their contract with the debtor.

There are various kinds of creditor who fall into this category. They range from moneylenders to trade creditors who supply goods or services to consumers who have paid a deposit to a company in exchange for a promise of a delivery of goods or services. Also included are the Inland Revenue and HM

---

4 Below at pp 20–21.

Customs, owed various taxes, and the employees of companies, who are owed arrears of wages and other benefits relating to their employment. Some of the problems that face such creditors in extending credit and what protections might be available to them are discussed in Chapter 19. Moneylenders are a group that encompasses debenture holders. Some might lend on a secured basis, but many do not. Trade creditors will supply goods or services on credit, with the arrangement involving a contractual deferment of a price obligation,[5] and this is known as sales credit.

It is this broad group of creditors that is going to be concerned about the kind of responsibilities that are studied in this book. They have no assets which they can grab, unless they have supplied goods subject to contracts which contain what are known as 'retention of title clauses'.

There are a number of different kinds of unsecured creditor that we can identify, and they are discussed in brief below.

Preferential creditors[6]

When a company enters administration or liquidation, unsecured creditors are treated equally and rateably when it comes to paying them out. This principle is known as *pari passu*. But there are some unsecured creditors who are given, by insolvency legislation, special treatment and a priority right when creditors are paid. Sections 175 and 386 with Sched 6 of the Insolvency Act 1986 detail the present categories of preferential debts for corporate insolvencies. The types of creditor covered are discussed below.

REVENUE AUTHORITIES

At one time in the UK the revenue authorities, principally the Inland Revenue Commissioners and HM Customs and Excise, were privileged creditors, as indicated in the previous section. But in the Enterprise Act 2002 provision was made for the abolition of the priority. Since losing preferential status in insolvency regimes such as liquidation, the Revenue has had to rethink its position as far as corporate debtors are concerned. When the Revenue had preferential status it was in a strong position. It could, except where it was aware that a company was hopelessly insolvent, wait and see what the company was going to do, or it could, if it was felt appropriate, seek a winding-up order against the company without regard for the company's future, and whether the company had a chance of rehabilitating itself if it was suffering financial difficulties. Now the Revenue is cast in the same position as all other

5   Finch, V, *Corporate Insolvency Law*, 2002, Cambridge: Cambridge University Press, p 61, n 4.
6   For a detailed discussion, including the history of the provision for these creditors, see Keay, A, and Walton, P, 'The preferential debts regime in liquidation law: in the public interest?' (1999) 3 *Company Financial and Insolvency Law Review* 84.

unsecured creditors and, arguably, has to monitor companies more closely and carefully.

Other countries around the world, such as Austria, Australia and Germany, have taken the same action as the UK and abolished the priority of revenue authorities. Revenue authorities in other countries, such as Ireland, France, Spain, Italy and South Africa, have decided that it is appropriate to retain a priority position in insolvencies.

EMPLOYEES

The justification for granting priority status to the wage claims of employees has been stated to be that:

> [S]alaries and wages are generally needed for, and generally expended in, the support and maintenance of the persons earning them, their wives and families and others dependent on them, and so may well be given priority, for a short period, over debts due to other creditors in the ordinary course of business and generally more nearly related to the profit and loss account of the creditor than his sustenance or that of those dependent upon him.
> (*Re Parkin Elevator Co* (1916) 41 DLR 123 at 125 per Meredith CJCP)

The employee has for a long time attracted the sympathy of the legislature, having been seen as being in a weak bargaining position compared to other creditors and investors. The employee priority is to 'ease the financial hardship caused to a relatively poor and defenceless section of the community by the insolvency of their employer'.[7] Employees, when negotiating the terms of their employment contract, do not usually insist upon a provision to protect them should the employer become insolvent; they usually do not even turn their minds to the possible insolvency of their employer. The reason given for priority to creditors is that the effect of an employer's insolvency on the employee is likely to be more serious than the effect on other creditors. Wages are likely to be the only source of income for an employee whilst other creditors are likely to have other sources of income.

Retention of title creditors

Some creditors, mainly suppliers of goods, will provide, as a term of the supply contract, that they retain title to the goods until they are paid. This means that if a debtor enters some insolvent regime, the supplier is able to demand the return of the goods from the insolvency administrator, as the

---

7   Insolvency Law Review Committee, *Insolvency Law and Practice* (commonly known as 'the Cork Report' after its chairman, Sir Kenneth Cork), Cmnd 858, HMSO (1982) at para 1428.

supplier still has title to the goods.[8] Retention of title creditors are not secured creditors, although they might be said to enjoy quasi-security.

Special relationship creditors

Envisaged here are those creditors who have a company as one of their main customers. Some creditors might even have more than half of their business with one company. Examples are suppliers of large companies, for instance those who supply components to the multinational carmakers. This kind of relationship might be lucrative, but these suppliers are in a potentially vulnerable position. If their main customer fails to pay on time or, even worse, clearly falls into a financial malaise, the supplier could well collapse, as it is so reliant on the one company. And, even if the supplier has a detailed contract, that might well offer no assistance, particularly if the company is heading for insolvency. Clearly, there are inherent dangers in not having a diversified customer base.

Involuntary creditors

This covers those who have not agreed to become creditors of the debtor, but who are creditors because of some action or inaction of the debtor. The prime candidate for this category is the person who is a victim of a tort committed by the debtor. To be able to have a claim against the tortfeasor/debtor, the creditor will have to obtain a judgment against the tortfeasor/debtor.

Customers

When thinking about risk one immediately focuses on those who have extended supplies or money to a company. Customers of companies are not usually considered in such a context. However, it is not unusual for customers to pay to companies a deposit for goods or services that they have ordered, or even in some areas, such as in the travel and mail order sectors, to pay the full price. Until those goods or services are delivered, the customer is a creditor of the supplier. In a sense, customers are involuntary creditors, because unless they provide the required payment in advance, they do not get the goods or services.

Creditor protection

In granting credit to companies, creditors are able to avail themselves of a number of protection measures, in order to ensure that they do not

---

8   The classic case that accepted these kinds of terms in English law was *Aluminium Industrie Vaassen BV v Romalpa Aluminium Ltd* [1976] 2 All ER 552, CA.

lose out from an extension of credit, or, if they do lose, they limit how much they lose. I do not want to say a great deal about this topic as it is the subject of a substantial amount of discussion in Chapter 19, and, to a lesser extent, Chapter 20. However, a few words are appropriate at this stage.

Contractual protection

First, creditors might seek to safeguard their position by including certain terms in their contract with the company. These terms are as varied as the ingenuity of man. But some are frequently used and are referred to here. One that has been referred to already in this chapter is the retention of title clause, which might enable a creditor to recover its goods or goods made with the materials that it supplied to the company, if the company collapses, on the basis that the creditor retained title in the goods/materials until the debt was paid.

A second protection, and one that is favoured by banks, is to require one or more of the directors of the company to provide a personal guarantee, whereby the director(s) covenants that if the company fails to pay the creditor, he or she will meet the obligations. This is a method that allows for dispensing with the limited liability rule, obviously a rule central to company law. Sometimes guarantees are taken to support the giving of security by the company. A third protection is where the contract states that the company is to disclose certain kinds of information to the creditor (over and above what the law requires).

Fourth, a creditor might require that the contract includes certain terms that place constraints on the company, known as restrictive covenants. Examples are: the company is not to change the nature of its business; the company is not to dispose of certain assets; or the company is limited in relation to the dividends that it can declare. Perhaps one of the most popular is the 'negative pledge clause', which provides that the company will not create security over some or all of the company's assets that are not already subject to security. A final protection to which we refer is where the contract provides that the creditor is given governance rights in relation to the company. Examples might be where a creditor obtains the right to nominate a director to the company's board.

The great majority of trade creditors, as well as other kinds of creditor, find it difficult to document transactions, and so often they end up providing goods and services on 'open account' terms without entering into a formal written contract containing agreed terms.[9] One reason for this, besides the time factor, is the fact that the preparation of formal and widely

---

9   Schwarcz, S, 'Rethinking a corporation's obligations to creditors' (1996) 17 *Cardozo Law Review* 647 at 652.

drawn contracts involves significant costs.[10] Such creditors can be quite vulnerable.

It should be noted that some creditors lack any, or sufficient, financial muscle to enable them to have specialist terms incorporated into contracts into which they enter. This is an issue that is taken further in Chapter 20.

Pre-contract checks

Before entering into a contract to extend credit the creditor might undertake certain checks in relation to the company to ascertain things like the capacity of the company to repay. Often creditors will ask their solicitors to undertake a search of the company at Companies House. This will disclose many of the key features of the company, although it will not, alone, determine whether the company is a good credit risk. Other checks that might be undertaken include making inquiries with credit reference agencies, enabling them to find out about a company's past credit history. Less formal action might include contacting present or former creditors of the company, if known.

Unfortunately, for many suppliers of goods and services, there is not sufficient time for them to undertake inquiries before they have to decide whether or not to supply the company on credit. Companies often need goods and services immediately, and if the supplier wants time in which to investigate the company in any depth, it is likely that the company will take its business elsewhere.

Security

Perhaps regarded as the most coveted form of protection, security (collateral) enables a creditor to depend not on the personal covenants of the company, which will most often require the need to go to court to enforce them if default occurs, and, of course, will not be particularly fruitful if the company is insolvent, but to depend on certain company property. That is, if the company fails to pay the creditor, the creditor can realise the property over which it has security and pay itself back from the proceeds of the realisation. In this type of situation the creditor is granted a proprietary right against the company. A classic way of creating security in relation to corporate debtors is through the charge. Some charges are fixed and others are floating, and still others are hybrid, that is, a combination of fixed and floating. A fixed charge

---

10 Butler, L, and Ribstein, H, 'Opting out of fiduciary duties: a response to the anti-contractarians' (1990) 65 *Washington Law Review* 1 at 28; Harvey, D, 'Bondholders' rights and the case for a fiduciary duty' (1991) 65 *St John's Law Review* 1023 at 1037; Whincop, M, 'Painting the corporate cathedral: the protection of entitlements in corporate law' (1999) 19 OJLS 19 at 28.

is taken over ascertainable property that is permanent or semi-permanent. The traditional view is that debtors are unable to deal in any way with property that is subject to a fixed charge. In contrast, a floating charge is a charge that is not fixed on any property; it hovers over property and fixes (the technical term being 'crystallises') on the happening of certain events, such as non-payment by the debtor. Floating charges are usually taken over circulating-type assets, such as stock in trade and book debts.[11]

One of the main advantages of taking security is that, under the Anglo-American models of law, the creditor retains its rights and can realise the secured property even after the commencement of some formal insolvency regime such as liquidation.

Monitoring

During the period when they are owed money by a company, a creditor can engage in monitoring the company and its financial position. Creditors often do this informally, but this is generally not sustained and its effectiveness is very problematic. Formal and substantial monitoring can be time-consuming and costly, and even then it might not be sufficient to keep the creditor well-informed.[12] The problem is that many creditors will not have the resources to carry out necessary monitoring. If a creditor decides that it will need to monitor a company, then it will have to build a cost factor into the price of its credit, because obtaining information and monitoring the affairs of a company are costly undertakings,[13] particularly if professional advice is sought. This might make the price of the goods or services uncompetitive.

Imposing higher interest

If a creditor is concerned about the company as a credit risk, it can demand that the company pays a higher rate of interest on credit extended. While this might compensate a creditor, it does not protect the creditor from a company failing and being unable to repay the debt owed.

Summary

'Creditors' is a very broad term and may include lenders who have been granted security (fixed, floating or both – chiefly banks), those holding

---

11 For further discussion, see Keay, A, and Walton, P, *Insolvency Law: Corporate and Personal*, 2003, Harlow: Pearson Education, pp 52–62.
12 See the comments in Cheffins, B, *Company Law: Theory, Structure and Operation*, 1997, Oxford: Clarendon Press, p 524.
13 Posner, R, 'The Rights of Affiliated Corporations' (1976) 43 *University of Chicago Law Review* 499 at 508.

long-term debt (holding publicly issued bonds or debentures), trade creditors, employees and those with tort claims, and it might, in some circumstances, include customers, such as those who have paid deposits for goods and/or services to be supplied in the future. This book will from time to time consider specific kinds of creditors, but generally when a reference is made to creditors the whole range of creditors that a company might have are in view.

Part B
Fraudulent trading

3 Fraudulent trading: background, aims and comparisons

Introduction

This chapter begins by considering the legislation and case law that has imposed certain responsibilities on company directors. Specifically in this chapter we will examine the advent, development and *raison d'être* for the provision dealing with what is known as 'fraudulent trading'. Following that, the chapter identifies the aims of the provision, finishing with a discussion of some comparable legislation in other jurisdictions. The ensuing chapters discuss aspects of the fraudulent trading provision, as well undertaking an assessment of it.

Background

For many years company legislation has made it an offence to carry on a business of a company with intent to defraud creditors. Also, the legislation has provided that a civil remedy is available where such activity can be proved. The first provision that was enacted to deal with what has been loosely referred to as 'fraudulent trading' was s 75 of the Companies Act 1928. There had been dissatisfaction in the first quarter of the last century at the ease with which the protection of limited liability could be abused by those who managed companies, and in 1926 the Greene Committee on Company Law Reform[1] had its attention directed particularly to the case, said to be encountered principally in private companies, 'where the person in control of the company holds a floating charge and, while knowing that the company is on the verge of liquidation, "fills up" his security by means of goods obtained on credit and then appoints a receiver' (at [61]). The Committee's recommendation, which with one small addition was originally embodied in s 75 of the 1928 Act, was that a new section should be inserted providing that where, in the course of winding up a company, it appeared that any business of the company had been carried on with intent to defraud

---

1 Report of the Company Law Amendment Committee, Cmnd 2697, HMSO, London, 1926.

creditors of the company, the court should have power, on application by the liquidator or any creditor or contributory, to declare that the directors responsible should be subjected to unlimited personal liability in respect of the debts or other liabilities of the company, and, further, that the court should be empowered to charge such liability upon any debt or obligation due from the company to the director, or upon any charge on any of the company's assets held by or vested in him or her or in any person on the director's behalf.

Section 75 shortly after its enactment became s 275 in the consolidated Companies Act 1929. The original section and its successors have been referred to as 'the most important incursion[s] into the principle of the separate personality of a company'.[2] The section imposed both criminal and civil liability and in both civil and criminal proceedings the elements of the section had to be established beyond reasonable doubt (*Re Maidstone Buildings Ltd* [1971] 1 WLR 1085 at 1094). Proceedings could be initiated by the official receiver, liquidator, creditors or contributories. Section 275 of the 1929 Act was followed by s 332 of the Companies Act 1948 which, as a result of the recommendations of the Cohen Committee in 1945,[3] expanded the pool of possible respondents to include those who had been parties to fraudulent trading.

The Report of the Insolvency Law Review Committee, *Insolvency Law and Practice* (commonly known, and similarly referred to here, as 'the Cork Report')[4] was of the opinion that the fraudulent trading provision as set out in s 332 of the 1948 Act possessed significant inadequacies in dealing with irresponsible trading, such as the fact that the criminal burden of proof applied to civil actions and, also, applicants were required to establish actual dishonesty and real moral blame on the part of respondents (*Re Patrick and Lyon Ltd* [1933] Ch 786). Consequently, the Cork Committee recommended that the provision be amended and that only criminal liability should apply in relation to fraudulent trading, with a new provision being introduced to allow for civil actions. The legislature took up these proposals, partly, and enacted s 214 of the Insolvency Act 1986 which covered civil action for wrongful trading, and fraudulent trading was left to be covered by two provisions, namely s 213 of the Insolvency Act and s 458 of the Companies Act 1985. The recommendations of the Cork Committee were not wholly implemented in that, against the views of the Committee, civil liability was retained for fraudulent trading, as well as criminal liability, and dealt with in s 213. But, unlike previous provisions, criminal liability is determined by a different provision, and this is s 458 of the Companies Act 1985. The two provisions, the one dealing with civil sanctions and the other with criminal sanctions, are essentially the

2   Williams, R, 'Fraudulent trading' (1986) 4 *Company & Securities Law Journal* 14.
3   Cmnd 6659 at para 149.   4   Cmnd 858, HMSO (1982).

same provision (*Bernasconi v Nicholas Bennett & Co* [2000] BCC 921 at 924). The main differences are as to the question of proof, the order of the court and the fact that with s 458 there is no need for the company to be in liquidation.

While the pre-1986 decisions related to a provision that could lead to both civil and criminal consequences, the courts in post-1986 decisions have not uttered any warning about using the older cases judiciously, and they certainly have not refused to hear argument based upon them. This seems reasonable, given the fact that the provisions are very similar.

When ss 213 and 214 were enacted, the latter was introduced to deal more with trading activity that was not fraudulent *per se*, but closer to negligent or irresponsible trading. Some of the discussion in this part overlaps with issues that are relevant to wrongful trading, which is discussed in Part C.

Some of the historical problems with fraudulent trading are manifested by the fact that Australia, which followed the UK and included a fraudulent trading provision, abandoned it in the 1960s. However, it has provided as part of its insolvent trading provision (Corporations Act 2001, s 588G), which is considered in the next part of the book, that if a director acts dishonestly in incurring debts while his or her company is insolvent, then the director can be subject to criminal sanctions.

At one stage the civil fraudulent trading provision was little used, as has been the case in Singapore (with only three cases in the history of that jurisdiction's equivalent provision until the year 2000)[5], and has led one commentator to say that the section is virtually obsolete,[6] but recent years have seen several cases brought successfully by liquidators. These cases feature in this part of the book. While civil cases have not been numerous at any stage of the history of fraudulent trading provisions, there have been quite a reasonable number of criminal prosecutions.

Aims

The paramount aim of s 213 is to compensate those who have lost out due to the actions of persons, who are identified in the section, engaging in fraudulent trading (*Bank of India v Morris* [2005] EWCA (Civ) 693 at [111]), while the aim of s 458 of the Companies Act 1985 is to impose penalties where the action is considered criminal. Also, the provisions are designed to prevent insolvent trading to the detriment of those who are induced to do business with the relevant company (*R v Smith* [1996] 2 BCLC 109 at 122, CCA).

---

5   Joyce, L, 'Fraudulent and insolvent trading in Singapore' (2000) 9 *International Insolvency Review* 121 at 128.
6   Finch, V, *Corporate Insolvency Law: Perspectives and Principles*, 2002, Cambridge: Cambridge University Press, p 511.

Comparisons

The legislations of several Commonwealth countries and Ireland have provided for proceedings where fraudulent trading has been perpetrated. Ireland's fraudulent trading provision is s 297A of its Companies Act 1963. The provision was introduced by s 138 of the Companies Act 1990 and is in very similar terms to the UK legislation. The provision also imposes liability for reckless trading, equivalent to wrongful trading in the UK, and this is discussed in Chapter 8. Section 297 of the 1963 Act, as a result of s 137 of the 1990 Act, imposes criminal liability for fraudulent trading. Section 297A imposes civil liability. Singapore includes in its Companies Act 1990 a fraudulent trading provision (s 340), which derives from the UK Companies Act 1928 via the Companies Act 1961 of the State of Victoria in Australia. Hong Kong's equivalent provision is s 275 of its Companies Ordinance (Cap 32).

Unlike the UK and Ireland, Australia, which abandoned a provision that dealt with fraudulent trading in the early 1960s, does not now have two different actions for fraudulent trading on the one hand and irresponsible trading on the other. There is only one kind of activity that is proscribed, namely insolvent trading. Whether a director was engaged in what the UK legislation terms as fraudulent or wrongful trading, directors in Australia will be held liable for insolvent trading. Insolvent trading involves, as we will see in Chapters 7 and 10, a director incurring debts when his or her company was insolvent and the director was aware at the time of the incurring of the debt that there were grounds for suspecting the insolvency of the company or a reasonable person in a like position in a company in the company's circumstances would have been aware of the company's insolvency (Corporations Act 2001, s 588G). Sections 588H–588Y of the Corporations Act 2001 provide the legislative regime that seeks to regulate insolvent trading. The legislation provides that directors have a duty to prevent their companies incurring debts at the time of insolvency. But, as indicated earlier, if it can be established that a director acted dishonestly, he or she can be found guilty of a criminal offence. There have been a number of such prosecutions brought, to which in many cases there have been pleas of guilty.[7]

South Africa does not have two sections. Section 424 of the Companies Act 1973 covers both fraudulent trading and reckless trading and is almost identical to s 213, providing liability where a company's affairs have been carried on with intent to defraud creditors or for a fraudulent purpose. The provision makes fraudulent trading punishable by both criminal and civil sanctions, therefore retaining the situation found in the UK Companies Act 1948.

---

7   See the Australian Securities and Investments Commission website, www.asic.gov.au.

European jurisdictions do include provisions which may be regarded, broadly, as analogous to s 213. For instance, sanctions may be imposed on directors in France who conduct the businesses of their companies improperly for personal gain, causing their companies to trade at a deficit and resulting in them being unable to pay their debts.[8] In this jurisdiction directors could be said to have committed the offence of *banqueroute* (criminal bankruptcy) where they are involved in managing a company that involves raising funds by reckless means or fraudulently increasing the company's debts.[9] More discussion concerning some European jurisdictions is to be found in Chapter 7 in the context of wrongful trading.

The next chapter considers s 213 and its scope, as well as a brief consideration of s 458.

8   Article L624-5-1 no 4, Commercial Code. See Omar, P, 'Defining insolvency: the evolution of the concept of "cessation de paiements" in French law' [2005] EBLR 311 at 312.
9   See art L626-2, Commercial Code and referred to in Omar *ibid* at 313–314.

4 The fraudulent trading provision and its scope

Introduction

As indicated in the last chapter, two provisions address fraudulent trading. They are the civil provision, s 213 of the Insolvency Act 1986, and the criminal provision, s 458 of the Companies Act 1985. They are essentially identical, the primary differences being procedural. The standard of proof for a s 213 action is the same as for any civil proceeding, namely the balance of probabilities, while the standard for the criminal proceeding remains beyond reasonable doubt. The applicant for a civil claim is the liquidator, while criminal proceedings must be initiated by the Crown. It has been stated that decisions on s 458 are relevant to a consideration of s 213 (*Re BCCI; Banque Arabe Internationale D'Investissement SA v Morris* [2002] BCC 407 at 413), so in Part B no distinction is made between the cases on the basis of the provision under which they were decided. The main focus of this part is, however, on s 213, although, of course, many of the things said here will be relevant to s 458, and occasionally reference will be made to the provision, either in the text or in footnotes. Also, there are a couple of sections of the chapter that include brief discussions of aspects of s 458.

This chapter involves an examination of the central elements of s 213, together with a discussion of the effect of its application. However, discussion of one of the main elements of the provision, namely the need to establish intent to defraud or acting for any fraudulent purpose, is postponed, for the most part, to Chapter 5.

At the outset we should note that at one time it was generally thought that s 213 would not be invoked frequently, given the advent of the action of wrongful trading in s 214 of the Insolvency Act 1986, but that is not the case. While s 214 has a lower threshold of proof, and the elements of the section appear prima facie easier to establish, s 213 is far from being a dead letter, and there have been several fraudulent trading actions in recent times with a number being reported (for example *Re Esal (Commodities) Ltd* [1997] 1 BCLC 705, CA; *Morris v Bank of America National Trust and Savings Association* [2000] BPIR 83, [2000] BCC 1076, [2001] 1 BCLC 771, CA; *Re Bank of Credit and Commerce International SA; Morris v State*

Bank of India [2004] 2 BCLC 236; *Morphitis v Bernasconi* [2003] EWCA Civ 289; [2003] Ch 552; [2003] BCC 540, CA; *Morris v Bank of India* [2004] BCC 404 and affirmed on appeal in [2005] EWCA Civ 693; [2005] 2 BCLC 328; [2005] BPIR 1067); many have revolved around the long-running liquidation of the Bank of Commerce and Credit International. There have also been, and continue to be, a respectable number of prosecutions under s 458, which is not, of course, affected by the presence of s 214 on the statute books.

Finally, in relation to interpretation, as mentioned earlier, while there have been some changes in the present fraudulent trading provisions compared with previous ones, it is clear that the cases decided under previous provisions are relevant to proceedings taken under the present provisions (*Re L Todd (Swanscombe) Ltd* [1990] BCC 125), although some of the cases have not been followed and some have even been overruled in light of the reform of the provisions. Also we should note that the interpretation of parts of s 213 has vexed courts and led the judge in one of the first reported cases dealing with the first fraudulent trading provision, *Re Patrick & Lyon Ltd* [1933] Ch 786, to say that the provision (in the 1929 Act) was 'a very remarkable section and one which is by no means easy to construe' (at 789–790).

The make-up of section 213

Section 213 sets out the civil provision in two subsections. Section 213(1) states the conduct that makes up fraudulent trading, that is, intent to defraud creditors or having a fraudulent purpose. The provision does not define the meaning of these two types of conduct; it is left to the courts to define them, and Chapter 5 primarily considers their meaning. After setting out what fraudulent liability entails, s 213(2) then states who may be liable in civil actions and for what they can be liable: first, that the persons who are able to be proceeded against are those who are knowingly parties to the carrying on of a business of a company with intent to defraud creditors; second, such persons are liable to make such contributions to the company as the court thinks proper.

The provision appears to be quite broad, in that it provides that it covers 'any business of the company [that] has been carried out'. This is broader than merely stating 'the business of the company' (*Hardie v Hanson* [1960] HCA 8; (1960) 105 CLR 451). The provision is designed essentially to safe-guard the interests of creditors. In *R v Smith* [1996] 2 BCLC 109 at 122, CCA Rose LJ, delivering the judgment of the court, said that 'creditor' is to be given its ordinary meaning and covers someone to whom money is owed; it is not material whether the debt can be sued for. The provision applies also where the intention is to defraud future creditors of the company (*R v Smith* at 122). While creditors are to be the primary ones protected, the fact is that the words 'carrying on a business for any fraudulent purpose' and 'creditors or any other person' give the provision a greater ambit, and it has been asserted that it is likely that this is to protect persons other than those regarded as classic creditors. Customers of a company may in fact be regarded as creditors of the company for the purposes of s 213 (*R v Inman* [1967] 1 QB 140, CCA; [1966] 3 All ER 414; *Re Sarflax Ltd* [1979] 1 Ch 592; *R v Smith* [1996] 2 BCLC 109) on the basis that they are prospective or contingent creditors, although this does not include all customers (*Re Gerald Cooper Chemicals Ltd* [1978] Ch 262). However, it is likely that the Secretary of State for Trade and Industry would seek to invoke s 124A of the Insolvency Act 1986 to wind up companies that were engaging in fraudulent activity that affected consumers, on the basis that it would be in the public interest to do so.[1]

The applicant

While individual creditors were able, under previous legislation, such as s 332 of the Companies Act 1948, to initiate applications for compensation on their own account, and it appears that a number of claims were initiated by persons other than liquidators (for example *Re Gerald Cooper Chemicals Ltd; Re Cyona Distributors Ltd* [1967] Ch 889 at 902; [1967] 1 All ER 281 at 284, CA), this cannot be done now, as only liquidators are entitled to apply for an order under s 213; applications are collective in that a liquidator is seeking compensation for the general body of creditors. Hence, courts are unable to direct that a specific creditor be compensated for losses sustained as a consequence of fraudulent trading (*Re Esal (Commodities) Ltd; London and Overseas (Sugar) Co Ltd v Punjab National Bank* [1993] BCLC 872 and affirmed on appeal at [1997] 1 BCLC 705, CA; *Morphitis v Bernasconi* [2003] EWCA Civ 289, [2003] BCC 540).

In common with previous UK legislation, other jurisdictions permit a wider category of applicants who can bring proceedings against directors, including creditors and members. For instance, under s 424 of the South African Companies Act 1973, s 275(1) of the Hong Kong Companies Ordinance (Cap 32), and s 340 of the Singaporean Companies Act 1990, creditors and members as well as liquidators are permitted to take action.

Arguably, the position that we have now in the UK is more equitable than was the former situation, as in the past one creditor might have been able to get paid following a fraudulent trading application, but as a result, the respondent might have been placed in an impecunious state, and unable to pay other creditors who either were slow in initiating proceedings or failed to do so.

It is submitted that there is a good case for administrators as well as liquidators being entitled to take proceedings pursuant to s 213, particularly now that administration has become far more popular (since the changes made by

---

1 On public interest petitions, see, Keay, A, 'Public interest petitions' (1999) 20 Co Law 296; Finch, V, 'Public interest liquidation: PIL or placebo?' [2002] Insolv L 157.

the Enterprise Act 2002).[2] While it is unlikely that they will want to issue many actions, it does broaden their options, and would mean that a company would not have to be converted from an administration to a liquidation merely to allow for proceedings under s 213 to be taken.

Persons liable

Unlike both the wrongful trading provision, discussed in Part C, which states that only directors are liable, and the fraudulent trading provision that pre-dated the version found in s 332 of the Companies Act 1948 which limited liability to directors past and present, any persons who are knowingly parties to the fraudulent trading can be the subject of proceedings under s 213. While it is probable, certainly based on history, that the most likely respondents to an action will be the directors and other officers of the company,[3] with the executive directors likely to be subject to action the most often, persons who are not involved in conducting the business of the company may be liable,[4] although this will not be something that occurs frequently. This is an approach also followed in the equivalent Irish provision (s 297A of the Companies Act 1963), where anyone who was knowingly a party to the fraudulent trading can be made the subject of proceedings. While this book focuses on directors and their responsibilities, it is appropriate here to discuss in brief the liability of others.

While it appears that anyone involved in the company can be liable under s 213, it can be said that in general terms, those who are merely employed by the company, and are simply carrying out orders, are not going to be liable, for liability should fall on those who are orchestrating and organising the business, and this would be, usually, the directors and senior managers (*Re BCCI; Banque Arabe Internationale D'Investissement SA v Morris* at 414). But the net of s 213 is broad and the respondent does not, necessarily, have be someone who performed a managerial or controlling role in the company. Each case must be judged on its own facts. In *Re Maidstone Building* the court held the company secretary of a company was not liable for failing to advise the directors that the company was insolvent and there

---

2   See Keay, A, 'What future for liquidation in light of the Enterprise Act reforms?' [2005] JBL 143.

3   There is every indication that the persons who can be said to be the 'directing mind' of the company are liable more often than not to be the subject of proceedings. See *R v Miles* [1992] Crim L R 657. Also, see *Re Supply of Ready Mixed Concrete (No 2)* [1995] 1 AC 456; *Meridian Global Funds Management Asia Ltd v Securities Commission* [1995] BCC 942.

4   For example, see *Re Gerald Cooper Chemicals Ltd* where a creditor was held liable. See Griffin, S, *Personal Liability and Disqualification of Company Directors*, 1999, Oxford: Hart Publishing, pp 45–46. For a more recent case, see *Morris v Bank of India* [2004] BCC 404 and affirmed on appeal in [2005] EWCA Civ 693; [2005] 2 BCLC 328; [2005] BPIR 1067 where a third party bank was held liable under s 213.

should be a cessation of business, yet this decision must be doubted given the enhanced role of the company secretary and the fact that such officers can bind the company to contracts that deal with administrative matters (*Panorama Developments (Guildford) Ltd v Fidelis Furnishing Fabrics Ltd* [1971] 2 All ER 1028). In a relatively recent criminal prosecution under s 458 of the Companies Act (*R v Waite* (2003) WL 21162167, CCA) a company secretary was successfully prosecuted.

In fact the language of s 213(2) seems to point also towards persons who were not employed by the company, but who were in fact outsiders (*Banque Arabe Internationale D'Investissement SA v Morris* at 411). So, a claim could be made against so-called 'outsider companies' that were involved with the company that is now in liquidation (*Bank of India v Morris*, CA, at [100]). In *Bank of India v Morris* (discussed more later) the respondent was a bank that was facilitating the company in liquidation in part of its operations, and it was held liable. In *Re Gerald Cooper Chemicals* a creditor was held liable, where he was aware that his debt was satisfied as a result of a fraud committed in relation to a customer of the company. In like manner, in *Banque Arabe Internationale D'Investissement SA v Morris* the court said that a company or other entity that was involved in, and assisted and benefited from, the action that was fraudulent, and did so knowingly, could be held liable (at 412, 414). Outsider respondents need not know all of the details of any fraudulent action perpetrated by the company nor how the fraud was to be carried out before they are held liable, provided that they knew, either from their own observations of what was being done or from what they were told, that the company was intending to carry out a fraud on creditors (*Re BCCI; Morris v State Bank of India* [2004] BCC 404). In *Re Augustus Barnett & Sons Ltd* (1986) 2 BCC 98,904 at 98,907, Hoffmann J opined, while not having to decide the point, that outsiders who were not carrying on, or assisting in carrying on, the business of the company, but who participated in some way in the fraudulent acts might be able to be cited as respondents. In Singapore it has been held there that outsiders can be liable if they are aiming to obtain illegal profits by conspiring with company officers in some activity that constitutes fraudulent trading (*Tan Hung Yeoh v PP* [1993] 1 SLR 93).

Professor Steve Griffin has criticised the decision in *Re Gerald Cooper Chemicals* to hold a creditor liable on the basis that the creditor was only acting in a passive way.[5] The learned commentator asserted that in light of the decision in *Re Maidstone Buildings Ltd* [1971] 1 WLR 1085, a person could only be found liable if he or she were participating in the company's trading activities in a significant manner.[6] Certainly in that case the judge said that a person, to be liable, had to act in a positive way (at 1093). With respect, could it not be argued with some force that a director or other person who fails to

---

5 Griffin, *ibid* at 45.   6 *Ibid* at 45–46.

alert the board to a particular issue which could lead to the defrauding of creditors is knowingly a party to the carrying on of a business in a way outlawed by s 213(1) even though he or she is not taking positive action? It is relevant to note that in the past 20 years the courts have become more and more severe on those directors who act passively, indicating that lack of action will not necessarily save them.

It was noted above that third party companies, namely companies involved in some way with the company in liquidation and its business, could be liable for engaging in fraudulent trading. A company could be held liable even if none of its board members had knowledge of the fraudulent trading activity, as otherwise that would defeat the policy behind the provision (*Bank of India v Morris*, CA, at [108], [129]) provided that someone of authority (granted by the board) had the requisite knowledge. Hence, a company employee's knowledge of fraudulent trading may be attributed to his or her employer company (*Bank of India v Morris*). Persons involved in third party companies will not be liable on the basis that they are acting for a company that has participated in the fraudulent trading unless they hold some role that involves managing or controlling the affairs of the company (*R v Miles* [1992] Crim LR 657 – a company salesman who acted under orders of management was not liable under s 458 of the Companies Act), that is, persons who can be said to be the directing mind of the company (*Bank of India v Morris* at [95]). Ascertaining who is the directing mind and will of the company and what was their knowledge, is never easy.[7] The company has, under this approach, attributed to it the mind and will of the natural person(s) who manages and controls its actions (*El Ajou v Dollar Land Holdings plc* [1994] BCC 143 at 150). According to Viscount Haldane in *Lennard's Carrying Co Ltd v Asiatic Petroleum Co Ltd* [1915] AC 707, the directing mind and will might be a person who is under the direction of the shareholders in general meeting, the board or someone who has, pursuant to the articles, an authority co-ordinate with the board (at 713). Hoffman LJ (as he then was) said in *El Ajou v Dollar Land Holdings plc* that 'a person held out by the company as having plenary authority or in whose exercise of such authority the company acquiesces, may be treated as its directing mind' (at 159). In closely held companies it is much easier to establish a directing mind. In general terms, whether attribution occurs, will depend on the terms of the legislation that are under examination and whether it is appropriate to attribute knowledge to the company, notwithstanding the fact that the employee has acted dishonestly (*Bank of India v Morris* at [116]). The Court of Appeal in *Bank of India v Morris* stated that

---

7   For example, see *Lennard's Carrying Co Ltd v Asiatic Petroleum Co Ltd* [1915] AC 707 at 713; *HL Bolton (Engineering) Co Ltd v TJ Graham & Sons Ltd* [1957] 1 QB 159 at 172–173; *Tesco Supermarkets Ltd v Nattrass* [1972] AC 153 at 170; *El Ajou v Dollar Land Holdings plc* [1994] BCC 143 at 150 and 158; *Meridian Global Funds Management Ltd v Securities Commission* [1995] 2 AC 500, PC.

there will be some situations where one cannot attribute an individual's knowledge of fraud to a company (at [114]). But it is not possible to argue that there should not be attribution merely because the participation in a fraud by an employee of an outsider company has caused potential harm to his or her company in that it has opened up the company to potential liability to fraudulent trading (at [114]). The court concluded that 'knowledge of fraud may be attributed to a company even though such attribution may expose it to the risk of liability under section 213' (at [114]), and in this case there was attribution. The court also indicated that attribution can occur where the person who has the requisite knowledge is a manager at below board level if the company involved is a large company [112]. It is submitted that if there was no attribution permitted in the kind of situations just adverted to, outsider companies would rarely, if ever, be liable under s 213. It should be noted that whether or not the knowledge of an employee will be attributed to a company will very much depend on the facts of each case, and where a company acts in good faith and has set up an appropriate and rigorous system of supervision, it is likely that the company will not be held liable (at [129]).[8]

Holding companies may be held liable where they clearly participate in the fraudulent trading, such as actively directing the activities of the subsidiary, particularly where there was some active encouragement on the part of the holding company for the subsidiary to conduct its business in a fraudulent manner.[9] But in proving a case against a holding company, a liquidator would have to provide clear evidence of the participation. It is not sufficient for the liquidator merely to point to the parent-subsidiary relationship and ask the court to infer participation, because the companies are separate legal entities and are to be treated accordingly (*Re Augustus Barnett & Son Ltd*).

There is a strong argument that a claim under the section would survive the death of a person allegedly liable under s 213, but who died before the initiation of proceedings. This argument is based on applying the law applicable to s 214. It would permit the liquidator to instigate proceedings against that person's personal representative, seeking an order that a payment be made out of the estate of the deceased (*Re Sherborne Associates Ltd* [1995] BCC 40).

Applications

Fraudulent trading actions may only be initiated when the company in relation to whose affairs the actions are being brought is in liquidation. But, in other jurisdictions, the legislation is not so limiting. For instance, in Singapore

---

8 See Cloherty, A, 'Knowledge, Attribution and Fraudulent Trading' (2006) 122 LQR 25 at 30–31.
9 *Op. cit.*, Griffin, fn 4 at 46–47.

action may be initiated in the course of any proceedings against the company (Companies Act 1990, s 340(1)). A reason for the limitation in the UK provision might be that it is envisaged that companies not in liquidation would be solvent and action could be taken against the company itself.[10] However, the fact that the company is solvent might be due to the success of its fraudulent activity.[11] Also, it should be noted that s 213 does not require the company to be in insolvent liquidation, so the provision could be invoked in relation to a company that has been wound up on a ground other than an inability to pay debts.

It is in order for a liquidator to take proceedings under s 213 where a company is being wound up as an unregistered company (*Re Howard Holdings Inc* [1998] BCC 549, a case involving an application under s 214). But a liquidator is unable to assign an action under s 213 so that someone else could institute or adopt proceedings, because it is an action given to him or her personally in the position of liquidator (*Re Oasis Merchandising Services Ltd* [1995] BCC 911). Actions cannot be taken under s 213 in relation to conduct that occurred between the date of the presentation of a winding-up petition and the making of a winding-up order as a company cannot be regarded as carrying on business when any transaction in the course of that business which amounts to a disposition of property is deemed to be void under s 127 of the Insolvency Act 1986 unless the court orders to the contrary (*Carman v Cronos Group SA* [2005] EWHC 2403 (Ch) at [37]–[38]). But it was held in the same case that people can be held liable under s 213 in relation to actions that occurred when the company had been dissolved at the time, but is later reinstated to the register under s 653(2) of the Companies Act 1985 (at [24]) on the basis that s 653 states that the company, when reinstated, is deemed to have continued in existence as if it had not been struck off the register (at [24]). Liquidators are required, before taking action, to secure approval from either the liquidation committee or the court (Insolvency Act 1986, s 165(2)(b) (creditors' voluntary liquidations) or s 167(1)(a) (compulsory liquidations); para 3A of Sched 4).

One of the major problems facing liquidators is the funding of litigation, a problem that is common to most, if not all, actions initiated by liquidators and administrators. This is an issue that is discussed in detail in Chapter 6, and much of the discussion in Chapter 10 in relation to the funding of wrongful trading actions, applies equally to fraudulent trading actions.

It has been held in relation to s 214 that, as the application can be categorised as a claim in respect of a sum of money within the Limitation Act 1980, a six-year limitation period applies (*Re Farmizer (Products) Ltd* [1997] 1 BCLC 589 at 598, CA). Proceedings pursuant to s 213 are of the same nature, so they must be commenced within six years of the last event which

---

10 Williams, R, 'Fraudulent trading' (1986) 4 *Company & Securities Law Journal* 14 at 17.
11 *Ibid*.

finalises the right of the liquidator to bring the proceedings, that is, when the cause of action accrued, and this will be either the resolution to wind up, in voluntary liquidation, or the making of a court order, in compulsory winding up (*Re Farmizer (Products) Ltd*). Unlike with actions under ss 238, 239 and 245, for instance, liquidators are not limited in how far back they go in the life of the company to identify periods of fraudulent trading, but in practice the period subject to inquiry will usually be the couple of years (at most) prior to the advent of winding up.

It appears that it would be in order for a liquidator to bring an action that relied on both ss 213 and 214. There is nothing in s 213 to prevent it, and s 214(8) specifically provides that s 214 is not to prejudice s 213. Recently it has been held in relation to an application under s 214, that such an application may be consolidated with disqualification proceedings (*Official Receiver v Doshi* [2001] 2 BCLC 235), and there is no reason to think that it is otherwise where fraudulent trading is involved.

The application for relief should plead fraud clearly and with particularity (*Re Augustus Barnett* at 98,908), that is, the actual conduct that constitutes an intent to defraud must be set out clearly (*Morris v Bank of America National Trust* [2001] 1 BCLC 771; [2000] BCC 1076; [2000] BPIR 83, CA, – an appeal relating to a strike-out application). But, unlike with wrongful trading, where it is critical that the liquidator pleads a date from which the wrongful trading is alleged to have commenced, and this date cannot be amended, courts have still held a respondent to be liable even if no date as to when the fraudulent trading occurred is stated, or where several alternate dates are alleged (*Re a Company No 001418 of 1988* [1991] BCLC 197).

The liquidator may give evidence at the hearing of an application (s 215(1)).

Criminal proceedings

Where criminal proceedings for fraudulent trading are brought under s 458, there are no requirements additional to a s 213 action that have to be proved for securing a criminal conviction, but, naturally, a different burden of proof will apply. Interestingly, while many jurisdictions impose both civil and criminal liability on those guilty of fraudulent trading, apart from the UK no other jurisdiction studied includes two separate provisions. One provision lays down both kinds of liability (for example Irish Companies Act, s 297, Singaporean Companies Act 1990, s 340, South African Companies Act 1973, s 424). This is probably a throwback to the position that existed in the UK before 1986. One jurisdiction, Australia, in s 588G(3) of the Corporations Act 2001, does define additional elements for a criminal prosecution. The Australian provision provides that directors can be liable for insolvent trading and they can be liable at both a civil or a criminal level. Directors are only liable at the latter level if there is a subjective suspicion of insolvency on the part of the director, and the director's 'failure to prevent the company incurring the debt was dishonest'. Whilst there are the inevitable difficulties of proof of such an issue as insolvency to the criminal standard, a number of such prosecutions have been brought, to which in many cases there have been pleas of guilty.[12]

Unlike where a civil claim is instituted, there is no need for the company to be in liquidation before a prosecution can be brought under s 458. This has changed the law, for it was held by the House of Lords in *DPP v Schildkamp* [1971] AC 1, when addressing fraudulent trading as regulated by 332 of the Companies Act 1948, that a prosecution cannot be initiated in relation to a company that was a going concern unless a liquidation had commenced.[13] The change may have been due to the fact that it was felt that the situation under the 1948 statute reduced the effectiveness of the provision.[14]

Putting the offence of fraudulent trading in context, while a charge on this ground is certainly regarded as serious, it is less serious than a specific charge of theft for fraud for an equivalent amount (*R v Smith and Palk* [1997] 2 Cr App R (S) 167). Naturally in a criminal action mounted under s 458 of the Companies Act 1985, if the prosecution is successful the court will order that the defendant be penalised by way of a criminal sanction. Schedule 24 to the Act sets out the parameters for any penalty. The penalty may be substantial, being up to seven years' imprisonment or a fine or both, if the proceedings are on indictment, and where proceedings are brought summarily the sanction is six months' imprisonment or the statutory maximum fine or both. The statutory maximum fine in England and Wales is at present £5,000 according to s 32 of the Magistrates' Courts Act 1980 as amended by s 17 of the Criminal Justice Act 1991.

The Court of Appeal has laid down guidelines on what are appropriate sentences to be visited upon defendants convicted under s 458 (*R v Gibson* [1999] 2 Cr App R (S) 52). Terms of imprisonment have ranged from 12 months in *R v Lockwood* (1986) 2 BCC 99,333, 15 months in *R v Grantham* [1984] 1 QB 675 (under s 332 of the Companies Act 1948), 18 months in *R v Smith* [1997] 2 Cr App R (S) 167 (reduced from three years), three years in *R v Ward* [2001] Cr App R (S) 14 (reduced from four years), and one defendant in *R v Waite* (2003) WL 21162167 was sentenced to five years' imprisonment. In *R v Kemp* [1988] QB 645 lesser penalties were imposed on the defendant, who was fined £500 on one count and on a second count was subject to a term of imprisonment of three months suspended for two years and a fine of £3,000.

Conditions for liability

There are three elements that need to be established by a liquidator for liability under s 213. These are:

---

12 See www.asic.gov.au.   13 Also, see *R v Rollafson* [1969] 1 WLR 815.
14 Certainly the view in Williams, *op. cit.* fn 10 at 17.

(a) the business of the company in liquidation has been carried on with intent to defraud creditors or for any other fraudulent purpose;
(b) the respondent participated in the carrying on of business;
(c) the respondent participated knowingly (*Re BCCI; Morris v Bank of India* [2004] 2 BCLC 236 at 243).

The first element has, perhaps, been regarded as the most critical, and certainly has been the subject of the most debate, so a whole chapter, Chapter 5, is devoted to examining it.

Party to the carrying on of business

First we must note that the respondent must be involved in the carrying on of business, that is, he or she was 'party to the carrying on of business'. According to *Re Maidstone Building* this means nothing more than participating, taking part or concurring in the business of the company. It might well exclude those who might know about the fraudulent conduct, but who do not get involved (at 1094), for instance in *Re Maidstone Building*, where the company secretary, knowing the company was insolvent, refrained from advising the directors to cease trading and was held not to be liable. This is the position in Singapore, where the court in the case of *Tan Hung Yeoh v PP* said that the phrase 'knowingly a party to the carrying on of the business' involved someone participating, concurring or taking some positive step in relation to the fraudulent transaction(s) the subject of the proceedings. I raised earlier the issue of whether a court today might be more ready to hold directors liable for inertia. In many of the wrongful trading cases, courts have indicated that directors were not liable because they sought to address their company's situation, and in others directors have been criticised for doing nothing. Courts might well adopt a similar position with respect to s 213 cases. One would think that it would be very difficult for a director, save where he or she registered unequivocal dissent to the action that the company has taken, to argue that he or she was not a party to the carrying on of business.

Carrying on business is interpreted broadly. For fraudulent trading to have been committed, it is not necessary for the liquidator to prove that there has been a course of conduct, as a single transaction or act is able to constitute the basis for action under s 213 (*Re Gerald Cooper Chemicals; R v Lockwood* (1986) 2 BCC 99,333 at 99,341, CCA; *Morphitis v Bernasconi* [2003] EWCA Civ 289; [2003] BCC 540).[15] Hence, where a company is doing nothing except for collecting and distributing its assets, it can be regarded as carrying on business within s 213, because carrying on trade is not required (*Re Sarflax*

---

15 It has been held in South Africa, where the fraudulent trading provision has been interpreted liberally, that a single action can constitute fraudulent trading (*Gordon & Rennie v Standard Merchant Bank Ltd* (1984) (2) SA 519 (C)).

Ltd [1979] 1 Ch 592; [1979] 1 All ER 529). In *Re Sarflax Ltd* a company had agreed to sell goods to buyers who were in Italy. The buyers asserted that the goods supplied were unsatisfactory and they rescinded the contract. Litigation commenced in England by the buyers and was not followed through but litigation initiated in Italy was, and judgment was secured against the company after the company had ceased trading and entered voluntary liquidation. The liquidator sought a declaration that the business of Sarflax had been carried on with intent to defraud creditors. This application was based on the fact that before the advent of liquidation the company had distributed its assets to some of its creditors (including Sarflax's parent company). The judge held that the company was carrying on business as there was a continuous course of active conduct.

Fraudulent trading can occur when business is being carried on to defraud just one creditor, but one cannot say that whenever a fraud on a creditor is perpetrated while carrying on business it is inevitable that a breach of s 213 occurs; critically, s 213 only applies where the business has been carried on with intent to defraud (*Morphitis v Bernasconi* at [46]–[47]). In this context, intent to defraud in the carrying on of business must be distinguished from misrepresentations and deception in general (*Morphitis* at [43]). A useful illustration was given in *Re Murray-Watson Ltd* (unreported, 6 April 1977, Ch D) by Oliver J when he said that a car dealer was not carrying on business to defraud creditors merely because every time that he sold a car he told lies about the car. Such a fraud was a fraud on the customer, but the dealer did not intend to defraud a creditor (*Re Gerald Cooper Chemicals Ltd* at 267). The dealer could be sued for misrepresentation by each individual customer, but the dealer was not carrying on fraudulent trading within s 213. The Court of Appeal in *Morphitis* (at [46]) made the point that Parliament had not sought to hold liable a person for fraudulent trading when any creditor had been defrauded in the course of carrying on business. The very business itself must be being conducted with the aim of defrauding creditors. The facts in *Morphitis* are worth recounting in outline form. T Ltd carried on business from leasehold premises owned by R. T Ltd was struggling mainly, so the respondents (the directors of the company at the time) thought, because of the high cost of renting the company's business premises. After seeking legal advice, the following plan was formulated. A new company was incorporated, with a similar style name to T Ltd, and it purchased the goodwill of T Ltd and operated the business once carried on by T Ltd. The respondents resigned as directors of T Ltd and became directors of the new company. The intention was to place T Ltd into liquidation, at which time the leases from R could be disclaimed as onerous property. However, so that the respondents did not fall foul of s 216 of the Insolvency Act 1986 (improper re-use of a company name), T Ltd had to operate for 12 months after the resignation of the respondents as directors of T Ltd. To ensure that this occurred the solicitors of T Ltd were instructed to stall R from taking legal proceedings that might lead to a winding-up order being made against T Ltd. The strategy implemented was for T Ltd's solicitors (acting also as the respondents' solicitors) to justify late payments and to seek extensions of time to pay. In response to threats by R to commence proceedings, T Ltd promised payment. T Ltd's solicitors did their job and T Ltd was not wound up until after the requisite 12-month period. When it was wound up, it was as a result of a petition presented by R. The liquidator initiated proceedings under s 213, but the Court of Appeal found that there was no fraudulent trading.

The decision in *Morphitis* is criticised on the basis that the Court of Appeal did not treat the expression 'intent to defraud' as a composite whole and defined 'intent' in isolation.[16] The court regarded the intent of the directors to be to avoid liability under s 216, and not to defraud R, the landlord, yet it has been argued that it would be equally acceptable to categorise the intent as being to permit the company to divest itself of onerous property, or minimise payments to R and seeking to delay the initiation of proceedings.[17] One might ask whether the situation covered in *Morphitis* is the type of single transaction situation envisaged by the court in *Gerald Cooper*, or is it like the illustration given in *Re Murray-Watson Ltd*? Arguably, it is like the former as the only creditor affected by what the directors in *Morphitis* did was the landlord of the premises leased by the company, and the business was being carried on in order to effect a fraud.

Knowingly

Once it has been established that the company's business has been carried on with intent to defraud or for a fraudulent purpose, and a person was a party to the carrying on of the business, the courts may only impose liability on the person provided he or she was knowingly a party to the carrying on of business. It has been held that the liquidator is required to demonstrate dishonesty on the part of the respondent (*Bank of India v Morris* [2005] EWCA Civ 693; [2005] 2 BCLC 328; [2005] BPIR 1067 at [8]), and if a person is found to have knowingly participated, then he or she is acting dishonestly (*Re BCCI; Morris v Bank of India* [2004] 2 BCLC 236 at 244). To be knowingly parties to the fraud, people do not have to know every detail of the fraud or how it is to be perpetrated (*Morris v Bank of India* [2004] 2 BCLC 279 at 297; [2004] BCC 404 at 419). But to be liable a person must have had the relevant knowledge contemporaneously with giving assistance to effect the fraud (*Morris v Bank of India* at 297, 419). What about where there is a series of transactions? The Court of Appeal in *Bank of India v Morris* (at [71]) said that it was appropriate to look at a respondent's conduct as a whole in determining his or her state of mind. But it would appear, from what the

---

16 Savirimuthu, A, '*Morphitis* in the Court of Appeal: some reflections' (2005) 26 Co Law 245 at 247.
17 *Ibid* at 247–248.

court went on to say, that a court must evaluate a person's state of mind in relation to each transaction (at [71]). It would appear that the way that a transaction is structured can go some way to indicating whether or not there was knowledge of fraud (*Morris v Bank of India*, Ch D). So, the fact that a transaction or set of transactions is artificial, or has never been heard of previously in the context of the particular trade being carried on, is likely to contribute to a finding of knowing participation in the fraud (*Bank of India v Morris*, CA, at [34–43]). This is consistent with what Lord Hoffman said in *Twinsectra Ltd v Yardley* [2002] UKHL 12; [2002] 2 AC 164 when dealing with an alleged assistance of a breach of trust that necessitated the proving of dishonesty. His Lordship said that he would not suggest that one cannot be dishonest without a full appreciation of the legal analysis of the transaction. In addressing the kind of action before him he said that a person may dishonestly assist in the commission of a breach of trust without any idea of what a trust means (at [24], 170).

In considering whether the respondent was knowingly a party to fraud, if liquidators could demonstrate that respondents had 'blind-eye' knowledge, namely deliberately shutting their eyes to the obvious, in that it was obvious to the respondents that fraud was involved, they could succeed (*Bank of India v Morris*, CA). Blind-eye knowledge involves a suspicion that a fraud exists and a deliberate decision being taken to avoid confirming that it exists, and that the suspicion is well-grounded (*Re BCCI; Morris v Bank of India*). In *Manifest Shipping Company Ltd v Uni-Polaris Company Ltd* [2003] 1 AC 469 at [116] Lord Scott put it this way when he said: 'In summary, blind-eye knowledge requires, in my opinion, a suspicion that the relevant facts do exist and a deliberate decision to avoid confirming that they exist.' But clearly the way that suspicion is interpreted is important. Lord Scott went on (at [116]), after making the point just adverted to, to sound a warning that:

> Suspicion is a word that can be used to describe a state of mind that may, at one extreme, be no more than a vague feeling of unease and, at the other extreme, reflect a firm belief in the existence of the relevant facts. In my opinion, in order for there to be blind-eye knowledge, the suspicion must be firmly grounded and targeted on specific facts.

In the Privy Council decision of *Royal Brunei Airlines Sdn Bhd v Tan* [1995] 2 AC 378, a case involving a claim that a person had dishonestly assisted in a breach of a trust, Lord Nicholls, on behalf of the Judicial Committee, indicated that it was dishonesty for a person 'deliberately to close his eyes and ears, or deliberately not to ask questions, lest he learn something he would rather not know, and then proceed regardless' (at 389).

It was accepted in *Re BCCI; Morris v Bank of India* [2004] 2 BCLC 236 at 243 that it is necessary to distinguish between a person who has a conscious appreciation of the true nature of the business that is occurring, and someone who fails, even negligently, to appreciate the fraud. Only the former is liable.

So, directors who are not intimately involved in the actions of the company that constitute fraudulent conduct, and who had suspicions, but did nothing about them, are not usually going to be able to extricate themselves from liability.

What constitutes fraudulent trading?

The fact that a company continues to engage in trading while it is insolvent does not constitute fraudulent trading, except where the company obtains credit when the directors know that there is no good reason for taking the view that funds will be available to pay the debt when it becomes payable (*R v Grantham* [1984] 2 QB 675 at 682–683; *R v Waite* (2003) WL 21162167 at [5], CCA). This can include the failure to pay trade creditors and not remitting moneys, deducted from employees' salary, to the revenue authorities, or the failure to pay VAT when receiving money for goods sold (*Re L Todd (Swanscombe) Ltd* [1990] BCLC 454), and continuing to incur liabilities when the company is clearly insolvent and with no chance of being able to discharge them as the company is obviously heading for administration or liquidation (*Re William C Leitch Bros Ltd* [1932] 2 Ch 71 at 77). Fraudulent trading can be made out even if it is not possible to establish that anyone has suffered a loss (*R v Grantham* [1984] QB 675 at 683–684). The critical issue is the intent to defraud or have a fraudulent purpose. This issue is discussed further in Chapter 5.

As mentioned earlier, not every fraud or fraudulent misrepresentation made by a company can constitute fraudulent trading within s 213 as the provision is aimed at carrying on business and not the execution of individual transactions (*Morphitis* at [43], [46]). For instance, if a retailer made misrepresentations to customers, he would not be committing fraudulent trading even though he is perpetrating a fraud on the customers, provided that he did nothing to prevent them from bringing an action and to recover their losses (*Re Gerald Cooper Chemicals Ltd* [1978] Ch 262 at 267). As Chadwick LJ explained in *Morphitis* (at [46]), it was not intended that the powers under s 213 were able to be exercised at any time a creditor was defrauded by a company in the course of the carrying on of business. In *obiter* comments in *Bernasconi v Nicholas Bennett & Co* [2000] BCC 921 at 925; [2000] BPIR 8 at 13 Laddie J said that 'closing a company down by methods which seriously, unfairly and impermissibly disadvantage creditors does not *per se* offend against' s 213. It is clear that, as indicated earlier, carrying on business within the section can be constituted by doing a single act provided that it is done in the course of carrying on business (*Re Gerald Cooper Chemicals Ltd; R v Lockwood; Morphitis*).

Loss

It has been stated, in *obiter*, that the liquidator, in order for a contribution to be ordered, has to establish a nexus between the loss caused to creditors because of the fraudulent trading and the contribution that is being sought from the person allegedly involved in the fraudulent trading (*Morphitis* at [53]). Chadwick LJ provided the following example in *Morphitis* (at [53]) as an obvious case for contribution, namely:

> [W]here the carrying on of the business with fraudulent intent has led to the misapplication, or misappropriation, of the company's assets. In such a case the appropriate order might be that those knowingly party to such misapplication or misappropriation contribute an amount equal to the value of the assets misapplied or misappropriated. Another obvious case would be where the carrying on of business with fraudulent intent has led to claims against the company by those defrauded. In such a case the appropriate order might be that those knowingly party to the conduct which has given rise to those claims in the liquidation contribute an amount equal to the amount by which the existence of those claims would otherwise diminish the assets available for distribution to creditors generally; that is to say an amount equal to that amount which has to be applied out of the assets available for distribution to satisfy those claims.

If the requisite nexus can be established, then the sum that is to be ordered to be paid is limited to the amount of the debts of the creditors proved to have been defrauded by the fraudulent trading (*Re a Company No 001418 of 1988* [1991] BCLC 197 at 203).

The position in the UK is to be contrasted with that in South Africa, where there has been no need to establish a causal connection between the allegedly fraudulent conduct and the relevant debts (*Howard v Herrigel* 1991 (2) SA 660 (AD) at 661).

The order

In civil actions under s 213, if the liquidator's case is proved, the court may make a declaration that the respondent was a person who was knowingly a party to the carrying on of business with intent to defraud or to effect a fraudulent purpose, and if it does it may then specify the sum that is to be paid by the respondent by way of contribution (*Re a Company No 001418 of 1988* at 202). As to the substance of the declaration, the court has a broad discretion. UK courts will be principally concerned about awarding a sum to the liquidator to compensate the creditors for the wrongful action of the respondent. But besides an order for compensation, courts have been willing, in the past, to include a punitive element in the order (*Re Cyona Distributors Ltd* [1967] Ch 889; [1967] 1 All ER 281, CA; *Re A Company (No 001418 of 1988)* at 202). *Re Cyona Distributors* was decided pursuant to the 1948 statute, and the position it espoused was followed in *Re a Company (No 001418)* where the court ordered a punitive amount of £25,000 in addition to a compensatory sum of £131,420. Notwithstanding the fact that s 213 is wider than its precursors, and there is case law to the effect that a punitive award as well as a compensatory award may be delivered if it is appropriate, recently, in *Morphitis v Bernasconi* (at [55]), the Court of Appeal said, in *obiter*, that there was no power in s 213 permitting a court to include any punitive element in the amount of any contribution ordered. It was the view of the court that the contribution to the assets, to be shared among the creditors, should reflect the loss which has been caused to the creditors by the carrying on of the business in the way that gave rise to the exercise of the power (at [55]). The court added (at [55]) that the power to punish a guilty party was preserved in the criminal form of fraudulent trading, s 458 of the Companies Act 1985. The position in other jurisdictions is different. For example, the view in Singapore appears to be that in a civil action the court can make a punitive order,[18] but it must be remembered that the provision is based on former UK legislation.

Even though it appears that a court cannot penalise the respondent, contribution orders can be high. For example, in the most recent decision involving s 213 and the BCCI liquidation, *Bank of India v Morris* (CA, at [1]), Patten J ordered the respondent to pay the liquidators £82,302,941, a sum that included interest and costs.[19]

Any court award must be in favour of the liquidator for the whole body of creditors, and not an individual creditor (*Re Esal (Commodities) Ltd* [1997] 1 BCLC 705, CA), something that is also applicable to s 214 (*Re Oasis Merchandising Services Ltd* [1995] BCC 911 at 918). The award is to be held by a liquidator for the purpose of making a distribution to the unsecured creditors (*Re Oasis Merchandising Services Ltd* affirmed on appeal [1997] 1 All ER 1009; [1997] BCC 282, CA) and is, therefore, not available for a secured creditor holding a charge over company assets. This is discussed in detail later in this chapter under 'The destination of the proceeds'.[20]

It is not always easy for a court to know what is an appropriate order of compensation. This is highlighted by the case of *Re L Todd (Swanscombe) Ltd*. In that case the liquidator of T Ltd applied for a declaration under s 630 of the Companies Act 1985, the immediate predecessor of s 213, for a declaration that a former director of the company, M, was liable for fraudulent trading. Specifically it was argued that M was knowingly a party to the carrying on of business with intent to defraud creditors. Prior to winding up it seems that M received substantial amounts of cash in relation to transactions involving the sale of company goods, but these transactions were not entered in the books of the company and VAT was not paid. Her Majesty's

---

18 Joyce, L, ' Fraudulent and Insolvent Trading in Singapore' (2000) 9 *International Insolvency Review* 121 at 133.

19 This still paled into insignificance when compared with the deficiency of BCCI at the time of its collapse – in the region of US$10 billion (*Bank of India v Morris* [2005] EWCA Civ 693; [2005] 2 BCLC 328; [2005] BPIR 1067 at [3]).

20 It remains the case that, in South Africa, creditors can make applications (*Bowman v Sacks* 1986 (4) SA 459 (WLD)) and obtain awards in their favour.

Customs and Excise discovered these facts when investigating the company. The precise amount of VAT, interest and penalties due to Customs was not proved before the court. The court did end up making a declaration that M was liable for fraudulent trading and that he was liable for debts, namely the VAT, interest and penalties, to the tune of slightly in excess of £70,000. It has been accepted that any order of contribution, while essentially compensatory, could only ever be a reasonable approximation either of the damage to which the actions of the led, or the damage to which he or she contributed (*Re BCCI; Morris v State Bank of India* [2004] 2 BCLC 279; [2004] BCC 404).

The judge, if he or she finds that the respondent is liable, may include an element of interest in the contribution ordered (*Re BCCI; Morris v State Bank of India* [2004] BCC 404 at 465). Also, where a court makes a declaration against the respondent to an application, it is, at its discretion, empowered to make further directions to give effect to its declaration (Insolvency Act 1986, s 215(2)). In particular, it may provide for the liability of the respondent under the declaration to be a charge on any debt or obligation due from the company to the respondent, or on any mortgage or charge or any interest in a mortgage or charge on assets of the company held by or vested in the respondent, or any person on behalf of the respondent, or any person claiming as assignee from or through the respondent (s 215(2)(a)). The court may, from time to time make such further or other order as may be necessary for enforcing any charge imposed under s 215 (s 215(2)(b)). Also, s 215(4) provides that in the case of a court declaration against a person that is liable for fraudulent trading, the court may direct that the whole or any part of a debt owed by the company to the guilty person is to rank after all other debts owed and interest payable on those debts.

Finally, it should be noted that besides imposing a criminal penalty under s 458 or ordering compensation under s 213, a court may disqualify the respondent from acting as a director or taking part in the management of a company (Company Directors Disqualification Act 1986, ss 4(1) and 10(1)), with the maximum period of disqualification being 15 years (ss 4(3), 10(2)).

The destination of proceeds

A critical issue for liquidators who recover sums of money pursuant to s 213 is to know how they should be distributed, assuming that the expenses and costs of winding up will not gobble up all that is recovered. In *Re William Leitch Bros Ltd (No 2)* [1933] Ch 261 the defrauded creditors argued that the amount recovered should be carried to a separate account to be applied in discharging their claims alone; Eve J rejected this contention and held instead that it formed part of the general assets of the company available for division among all unsecured creditors (at 266). The judge based this conclusion in part upon the problem of establishing any other way of applying the funds, coupled with the absence of any machinery in the section itself, and in part upon the analogy provided by *Webb v Whiffin* (1872) LR 5 HL 711.

However, it would seem that, notwithstanding the view of Eve J, any award ordered to be paid is not available to a chargeholder who has a charge over the present and future assets of the company. This is because the liquidator, in taking proceedings under s 213, is proceeding in his or her own capacity and not on the company's behalf. This is the same situation as liquidators taking action under the wrongful trading ground and the courts have made it plain that any funds recovered are to be distributed amongst the unsecured creditors alone (*Re Oasis Merchandising Services Ltd* [1995] BCC 911 and affirmed on appeal by the Court of Appeal at [1997] 1 All ER 1009; [1997] BCC 282; *Morphitis v Bernasconi*). This issue is discussed in more detail in relation to wrongful trading in Chapter 8 ('The effects of an order'). So, the amount of any recovery is to be distributed among all creditors pursuant to the statutory scheme.

5 Intent to defraud and fraudulent purpose

Introduction

The primary element of the fraudulent trading provision is that the respondent must be proved to have carried on business with intent to defraud creditors or for any fraudulent purpose, that is, the intention to defraud or acting for any fraudulent purpose must accompany the carrying on of the business. The main issue that has dogged the provision, ever since its advent, has been what is meant by 'intent to defraud', and 'fraudulent purpose', and what actually has to be proved by a liquidator in order to establish that the respondent has engaged in one or the other. These phrases have never been defined statutorily and there has been judicial inconsistency concerning which test should be applied. In one of the first reported cases dealing with the first fraudulent trading provision, *Re Patrick & Lyon Ltd* [1933] Ch 786, Maugham J said that the words 'defraud' and 'fraudulent purpose' are words that connote actual dishonesty and encompass real moral blame (at 790). Ascertaining a meaning of these words is far from easy as 'there has been a lack of consistency over the years in the judicial approach to formulating a test for fraudulent conduct'[1] in relation to s 213. This chapter traces the way that the courts have interpreted the expressions, focusing on the most recent case law, and seeks to ascertain what the present tests are for establishing 'an intent to defraud'.

It has been suggested, adroitly, it is respectfully submitted, that the greatest obstacle to the use of fraudulent trading proceedings is the requirement of fraud or dishonesty.[2] The onus of proving an intent to defraud, which involves dishonesty (*R v Grantham* [1984] QB 675; [1984] 2 WLR 815; [1984] BCLC 270, CCA), can be extremely hard to discharge (*Bank of India v Morris* [2005] EWCA (Civ) 693; [2005] 2 BCLC 328; [2005] BPIR 1067 at [101]), and is one important reason why wrongful trading was introduced. Notwithstanding this, as we saw in Chapter 4, apparently there has been some resurgence in the use of s 213 in recent times.

---

1 Fletcher, I F, *The Law of Insolvency*, 3rd edn, 2002, London: Sweet and Maxwell, para 27.015.
2 Oditah, F, 'Wrongful trading' [1990] LMCLQ 205 at 206.

Intent to defraud

The first matter to consider in relation to this expression is the interpretation which is to be given to the meaning of 'fraud' in the context of the section. This has been the main issue facing courts over the years, and, as is generally well known, fraud is difficult to define for it has different meanings in different contexts,[3] although in *R v Terry* [1984] AC 374 at 380–381 the House of Lords did indicate that in some cases, such as the House of Lords' decision in *Welham v DPP* [1961] AC 103, comments are made with an intention to cover fraud generally. It is submitted that one of the causes of the problem that faces the courts is that judges in summing up to juries in fraudulent trading prosecutions have had to try and explain what fraud involves in the context of s 458, and these difficulties have been transferred to civil cases. Although focusing on Australian provisions in insolvency law that enable liquidators to avoid pre-liquidation transactions, such as preferences and uncommercial transactions,[4] what Pincus JA of the Queensland Court of Appeal had to say in *World Expo Park v EFG* (1995) 129 ALR 685 at 708 is most apposite. Speaking of fraud, his Honour said that it is:

> . . . [a] legal curiosity that after 400 years of judicial exposition of the statutes which have reproduced part or all of the substance [of bankruptcy and insolvency fraud provisions] there remains room for argument as to the nature of the fraud which must be proved, under such provision in order to set aside a transaction.

Dishonesty

First we must note that for a person to be liable for fraud, he or she must be proved to have been engaging in dishonesty (*Re Cox and Hodges* (1982) 75 Cr App R 291, CCA; *R v Grantham; Bank of India v Morris* at [8]), a concept that is associated with fraud. Fraud is said to connote dishonesty involving, according to current notions of fair trading among commercial men, real moral blame (*Re Patrick & Lyon Ltd* at 790; *R v Grantham; Re a Company No 001418 of 1988* [1991] BCLC 197). Where s 458 is concerned, the notion does not appear to be different from the concept of dishonesty in general criminal cases (*R v Lockwood* [1986] 2 BCC 99,333 at 99,340, CCA).

In *Bernasconi v Nicholas Bennett & Co* [2000] BPIR 8 at 12, 13; [2000] BCC 921 at 924, Laddie J stated that dishonesty was a critical element in an action under s 213. In fact the judge said that it was the dishonesty factor

---

3   Farrar, J, 'Fraudulent trading' [1980] JBL 336 at 339.
4   The UK provisions covering these kinds of transactions are Insolvency Act 1986, ss 239 and 238 respectively.

which distinguished s 213 from an action for wrongful trading (at 13; 925). All of this is consistent with the general view that dishonesty is an essential element of fraud (*Scott v Commissioners of Police for the Metropolis* [1975] AC 819).

The issues

There are two primary issues that need to be resolved when considering the meaning of fraud in the context of s 213. First, can a court only consider what a respondent says about his or her state of mind, namely applying a purely subjective test, or can any objective considerations be taken into account in determining whether the respondent was dishonest, such as whether a court is able to infer what the respondent's state of mind was from the actions of the respondent and the circumstances surrounding the alleged fraudulent trading. Second, what standard of honesty is to be applied? Is it that of the respondent according to his or her testimony, namely what he or she regarded as honest conduct, or is it some other standard? Undoubtedly the two issues are related, but for analytical and expositional purposes it is better to separate them.

The state of mind

The test for intent to defraud is a subjective one (*Bernasconi v Nicholas Bennett & Co; Re BCCI; Morris v Bank of India* [2003] BCC 735): namely the state of the mind of the respondent at the time of the alleged fraudulent trading is the decisive issue (*R v Ghosh* [1982] QB 1053, CCA, a case dealing with the Theft Act). So, if it was established that the respondent had knowledge of fraud, then it follows that the respondent was acting dishonestly (*Re BCCI; Morris v State Bank of India* [2004] BCC 404).

While the test for intent to defraud is subjective and not objective, in that the state of the mind of the respondent is the critical factor, we have case law right from the time of the first fraudulent trading provision that indicates that objective considerations are not irrelevant. The issue is, however, in what circumstances may objective factors be taken into account by a court, and to what extent may these factors be used?

An examination of the meaning of 'carrying on business with intent to defraud' must start with two judgments of Maugham J in the 1930s which were, it has been suggested, inconsistent. In the first of the cases, *Re William C Leitch Bros Ltd* [1932] 2 Ch 71, the judge gave 'intent to defraud' a wide meaning and, in effect, indicated that courts could infer the requisite state of mind. His Lordship said (at 77):

> If a company continues to carry on business and to incur debts at a time when there is, to the knowledge of the directors, no reasonable prospect of the creditors ever receiving payment of those debts, it is, in general,

a proper inference that the company is carrying on business with intent to defraud.[5]

The case in question fell directly within the mischief which the section was designed to suppress, for it was one in which the governing director of the company had, at a time when the company was, to his knowledge, unable to pay its debts, ordered goods on credit which thereupon became subject to a floating charge in favour of the director.[6] His Lordship's statement suggested that where the relevant conduct of the director could be regarded '. . . as dishonest *per se*, the inference will be that the conduct was dishonest and thus constitutes on the part of the director intent to defraud'.[7] The suggestion from the case is that intent to defraud could be inferred even if the respondent states that he or she had no such intent. In view of this, the proposition laid down by Maugham J may have been framed rather more widely than was strictly necessary for the decision of the case, and it may not be without significance that in the subsequent case of *Re Patrick & Lyon Ltd* the same judge declined to make a declaration of personal liability against a director who had deliberately delayed in despatching notices of intention to wind up voluntarily with the object of protecting his charge from invalidity under the precursor of s 245 of the Insolvency Act 1986 (a provision that permits, in certain circumstances, the invalidation of floating charges in a liquidation or administration). It is often said that the judge favoured a narrower approach than that which he articulated in *Leitch*. While in *Patrick & Lyon* the judge clearly found for the defendant, and did not consider whether intent could be inferred, his Lordship did not say anything that indicated a retraction of what he had said in the earlier case. The judge simply did not think that the defendant was deliberately intending to defraud. Certainly, in *Patrick & Lyon*, the facts, as far as they are reported, do not disclose the same questionable activities on the part of the defendant when compared with the defendant in the earlier case, and might be explained accordingly. However, in *Hardie v Hanson* (1960) 105 CLR 451, the Australian High Court expressed grave doubts as to the validity of the proposition of Maugham J in *Leitch*, quoted earlier, being regarded as a rule of substantive law, and thought it was, at most, a proposition of evidence of proof which was only 'in general' true (at 460 per Dixon CJ; Kitto J agreed at 464). The court seemed disposed to regard it as essential that a party charged under the section should be shown to have intended to benefit or protect himself or herself at the expense of the company's creditors (at 461–462, 464, 467),[8] and this, in the opinion of one of

---

5   See also *R v Wax* 1957 (4) SA 399 and *Re Gerald Cooper Chemicals* [1978] 2 All ER 49.

6   The director was declared personally liable for £6,000, the amount of the debts incurred, which was charged on a debenture held by him.

7   Scanlan, G, 'The criminal liabilities of directors to the creditors of the company' (2003) 24 Co Law 234 at 239.

8   Compare *Re Gerald Cooper Chemicals Ltd* [1978] Ch 262.

the judges (Kitto J), was not established by proving simply that he had 'acted with blameworthy irresponsibility, knowing that he was gambling in effect with his creditors' money as well as his own, and with much more of their money than of his own' (at 464).

In the unreported decision of *Re White and Osmond (Parkstone) Ltd* (30 June 1960), Buckley J appears to have sought to reconcile any perceived divergence in the two decisions of Maugham J. Buckley J said, in rather descriptive language:

> In my judgment there is nothing wrong in the fact that directors incur credit at a time when, to their knowledge, the company is not able to meet all its liabilities as they fall due. What is manifestly wrong is if directors allow a company to incur credit at a time when the business is being carried on in such circumstances that it is clear that the company will never be able to satisfy its creditors. However, there is nothing to say that directors who genuinely believe that the clouds will roll away and the sunshine of prosperity will shine upon them again and disperse the fog of their depression are not entitled to incur credit to help them to get over the bad time.[9]

So, Buckley J seems to accept that the requisite state of mind could be inferred. But his Lordship drew a distinction between inferring intent in the case where the respondent knows that the company will never be able to pay debts that are incurred, as opposed to the case where debts are incurred when it is known that the company cannot satisfy debts as they fall due, but the person has a genuine belief that the debts may well be satisfied in due course. According to the learned judge, only in the former case is the respondent liable under s 213. Consequently, this approach does not lead to liability for a person who is possessed by unfounded optimism. There appears to be little in the case law that is against the first of the two positions proposed by Buckley J. It is in relation to the latter that there is some divergence.

At about the time of Buckley J's judgment, the Australian High Court in *Hardie* rejected the idea that a person is liable if he or she incurs debts without any reasonable prospect of being able to pay. The court said that personal dishonesty needed to be established. One of the judges, Menzies J, said (at 467):

> [E]ven if the chances of payment of all creditors in full were so remote that it belonged to the realms of hope rather than belief, it seems to me that the fault, grievous though it may be, falls short of fraud unless it is coupled with something else, such as misrepresentation of the position or

---

9   Quoted in Davies, P, *et al*, *Palmer's Corporate Insolvency Law*, London: Sweet and Maxwell, p 1249.

an intention to use goods on credit for the purposes of dishonest gain, which gives it a fraudulent character.

However, the Court of Appeal in *R v Grantham* (and followed in *Re a Company (No 001418 of 1988)*) took a more robust approach, and it indicated that a person may be liable if, when obtaining credit, it was known that there was no reason for thinking that the debt would be able to be paid when it became due or shortly afterwards. A similar position was taken in *Re Gerald Cooper Chemicals Ltd* [1978] Ch 262 at 268. In *Re Gerald Cooper* it was said that a company was being carried on with an intent to defraud if it accepted payments for goods and it was known that the company could not supply the goods, and the directors knew that the company was insolvent (at 267–268). Templeman J also stated that the word 'intent' is employed in the sense that a person must be taken to intend the 'natural or foreseen consequences of his act' (at 267), clearly accepting the fact that intent can be inferred. This view received the implicit imprimatur of the Court of Appeal (Criminal Division) in *R v Grantham* [1984] QB 675, when it approved of the following (at 681), taken from the summing-up in the trial:

> A man intends to defraud a creditor either if he intends that the creditor shall never be paid or alternatively if he intends to obtain credit or carry on obtaining credit when the rights and interests of the creditor are being prejudiced in a way which the defendant himself has generally regarded as dishonest . . . a trader can intend to defraud if he obtains credit when there is a substantial risk of the creditor not getting his money or not getting the whole of his money and the defendant knows that is the position and knows he is stepping beyond the bounds of what ordinary decent people engaged in business would regard as honest.

In these decisions the courts were, in effect, inferring intent to defraud, based on something close to recklessness. More recently, Laddie J seemed to accept this view as he said that to be liable the respondent had to evince an intent or, as an alternative, a reckless indifference whether creditors were defrauded (*Bernasconi v Nicholas Bennett & Co* at 12; 924). All of this suggests a more severe approach than that taken in *Hardie*. In *Grantham* the court referred to an earlier decision of the Court of Appeal (Criminal Division) in *R v Sinclair* [1968] 1 WLR 1246, a case involving a prosecution for fraudulently using a company's assets for purposes other than those of the company, and where the Court of Appeal upheld the statement of the trial judge (at 1250) that:

> To prove fraud it must be established that the conduct was deliberately dishonest. In the circumstances of this case what sort of test should be applied as to whether the conduct was dishonest? It is fraud if it is proved

that there was the taking of a risk which there was no right to take which would cause detriment or prejudice to another.

On the basis of this case it might be argued that a respondent has committed a breach of s 213 if he or she incurred debts in such a way that there was a significant risk that there would be no repayment, even if there was no subjective intent to defraud. The use in *Sinclair* of the phrase, 'the taking of a risk which there was no right to take' suggests recklessness. This is to be contrasted with a situation like that found in *Re Augustus Barnett & Sons Ltd* [1986] 2 BCC 98,904 where the respondents were held not to be liable, for when they incurred liabilities they believed that their company would be supported by the company's holding company, and this belief was reasonable, because, *inter alia*, the holding company had provided large subsidies in the past. In terms of the test in *Sinclair*, there was no taking of a risk that there was no right to take.

In the Hong Kong case of *Aktieselskabet Dansk Skibsfinansiering v Brothers* [2001] 2 BCLC 324 Lord Hoffmann, sitting as a member of the Court of Final Appeal and delivering a judgment that was agreed to by the other four members of the court, did not express his views in the same terms as the judges in the decisions just considered. His Lordship emphasised other factors, and agreed with the High Court of Australia that the statement in *Leitch* which was quoted above was a not a helpful generalisation (at 331), and went on to accept the view of the trial judge in the case on appeal before him that whether a person was or was not dishonest was dependent on an assessment of all of the facts. But his Lordship did think that there was adequate evidence in *Leitch*, namely the defendant ordering goods greatly in excess of the company's usual requirements so that the value would reduce the extent of the defendant's guarantee to the bank which had a charge over the assets of the company, to permit Maugham J to find that fraudulent trading had occurred. Lord Hoffmann indicated that for a person to be liable under s 213, where he or she ordered goods or services from a creditor, an applicant had to establish that the respondent was seeking to gain a personal advantage and was deceiving the creditor (at 331), and this is consistent with *Leitch* where emphasis was placed on the fact that the respondent deliberately went on trading in the name of the company in order, as he hoped, to safeguard his own position, and without any regard to the interests of the creditors. It is also reminiscent of the views expressed in the Australian case of *Hardie*. The corollary of the view of Lord Hoffmann might be that directors who order goods for their company are not going to be liable necessarily for fraudulent trading merely because there is a risk that the supplier is not going to get paid. The directors must be gaining a personal benefit from the ordering of the goods for liability to be imposed. Certainly, Lord Radcliffe in *Welham v DPP* [1961] AC 103, HL (a case involving consideration of s 4 of the Forgery Act 1913 and one of the leading cases on the issue of fraud) said that fraud invariably is associated with the obtaining of an advantage for the perpetrator, but his Lordship indicated (at 123) that the effect on the party who is the object of an alleged fraud is the critical element, a point accepted in *Grantham* (at 683–684) and *Re a Company (No 001418 of 1988)* (at 198). The court in *Grantham* (at 683–684) actually stated that fraudulent trading can be made out even if it is not possible to establish that anyone has suffered a loss.

A matter with which Lord Hoffmann was deeply concerned was the fact that he felt that precedent was being used improperly in fraudulent trading cases. His Lordship stated that while precedent can be used to establish principles in relation to dishonesty, each case must be assessed on its own facts (at 331–332). The position of the learned judge (at 331–332) is that one cannot say, by way of generalisation, that anyone who incurs debts, for example, at a time when there is no likelihood of being able to pay, is necessarily liable for a breach of s 213. This concern is consistent with what his Lordship said in the earlier case of *Re Augustus Barnett & Sons Ltd* (at 98,909), where he said that it is not permissible to translate the actual facts pleaded in a fraudulent trading action into generalities and then draw inferences from the generalities instead of from the facts themselves. In *Aktieselskabet Dansk Skibsfinansiering* Lord Hoffmann expressed the need for caution when employing statements about objective considerations. He said that courts must be careful in invoking the concept of the hypothetical decent honest man and what that person would have done in the circumstances, as there might be a temptation to treat the respondent's shortcomings as a failure to comply with the necessary objective standard of conduct. Lord Hoffmann went on to say that dishonesty depended on an assessment of all the facts and stated that it was much safer to focus on the respondent before the court and to ask whether that person had been dishonest.

The above analysis seems to suggest some difference in the view of Lord Hoffmann and that of the Court of Appeal in *Grantham*, although his Lordship did not take issue with anything said in *Grantham* when he referred to it in his judgment, and in fact he was of the opinion that the defendants in *Grantham* should have been found liable. Lord Hoffmann in *Aktieselskabet Dansk Skibsfinansiering* emphasised the fact that for the respondent to be liable, he or she must have benefited personally from the alleged fraud, a point also taken in the *Hardie* case, while in *Grantham*, and other decisions, including the important case of *Welham*, injury to the creditors was regarded as the essential requirement for liability. Lord Hoffmann and the Australian High Court in *Hardie* seem to be of the view that inferences can only be made where the respondent actually benefits personally from the allegedly fraudulent trading, hence, it follows that if a respondent is able to claim without challenge that he or she had no intent to defraud, and the respondent did not benefit from the incurring of debts on behalf of the company, he or she should not be held liable. Also of note is the fact that both the Australian High Court in *Hardie* and Lord Hoffmann in *Aktieselskabet Dansk Skibsfinansiering* expressed concern about making the right to infer intent a rule of law; rather, the focus should be on the facts of each case.

A similar approach to that advocated in *Grantham*, has been implemented in a cognate field, namely where a person is alleged to have put assets beyond the reach of his, her or its creditors, which involves a breach of s 423 of the Insolvency Act 1986. The Australian High Court in *Cannane v Cannane* (1998) 192 CLR 557, a case dealing with the Australian equivalent of s 423, s 121 of the Bankruptcy Act 1966, involved three of the five judges saying that intent to defraud could be established by inference, and whether a court was able to infer depended on all the circumstances (at 566–567 and 591–593). This approach has been utilised for many years, and certainly as far back as *Freeman v Pope* (1870) LR 5 Ch 538 where Lord Hatherley LC permitted inferences to be drawn in evaluating whether there had been an intent to defraud in relation to a precursor of s 423. In recent times, in giving the leading judgment of the Court of Appeal in the s 423 case of *Inland Revenue Commissioners v Hashmi* [2002] 2 BCLC 489, Arden LJ indicated that judges may draw inferences. The Report of the Insolvency Law Review Committee, *Insolvency Law and Practice*,[10] supported allowing courts to infer purpose where this would be the natural and probable consequences of the debtor's actions (at [1283]).

When it comes to consideration of the phrase, 'intent to defraud' in a prosecution under s 458, it should be seen in light of s 8(1) of the Criminal Justice Act 1987 which provides that a court is not bound to infer that the defendant intended or foresaw a result of his or her actions. It must decide whether the defendant did intend or foresee the result by reference to all of the evidence, drawing such inferences from the evidence as appears fit and proper. But arguably this is no different than the position that the courts have taken under s 213. All of this is not surprising, for there are a number of criminal cases in which it has been stated that courts may draw inferences concerning the state of mind of a director (for example, *R v Berrada* (1990) 91 Cr App R 131, CCA).

In sum, the preponderance of authority, including notably *Grantham*, seems to hold to the view that a court may infer that the respondent had an intent to defraud either where the respondent, when incurring a debt, was aware that there was no good reason for thinking that the debt could be satisfied, or where the respondent knew that there was a risk that the creditor might not get paid. Lord Hoffmann, primarily in *Aktieselskabet Dansk Skibsfinansiering*, and the Australian High Court in *Hardie*, seem to require the respondent to receive a personal gain from a transaction before they would acquiesce to the making of any inference. While his Lordship's view, in particular, is of strong persuasive force, it is not binding on a High Court judge, and one would think that the *Grantham* approach would prevail.

10 Cmnd 858, HMSO (1982), and known as the Cork Report.

The standard of honesty

The issue to which we now turn is whether respondents are able to say that they are not liable because they believed that what they did was not fraudulent, or whether some other standard is relevant. Lord Lane CJ in the case of *Ghosh*, which dealt with a prosecution for obtaining property by deception in breach of the Theft Act, said that defendants would be acting dishonestly where they act in ways that they know are considered by ordinary people to be dishonest, even if they assert that they believed that what they were doing was morally justified (at 1064). The Court of Appeal in *R v Lockwood* [1986] 2 BCC 99,333 at 99,340, a fraudulent trading case, said that the definition[11] of dishonesty given in *Ghosh* was of general application. This is consistent with the approach sanctioned by both the Privy Council and the House of Lords in two cases that have addressed the concept of dishonesty in a civil setting. The cases, *Royal Brunei Airlines Sdn Bhd v Tan* [1995] 2 AC 378 and *Twinsectra Ltd v Yardley* [2002] UKHL 12; [2002] 2 AC 164,[12] considered the issue of dishonesty in the context of a claim that the respondents were involved in dishonestly assisting a breach of trust. It is not intended to undertake an exposition of these two cases, but what they have to say about dishonesty is on point. In *Twinsectra*, Lord Hutton (with whom three of the Law Lords agreed) said that there were three tests that could be applied to determining whether someone acted dishonestly or not. The first two tests were the standard subjective and objective tests. But his Lordship applied the third test, which he called 'the combined test'. This is a 'standard which combines an objective test and a subjective test, and which requires that before there can be a finding of dishonesty it must be established that the defendant's conduct was dishonest by the ordinary standards of reasonable and honest people and that he himself realised that by those standards his conduct was dishonest' (at 171, [27]). In a similar manner, Lord Nicholls said in *Royal Brunei Airlines* (at 389) (and this was approved of by a majority of the House of Lords in *Twinsectra*) that:

> Honesty has a connotation of subjectivity, as distinct from the objectivity of negligence. Honesty, indeed, does have a strong subjective element in that it is a description of a type of conduct assessed in the light of what a person actually knew at the time, as distinct from what a reasonable person would have known or appreciated. Further, honesty and its counterpart dishonesty are mostly concerned with advertent conduct, not inadvertent conduct. Carelessness is not dishonesty. Thus for the

---

11 One might quibble with the use of this word, as courts have been at pains to say that they will not attempt to define dishonesty.

12 It is interesting that in this case, involving the issue of whether the respondent was liable for being an accessory to a breach of trust, Lord Millett, who dissented, favoured a totally objective test.

most part dishonesty is to be equated with conscious impropriety. However, these subjective characteristics of honesty do not mean that individuals are free to set their own standards of honesty in particular circumstances. The standard of what constitutes honest conduct is not subjective. Honesty is not an optional scale, with higher or lower values according to the moral standards of each individual. If a person knowingly appropriates another's property, he will not escape a finding of dishonesty simply because he sees nothing wrong in such behaviour.

Lord Hoffmann, who as we saw earlier, sounded warnings in *Aktieselskabet Dansk Skibsfinansiering v Brothers* about employing objective considerations, accepted the statement of the trial judge that the further a person moves away from objective standards of honesty, the more likely it is that he or she is dishonest (at 330). His Lordship seemed to agree that while respondents are not liable unless they knew that they were acting dishonestly, the standard of honesty is not the respondents'; it is the ordinary standards of reasonable and honest people (at 333). It is notable also that Lord Hoffmann sat on the appeal to the House of Lords in *Twinsectra*. The position of the Court of Appeal in *Grantham* is also consistent with the approaches adopted in *Royal Brunei* and *Twinsectra*.

Therefore, it seems that the case law suggests that the combined approach, as Lord Hutton put it, is to be followed in relation to fraudulent trading as this maintains the subjectivity of the respondent's state of mind and does not invoke the hypothetical reasonable person, but ensures that the ordinary standards of reasonable and honest people are not excluded, ensuring that respondents cannot impose their own standards.

What actions can constitute fraud?

It is worthwhile setting out some actions that are and are not regarded as fraud for the purposes of s 213. First, the payment of preferences, that is, entering into transactions that can be classified as giving preferential payment to creditors, and which are within the scope of s 239 of the Insolvency Act 1986, will not generally be deemed to be fraud (*Re Sarflax Ltd* [1979] 1 All ER 529 at 535, 545), the reason being that a debtor is entitled to pay its creditors in whatever order it sees fit. It is not until administration or liquidation eventuates that that action may be impugned, and that is done retrospectively. When a preference is given, it might well be that the officers had no way of expecting the company to enter liquidation or administration. It is well recognised that the giving of a preference is not illegal for when it occurred the provisions in the Insolvency Act that deem transactions to be preferences did not apply.[13] But if a company were to pay uncommercial sums

---

13 Notwithstanding this, directors could be attacked for the payment of preferences on the basis

to a party with the intention of ensuring that property were put out of the reach of creditors, then this could be regarded as fraudulent trading, and possibly a breach of s 423 of the Insolvency Act.

As we saw in Chapter 4, inaction cannot constitute fraud: some positive action must have been taken (*Re Maidstone Buildings Ltd* [1971] 1 WLR 1085). Hence, if an officer of, or adviser to, the company, such as the company secretary, neglects to inform the directors that the company is insolvent, and what the consequences are in continuing to trade, that person is not liable, as there is no positive conduct. While, for the most part, a respondent is not liable except where he or she has committed a positive act, a respondent who is a third party as far as the company in liquidation is concerned may be held liable notwithstanding the fact there was neither ·a positive act on the part of the third party nor involvement in the carrying on of business if the third party is knowingly a party to a fraudulent act (*Re Augustus Barnett & Sons Ltd* at 98,907). For instance, a creditor who receives a payment from the company at a time when he or she knew that the payment was made possible because a controller of the company was carrying on business with an intent to defraud, may be held liable (*Re Gerald Cooper Chemicals Ltd*). As indicated in the previous chapter, a single transaction or act may be the basis for a successful action under either s 458 or s 213 (*Gerald Cooper*). So, if a director were to get a trade supplier to provide goods with the intention of deceiving the supplier in that the director had no intention of paying for them, this would constitute an intent to defraud (*Gerald Cooper*).

Fraudulent purpose

When addressing the expression, 'fraudulent purpose', the first thing to ask is whether it should be read *ejusdem generis* with 'intent to defraud creditors'? The court in *R v Kemp* [1988] 1 QB 645 at 654, CCA, thought not. This conclusion is supported by the fact that in *R v Inman* [1967] 1 QB 140 it was said that there were two offences covered by the provision, namely carrying on business with intent to defraud creditors, and carrying on business for any fraudulent purpose. The expression should not be seen in any way to be restricting the application of s 213. On the contrary, the expression is extremely wide (*R v Kemp* at 654–655), a position also taken in Singapore (*Rahj Kamal bin Abdullah v PP* [1998] 1 SLR 447).

A person is not liable merely because he or she nominated a person as a director who committed fraudulent trading, or because he or she had the opportunity of influencing the conduct of the affairs of the company. Company officers will not, necessarily, be liable for trading while the company

of engaging in misfeasance but such proceedings are usually only taken where there is a flaw in a preference action against the recipients of the preferences, and proceedings are only likely to succeed where the directors knew clearly that the company was insolvent at the time. For an example, see *Liquidator of West Mercia Safetywear Ltd v Dodd* [1988] 4 BCC 30.

is insolvent. As indicated earlier in the chapter, it may well depend on whether the directors have been reckless in incurring debts. If there is no recklessness, and there is no intent to defraud involved, a liquidator might well prefer to proceed against directors under the wrongful trading provision.

Conclusion

Professor Ian Fletcher has stated that:

> [I]n the absence of reasonably clear indications that the requisite intent to defraud was present at the time of the conduct in question, there remains a degree of uncertainty whether civil or criminal proceedings for fraudulent trading will prove to be successful in any given case.[14]

With respect, this appears to be true, for we do not have a clear articulation of the relevant principles in one or two recent cases. To ascertain what the present position is requires a substantial study of the cases, and even then there is a lack of certainty. It is submitted that we have general acceptance, as noted in this chapter, that while the test for fraud is a subjective one, the courts do not take the respondent's standard of honesty, but the standards of ordinary people. Whether, and if so when, courts can infer intent to defraud with respect to a respondent is not without some doubt, but it is submitted that courts can do so either where respondents incur debts at a time when they know that their company will clearly not be able to make repayment, or where there is considerable risk in not being able to repay the creditor(s) when the debts are due or shortly thereafter.

---

14 Fletcher, I F, *The Law of Insolvency*, 2nd edn, 1996, London: Sweet & Maxwell, p 660.

6 Fraudulent trading: an assessment

Introduction

While there has already been in earlier chapters some assessment of the fraudulent trading provision, this chapter endeavours to focus solely on assessing the provision, the effect that it has had on company and insolvency law, and what reforms might be implemented.

The uncertainty which has existed with aspects of s 213, and particularly, the meaning of 'intent to defraud' has led to suggestions that a liquidator might be far more inclined, where possible, to initiate proceedings pursuant to s 214, because it has a lower threshold of proof, and the elements of the section appear, prima facie, easier to establish. But, while at one time it was generally thought that s 213 would not be used frequently, especially in light of the emergence of wrongful trading in s 214, that is not the case, and there have been several fraudulent trading actions in recent times, as was mentioned in Chapters 4 and 5. Also, it might be said that there have been, relatively speaking, few wrongful trading cases, and that given the way that the wrongful trading proceedings have been dealt with, success under s 214 is far from assured, and might not even present a better opportunity of succeeding when compared with actions under s 213. But of course much will depend on the facts. A claim under s 213 must involve proof of fraud, and not every instance of directorial misconduct will involve fraud.

Actions available before liquidation?

As was discussed in Chapter 4, while a prosecution under s 458 of the Companies Act 1985 may be initiated before the company enters liquidation, this is not the case with s 213 of the Insolvency Act 1986. While it is upon liquidation that creditors will be most concerned about getting some compensation, being able to initiate proceedings before liquidation has advantages. For example, if a creditor has evidence about a course of trading that is fraudulent and he or she can see that if things continue as they are the company will end up in liquidation, the ability to set in motion proceedings as a sort of pre-emptive strike is beneficial. Of course, creditors are able, in the

UK, to rely on s 423 of the Insolvency Act 1986 which prohibits the putting of assets out of the reach of creditors so as to defraud creditors, but that would not cover every kind of action that might constitute fraudulent trading.

The Singaporean provision that permits proceedings prior to the liquidation of the company (Companies Act 1990, s 340(1)) might be regarded as attractive, certainly to some creditors, in that creditors can take action to prevent loss, in some cases, before the company collapses totally. Also, as Lee Suet Joyce states:

> If insolvent liquidation of the company had been a prerequisite to trigger the fraudulent and insolvent trading provisions, corporate managers would be given the incentive to take any risks so long as they are able to avoid insolvent liquidation at the end of the day.[1]

The problem with allowing creditors to take action before liquidation is that their action might leave directors impecunious and unable to satisfy any later claims that are made against them if the company does enter liquidation. The points both in favour and against allowing creditors to take proceedings are canvassed in Chapter 11 in relation to wrongful trading. The issues tend to overlap both the wrongful and fraudulent trading provisions.

Other applicants?

As we saw in Chapter 4, s 213 can only be relied upon by the liquidator to bring proceedings for fraudulent trading, whereas in other common law jurisdictions, such as South Africa and Singapore, the creditors and/or members can bring proceedings. It is unlikely that the members would have any interest in issuing proceedings. Any award from an action commenced by a member is likely to go to the creditors and not benefit the members, where a company is insolvent. Even if proceedings could be issued outside of liquidation, it is highly unlikely that members would consider issuing proceedings. Also, any action taken against directors might precipitate the company becoming subject to some insolvency regime, ending the trading of the company, and, hence, terminating the chance of the members receiving a return of their investment, let alone making any further money out of the company.

As far as creditors are concerned, they would not be willing to bring proceedings unless they could be sure that they would get some benefit from them. Even if they did successfully bring proceedings, the award would be distributed amongst all of the unsecured creditors. While the applicant creditor would receive a share, he or she might reason, with some justification,

---

1   Joyce, L, 'Fraudulent and insolvent trading in Singapore' (2000) 9 *International Insolvency Review* 121 at 125.

that it is not worth his or her while bringing proceedings and taking on considerable risk where the fruits of the action have to be shared with others who engage, in effect, using economic language, in freeriding. Any creditors issuing proceedings have, of course, the risk of paying out indemnity costs if they lose as well as not being able to recover all of their own costs, even if they are successful. Creditors have the option to freeride on the litigation of other creditors, and that could mean that no one would take proceedings as they will hope that someone else will take the initiative. This is a form of brinkmanship, for creditors could wait until the last minute before deciding whether to commence proceedings, in case someone else is minded to do so and bear all of the risks associated with litigation.

The arguments against permitting a creditor to take action and benefiting solely from the fruits of it are, in essence, that it might lead to an avalanche of litigation, one or a few creditors might succeed in proceedings which leaves the directors impecunious and unable to pay any other creditors, and it is far from clear what kind of order could be, or should be, made by a court if the claim(s) is successful. What permitting creditors to bring actions does not do, as has been asserted by one commentator,[2] is to affect pre-liquidation entitlements, as company funds will not be diminished for the money to pay any award will be coming from the director(s). These and other issues are discussed in more detail in Chapters 15 and 16 in relation to allowing creditors to take proceedings at common law against directors who fail to discharge their duty to creditors. One sound argument that might be used to support the right of creditors to bring an action and retain the benefits of any award, is that it might lead to better standards of corporate governance[3] as directors would be more concerned about actions being brought against them.

The public element

Clearly s 213 has both a private law and a public law function. In relation to the former, the intention behind the private law function is to compensate creditors who have lost out because of the actions of people involved with the company, and, ultimately, because of the liquidation of the company. But, at present the action is not meeting any public function. Also, although wrongful trading was introduced to overcome problems with fraudulent trading, it would seem that directors are not being subject frequently to wrongful trading proceedings, as envisaged by the Insolvency Law Review Committee in its report, *Insolvency Law and Practice*,[4] possibly because of the problems that afflict that provision, and discussed later in Part C of the book.

The public function of s 213 is marked by the fact that it is linked to

---

2 *Ibid* at 127.   3 *Ibid*.
4 Cmnd 858, HMSO (1982) and known as the Cork Report.

directors' disqualification, in that under s 10(1) of the Company Directors' Disqualification Act 1986 a court is able to disqualify a director if he or she has been in breach of s 213, and this is a process intended to protect the public from reckless and/or dishonest directors. It is difficult for any provision to fulfil both private and public functions, and it is doubtful whether s 213 comes near to doing so.[5] This problem might be overcome by granting to a public official, say the Secretary of State for Trade and Industry, the power to commence fraudulent trading proceedings with the aim of securing a disqualification order against the director. This issue is discussed more in Chapter 11 in the context of wrongful trading.

One other possible innovation that might bear fruit, from a public perspective, is to permit a public official, again say the Secretary of State for Trade and Industry, to be entitled to institute proceedings against directors under s 213 with the object of seeking a civil penalty order against miscreants. Australian law has taken this approach in relation to a number of actions involving 'white collar' corporate misconduct. The purpose behind that policy was to allow corporate regulation to be pursued unconstrained by the real difficulty, indeed near impossibility in many cases, of proving complex commercial claims to the high criminal standard. Whilst the breach of a civil penalty provision is not a criminal breach, and no prison sentence can be ordered, civil penalties can be considerable.[6] So civil penalty orders, with their lower standard of proof, could be used in the UK to enable miscreants in appropriate cases to be penalised for their actions. This runs counter to the approach espoused recently in the Court of Appeal in *Morphitis v Bernasconi* [2003] EWCA Civ 289, [2003] Ch 552; [2003] BCC 540, where the court said that it had no power to make a punitive award. But, for many years, courts felt that this could be done, and was, in some cases, appropriate, and, more pertinently, if s 213 were amended to permit action to be taken by the Secretary of State for Trade and Industry, *Bernasconi* could be overcome.

Where proceedings have already been commenced by a liquidator, the Secretary of State for Trade and Industry could be given the power to apply to be joined as an applicant, in order to seek a civil penalty, but only in those cases where it is felt proper. The result, if the action were successful, would be that compensation could be ordered to be paid to the liquidator on behalf of the creditors, and the court could also make a penalty order by way of punishment on the application of the Secretary of State. After deducting the costs and expenses of the Secretary of State, the balance could be used by the

---

5 See the comments in Schulte, R, 'Enforcing wrongful trading as a standard of conduct for directors and a remedy for creditors: the special case of corporate insolvency' (1999) 20 Co Law 80.

6 Corporations Act 2001, Part 2D.6. Proceedings can be commenced by the Australian Securities and Investments Commission. See Keay, A, and Murray, M, 'Making company directors liable: a comparative analysis of wrongful trading in the United Kingdom and insolvent trading in Australia' (2005) 14 *International Insolvency Review* 27.

liquidator to pay the creditors further sums. The argument against this course might be that the creditors are enjoying a windfall. But, provided that the creditors are not receiving more than 100p in the pound on the debts owed to them by the company, the windfall would not be, arguably, unfair or unjust. Furthermore, besides fulfilling the public function adverted to above, the suggested reform would mean that the Secretary of State for Trade and Industry could institute proceedings in cases where the liquidator could not obtain the necessary funding, a real problem for liquidators (discussed further in Chapter 11).

Interpretation of the provision

While there are undoubtedly still some problems with the interpretation of aspects of s 213, it is arguable that common law developments in the past few years have ameliorated the position. Having said that, while, as argued in Chapter 5, it is possible to find some consensus running through a line of cases dealing with the meaning of 'intent to defraud', there is still room for achieving greater clarity. While we have had recent s 213 cases addressing and clarifying issues revolving around the meaning of 'knowingly a party to carrying on business', the same cannot be said for the meaning of 'intent to defraud'. Also, while we have seen some clarification of the meaning of knowingly a party to the carrying on of business 'in a fraudulent way', the recent case of *Morphitis v Bernasconi* does leave open some issues. On the positive side, though, there are cases in other areas, such as claims involving dishonestly assisting a breach of trust, which have, arguably, provided some guidance.

Substituting the incurring of debts for fraudulent trading?

It is submitted later in Part C, and particularly in Chapter 11, that the wrongful trading provision ought to be reformed along the lines of proscribing the incurring of debts by directors when the company is insolvent, that is, outlawing insolvent trading. Prima facie, if that approach were adopted it might make sense also to reform s 213 by tying the action that would lead to the invoking of the provision to incurring debts when insolvent, with the distinction between s 213 and s 214 being that one could only be liable under the former if the respondent had acted dishonestly (the position that exists in Australia). But, if that were done, it might be argued that some actions could not be caught by the provision. A prime example is the activity documented in the case of *Bank of India v Morris* [2005] EWCA (Civ) 693; [2005] 2 BCLC 328; [2005] BPIR 1067, where, before its collapse, the central treasury division of BCCI had embarked on an operation that involved the manipulation of account balances to conceal losses incurred by BCCI, and where the respondent bank had been employed to assist in this deception and some of the employees of the respondent knew about the dishonesty being perpetrated. This might not be a major problem, as in some cases creditors might be able to take action on other bases, such as for deceit. Also, reforming s 213 in the way suggested would not prevent s 458 prosecutions being initiated in the appropriate situations. We would end up with a situation that was advocated by the Cork Committee, namely that fraudulent trading as far as civil law goes should be repealed, leaving s 458 of the Companies Act to cover blatant fraudulent activities and s 214 to deal with civil law issues.

Conclusion

In the fourth edition of his renowned text on company law, Professor LCB Gower stated that the then fraudulent trading provision, s 332 of the Companies Act 1948, was a potent weapon and 'the mere threat of proceedings under it has been known to result in the directors agreeing to make themselves personally liable for part of the company's debts'.[7] The learned author was referring to a provision that encompassed both criminal and civil sanctions. While the comment could well be relevant to s 458 of the Companies Act 1985, under which there have been a number of successful prosecutions, it might be argued that until recently, it had little relevance to s 213. In recent times we have seen several high-profile cases that have been decided in favour of the liquidator, and this might well cause directors in particular to demonstrate some circumspection in how they operate. The caveat that should be sounded concerning the number of s 213 cases that we have seen is that the majority of them have resulted from the litigation in the winding up of BCCI and it remains to be seen whether there will be regular use of the provision in other liquidations, or whether the statements by several commentators[8] that the provision is employed rarely is predictive of the future.

---

7   *Principles of Modern Company Law*, London: Sweet and Maxwell, p 115.
8   For instance, Finch, V, *Corporate Insolvency Law*, 2002, Cambridge: Cambridge University Press, p 511.

Part C
Wrongful trading

7 Wrongful trading: background, aims, rationale and comparisons

Introduction

This part deals with an action that might be taken by liquidators against directors of a company who engaged in what is known as 'wrongful trading' before the company entered insolvent liquidation. The action is taken to obtain some contribution from the directors towards the payment that is made to the creditors, who, of course, in an insolvent liquidation are not going to get back what they were owed by the company. This action is initiated pursuant to s 214 of the Insolvency Act 1986. Section 214 provides, in effect, that the liquidator of a company that is in insolvent liquidation – effectively the situation where a company's assets are not sufficient to pay its debts at the time of liquidation (s 214(6)) – may commence proceedings against the company's directors, and these proceedings may seek an order that the directors make such contribution to the company's assets as the court thinks proper (s 214(1)). Directors may only be liable where at some time before the commencement of the winding up of the company, they knew or ought to have concluded that there was no reasonable prospect that the company would avoid going into insolvent liquidation (s 214(2)). Courts are not to make an order against directors if satisfied that, after the directors first knew or ought to have concluded that there was no reasonable prospect that the company would avoid going into insolvent liquidation, they took every step with a view to minimising the potential loss to the company's creditors that they ought to have taken (s 214(3)). It is worth pointing out that s 214 does not use the words, 'wrongful trading'; it is a description that is only employed in a marginal note, and there is clear authority that a marginal note is not to be used as an aid to interpretation of legislation (*Chandler v DPP* [1964] AC 763). The trading that offends against s 214 is, perhaps, better referred to as 'irresponsible' or 'illicit'.[1]

---

1   The latter term was employed by Michael Murray and myself in our article: 'Making company directors liable: a comparative analysis of wrongful trading in the United Kingdom and insolvent trading in Australia' (2005) 14 *International Insolvency Review* 27.

This chapter is effectively an introduction to wrongful trading. Chapter 8 then explains the scope of s 214, and Chapter 9 discusses the sole defence that is available to respondents to proceedings. Finally, in this part, Chapter 10 assesses the provision.

Background

It must be noted from the outset that the advent of wrongful trading was due primarily to the perceived inadequacies of the fraudulent trading provision. The Report of the Insolvency Law Review Committee, *Insolvency Law and Practice* (commonly known as, and similarly referred to here, as 'the Cork Report')[2] was of the opinion that the fraudulent trading provision, which was at the time that the Committee was considering insolvency law set out in s 332 of the Companies Act 1948, possessed significant inadequacies in dealing with irresponsible trading (paras 1776–1780), such as the application of the criminal burden of proof applied to civil actions and, also, applicants were required to establish actual dishonesty and real moral blame on the part of the respondent (*Re Patrick and Lyon Ltd* [1933] Ch 786). Courts were hesitant to find defendants liable, given the nature of the provision. For instance, in *Re Maidstone Building Provisions Ltd* [1971] 1 WLR 1085 at 1095 the judge, who held the defendant not guilty of fraudulent trading, emphasised the fact that the provision was a penal one. The Cork Committee was concerned that unsecured creditors were not protected adequately and it took the view that compensation ought to be available to those persons who experience loss due to unreasonable behaviour as well as fraudulent action (at [1777]). It was concerned that the existing fraudulent trading provision had failed in curbing directors running up losses when their companies were in deep financial difficulty (at [1776–1778]). Consequently, the Cork Committee recommended that a new provision be introduced to provide civil actions for unreasonable trading where only the civil burden of proof would apply (at [1777]). Hitherto, directors were only liable if they were proved to have intent to defraud creditors. The Committee wanted to see it provided in legislation that a director, otherwise honest but who sees insolvency coming and does nothing to arrest it, should lose the benefits of limited liability along with those directors who are fraudulent.[3] To this end the Committee advocated an objective test to determine liability (at [1782–1783]). It advocated liability if the directors incur liabilities when their company is insolvent without having a reasonable prospect of satisfying the debts. What the Committee envisaged was legislation that acted so as to encourage company directors to satisfy themselves concerning the company's ability to discharge commitments. The Committee

---

2   Cmnd 858, HMSO (1982).
3   Walters, A, 'Enforcing wrongful trading – substantive problems and practical incentives' in Rider, BAK (ed), *The Corporate Dimension*, 1998, Bristol: Jordans, p 146.

recommended that only criminal liability should continue to apply in relation to fraudulent trading.

While, in 1984, the government stated in a White Paper, entitled 'A Revised Framework for Insolvency Law' (Cmnd 9175) that it agreed that there had to be a tighter rein on directors' activities in order to prevent irresponsible trading where insolvent companies were concerned, it declined to take up many of the recommendations of the Cork Report relating to wrongful trading. This view had not changed by the time that the Insolvency Bill was introduced in late 1984 (later to become the Insolvency Act 1985). The reason that the government gave for this attitude was that the Cork Report's approach imposed too severe a responsibility on directors for their companies' liabilities. The provision, first finding life as s 15 of the Insolvency Act 1985, provided for a concept that was more limited than that recommended by the Cork Committee and it reflected legislative caution against watering down the law of limited company liability. The provision focused on making directors liable for creditor losses when they failed to take appropriate steps where the avoidance of insolvent liquidation was not a reasonable prospect. Professor Len Sealy records that one reason that was given for the decision not to follow the Cork Report proposal was that it was not envisaged that the conduct covered should be restricted to the incurring of liabilities when insolvent.[4] Sealy notes that it was suggested that the provision might well encompass the situation where there is a loss of company assets in order to pay excessive directors' fees.[5] As we have seen, the government decided, contrary to the Cork Report's recommendations, to retain a civil liability provision dealing with fraudulent trading (s 213).

Provisions like s 214 are, in effect, exceptions to the fundamental principle of corporate law that if a corporation is liable for debts it, and it alone, is liable for them. This rule is based, of course, on the inveterate principle emanating from *Salomon v Salomon & Co Ltd* [1897] AC 22 that a company is a legal entity which is separate from its members and controllers and consequently it, and not its directors, is liable, *inter alia*, for its contracts and debts generally. Section 214 involves, in essence, a piercing of the corporate veil.

Aims

Patently, s 214 can be characterised as a regulation that is intended to control corporate activities. The objective of a regulation is to affect the demeanour

---

4   'Personal liability of directors and officers for debts of insolvent corporations: a jurisdictional perspective (England)' in Ziegel, J (ed), *Current Developments in International and Comparative Corporate Insolvency Law*, 1994, Oxford: Clarendon Press, p 491.

5   *Ibid.*

of someone so as to precipitate a particular outcome.[6] In this regard, the wrongful trading provision was introduced in order to require directors to take some action to arrest their companies' slide into insolvency; directors were to be forced to engage in more rigorous monitoring of their companies' health. The section was designed not to penalise directors for taking a company into a state of insolvency, but to address the situation where directors can see that their company is in difficulty, perhaps insolvent, and they do nothing to protect creditors' interests. Effectively, it is a stick approach to induce the raising of directorial standards. Also, the purpose of s 214 is to 'recoup the loss to the company so as to benefit the creditors as a whole' (*Re Purpoint Ltd* [1991] BCLC 491 at 499 per Vinelott J).

A similar rationale was given for the Australian counterpart of s 214 (Corporations Act 2001, s 588G) by Barrett J in the New South Wales Supreme Court case of *Woodgate v Davis* (2002) 42 ACSR 286 at 294, when he said:

> Section 588G and related provisions serve an important social purpose. They are intended to engender in directors of companies experiencing financial stress a proper sense of attentiveness and responsible conduct directed towards the avoidance of any increase in the company's debt burden. The provisions are based on a concern for the welfare of creditors exposed to the operation of the principle of limited liability at a time when the prospect of that principle resulting in loss to creditors has become real.

Wrongful trading is not intended to deal with mismanagement *per se*. It is designed to address the situation where directors can see that their company is in difficulty and they do nothing to protect creditors' interests. The provision is an attempt not to have creditors compensated through laws proscribing wrongful trading, but to try to ensure that wrongful trading does not occur in the first place so that such compensation is unnecessary. The provision can be seen as an attempt to 'align the interests of managers of firms [although it is not limited to the managers alone] on the verge of insolvency with the interests of the firm's creditors'.[7] The Australian insolvent trading provision that became operative from mid-1993 (as a result of the Corporate Law Reform Act 1992) also focused on a similar concern, identifying the need to prevent insolvent trading rather than emphasising compensation for breaches. In a similar manner, the Singaporean provision, found in s 339 of its Companies Act 1990, aims to prevent a company unjustifiably running up debts when there is no prospect of paying them.[8]

---

6   Yeung, K, 'Private enforcement of competition law' in McCrudden, C (ed), *Regulation and Deregulation*, 1999, Oxford: Clarendon Press, p 40.
7   Mokal, R, 'On fairness and efficiency' (2003) 66 MLR 452 at 461.
8   Joyce, L, 'Fraudulent and insolvent trading in Singapore' (2000) 9 *International Insolvency Review* 121 at 125.

Rationale

Regulating directors through the use of s 214 was an attempt to stop directors from externalising the cost of their companies' debts and placing all of the risks of further trading on the creditors. For, if a company is heading for insolvent liquidation, the creditors of the company are effectively the ones who have a residual claim (the claim of those whose wealth directly rises or falls with changes in the value of the company[9]) over the company's assets,[10] and so the directors should be taking actions to minimise the losses of the creditors. The provision covering wrongful trading requires the directors' allegiance to shift from the shareholders to the directors (assuming that the directors are to run the company for the benefit of the shareholders according to the shareholder primacy principle,[11] or the enlightened shareholder value approach proposed by the Company Law Reform Bill[12]).

It is generally accepted that directors can be expected, when their companies are in difficulty, to embrace actions which involve more risk,[13] because the shareholders, given the concept of limited liability, have little to lose where their company is in financial distress. If the risk-taking pays off, then the shareholders will see their wealth maximised, but if it does not, then they have lost nothing more; it is the creditors who will bear the cost. Many would argue that corporate regulations are introduced because of market failure,[14] and s 214 might be seen as a response to the fact that market forces have failed to discipline directors and, thereby, prevent creditors losing out. The wrongful trading provision is an attempt to stop directors from abusing the privilege

9 Baird, D, 'The initiation problem in bankruptcy' (1991) 11 *International Review of Law and Economics* 223 at 228–229; Gilson, S, and Vetsuypens, M, (1994) 72 *Washington University Law Quarterly* 1005 at 1006. This seems to be what was being said in *Brady v Brady* [1988] 3 BCC 535. Mr Leslie Kosmin QC (sitting as a Deputy Judge of the Chancery Division) in *Gwyer v London Wharf (Limehouse) Ltd* [2003] 2 BCLC 153; [2002] EWHC 2748 (Ch) specifically stated that creditors' interests should be paramount at the time of insolvency (at [74]). Overall the cases provide little guidance.

10 Schwarcz, S, 'Rethinking a corporation's obligations to creditors' (1996) 17 *Cardozo Law Review* 647 at 668.

11 This is the prevailing approach in Anglo-American corporate governance, namely that directors' primary duty is to the shareholders of their companies. For a discussion, see Armour, J, Deakin, S, and Konzelmann, S, 'Shareholder primacy and the trajectory of UK corporate governance' (2003) 41 *British Journal of Industrial Relations* 531.

12 Introduced into the House of Lords on 1 November 2005.

13 Adler, B, 'A re-examination of near-bankruptcy investment incentives' (1995) 62 U Chi L Rev 575, 590–598; Barondes, R, 'Fiduciary duties of officers and directors of distressed corporations' (1998) 7 George Mason L Rev 45 at 46, 49; Daigle, K, and Maloney, M, 'Residual claims in bankruptcy: an agency theory explanation' (1994) 37 *Journal of Law and Economics* 157. See Company Law Review Steering Group, *Modern Company Law for a Competitive Economy: Final Report* Vol 1 (DTI, London, 2001), at para 3.15.

14 For example, Professor Ian Ramsay in 'Models of corporate regulation: the mandatory/enabling debate' in Rickett, C, and Grantham, R, *Corporate Personality in the 20th Century*, 1998, Oxford: Hart Publishing, p 219.

of limited liability by making them liable if they do so (Cork Report at para 1805). The issues raised here are discussed further in Chapter 19, in the context of a duty to creditors.

Comparisons

Although this chapter begins a part that focuses on wrongful trading in the UK, it must be emphasised that several common law jurisdictions have similar provisions. First, Ireland provides for what it refers to as 'reckless trading' in s 297A of its Companies Act 1963 (introduced by s 138 of the Companies Act 1990). Notwithstanding the different terminology used, the provision is similar to the wrongful trading provision; the provision is compared more with the UK provision in the next chapter. Other jurisdictions also use the concept of reckless trading. These are New Zealand (Companies Act 1993, s 135 – a remarkably brief section) and South Africa (Companies Act 1948, s 424). The use of the term 'reckless' suggests that with the legislation of all of these jurisdictions, the actions of the creditors must be more culpable than negligent. The South African legislation actually makes reckless trading a criminal offence, just as fraudulent trading can be in the UK. Interestingly, it is likely that the aforementioned jurisdictions employed 'reckless trading' as it was recommended by the Jenkins Committee in the UK (*Report of the Company Law Committee*, London, 1962, Cmnd 1749). Ironically, of course, the UK did not adopt the recommendations. Perhaps the main odd ones out when it comes to this area are Australia and Singapore, whose provisions (Corporations Act 2001, s 588G-Y and Companies Act 1990, s 339, respectively) do not refer to the proscription of reckless trading, but action which has been called 'insolvent trading'. These two jurisdictions make directors liable when they cause their companies to incur debts when there is no reasonable expectation of being able to repay the creditors. More will be said about the law in Australia, New Zealand, Singapore and South Africa in the remaining chapters of this part.

Interestingly, two other common law jurisdictions, the US and Canada, that share similar laws to the UK, do not include a wrongful trading-type provision in either their corporations or bankruptcy legislation. However, some of the Canadian provinces do provide a safeguard for creditors in that they allow creditors to take action against the company where the creditors have been oppressed by a company's action. Also, in the United States, the tort of deepening insolvency has been employed increasingly.[15] This tort involves the wrongbeing to prolong, improperly, the life of an insolvent

---

15 Heaton, J, 'Deepening insolvency' available on the Social Science Research Network at www.papers.ssrn.com/sol3/papers.cfm?abstract_id=622561; Ho, LC, 'On deepening insolvency and wrongful trading' (2005) 20 *Journal of International Banking Law and Regulation* 426.

company so as to exacerbate the losses of creditors as the company becomes more insolvent (*Official Committee of Unsecured Creditors v R F Lafferty & Co* 267 F 3d 340 at 349 (2001); *Re Del-Met Corp* 322 BR 781 at 812 (2005) (TN)). However, there is clearly some difference between the tort and wrongful trading, such as the fact that the former may apply to a wider group of people than the latter, as the latter only applies to directors.

Still other jurisdictions, which do not have a provision that can be regarded as similar to s 214 in terms of the way that it is drafted, do have a provision which is designed to achieve similar aims, by requiring directors to take their company into some form of insolvency regime with the onset of insolvency. In France, under Book II of the Commercial Code 2000, there is the need to enter *redressement judiciare*, with the requirement that directors provide a *déclaration de cessation des paiements* (a declaration of insolvency when their company is unable to pay its debts).[16] Likewise, the Belgian Commercial Code requires directors to notify the court on the cessation of payment of debts within three days of their company failing to pay debts (art 440). This failure is assumed to have occurred when the company is only able to pay its debts with money and loans obtained in an irregular fashion.[17] Where directors breach art 440 the company's liquidator is entitled to commence proceedings against the directors, under art 1382 of the Civil Code, on behalf of all creditors, and he or she has to establish that the directors could and should have been aware that their company was insolvent.[18] If the directors are unable to defend the proceedings, by proving that either they did not know or they should not have known that the company was insolvent, a liquidator may be awarded damages covering the increase of the amount owed to creditors after the date of the cessation of payments.[19]

In Germany the directors of the managing board (equivalent to executive directors in the UK) in open or public corporations[20] and the general manager of closed corporations[21] must take the corporation into the statutory insolvency process if their company is insolvent, as must directors of both open and closed corporations in Switzerland.[22]

---

16 Article L624-5-1 no 4. See Omar, P, 'The European initiative on wrongful trading' [2003] *Insolvency Lawyer* 239 at 245; Omar, P, 'Defining insolvency: the evolution of the concept of "cessation de paiements" in French law' [2005] EBLR 311 at 312.

17 Boschma, H, and Lennarts, L, 'Wrongful trading in a comparative perspective' in Wouters, J, and Schneider, H (eds), *Current Issues of Cross-Border Establishment of Companies in the European Union*, 1995, Antwerp: Maklu, p 208.

18 *Ibid*.   19 *Ibid* at 209.   20 Aktiengesetz (Public Companies Act), s 92.

21 Gesetz betreffend die Gesellschaften mit beschränkter Haftung (Limited Liability Company Act), s 64.

22 Code de Commerce, art L 621-1 and referred to in Hertig, G, and Kanda, H, 'Creditor protection' in Kraakman, R, *et al* (eds), *The Anatomy of Corporate Law*, 2004, Oxford: Oxford University Press, p73.

Obviously, the approach taken in France, Belgium, Germany and Switzerland is somewhat different to that taken in the common law jurisdictions mentioned earlier. In the common law jurisdictions mentioned above, seeking some formal insolvency regime for their company is sometimes going to be the action that directors take, but it is not obligatory, as it is in the European countries that have been mentioned.

Other European jurisdictions tackle things differently. Directors in the Netherlands[23] are not required to place their company in some form of insolvency administration when the company becomes insolvent. But if a company goes into liquidation, the directors will be liable for the deficit owed to creditors if they performed their duties improperly and it is found that it is likely that this action was an important cause of the liquidation (art 2:248, Civil Code). Also, a director is liable if he or she were to enter transactions for the company when he or she knows or could reasonably be expected to know that the company will not be able to meet its liabilities, for in doing this the director is said to be in breach of a duty of care to creditors (art 6:162, Civil Code).

Provisions akin to wrongful trading might become more numerous in Europe in the not-too-distant future. A high-level group of experts on company law have recommended to the European Union that it introduce a framework rule proscribing wrongful trading.[24]

It might be felt that having to embrace insolvency procedures when a company is insolvent, as is the case in jurisdictions like France, is premature and could lead to a company having to reduce its workforce. It does have the possible advantage for creditors of protecting them, although, of course, the commencement of insolvency regimes prematurely might, in some cases, thwart any potential rescue action which might lead to greater repayment of creditors.

---

23 See above fn 17, at 202–204.
24 *Report of the High Level Group of Company Law Experts on a Modern Regulatory Framework for Company Law in Europe*, 126, and available at www.europa.eu.int/comm/internal_market/en/company/company/modern/consult/report_en.pdf.

8 The wrongful trading provision and its scope

Introduction

This chapter focuses on the terms of the wrongful trading provision, s 214 of the Insolvency Act 1986, and it endeavours to ascertain its scope. Specifically the chapter considers who can bring proceedings, who can be sued, the nature of the proceedings, the elements of liability, what loss must be established, the nature of the orders that can be made, and their effect, and what relief might be available to any directors who are found liable. In addition, some comparisons are drawn with similar provisions in other common law jurisdictions.

The applicant

Unlike most other common law jurisdictions, the UK provision only permits liquidators to initiate proceedings under s 214. Other common law jurisdictions that have a similar provision generally permit other parties to commence proceedings. In Ireland action can be taken by a receiver, examiner, creditor and a contributory, in addition to a liquidator (Companies Act 1963, s 297A). Under s 424 of the South African Companies Act 1973, creditors and members as well as liquidators are permitted to take action. The same can be said about both the New Zealand provision (Companies Act 1993, s 135) and the Singaporean (Companies Act 1990, s 340(2)). There may be some limit on when proceedings can be brought by some applicants. For example, in Australia before creditors can bring proceedings, they must obtain the consent of the liquidator (Corporations Act 2001, s 588R) or give notice to the liquidator after six months from the commencement of the winding up that it is intended to begin proceedings against a director and asking the liquidator to give to the creditor, within three months, either a consent or a statement of reasons why the liquidator is of the opinion that proceedings should not be initiated (s 588S). If no consent is given within the three months, the creditor may proceed against the director (s 588T(2)).[1] If a reason for not proceeding

---

[1] For a case where proceedings were initiated by a creditor, see *Metropolitan Fire Systems Pty Ltd v Miller* (1997) 23 ACSR 699.

is given by the liquidator, it must be produced to the court in the action in which proceedings have been or are initiated (s 588T(3)). There has not been a huge number of cases initiated by creditors under the present regime, commenced in 1993, but creditors' actions do constitute over 40 per cent of all actions.[2] The reason for the UK legislation not permitting creditors to bring proceedings is probably in order to avoid a multiplicity of actions.

In both Ireland and Australia, a government agency is entitled to initiate proceedings against directors. In Ireland action may be taken by the Director of Corporate Enforcement (an office created by s 7 of the Company Law Enforcement Act 2001), and in Australia action may be initiated by the Australian Securities and Investment Commission (a body created originally by the Australian Securities Commission Act 1990). The issue of permitting a government body to bring proceedings is discussed further in Chapter 10.[3]

The Insolvency Law Review Committee in its report, *Insolvency Law and Practice* (the 'Cork Report'),[4] actually advocated that administrators and administrative receivers as well as liquidators be given the right to take proceedings ([1792]). It is submitted that while giving the right to administrative receivers would be rather redundant in light of the fact that administrative receivership is being phased out, save in a few cases, by the provisions of the Enterprise Act 2002, administrators should be able to take actions. Examiners in Ireland, who fulfil a similar role to administrators in the UK, are given, as we noted above, the right to do so. As it is at the moment, if an administrator believes that directors of the company have been engaged in wrongful trading, he or she has to recommend that the company move from administration to liquidation, when a liquidator can initiate proceedings. This is time-consuming and adds costs. Another possible drawback in not permitting actions by administrators is that any creditor who is concerned that wrongful trading has occurred or is occurring might push for liquidation rather than administration because that is the only way that he or she is going to enhance what is to be received. Yet, conceivably, if an administrator could take proceedings, the company could be placed in administration, action taken against the directors and the company might still be able to be rescued.

While creditors are not entitled to bring proceedings in the UK, they are not completely eliminated from the equation as it is submitted that in some circumstances creditors could apply to the courts for a review of the decision of the liquidator if he or she chooses not to proceed with an action. This could be done pursuant to s 168(5) of the Insolvency Act 1986 for

2   James, P, Ramsay, I M, and Siva, P, 'Insolvent trading – an empirical study' (2004) 12 *Insolvency Law Journal* 210 at 235–236, and an earlier version is also available on the website of the Centre for Corporate Law and Securities Regulation, University of Melbourne, www.cclsr.law.unimelb.edu.au/research-papers/monograph%20series/ Insolvent%20Trading%20final.pdf>.
3   See pp 122 and 133.   4   Cmnd 858, HMSO (1982).

compulsory liquidations, and under s 112 for voluntary liquidations. But, of course, absent those situations where the threat of creditors to seek a court review may cause a liquidator to think again, creditors will have to expend time and money on court proceedings, and it might be thought that it is not worth doing so.

Claims

Section 214(8) provides that the section is without prejudice to s 213 (the fraudulent trading provision), so there is nothing to prevent a liquidator, in an appropriate case, from mounting proceedings which claim relief under s 214 and, in the alternative, under s 213. The liquidator in *Re Produce Marketing Consortium Ltd* (1989) 5 BCC 569 commenced his action relying on both ss 213 and 214, and while the s 213 claim was dropped (clearly because the directors were not guilty of intending to defraud creditors (at 594), the judge did not comment adversely on bringing proceedings under both of the aforementioned sections.

It is likely that in some situations liquidators may choose to couple a claim under s 214 with other claims, such as a claim under s 212 (misfeasance proceedings), as occurred in *Re Brian D Pierson (Contractors) Ltd* [1999] BCC 26; [2001] BCLC 275, arguing that directors have breached their duties. If a liquidator were to launch proceedings under both ss 214 and 212, the respondent's liability will be regarded as concurrent (*Re DKG Contractors Ltd* [1990] BCC 903), except where the conduct leading to liability under each heading was different, and in such a case the court might order cumulative awards (*Re Purpoint Ltd* [1991] BCC 121; [1991] BCLC 491). The difficulty that might arise where there is a concurrent award is that any award pursuant to s 214 is to be distributed amongst the general body of unsecured creditors, while an award under s 212 goes to the company (*Re Anglo-Austrian Printing & Publishing Co* [1985] 2 Ch 891) and this might enable a holder of a charge over company property to have priority in payment out of this latter award. The issue of priority in relation to an award under s 214 is discussed later in the chapter.

Claims under s 214 are regarded as claims for the recovery of sums recoverable under any enactment, so the limitation period is six years from the date of the accrual of the cause of action (Limitation Act 1980, s 9(1)), and runs from the date when the company entered insolvent liquidation (*Re Farmizer (Products) Ltd* [1997] BCC 655, CA), namely either the date of the resolution to wind up for voluntary liquidation or the date of the winding-up order for compulsory liquidation. The court in *Re Farmizer* rejected the idea that the commencement of the action was the time when it appeared to the liquidator that s 214(2) applied (at 661). In any event, unreasonable delay in initiating proceedings by a liquidator could see the proceedings struck out (*Re Farmizer*).

It must be pointed out that the provision that provides for wrongful trading neither includes the words 'wrongful trading' within it (the term was used by the Cork Report), nor sets out the kind of conduct which will constitute wrongful trading.[5] This suggests that the section is very wide and can catch all sorts of activity or inactivity which involved directors' misconduct in the affairs of their companies. However, the kind of conduct which will mean that directors fall foul of the section is restricted by s 214(2). The subsection provides, *inter alia*, that a director will only be liable if he or she knew or ought to have concluded that there was no reasonable prospect of the company avoiding going into insolvent liquidation. Professor Steve Griffin has said that the type of conduct caught by s 214 includes the paying of over-generous dividends, selling company assets at an undervalue and the payment of excessive remuneration to directors, as well as the incurring of liabilities when the directors knew or ought to have known that the company was likely not to be able to satisfy those liabilities and existing liabilities.[6] As the word 'trading' is not expressly mentioned in s 214, there is no reason why activity short of actual trading cannot be the subject of an action, such as selling assets with a view to winding up the company or failing to collect debts owed.

A claim pursuant to s 214 may be continued against a director's estate in the event of his or her death as there was reason to suppose that Parliament had intended that such a claim should not be defeated by death (*Re Sherborne Associates Ltd* [1995] BCC 40 at 46), but in *Re Sherborne Associates* the judge issued the caveat that if the director had lived, he or she might have been able to provide a credible explanation for what had been done or not been done, and consequently a judge should have in mind the fact that the director might have been able to rebut the liquidator's claims had he or she lived (at 47).

One practical issue that is worth raising is that it might be worthwhile for liquidators, assuming that they have not sought a private examination of the directors under s 236 of the Insolvency Act 1986, to seek to arrange, before initiation of proceedings, a conference with the directors against whom they are contemplating making a claim. This would enable the liquidators and their advisers to assess the directors. Park J makes the point in *Re Continental Assurance* [2001] BPIR 733 at 764 that if the liquidators had seen the directors they would have discovered that the directors were not irresponsible or roguish, and that might have affected their decision to take proceedings. Another way forward might be to apply to examine the directors under s 236, but that can be costly and could not be recommended, except where a claim is likely to be very high, if the sole reason for examination is to assess the nature of the likely respondents. Liquidators also have to think seriously

---

5   See the criticism of the fact that the section does not set out what activity is proscribed in Doyle, L, 'Anomalies in the wrongful trading provisions' (1992) 13 Co Law 96.

6   *Personal Liability and Disqualification of Company Directors*, 1999, Oxford: Hart Publishing, p 64.

about issuing proceedings against a number of respondents. In *Re Continental Assurance* the trial lasted for 72 days, and much of this was due to the fact that the applicants' case had to be put to all of the respondents and each of the respondents had to be cross-examined thoroughly (at 765).

Although there are no guidelines on how liquidators should act prior to initiating proceedings, Park J in *Re Continental Assurance* was clearly unimpressed with the way that the liquidators and their solicitors had conducted themselves. For instance, proceedings were commenced just before the elapse of the limitation period and the liquidators' solicitors had not been in contact with the directors for in excess of five years. Furthermore, the solicitors did not acknowledge the fact that the directors had answered, in some detail, the allegations of the liquidators quite early in the liquidation process. As Professor Adrian Walters has said:

> The message seems to be that although insolvency litigation is not the subject of a pre-action protocol, the liquidator and his legal team will be expected to conduct the pre-action phase of wrongful trading proceedings in accordance with the spirit of the Civil Procedure Rules.[7]

In assessing whether to bring proceedings a liquidator would do well to consider the following issues:[8]

(a) how strong is the evidence against the directors? Recent case law such as *Re Continental Assurance* makes it clear that judges are not going to be impressed unless the evidence demonstrates irresponsibility;
(b) is the loss due to wrongful trading worth chasing?
(c) are directors clearly culpable?
(d) are the directors people of substance or are they likely to be impecunious?
(e) how do the largest creditors view proceedings?

The burden of making out a case is, as one would expect, on the liquidator (*Re Sherborne Associates*). If the liquidator is able to establish that there was no reasonable prospect of avoiding insolvent liquidation, then the burden of proof is transferred to the director, who must make out a defence pursuant to s 214(3), a matter discussed in Chapter 9.

It has been held that an application under s 214 may be consolidated with disqualification proceedings (*Official Receiver v Doshi* [2001] 2 BCLC 235). Liquidators are required by the Insolvency Act 1986, before taking action, to secure approval from either the liquidation committee or the court – s 165(2)(b) (creditors' voluntary liquidations) or s 167(1)(a) (compulsory

---

7 'Wrongful trading: two recent cases' [2001] Insolv L 211 at 214.
8 These are based on those stated by Goode, R, *Principles of Corporate Insolvency Law*, 2nd edn, 1997, London: Sweet and Maxwell, p 477.

liquidations); para 3A of Sched 4. Unlike with many actions that can be initiated by a liquidator, there is no limit on the time period when the wrongful trading took place, although in most cases it will be the period immediately before the commencement of winding up.

The liquidator may give evidence at the hearing of an application (s 215(1)).

The elements required for liability

Insolvent liquidation

The first point to note is that the company must have entered insolvent liquidation (s 214(2)(a)). According to s 214(6), insolvent liquidation means that the company, at the time of winding up, was in a position where its debts and liabilities together with the expenses of winding up exceeded its assets. So, a balance sheet test is employed rather than a cash flow test.[9] While the majority of liquidations involve insolvent companies, we must note that if a company was not insolvent within the meaning of s 214(6), no proceedings could be brought. As balance sheet insolvency is the test, in determining whether the assets are outweighed by the liabilities a court is able to take into account contingent and prospective liabilities, but not contingent and prospective assets (*Byblos Bank SAL v Al-Khudhairy* (1986) 2 BCC 99,549, CA), so this potentially makes things easier for a liquidator in establishing insolvency. 'Liabilities' is broader than 'debts' (*Re A Debtor (No 17 of 1966)* [1967] Ch 590; [1967] 1 All ER 668) and is defined for the purposes of winding up in r 13.12(4) to mean 'a liability to pay money or money's worth, including any liability under an enactment, any liability for breach of trust, any liability in contract, tort or bailment, and any liability arising out of an obligation to make restitution'. According to r 13.12(3) it is immaterial whether the liability is present or future, whether it is certain or contingent, or whether its amount is fixed or liquidated, or is capable of being ascertained by fixed rules or as a matter of opinion.

Proceedings in other jurisdictions are not so limited. For instance, in Singapore equivalent actions may be initiated in the course of any proceedings against the company (Companies Act 1990, s 339(3)). So, action could be commenced while the company is still discharging its obligations to creditors.

Directors

Besides the fact that the company must be in insolvent liquidation, the two primary elements for liability of a person are that:

---

9   For a discussion of these tests, see Goode, *ibid* at pp 67–70 and 77–100; Keay, A, *McPherson's Law of Company Liquidation*, 2001, London: Sweet and Maxwell, pp 84–91.

(a) at some time prior to the commencement of winding up the person knew or ought to have concluded that there was no reasonable prospect of the company avoiding going into insolvent liquidation; and

(b) he or she was at that time a director of the company.

We will deal with the second point first. Unlike fraudulent trading which may apply to a broad range of persons, s 214 only applies to directors. It is interesting to note that some jurisdictions are broader than the UK section in that they impose liability on an officer of the company, and not just directors. Examples are the Irish provision, that covers 'reckless trading' (s 297A of the Companies Act 1963) and the Singaporean provision that covers 'insolvent trading' (s 339 of the Companies Act 1990). Under the Irish legislation, 'officer' includes auditors, liquidators, receivers as well as directors and shadow directors (ss 33 and 138(10) of the Companies (Amendment) Act 1990), and under the Singaporean provision the term covers the company secretary, persons employed in an executive capacity by the company, receivers and liquidators of the company in voluntary liquidation (Companies Act 1990, s 4). The Cork Committee had advocated that any person party to the carrying on of the company's business when it was wrongful could be held liable if he or she knew or ought to have known that the trading was wrongful (at [1787]), but this was one of a number of recommendations not taken up by the government.

Returning to who may be the subject of a UK wrongful trading suit, 'director' is defined in s 214(7) to include a shadow director. Persons who give advice in a professional capacity or business relationship are not included within the definition of 'shadow director', even though the directors may act on his or her directions or instructions (s 251). Notwithstanding this exclusion of professionals, investigating accountants put into a company by influential creditors, and accountants involved in an informal corporate rescue, must be especially careful that they are not seen as running the company and, therefore, being regarded as shadow directors. Such persons must be seen as advising the board and permitting it to make a decision after assessing their advice. It has been held that companies can be regarded as shadow directors for the purposes of s 214 (*Re a Company (No 005009 of 1987)* (1988) 4 BCC 424).

There is authority for the proposition that liability may extend to *de facto* as well as *de jure* directors (*Re Hydrodan (Corby) Ltd* [1994] BCC 161 at 162). As Millett J stated in *Hydrodan*:

Liability cannot sensibly depend on the validity of the defendant's appointment. Those who assume to act as directors and who thereby exercise the powers and discharge the functions of a director, whether validly appointed or not, must accept the responsibilities which are attached to the office (at 162).

A claim may be initiated against foreign directors of a foreign company being wound up in England or Wales, but in assessing the claims, courts must have regard for the relevant foreign law under which the directors were acting and the obligations imposed on a director as far as minimising losses to the company's creditors under that law (*Re Howard Holdings Inc* [1998] BCC 549 at 552; *Stocznia Gdanska SA v Latreefers Inc (No 2)* [2001] 2 BCLC 116 at 142, CA). Where the foreign law does not impose obligations that are similar to s 214, the English court will decide that it is not appropriate to make an order under s 214 (*Re Howard Holdings Inc* at 554). However, Chadwick J did go on to say in *Re Howard Holdings* (at 555) that he found it difficult:

> ... to envisage any developed system of corporate law which does not impose some obligations on those charged with responsibility off [*sic*] the management of a company's affairs to pay regard to the question whether or not it is, from time to time, solvent and, if insolvent, to consider what should be done about it.

Knowledge

The primary condition for wrongful trading is that at some time prior to the commencement of winding up the person knew or ought to have concluded that there was no reasonable prospect of the company avoiding going into insolvent liquidation. The main element of wrongful trading relates to actual or deemed knowledge that the director had of the fact that insolvent liquidation was likely to occur.

Section 214 has ditched the concept of dishonesty that proved so troublesome in relation to claims for fraudulent trading,[10] and has introduced an objective standard. In fact, s 214(4) includes both objective and subjective tests. The subsection sets out the approach that a court must take in assessing a claim, and provides that the facts that a director ought to know or ascertain, the conclusions which ought to be reached and the steps which the director ought to take, are those that a reasonably diligent person would take or have taken. So, the objective element of the provision is marked by the reference to the reasonably diligent person. This concept is used to refer to one who has the general knowledge, skill and experience that may reasonably be expected of a person who carries out the same functions as are carried out by the respondent director. The subjective element introduces the general knowledge, skill and experience of the director, namely something that is specific to the respondent director. But this does not serve to reduce the standard of knowing or ascertaining, rather it heightens it if the director is experienced. So, if a director is not very experienced or has qualities that do

---

10 See above at pp 50–59.

not match that of the reasonable person, he or she is not able to take advantage of that fact and be protected from liability; ignorance is not an excuse (*Re Brian D Pierson (Contractors) Ltd* [1999] BCC 26 at 55; [2001] BCLC 275 at 309). A director is not able to argue that he or she left all management functions to others without question; there are minimum responsibilities that must be met and there is no such thing as a 'sleeping director' (*Re Brian D Pierson* at 55; 309). It should be noted that if a director is involved in what the Cork Committee called (at [1788]) 'wilful blindness' – resolutely shutting one's eyes to the obvious, or refraining from asking obvious questions in case one discovers the truth – the director will be regarded as having the requisite knowledge. If a person is designated as the 'sales director', 'marketing director' or 'finance director', then special skills must be expected of that person (*Brian D Pierson* at 55; 309). This follows in any event from s 214(5), which provides that the reference to functions carried out by directors in s 214(4) includes functions that were entrusted to them but which they failed to fulfil.

All of this means that a director will be judged by two tests and the director has to attain the higher of the standards set by the tests. So, if a director were to meet the standard of a reasonable person carrying out his or her functions in relation to the company, but a court took the view that the director did not act in such a way as one would expect of someone with his or her knowledge, skill and experience (an experienced and well-qualified director, for example), the director could be held liable under s 214. In the reverse situation, where a director does act consistently with his or her knowledge, skill and experience, but cannot be said to have acted in line with how the reasonable person would have acted (perhaps a poorly qualified director with little experience), the director again will be liable, not being able to hide behind his or her lack of expertise. The director must fulfil both tests to avoid liability. This prevents a highly experienced director being saved from liability where he or she might act as a reasonable director, but fails to live up to the standard that one would expect of a person of his or her experience. Likewise, the tests mean that very inexperienced directors are not able to duck liability merely because they did what persons of their experience would have done, if their conduct falls below that expected of a reasonable director. For instance, in *Re DKG Contractors* one of the directors said that he did not know about companies and had no idea what was involved in being a director. But this did not save him (at 912).

Obviously, the concern of the legislature would be that neither inexperienced nor incompetent directors are to be protected because of the mere fact that they are inexperienced or incompetent, and those who are experienced are not able to say that while they did not live up to their standards, they did what an average person would have done. In New Zealand, a recent case (*Re Global Print Strategies Ltd* (unreported, High Court, 24 November 2004, Salmon J)) has (at [39]) emphasised the fact that there 'must be some element of subjectivity in determining whether what a director has failed to do constitutes reckless trading' as well as an objective element. The court also indicated that higher standards would be expected of professional directors. Although not saying this in *Re Sherborne Associates Ltd* [1995] BCC 40, the judge did indicate (at 55) that two of the directors against whom proceedings had been brought, being non-executives, were entitled to rely on the third director sued, a highly experienced chairman, because he had greater involvement with the company and the accounts. The judge went on to accept (at 55) that where a director relies on another director, the latter's views or conclusions are matters to be taken into account in making the assessment required by s 214(4).

The objective test laid down in s 214(4) was new as far as directors and their duties were concerned. Prior to this provision directors were not subjected to an objective test as far as their care and skill was concerned, although in *Re D'Jan of London Ltd* [1993] BCC 646, Hoffmann LJ did say that s 214 encapsulated the common law duty of care owed by a director.

The following aptly summarises the position:[11]

> The court is thus required to arrive at a conclusion as to the appropriate conduct and acumen of a hypothetical person assuming him to have possessed in combination the levels of general knowledge, skill and experience which the director in question subjectively did possess and which objectively he ought to have possessed in view of the position held.

It is likely that liquidators will rely more often on establishing that the directors ought to have concluded that the company was heading for insolvent liquidation (for example, *Re Continental Assurance* at 766), rather than proving that the directors knew that that was the company's fate, the latter being, obviously, more difficult to establish.

It needs to be emphasised that the liquidator is not required to prove that a director participated in irresponsible conduct; all that he or she has to do is to establish that the director knew or ought to have concluded that there was no reasonable prospect of the company not going into insolvent liquidation.

In bringing proceedings, a liquidator must specify a date from which he or she maintains the director should have realised that insolvent liquidation was inevitable. So, the key issue is clearly: at what time did the director know or should have concluded that there was no reasonable prospect of the company avoiding insolvent liquidation? The point of time when liability fixes has been referred to as 'the moment of truth'.[12] Professor Harry Rajak explains this as the point 'when the reasonably diligent person would have said, "Oh dear

11   Davies, P, *et al* (eds), *Palmer's Corporate Insolvency Law*, Vol 1, London: Sweet and Maxwell, p 1256.

12   Boschma, H, and Lennarts, L, 'Wrongful trading in a comparative perspective' in Wouters, J, and Schneider, H (eds), *Current Issues of Cross-Border Establishment of Companies in the European Union*, 1995, Antwerp: Maklu, p 205.

(or words to that effect), while yesterday I thought that we could pull through, today I see that that is highly unlikely" ',[13] and Professor Sir Roy Goode states that this is the time 'when the writing is on the wall'.[14] The fact that directors might be able to get a bank to extend more credit should not be seen as a 'green light' and an indication that everything is all right, for, as Cooke and Hicks have stated: 'It is far easier to persuade a bank to support trading than it may be to persuade a court that there was a reasonable prospect of avoiding insolvent liquidation.'[15] In *Re Produce Marketing Consortium* the judge did not regard the fact that the company's bank had continued to make finance available as relevant to his decision, although that was primarily due, probably, to the fact that the bank was not aware of the company's financial problems. The likely provision of funds might be sufficient for directors to have confidence that insolvent liquidation can be avoided, but circumstances might be such, as they were in *Rubin v Gunner* [2004] EWHC 316 (Ch); [2004] BCC 684; [2004] 2 BCLC 110, where eventually the respondent directors' reliance on that became inappropriate.

Clearly a director is not going to be able to rely solely on a 'feeling' that things would get better. He or she would have to be able to point to something that indicated, to the reasonable person in his or her position, that the company's position would either improve or, at least, not deteriorate. Of course, a court might well feel that the views of directors are not reasonable. For instance, in *Rubin v Gunner* the judge described (at [112]) the notion that the company, later to be liquidated, would receive sufficient funds to bail it out of its problems from the flotation of a new company in a very short period of time as 'fantastic'.

Notwithstanding the fact that s 214(4) provides that directors can be liable if they ought to have known that the company was destined for insolvent liquidation, there are suggestions that courts are more concerned with the belief held by the directors. For instance, in *Re Continental Assurance* Park J, in considering the fact that the figures of the company presented at a board meeting were worrying, said that he was of the opinion that the directors were not expecting figures which showed a bad financial situation, and this appears to have been weighted by his Lordship in the favour of the directors. This is notwithstanding expert evidence from one of the liquidator's witnesses that indicated that the figures suggested a worse financial position (at 753).

In this context it is worth noting that while s 297A of the Irish Companies Act 1963 (amended by s 138 of the Companies Act 1990) uses similar language to the wrongful trading provision, there is no need for an Irish applicant to establish that the respondent knew or ought to have concluded that insolvent liquidation could not be avoided. It is merely sufficient to establish that the respondent, given the general knowledge, skill and experience that

---

13 'Wrongful trading' (1989) NLJ 1458 at 1459.   14 *Op. cit.* Goode fn 8 above at 204.
15 Cooke, T, and Hicks, A, 'Wrongful trading – predicting insolvency' [1993] JBL 338 at 340.

might reasonably be expected of a person in his or her position, ought to have known that his or her actions would cause loss to the creditors (s 297A(2)(a)). Prima facie, this seems to enable Irish claimants more leeway in proving their case, for all they have to do is to establish that the respondent ought to have known that the creditors would lose out, not that the company was heading for collapse. However, in *Re Hefferon Kearns Ltd (No 2)* (unreported but noted in (1993) JIBL 93) Lynch J held that for the respondent to be liable, he had to be shown to be actually aware of the risk of the company's insolvency with little regard for the creditors and it would not be sufficient to prove only that the officer was uncertain that all creditors might not be able to be paid.

In determining whether a director knew or ought to have concluded that there was no reasonable prospect of avoiding insolvent liquidation, courts are not restricted to a consideration of the material available to the director during the period of the alleged wrongful trading; reference may be had to material that was able to be accessed by a person exercising reasonable diligence and an appropriate level of general knowledge (*Re Produce Marketing Consortium Ltd* (1989) 5 BCC 569 at 595).

If a liquidator can establish the fact that directors knew or ought to have known that there was no reasonable prospect of the company avoiding insolvent liquidation, the directors' liability will be based on the losses incurred by the company after this time.

The approach adopted by the UK provision of combining both subjective and objective considerations is consistent with what has occurred in other jurisdictions, such as Australia. However, South Africa has eschewed any subjective factor. Under its legislation a person can be liable for reckless trading based solely on an objective test. Liability is imposed on a person if he or she is guilty of negligence, albeit gross negligence (and not mere negligence), a view also taken in New Zealand (*Re Global Print Strategies Ltd* (unreported, High Court, 24 November 2004, Salmon J)) where an applicant does not have to establish the traditional meaning of recklessness, namely 'the existence of a subjective foresight as to the probability or possibility of harm resulting from conduct but, nevertheless, a persistence in that conduct'.[16]

It is interesting that it has been asserted that even though s 214 enables a liquidator to establish that a director failed to meet an objective test, it has been said that practitioners have found that in practice a wrongful trading action is almost as difficult to prove as fraud.[17]

It is not possible to catalogue the circumstances that might lead a court to say that the directors knew or ought to have concluded that the company had

---

16 Dabner, J, 'Insolvent trading: recent developments in Australia, New Zealand and South Africa' [1995] JBL 282 at 291.
17 McGee, A, and Williams, C, *A Company Director's Liability for Wrongful Trading*, 1992, London: Certified Accountants Educational Trust, p 10.

no reasonable prospect of avoiding insolvent liquidation. The cases are of limited assistance. The loss of a major customer or contract on the one hand, or the withdrawal of credit by a primary supplier, as was the case in *Re DKG Contractors* [1990] BCC 903, on the other, might suffice.

No reasonable prospect of avoiding insolvent liquidation

As Dr Fidelis Oditah has said, the phrase 'reasonable prospect' is elusive.[18] It is difficult for directors in many situations, leaving aside those cases where their company is clearly hopelessly insolvent and cannot possibly recover, or the slide into insolvency appears to be inexorable, to gaze into the future and determine whether insolvent liquidation is the company's lot. Much is likely to turn on what the directors are doing, what are the company's prospects as far as its business goes, what is the general commercial milieu as far as it affects the company and its business, and whether funds are likely to be received in the short term. Certainly temporary cash-flow problems should not be seen as meaning, necessarily, that the company is heading for insolvent liquidation,[19] but obviously continual problems in this regard must be seen as warning signs.

It has been suggested by Oditah that 'the question whether directors ought reasonably to conclude that their company has no reasonable prospect of avoiding insolvent liquidation so as to avoid liability . . . can only be answered by identifying the cause of the particular insolvency'.[20] This is an adroit comment, although, with respect, the company does not necessarily have to be insolvent at the point when wrongful trading actually commences, but clearly one would expect the company was not far from it if the liquidator is to succeed.

The point of liability

The liquidator will need to decide on a point of time from which it is alleged the director knew or ought to have concluded that there was no reasonable prospect of the company avoiding going into insolvent liquidation, for s 214(2)(b) requires that 'at some time' before the commencement of the winding up the respondent must have known or ought to have known that insolvent liquidation could not be avoided. Liquidators will have to weigh up a number of factors in determining from which time wrongful trading commenced.[21] It has been said that identifying the point might well be an extremely difficult task.[22]

It has been held that a liquidator is not entitled, where the case presented is not made out in relation to the dates pleaded in the claim, to argue for

---

18 'Wrongful trading' [1990] LMCLQ 205 at 208.   19 *Ibid*.   20 *Ibid* at 210.
21 In this regard, see Hicks, A, 'Advising on wrongful trading: Part 1' (1993) 14 Co Law 16 at 17.
22 Simmons, M, 'Wrongful trading' (2001) 14 *Insolvency Intelligence* 12 at 13.

wrongful trading in respect of other dates once the evidence has been heard, as this would be unfair on the respondent(s) (*Sherborne Associates* at 42; *Re Continental Assurance* at 766–767). However, in *Re Brian D Pierson (Contractors) Ltd* (at 49–50; 302–303) Hazel Williamson QC (sitting as a deputy High Court judge), while not disagreeing with this viewpoint, seemed to suggest that she would not be averse to a liquidator being able to point to events that establish liability around about the date that has been pleaded. The court is able, it seems, to impose its own starting point for wrongful trading, certainly where the company's affairs are in a total shambles (*Re Purpoint Ltd* at 128; 498–499). In *Official Receiver v Doshi* [2001] 2 BCLC 235 at 281 Hart J held that the respondent was engaging in wrongful trading from November 1992, and the fact that the liquidator had alleged that the trading had commenced in February 1992, did not seem to matter. The same goes for *Rubin v Gunner* where the liquidator had argued that wrongful trading began in May or June 1998, while Etherton J found that it began from 15 October 1998, and held the director liable accordingly from that date.

What date will be chosen? It has been suggested that the point from which liability commences is likely to be a crisis point in the life of the company when directors have to acknowledge the inevitable.[23]

It is likely that the further back that a liquidator seeks to push the point of liability, the greater the difficulty of establishing that fact. A liquidator will have to balance the weight of evidence against the quantum of a possible contribution order. It might be wise of a liquidator to be conservative and nominate a date from which the directors clearly knew or ought to have concluded insolvent liability was inevitable.

What should directors be doing?

Professor Len Sealy has submitted that the drafting of the provision is so broad that it is able to render liability for 'incompetence, ignorance and indifference' as well as conscious wrongdoing,[24] so directors must be careful how they act. Critically, directors must keep on top of the financial position of their company, and, in accordance with what the law now requires of directors, they must be able to understand company accounts.[25] If they are not able to do so, then they must employ someone who can advise them appropriately (*Re Hitco 2000 Ltd* [1995] 2 BCLC 63). Even conscientious and

23 *Op. cit.* fn 15 at 339.
24 'Personal liability of directors and officers for debts of insolvent corporations: a jurisdictional perspective (England)' in Ziegel, J (ed), *Current Developments in International and Comparative Corporate Insolvency Law*, 1994, Oxford: Clarendon Press, p 491.
25 See the comments in *Re DKG Contractors Ltd* [1990] BCC 903 and referred to in Milman, D, 'Strategies for regulating managerial performance in the "Twilight Zone" – familiar dilemmas: new considerations' [2004] JBL 493 at 497.

competent directors can be placed in difficult positions when they become aware that their company's finances are not too healthy. They must not be cavalier, but nor must they be overly cautious, because the latter could see them do something that would not benefit creditors. For example, the immediate cessation of business could well be the worst thing for all concerned. The directors also might be in breach of their duties to shareholders.

Rarely, where directors have made an effort to understand the position of their company, and where they have decided to continue doing business, will they be held liable (see *Re Sherborne Associates; Re Continental Assurance*). Indeed in *Re Continental Assurance* Park J said (at 769) that in the typical case in which directors have been held to be liable, the directors have:

> . . . closed their eyes to the reality of the company's position, and carried on trading long after it should have been obvious to them that the company was insolvent and that there was no way out for it. In those cases the directors had been irresponsible, and had not made any genuine attempt to grapple with the company's real position.

Admittedly, what is required of directors is some 'crystal ball gazing' as to the future of their company, and this, in many cases, might be difficult to do. It has been judicially recognised that 'directors immersed in the day-to-day task of trying to keep their business afloat cannot be expected to have wholly dispassionate minds' (*Re CU Fittings Ltd* [1989] BCLC 556 at 559 per Hoffmann J). But the same judge also acknowledged that 'there comes a point at which an honest businessman recognises that he is only gambling at the expense of his creditors on the possibility that something may turn up' (*Re CU Fittings Ltd* at 559).

Importantly, it would seem that directors should be recording all their decisions and what information they have sought and considered. Also, they should obtain all available information about the company, which should include not only what is available to them, but what ought to be available,[26] and that which they could have reasonably obtained (*Re Produce Marketing* at 595), such as documents or information concerning the financial state of the company. For instance, the directors are deemed to know what is to be found in the company's accounting records. It should be noted that the knowledge that is imputed to directors is not limited to any documents that are available at the relevant time (*Re Produce Marketing* at 595).

In New Zealand the courts seem to have distinguished between those actions which involve legitimate business risks and those which are illegitimate (*Re South Pacific Shipping Ltd* (2004) 9 NZCLC 263,570; *Walker v Allen*, unreported, High Court, 18 March 2004, France J). The latter can constitute reckless trading, and could be marked by a significant departure

---

26 Fidler, P, 'Wrongful trading after *Continental Assurance*' (2001) 17 I L & P 212 at 215.

from orthodox business practice and extensive risks for creditors (*Re South Pacific Shipping Ltd*).

Court considerations

Obviously, when hearing a wrongful trading case the courts are hearing it retrospectively and must realise that and the fact that the director respondent did not have the benefit of hindsight when making decisions. It has been judicially recognised that there is always the danger of the courts taking the view, because of hindsight, that it can be assumed that what in fact occurred was always bound to happen and was apparent, and courts must be wary of making such an assumption (*Re Sherborne Associates* at 54; *Re Brian D Pierson (Contractors) Ltd* at 50; 303). The decisions of the director must be taken in the context of the material available to him or her and the situation that existed at the relevant time. It is submitted that the judicial decisions that we have available to us manifest the fact that the courts have not used hindsight to the detriment of respondents. Indeed, courts have tended to give respondents the benefit of any doubts.

Clearly, courts are to have regard for the kind of company managed by the director, as well as the type of business in which it was involved (*Re Produce Marketing Consortium Ltd* (1989) 5 BCC 569 at 594; *Re Sherborne Associates* at 54; *Re Brian D Pierson* at 50; 303). Consequently, the courts will expect less general knowledge, skill and experience of a director of a small company which has modest systems, simple accounting processes and equipment, and which is involved in a modest amount of business, than a person whose company has well-developed systems and practices and is conducting a large-scale business (*Re Produce Marketing* at 594–595). According to Professors Len Sealy and David Milman, s 214(4) should 'give scope for the courts to make some allowances in the case of non-executive and part-time directors'.[27] But courts will assume that certain minimum standards are assumed to be attained in whatever the company or its business, for example, to cause accounting records to be maintained (*Re Produce Marketing* at 595). Probably more might be expected of some directors, with particular knowledge and/or experience in specialist fields, such as accounting or law.

Directors will not be held liable, it would seem, merely because their company was insolvent at the time when they are alleged to have engaged in wrongful trading (*Re Sherborne Associates Ltd*). In *Rubin v Gunner* the court absolved the respondents from liability because it was satisfied that the respondents had a genuine and reasonable belief that liquidation could be avoided because of the fact that sufficient funding was going to eventuate ([79]). In a director disqualification case, *Secretary of State for Trade and*

---

27 *Annotated Guide to the Insolvency Legislation*, 2nd revised 7th edn, 2004, London: Sweet and Maxwell, p 227.

Industry v Gash [1997] 2 BCLC 341, Chadwick J (as he then was) said that directors are entitled, even when their company is insolvent, to continue to trade in order to try and trade out of its difficulties, on the basis that it is in the interests of the creditors to do so (see *Secretary of State for Trade and Industry v Taylor* [1997] 1 WLR 407). This might be done where the directors take the view that it is in the interests of creditors that some loss-making activity should be accepted in anticipation of the company enjoying profitability in the future. Of course, this might, as the judge acknowledged, lead to personal liability on one or more of the bases discussed in this book.

Clearly, directors are not stopped from taking some risks. For instance, in *Facia Footwear Ltd (in administration) v Hinchliffe* [1998] 1 BCLC 218, a case involving a claim that directors had failed to take into account creditors' interests, Sir Richard Scott V-C acknowledged that, in continuing trading the directors were taking a risk, but his Lordship went on to say (at 228) that 'the boundary between an acceptable risk that an entrepreneur may properly take and an unacceptable risk . . . is not always, perhaps not usually, clear cut'.

Section 214(5) assists courts in the interpretation of s 214(4). It provides that the reference in the latter subsection to the functions carried out in relation to the company by the director includes any function that the director does not carry out but were entrusted to him or her. This, therefore, makes a director responsible for omitting to do that which he or she should have done, and is in contrast with the common law on care and skill which tended to absolve directors when they did not do something, such as attending board meetings.

In determining whether there was no reasonable prospect of a company avoiding insolvent liquidation, courts will take into account a broad range of factors which may be presented to them through evidence. This may include pressure from creditors owed debts, the withdrawal of support from banks, the loss of contracts, the fact that fresh contracts cannot be obtained, the failure to pay Crown debts,[28] and the loss of a major supplier (for example, *Re DKG Contractors Ltd* [1990] BCC 903).

The courts do not appear readily to impose liability on directors. For instance, in *Re Purpoint Ltd* it was stated that even if it might be said that a reasonably prudent director would not have permitted his or her company to commence trading at the time when it in fact did, because the company was poorly set up, it is probably too harsh to conclude that the director ought to have known that the company had no chance of keeping out of insolvent liquidation (at 127; 498). Courts appear to look favourably on respondents when they sought and obtained advice from professionals. In most cases where directors have been held liable they have been found to have acted irresponsibly. Arguably though, given the legislation, liability should have nothing to do with irresponsibility. The issue is: did the director know or

---

28 *Op. cit.* fn 6 above at 66.

ought the director to have concluded that there was no reasonable prospect of the company avoiding insolvent liquidation? A director could have been responsible in taking advice, monitoring the company and undertaking checks and still he or she might fall foul of s 214 as he or she ought to have concluded that there was no reasonable prospect of the company avoiding insolvent liquidation. It is not totally about what the directors actually did, but is about what they knew or ought to have concluded. Directors might be conscientious (as the directors were said to have been in *Re Continental Assurance* (at 769)), but then they might totally miss the fact that their company is doomed. In such cases should they be kept from liability?

It is respectfully submitted that Park J in *Re Continental Assurance* missed the point when he noted that the directors did not ignore the fact as to whether the company should continue to trade (at 769), for that is not the essential issue. The issue is: should they have concluded that there was no reasonable prospect of the company avoiding insolvent liquidation? Admittedly, the fact that the directors 'reduced the scale of trading to minimal and cautious levels' (at 769) as the financial position became more bleak, should be an issue to be taken into account, but only as to whether the defence mentioned in s 214(3) can be made out, namely it should go towards whether the directors took every step to minimise the potential loss to creditors and not to whether they knew or ought to have concluded that there was no reasonable prospect of the company avoiding insolvent liquidation. Indeed, counsel for the liquidators in *Re Continental Assurance* argued that while the directors tried their best, they got things wrong, and it was their fault that they got things wrong (at 770). Park J felt that that was an 'austere attitude' (at 770) and had sympathy with the view that the liquidators relied on hindsight and they failed to appreciate the realities of being a director (at 770). His Lordship noted that the directors questioned figures that were presented to them, but while that is a laudable course of action to take, it is surely not directly relevant to the issue of whether they could not have concluded that their company could not avoid liquidation. The asking of questions alone is not the critical issue. The critical issue is what answers were given, if any, and whether they should have been in a position to know or conclude that liquidation was not able to be avoided, if they had not been in a position beforehand. Equally of course the answers might, or could, not have taken them any further in knowing where the company was heading. For instance, his Lordship notes that the answers given might have been incorrect (at 812). I do not take issue with the conclusion that Park J drew, namely that the directors were not liable for wrongful trading, but I contend that some of the factors that he took into account were erroneous. His Lordship seemed to be looking for some clear wrongdoing on the part of the directors, and found none, and that meant that they were not liable. With respect, the provision does not require the establishing of any wrongdoing, certainly in the sense of blameworthiness. Applying the approach taken by the judge to, say, a student enrolled in a university course who works very hard, reads all of the prescribed readings, attends classes and asks all the right questions, but in the final examination performs poorly, should the student pass for all of the hard work done? The answer is clearly 'no', if the examination answer script does not satisfy the pass criteria.

The concern that I would have is that the approach in *Re Continental Assurance* appears to circumscribe the scope of s 214, by indicating that blameworthiness is an issue that can be taken into account in determining liability. It is submitted that if anything, it should only go to the issue of the amount of contribution ordered to be paid.

The types of company involved in actions

Let us return briefly to the cases where an order in favour of a liquidator has been made. To date, the cases have involved exclusively small, closely held companies, such as in *Re DKG Contractors Ltd* [1990] BCC 903, *Re Purpoint Ltd* [1991] BCC 121; [1991] BCLC 491, *Re Brian D Pierson (Contractors) Ltd* [1999] BCC 26, and *Rubin v Gunner* [2004] BCC 684; [2004] EWHC 316 (Ch), a phenomenon that also appears to exist in Australia, according to some empirical work done recently.[29] Dr Rizwaan Mokal has said that 'the section 214 duty is most relevant to companies whose directors themselves own a substantial chunk of the firm's equity'.[30] There is not a single instance of the directors of a larger company being held liable. Why is this? Mokal states that 'companies large enough to have professional non-executive directors are highly unlikely to engage in wrongful trading'.[31] Perhaps the directors of larger companies are more ready to seek professional advice, and to act on it, rather than directors of closely held companies who may be fiercely independent and intolerant of such advice, partially on the basis that they, the professionals, do not know the business as well as the directors, who might rely on 'gut feeling' founded on experience (*Re Brian D Pierson* at 50; 303) on many occasions. Another reason might be that information about the company's financial position might be more readily available in large companies. A substantial reason, in relation to a goodly number of cases, is likely to be that the directors of a large company are not so wedded to the company and its mission as those who start small businesses, who often put their heart and soul into ventures and find it hard to admit that they might not be able to achieve success,[32] often leading to what can only be described as 'wishful thinking'. An example is the male respondent in *Re Brian D Pierson*.

---

29 *Op. cit.* above, fn 2.

30 *Corporate Insolvency: Theory and Application*, 2005, Oxford: Oxford University Press, p 266.

31 *Ibid* at 283 fn 97.

32 Mokal, R, 'An agency cost analysis of the wrongful trading provisions: redistribution, perverse incentives and the creditors' bargain' (2000) 59 CLJ 335 at 353–354.

Whereas directors of large companies have to ensure, as much as possible, they do not damage their reputation for the future as they will, ordinarily want to go and be involved in, and even manage, other companies. And as Professor Ron Daniels has stated in relation to the executive directors of larger companies:

> [I]n light of their imminent re-entry into the job market, managers may reason that the best strategy to adopt in a distress situation is one of honesty and integrity. Rather than using wrongdoing as a way of gambling the company back to success, the managers may decide to avoid unscrupulously any hint of wrongdoing out of a concern for inflicting irrevocable damage to their reputational capital in the managerial market.[33]

Another reason could be that the directors of small companies do not always separate their personal affairs from their business affairs, again a criticism made of the male respondent in *Re Brian D Pierson* (at 39; 290).

Loss

Although not deciding the issue, it has been assumed that it may not be necessary to prove a causal link between the wrongful trading established, and any particular loss (*Re Simmon Box (Diamonds) Ltd* [2000] BCC 275; [2001] 1 BCLC 176, CA). However, subsequently in *Re Continental Assurance* (at 844) Park J said that it was necessary to establish some connection between the wrongfulness of the directors' conduct with the company's losses which the liquidator seeks to recover. This later view is in accord with the argument of counsel for the liquidator in *Re Produce Marketing Consortium Ltd*, an argument that appeared to have been accepted by the judge in that case. This argument was essentially that the test of liability is analogous to the assessment of tortious damages, liability for which is dependent on causation. Nevertheless, Park J in *Re Continental Assurance* said that more had to be established than a mere nexus between an incorrect decision to carry on trading and a particular loss sustained by the company (at 844). Park J pointed out that the required nexus will often be obvious, such as where a director turns a blind eye to inherent loss-making (at 844).

Not all losses suffered by a company after the directors wrongly decide to continue trading can necessarily be claimed by a liquidator (*Re Continental Assurance* at 844; *The Liquidator of Marini Ltd v Dickensen* [2004] BCC 172; [2003] EWHC 334 (Ch) at [68]). The law will limit liability to those consequences which are attributable to the wrongful action(s) (*Re Continental*

---

33 Daniels, R, 'Must boards go overboard?' (1994–1995) 24 Can Bus L J 229 at 241.

Assurance at 845). This position diverges from that in South Africa, where it has been said that there is no need to establish a causal connection between the allegedly reckless conduct and the relevant debts (*Howard v Herrigel* 1991 (2) SA 660 (AD) at 661).

Liquidators are required to show that there was a net deficiency in company assets when comparing the company's position as at the time when wrongful trading is alleged to have commenced (and trading should have stopped) and the position when trading actually ceased (*Re Continental Assurance* at 821, 844; *The Liquidator of Marini Ltd v Dickensen* at [68]). This, as evidenced by what occurred in *Re Continental Assurance* (at 821–822), is often going to be a difficult task. In *Marini Ltd* (at [68]) Judge Seymour QC (sitting as a High Court judge) agreed with Park J in *Re Continental Assurance* that in determining loss, the appropriate test was not whether new debt was incurred after the date on which it was decided that the respondent knew or ought to have concluded that the company could not avoid insolvent liquidation, but whether the company was in a worse position at the date of liquidation than it would have been if trading had ceased at the time it is alleged was appropriate. It has been suggested that in calculating the net deficiency, the court will not take into account the costs of the liquidation.[34]

The order

The provision states that if satisfied that the respondent engaged in wrongful trading, the court, as with claims under s 213 for fraudulent trading, may declare that the respondent is to be liable to make such contribution to the company's assets as is thought proper; it is a matter left to the court's discretion (*Re Produce Marketing Consortium* at 597), so that it appears that it is able to award any sum that it thinks is appropriate. The court may in fact refrain from ordering any contribution. Notwithstanding the fact that the court has a discretion, in *Re Continental Assurance* Park J noted that while there is a major element of discretion, it is not entirely at large (at 821). His Lordship appeared to accept that a judge has to determine what is the maximum amount that could be ordered, and then he or she could exercise discretion to reduce that amount. The maximum amount would appear to be the net deficiency in the company's assets.

In relation to s 213, it was noted in Chapter 4 that the Court of Appeal in *Morphitis v Bernasconi* [2003] EWCA Civ 289; [2003] BCC 540, when dealing with the same wording as in s 214(1), said that the contribution to the assets to be shared amongst the creditors should reflect the loss which has been caused to the creditors by the carrying on of the business in the way that gives rise to the exercise of the power (at [55]), and this appears to limit the discretion of judges, certainly when it comes to ascertaining loss.

---

34 Walters, A, 'Wrongful trading: two recent cases' [2001] Insolv L 211 at 212.

Determining what order of contribution should be made is often a difficult matter and might require the judge hearing further argument and evidence (as in *Official Receiver v Doshi* [2001] 2 BCLC 235 at 289). In *Rubin v Gunner* (at [125]) the court, after making the required declaration, ordered an account so as to ascertain what contribution should in fact be ordered.

As far as any order made, is a court limited to ordering compensation, or may it make an order that is penal? In *Re Produce Marketing Consortium*, Knox J, while accepting that the contributions should be the amount by which the company's assets can be regarded as being depleted by the wrongful trading of the directors, seemed to leave open the possibility of being able to take into account the fact that a director was culpable, with the result that courts may treat directors who have been reckless more harshly than those who have acted honestly, and perhaps naively (at 597–598). This position was favoured in *Re Brian D Pierson* (at 55; 310). The judge in *Re Produce Marketing Consortium* said (at 597) that the jurisdiction under s 214 is '*primarily* compensatory' (my emphasis). It has been asserted, on the basis that the courts have a broad discretion, that the courts may take into account the fact that a director was culpable when considering the wrongful trading.[35] So, the making of untruths by directors may be taken into account, as might the ignoring of warnings from the company's auditors. Other factors that might be taken into account in determining the amount of the contribution are: the fact that the company's position was worsened by issues outside of the directors' control or reasonable anticipation; the directors received no warnings from advisers; the attitude of the directors to advice; and whether a director relied on the experience and dominance of other directors (*Re Brian D Pierson* at 56–57; 310–311). But, the Court of Appeal in *Morphites v Bernasconi*, in dealing with a s 213 case, rejected any notion of providing for a penal award, and this does accord with the opinion of Knox J in *Re Produce Marketing Consortium Ltd* (at 597) when he was dealing with s 214, namely that the provision envisaged a compensatory award (something supported by the Court of Appeal in *Re Farmizer (Products) Ltd* [1997] BCC 655 at 662). So, while no actions of the directors will, it appears, lead to penal awards, if directors act honestly, the award might be reduced.

As with the UK provision, the NZ provision allows for compensatory orders and not penal ones. For instance, in *Re South Pacific Shipping Ltd* (2004) 9 NZCLC 263,570, Young J ordered the director against whom proceedings were issued to pay 26 per cent of the company's liabilities owed to the unsecured creditors. This, nevertheless, amounted to a large sum, namely NZ$7m.[36] The equivalent Singaporean provision also reflects the same approach (Companies Act 1990, s 339).

---

35 *Op. cit.* fn 6 above at 83.

36 Although a finding against a director may mean that an order of disqualification from acting as a director may be imposed by the courts: Company Directors' Disqualification Act 1986, s 10.

As with s 213, courts cannot make orders in favour of particular creditors because the objective is to assist the liquidator to recoup the loss to the company so as to benefit all of the creditors of the company (*Re Purpoint Ltd* at 129; 499; *Re Oasis Merchandising Services Ltd* [1995] BCC 911 at 918). Furthermore, it has been held that creditors whose debts are incurred after the point when the directors are said to have begun to engage in wrongful trading have no better claim than the pre-wrongful trading creditors as both classes of creditor suffer to the extent that assets are depleted by the wrongful trading (*Re Purpoint* at 129; 499). The criticism of the present system of compensation has been that the persons who have been the real victims of the wrongful trading, namely those who became creditors subsequent to the time when wrongful trading commenced, do not receive all of the compensation, for some of it will go to persons who had become creditors prior to the advent of wrongful trading.[37] The extant UK approach is not followed in many other jurisdictions. For example, the equivalent Irish provision (Companies Act 1963, s 297A) provides that the court may determine that 'sums recovered under this section [s 297A] shall be paid to such persons or classes of persons, for such purposes, in such amounts or proportions at such time or times and in such respective priorities among themselves . . .' (s 297A(7)(b)). This permits the courts to do justice by directing to whom money should be paid. The position in Singapore seems to be similar to the Irish situation, for as Singapore permits creditors to bring wrongful trading type actions, it would appear arguable that an order could be made that rewarded the applicant creditor alone.

Where a claim is made pursuant to both s 212 and s 214, not an unusual occurrence, there is no injustice in ordering payments under both provisions provided that the liquidator did not recover more than was required to satisfy the liabilities of the company (*Re Purpoint Ltd* at 128; 499). Professor Sir Roy Goode points out that 'to the extent that recovery for an unconnected loss under section 212 reduces the net deficiency below the amount of the loss caused by the director's breach of section 214 his liability under that section will abate'.[38]

Where more than one director is subject to proceedings, the court has a discretion whether to hold that the directors are to be jointly and severally liable on the one hand, or severally liable on the other (*Re Brian D Pierson* at 57; 311; *Re Continental Assurance* at 847). The courts in *Re Produce Marketing* (at 598) and *Re DKG Contractors Ltd* ([1990] BCC 903 at 912) made orders encompassing the first alternative. In *Re Continental Assurance*, the judge did not hold the directors liable, but he said that if he had held them liable it would not have been appropriate to embrace the first alternative; he saw several liability as the starting point and then a court could exercise its discretion and make the director jointly and severally liable if it chose to do

---

37 *Op. cit.* fn 21 above at 17.   38 *Op. cit.* fn 8 above at 462.

so (at 846, 847). Park J's reason for this view (at 846) was that the provision's focus is on 'an individual director and his conduct, not on the joint conduct of a board of directors as a whole', hence he would have ordered several liability in the case before him if he felt that the directors were indeed liable (at 847). Where more than one director is involved in an action, a judge can order the various respondents to pay different amounts, depending on their position, knowledge and experience (*Re Continental Assurance* at 847).

A judge may include in the contribution awarded against a respondent an amount covering interest in order to compensate the creditors for the time that has elapsed (*Re Produce Marketing*).

Where a court makes a declaration against the respondent to a s 214 application, it is, at its discretion, empowered to make further directions to give effect to its declaration (s 215(2)). In particular it may provide for the liability of the respondent under the declaration to be a charge on any debt or obligation due from the company to the respondent, or on any mortgagee or charge or any interest in a mortgage or charge on assets of the company held by or vested in the respondent, or any person on behalf of the respondent, or any person claiming as assignee from or through the respondent (s 215(2)(a)). Also the court may, from time to time, make such further or other order as may be necessary for enforcing any charge imposed under s 215 (s 215(2)(b)). Section 215(4) provides that, in the case of a court declaration against a person that is liable for wrongful trading, the court may direct that the whole or any part of a debt owed by the company to the guilty person is to rank after all other debts owed and interest payable on those debts.

Some jurisdictions, such as Singapore (Companies Act 1990, s 339(3)) and South Africa (Companies Act 1973, s 424), provide that a breach of their equivalent of wrongful trading can lead to both civil and criminal liability, whereas, of course, there is no criminal liability linked to wrongful trading.

The effects of an order

Liquidators are entitled to accept property other than money from directors when the latter seek to satisfy any award against them, even though s 214 is an action for the recovery of a sum of money which a court declares a respondent liable to contribute (*Re Farmizer (Products) Ltd* [1997] BCC 655 at 662, CA).

Perhaps one of the major issues facing a liquidator who is granted an award of funds as a result of litigation is to know to whom the funds should be distributed. One of the primary questions is whether a holder of a charge over company assets is given any priority in relation to the funds. While in the judgment in *Re Produce Marketing Consortium* Knox J stated (at 598) that the chargeholder would have a charge over anything that the respondents paid under his order, his Lordship did indicate that he disagreed with this state of affairs and that if 'this jurisdiction is to be exercised, as in my judgment it should be in this case, it needs to be exercised in a way which will benefit unsecured creditors' (at 598). Subsequently the Court of Appeal stated that the discretion given to courts under s 214 is to be exercised in order to benefit unsecured creditors (*Re Oasis Merchandising Ltd* [1997] 1 WLR 764 at 773–777). The court indicated that any award would not constitute property of the company; a liquidator is taking proceedings under s 214 on behalf of the creditors and contributories of the company, so any money recovered will be paid to them and not paid out first to creditors who hold charges. This accords with the thinking of the Cork Committee and overturns the decision in *Produce Marketing Consortium*. As a consequence of the recent law, chargeholders will merely rank with all other creditors in relation to any pay-out, and only in so far as they are not secured. Mokal makes the point that if secured creditors were able to participate in any award then this would be likely to attenuate their monitoring activities.[39] However, Dr Rebecca Parry has pointed out that it could be argued that a chargeholder would be prejudiced by wrongful trading just as much as any other creditor, as demonstrated by many disqualification cases where companies have traded on while insolvent, doing so at the expense of the Crown.[40] This has often involved companies using unremitted deductions of tax from employees' wages to enable them to continue to do business, a practice that has been condemned by the courts (*Re Stanford Services Ltd* [1987] BCLC 607; *Re Lo-Line Electric Motors Ltd* [1988] Ch 477 at 486) and it might lead to the making of a director's disqualification order under s 6 of the Company Directors' Disqualification Act 1986 (*Re Bath Glass Ltd* [1988] BCLC 329 at 333; *Re Sevenoaks Stationers (Retail) Ltd* [1991] 1 Ch 164 at 183–184, CA). The thrust of this observation of Parry was that the Crown had preferential status and would be able to recover from company funds what was owed before the chargeholder. Of course, now the Crown does not have any preferential right, the right being taken away (from 15 September 2003) by the Enterprise Act 2002. But, the chargeholder is only prejudiced if the funds of the company are reduced below what the chargeholder is owed, and the chargeholder, if holding a charge over the whole, or substantially the whole, of the company's assets, is able to protect itself as it is entitled to appoint either an administrative receiver (if the charge pre-dates 15 September 2003) or an administrator. In contrast, unsecured creditors cannot appoint either of these office-holders, although they could apply for an administration order from the court.

It has been argued that it is inconsistent to say that the award under s 214 does not belong to the company (and, therefore, the chargeholders cannot claim priority) when the courts, notably those in *Re Purpoint Ltd* and

---

39 *Op. cit.* fn 30 above at 300.
40 'The destination of proceeds of insolvency litigation' (2002) 23 Co Law 49 at 55.

Re Continental Assurance, recognise that wrongful trading causes loss to the company, and it is the company that is the victim of the wrongful trading.[41] It is further argued that the section itself states that directors can be ordered to make a contribution to 'the company's assets',[42] which is the same word formula used in s 212. Admittedly, the courts say, as we have seen, that loss is calculated on the increase in the net deficiency which reflects the loss to the company. But that is merely an equitable way of devising what directors should pay; there is no other fair way of calculating the liability of the directors. In relation to the point about the provision including a reference to a contribution to the company's assets, it might be argued by way of riposte that at the time when wrongful trading is said to have occurred, the company's assets belong to the creditors, as they are the owners of the residual value of the firm, having transplanted the shareholders. Further, it has been suggested that while s 214 actions are actionable at the suit of the company acting by its liquidator,[43] the provision is bestowed specifically on the liquidator. Furthermore, the provision is regarded as having a penal element to it (*Re Oasis Merchandising Services Ltd*), because it can lead to a director's disqualification, and it cannot be said that the action is the company's, for it must be that of someone who is acting independently and enforcing commercial morality. Oditah points out that the right of action never vests in the company at any stage, so, he asks, how can a chargeholder establish entitlement to the action?[44] Also, as the action is not the company's, the fruits of it should not fall to the company.[45] The action under s 214 is akin, in some ways, to a claim under s 239 for a restoration order when a preference is found to have been given by the company before liquidation, for both claims emanate from a statutory right granted to the liquidator, and any fruits of an order pursuant to s 239 go to the unsecured creditors (*Re MC Bacon Ltd (No 2)* [1990] BCC 430 at 434). Another interesting point is that a liquidator's actions are not treated as corporate actions for the purposes of the security for costs jurisdiction in s 726 of the Companies Act 1985. So,

> . . . if both the action *and* the recoveries vest exclusively in the liquidator then it stands to reason that the recoveries will be outside the scope of any charge granted by the company over its property. . . . The fact that recoveries comprise 'assets of the company' for the purposes of the Insolvency Act 1986 is of no consequence. In light of the House of Lords' decision in *Buchler v Talbot* [2004] UKHL 9; [2004] 2 AC 298, this wording simply denotes the fund of assets available for distribution under the statutory winding-up scheme.[46]

41 Ho, L C, 'On deepening insolvency and wrongful trading' (2005) 20 *Journal of International Banking Law and Regulation* 426.
42 *Ibid.*   43 *Ibid.*   44 *Op. cit.* fn 18 above at 218.   45 *Ibid.*   46 *Ibid.*

One further argument from a policy point of view in favour of allowing chargeholders to participate in any award under s 214 is that now, under the changes effected by the Enterprise Act 2002, where there is a floating charge created after 15 September 2003, the unsecured creditors are entitled, except where company property is less than £10,000, to share in a pre-scribed part of the company's net property (Insolvency Act 1986, s 176A), a process known as 'top-slicing'. However, this process is seen as the *quid pro quo* for the government relinquishing the Crown's right to preferential treatment.

A disadvantage that follows from the view that a floating chargeholder receives no priority in relation to any order made is that the chargeholder will not be inclined to assist in funding a wrongful trading action, and this removes a significant potential source for funding.

If the fruits of a claim go to the unsecured creditors in the normal course of events, it would appear possible for a court, given the broad discretion granted to it, to order that a certain portion of the contribution should go to the chargeholder(s) if that was thought appropriate.[47] Another approach that could be adopted in order to resolve any doubt, and assuming that it is thought that unsecured creditors, as a matter of policy, should not see the chargeholder gobble up any award, is to implement the position that is extant in Australia. The Australian Corporations Act 2001 in s 588Y expressly pro-vides that any amount recovered is to be paid to satisfy unsecured debts in the first instance.

One issue that might be worth raising is whether those who became cred-itors during the period of wrongful trading warrant being paid the funds recovered as they have been, arguably, most wronged by the directors' actions. But, as mentioned earlier, the courts have held that they cannot make orders in favour of particular creditors as the objective is to assist the liquidator to recoup the loss to the company so as to benefit all of the creditors of the company (*Re Purpoint Ltd* at 129; 499; *Re Oasis Merchandising Services Ltd* at 918). In *Re Purpoint Ltd* Vinelott J said that those who became creditors before the commencement of wrongful trading are equally prejudiced by the loss of funds. This view can be justified on the basis that earlier creditors would receive more on a distribution in the liquidation if the directors had not engaged in wrongful trading, because for liability for wrongful trading to be found, the company must have incurred losses from the point when wrongful trading commenced.

If a person is found to have been involved in wrongful trading and is liable to make a contribution to the assets of the company, then the court may, on application or of its own volition, and pursuant to s 10 of the Company Directors' Disqualification Act 1986, make a disqualification order thereby disqualifying the person from acting as a director or taking part in

---

47 *Op. cit.* fn 21 above at 20.

the management of a company.[48] This occurred in *Re Brian D Pierson (Contractors) Ltd* [1999] BCC 26. As mentioned earlier, it is possible for an application under s 214 to be consolidated with disqualification proceedings (*Official Receiver v Doshi*).

What if an order is made under both s 212 and s 214 and the director against whom the order is made is unable to satisfy the amount involved? This is a relevant issue because of the fact that those with charges over company property are going to be entitled to be paid first out of funds recovered under the former provision, but not, arguably, under the latter. Goode has stated that the court has a discretion in making an order and it is for it to consider what effects justice in the matter.[49] However, when the court makes an order it will not know whether the director is able to pay the sum ordered to be paid. But Goode has suggested, adroitly, it is respectfully submitted, that:

> [T]he most appropriate solution would seem to be to respect the debenture holder's rights as regards assets recovered in a proprietary claim and to divide the total sum awarded in respect of the director's personal liability between the two heads of claim in the proportion which each bears to the total.[50]

The point should be made that directors held liable are not able to set off any payment which they are owed by the company against the amount awarded by the court. The reasons for this are: first, there is an absence of mutual dealings as the debt owed by the company involves a dealing between the director and the company, and the wrongful trading issue is between the director and the liquidator (*Guinness plc v Saunders* [1988] 1 WLR 863 and affirmed on appeal [1990] 2 WLR 324), reasoning that has applied in relation to the recovery of preferences paid to company creditors (*Re A Debtor* [1927] 1 Ch 410 at 419); second, s 214 creates 'a liability to contribute to the general assets of the company, and, since they do not give a right of set-off, the statutory ability to contribute extends to the whole amount ordered to be paid';[51] third, on policy grounds it would be wrong, for as Oditah has stated: 'it is not right that a director . . . guilty of wrongful . . . trading should have his liability to contribute converted into a debt so as to provide him with a right of set-off'.[52]

---

48 The maximum period of disqualification is 15 years: s 10(3). See *Re Brian D Pierson (Contractors) Ltd* [1999] BCC 26 for a case where the respondents were found to have been guilty of wrongful trading and were disqualified from acting as directors as a result.

49 *Op. cit.* fn 8 above at 464.   50 *Ibid.*

51 *Op. cit.* fn 18 above at 222 and referring (*inter alia*) to *Re Anglo-French Co-operative Society* (1882) 21 Ch D 492.

52 *Ibid.*

The public factor

While the main thrust of s 214 is to compensate creditors of companies in insolvent liquidation, it also plays a public role. If a person is guilty of wrongful trading, there is no criminal sanction to be imposed. If it is thought that what a person has done is fraudulent then proceedings may be initiated under s 458 of the Companies Act 1985. But the fact that wrongful trading does not lead to criminal liability should not be seen as an indication that s 214 has no public role to play. On the contrary, it is intended to play a public as well as a private role. If wrongful trading is found to have occurred, the court is at liberty, of its own volition, to disqualify the director from being involved in the management of companies for a period of up to 15 years (Company Directors Disqualification Act 1986, s 10(2)). This has occurred in a number of cases, with *Re Brian D Pierson (Contractors) Ltd* being one prime example. Clearly s 214 has both a private law and a public law function. In relation to the former, the intention is to compensate creditors who have lost out because of the liquidation of the company. Robert Walker J in *Re Oasis Merchandising Services Ltd* (at 918) adverted to the public element in s 214 proceedings, which involves an attempt to prescribe a minimum standard of conduct of directors in managing the affairs of companies. The public function is marked by the fact that it is linked to disqualification, the latter being an attempt to protect the public from reckless and/or dishonest directors. This issue is taken up in Chapter 10.

9   A defence to wrongful trading

Introduction

In the previous chapter we examined the scope of the provision and focused on when a director might be held liable. We now turn to consider when a director might be able to defend successfully any action brought against him or her. The director need only establish the defence in s 214 once the liquidator's case has been made out (for example, *Re Produce Marketing Consortium Ltd* (1989) 5 BCC 569 at 596). But it should be noted that the liquidator is not required to prove that a director participated in irresponsible conduct, for all that he or she has to do is to establish that the director knew or ought to have concluded that there was no reasonable prospect of the company not going into insolvent liquidation. Once that has been established, then the burden is thrown on the respondent to extricate himself or herself by making out the defence provided.

This chapter explores what is entailed in establishing the defence, and what issues result from it for directors and liquidators alike. Particular emphasis is placed on ascertaining the meaning of 'every step' in s 214(3). The subsection is explained in the first part of the chapter. The chapter also examines whether a director can be relieved of liability under s 727 of the Companies Act 1985 when he or she has been found liable.

The substance of the defence

The solitary defence to a wrongful trading action is found in s 214(3), which provides that a director is not liable for wrongful trading where the court is satisfied that, after becoming aware that the company was bound for insolvent liquidation, the director took 'every step with a view to minimising the potential loss to the company's creditors as (assuming him to have known that there was no reasonable prospect that the company would avoid going into insolvent liquidation) he ought to have taken'. So, once a liquidator has made out a case, the respondent has a positive burden placed on him or her of establishing the elements of the defence, on the balance of probabilities. The critical issue is, as we shall see, what 'every step' entails.

In determining whether the defence is made out or not, the court is required by s 214(4) to consider if the director took the steps which a reasonably diligent person who has the general knowledge, skill and experience that may reasonably be expected of a person who carries out the same functions as are carried out by the respondent director, and, the general knowledge, skill and experience that the respondent director has. This is the same factor that applies in deciding whether or not a director falls within the condition for liability. Again, a director is not able to rely on his or her inexperience. Nor is the experienced director who is above average able to argue that he or she did what the person with average experience would have done. In this case, where the standard expected of a reasonable person would be less than for a person with the director's experience and skill, then the higher standard will be used to judge the director.

The difficulty with the defence is that there is nothing in s 214 which tells us what will excuse a director from liability: what are the steps that should be taken by a director? Of course, what is to be done is heavily dependent on the particular situations facing directors. What might be entirely appropriate in one case might be totally inappropriate in another. It is possible to say that what directors must not do is nothing. The 'head in the sand' approach is unforgivable in the context of s 214. The directors must be seen to be engaging in some action in light of the company's financial problems.

Every step: meaning

Introduction

Initially, we should acknowledge the fact that, when faced with a company that is insolvent or rapidly heading that way, directors find themselves, very often, in the dilemma explained by Park J in *Re Continental Assurance* ([2001] BPIR 733 at 817):[1]

> An overall point which needs to be kept in mind throughout is that, whenever a company is in financial trouble and the directors have a difficult decision to make whether to close down and go into liquidation, or whether instead to trade on and hope to turn the corner, they can be in a real and unenviable dilemma. On the one hand, if they decide to trade on but things do not work out and the company, later rather than sooner, goes into liquidation, they may find themselves in the situation of the respondents in this case – being sued for wrongful trading. On the other hand, if the directors decide to close down immediately and cause the company to go into early liquidation . . . they are at risk of being criticised on other grounds. A decision to close down will almost certainly

---

1   Also, see *Re Uno plc* [2004] EWHC 933 (Ch) at [155].

mean that the ensuing liquidation will be an insolvent one . . . They [the creditors] will complain bitterly that the directors shut down too soon; they will say that the directors ought to have had more courage and kept going. If they had done, so the complaining creditors will say, the company probably would have survived and all of its debts would have been paid. Ceasing to trade and liquidating too soon can be stigmatised as the coward's way out.

Blackburn J, when giving judgment in a disqualification case, *Secretary of State for Trade and Industry v Gill* [2004] EWHC 933 (Ch) at [154], agreed with these sentiments.

'Every step' was 'intended to apply to cases where, for example, the directors take specific steps with a view to preserving or realising assets or claims for the benefit of creditors, even if they fail to achieve that result' (*Re Brian Pierson Ltd* [1999] BCC 26 at 54; [2001] BCLC 275 at 308). The provision does not enumerate actions that may constitute the step(s) which a director ought to take, and therein lies the problem for directors and their advisers. Professor Len Sealy mentioned in 1994 that guidelines had not been developed in the cases as to what directors should do.[2] Over a decade a later, the same can still be said, with little in the way of judicial statements on the defence and the scope of 'every step'.

One thing is clear, in terms of general principle, and that is the director:

> . . . will ordinarily be required to establish that his participation in the company's affairs was, as from the date upon which he realised that there was no reasonable prospect of the company avoiding liquidation, both active and geared to the protection of the interests of corporate creditors.[3]

The use of the words 'every step' might be said to be too strong, for if one wanted to be strict, the defence is, except in rare cases, almost impossible to establish. Sealy has said that it suggests that there is no room for any conduct that falls 'short of the very best'.[4] Andrew Hicks' survey of insolvency practitioners and solicitors in 1993 suggested that it was not an insuperable hurdle for liquidators in making claims. Also, as Professor Sir Roy Goode has said, in relation to the words 'every step', this may mean no more than, given the reference in s 214 to the reasonably diligent person, requiring the taking of

---

2 'Personal liability of directors and officers for debts of insolvent corporations: a jurisdictional perspective (England)' in Ziegel, J (ed), *Current Developments in International and Comparative Corporate Insolvency Law*, 1994, Oxford: Clarendon Press, p 492.

3 Griffin, S, *Personal Liability and Disqualification of Company Directors*, 1999, Oxford: Hart Publishing, pp 74–75.

4 *Op. cit.* Sealy above fn 2.

'every reasonable step'.[5] With respect, this can be the only way that the expression is to be interpreted.

Professional advice

The courts appear to manifest sympathy for any director who seeks professional advice. This was the case in two disqualification cases, *Re Bath Glass Ltd* [1988] BCLC 329 and *Re Douglas Construction Services Ltd* [1988] BCLC 397. Furthermore, in *Re Continental Assurance*, Park J placed a lot of emphasis on the fact that the directors did seek and listen to professional advice at critical points. But if advice is not heeded, then directors are likely to find it more difficult to defend s 214 actions. In *Re Brian D Pierson Ltd*, the director who was subject to proceedings had ignored indications, although not warnings, from professional advisers concerning the financial malaise of the company. In the earlier case of *Re Purpoint Ltd* [1991] BCC 121; [1991] BCLC 491 the respondent was found liable when professional advice was not heeded. Notwithstanding being given professional advice concerning the parlous state of the company's affairs, the director in this case did not cease trading for six months and did not place the company in liquidation for nearly a year (at 125; 495).

What if a director takes professional advice, follows that advice as best as he or she could and, notwithstanding that, the company enters insolvent liquidation? Can the director be held liable? It is submitted that the answer is 'yes', for following the advice of a professional adviser is not guaranteed to absolve a director, but it should go some way to doing so.[6]

One respondent to the Hicks' survey, to which reference was made earlier, suggested that if directors take advice from an insolvency practitioner, that should be regarded as an absolute defence to an allegation of wrongful trading.[7] My concern with this is three-fold. First, the process of taking advice might just be regarded as paying lip service to a requirement and provide the directors with immunity from liability. Second, the directors might not take the advice of the practitioner, so nothing has been gained. Third, there is no guarantee that a practitioner will provide appropriate advice. Should the creditors' position depend, effectively, on the advice given by just one practitioner?

But what if there are no professional warnings about the state of the company's finances? In *Re Brian D Pierson* the judge indicated that that does not absolve a director from liability, if there are other factors that suggested problems for the company (at 54; 308).

---

5   *Principles of Corporate Insolvency Law*, 2nd edn, 1997, London: Sweet and Maxwell, p 471.
6   See Oditah, F, 'Wrongful trading' [1990] LMCLQ 205 at 208, where the learned commentator argues that, if a director acts on the informed advice of an auditor, a strong case should be able to be mounted against the director being held liable.
7   Hicks, A, 'Wrongful trading – has it been a failure?' (1993) 8 I L & P 134 at 136.

It is probably the case that if the directors can demonstrate that when they were aware of financial difficulties they adopted a frugal approach to business, as well as in relation to their own salary entitlements,[8] this might well impress a court. Likewise, courts might be impressed by directors who pay money into the company from their own funds.

Resignation

Resignation might be considered by individual directors, but it should be seen, in most cases, as the last straw, for if a director does resign, he or she loses the opportunity to influence at board meetings, to obtain confidential information, and the director cannot any longer influence the direction of the company's affairs. Also, if a director who has resigned is later held to be liable for wrongful trading, his or her liability could be greater because of what has been done post-resignation. Moreover, it might be said that resigning is 'designed to protect the interests and integrity of the individual director, rather than seeking to confer any benefit on the company in respect of minimising the potential loss of its creditors'.[9] Although resignation has never been regarded as a foolproof way of extricating oneself from liability for wrongful trading, one would think that it is often going to be a consideration in a director's favour, particularly where he or she has found that his or her advice or recommendations have not been heeded. In fact in *Secretary of State for Trade and Industry v Taylor* [1997] 1 WLR 407 at 414 Chadwick J said, while hearing a director disqualification case, that in such a situation it was prudent for a director to resign (at 412). It must be said that what his Lordship went on to say makes it clear that just because a director does not resign does not necessarily mean that he or she will be held liable. Resignation may be the only action that a director can take if he or she has made proposals to the board for the arrest of a company's demise, and the board has refused to implement them or any other efficacious alternatives.[10] Obviously, a court will have to weigh up what was the reason behind the resignation and what other options might have been available to the director. If a director is of the view that the company is heading for insolvent liquidation, but he or she is alone in this view, then the director faces an uphill battle. So, resignation might be the most appropriate action for the director to take. This action should follow only after the director has expressed his or her concern at a board meeting or in some other formal way, and he or she has ensured that what he or she has to say is minuted or recorded in some fashion, and can be perused by a liquidator if the company does fall into liquidation.

---

8 Milman, D, 'Strategies for regulating managerial performance in the "twilight zone" – familiar dilemmas: new considerations' [2004] JBL 493 at 505.
9 *Op. cit.* fn 3 above at 77.
10 Griffin has submitted that resignation, in the majority of cases, will probably be viewed as an indication of the fact that the director has failed to take every step: *ibid* at 76.

Placing the company into a formal insolvency regime

It might be thought that liquidation is the step that should be taken. While liquidation might minimise further company losses, it might not be the most beneficial action as far as the creditors are concerned. For instance, in liquidation if assets are sold off piecemeal, in what is often referred to as a 'fire sale', the liquidator will recover less than if the assets were sold off strategically, or as part of a sale of the business. If liquidation is thought to be the appropriate step to take, it may be necessary, in some cases, to seek the appointment of a provisional liquidator after lodging a petition for winding up.

Perhaps one of the safest courses of action is to place the company into administration, and this can now be done quite swiftly under Sched B1 to the Insolvency Act 1986, and it is a relatively costless exercise, compared with previous times, because no court involvement is necessary if the company complies with the Schedule. In Australia, voluntary administration, the equivalent of administration in the UK, has been used regularly by directors to prevent liability for insolvent trading, the equivalent of wrongful trading. In fact in Australia, where it is a defence that one took all reasonable steps to prevent the incurring of further debts (when the company was insolvent), the legislation goes on to say that steps taken by a director to place his or her company in administration can be taken into account in deciding whether an adequate defence had been made out.

Directors might, quite properly, now regard administration more favourably as an escape route from possible wrongful trading. It appears that this might have been done in *Re Chancery plc* [1991] BCC 171 at 172, one of the few instances we have in case law of the directors of a public company going close to engaging in wrongful trading, but because of the time and cost involved in obtaining an administration order, directors might have been discouraged in the past from seeking administration where they were concerned about the issue of wrongful trading. In favour of directors taking their companies into administration now is the fact that the administration process can be initiated more cheaply and quickly, and the administrator is still not, as we have considered earlier, in Chapter 8, able to bring wrongful trading proceedings against the directors. It is interesting to note that in *Re Farmizer*, the liquidator was only seeking contribution up until the time when the company entered administration, so at least that step might restrict the liability of a director. By way of caution, we must note that appointing an administrator will not necessarily save a director from liability if the company subsequently enters liquidation and wrongful trading proceedings are commenced by the liquidator. But the advantage of administration is that it permits an assessment of the company's position free from attack, as there is a moratorium on the initiation or continuation of legal proceedings against the company, by an independent insolvency practitioner who is experienced in handling insolvency or near-insolvency situations.

The danger with placing the company in some form of formal insolvency regime is that the company may not be 'finished' or even in need of rescue, and so its placement in administration or liquidation may be premature; the company might have been able to carry on and the directors might have felt that there was a fair chance of survival, but the fear of personal liability could cause them to embrace what might be seen as the safe alternative. If directors did place their company in an insolvency regime, then in some situations, and it is suggested that they would have to be fairly extreme, directors might be subject to liability for wrongful trading as the action might not be regarded as minimising creditor losses. Liability would, it is submitted, only be imposed in cases where the directors panicked or totally misread the situation and the company clearly could have returned to profitable trading if appropriate action had been taken, but entering an insolvency regime meant that that was never going to be possible.

It should be said at this point that it is far safer for directors to place the company in administration rather than to embark on some form of rescue process. For instance, the process of seeking to put in place some arrangement with creditors, such as a company voluntary arrangement or an informal scheme is fraught with danger in the sense that they could take a while to finalise and during this period any one of the creditors could obtain a winding-up order.

Cessation of business

The termination of business, while it may seem to be the most sensible and proper thing to do, can in fact be the worst thing, especially in the short term, as it may be detrimental for all concerned, particularly the creditors, a point made in *Re Hefferon Kearns Ltd (No 2)* (1993) 3 IR 191 by Lynch J when discussing the equivalent Irish provision. This is especially the case where the company can make gains in the short term and this might rescue the company from its parlous state. But in some cases the cessation of business might be the most appropriate thing to do. Too often, companies trade on for too long. This is particularly the situation with closely held companies set up by an entrepreneurial director-owner who identifies with the company and its business and will do all that he or she can to ensure that the company remains in business.[11]

If the directors decide to cease trading, it would usually be proper to instigate some formal insolvency regime, such as administration or liquidation. Given the law as it now stands the former is probably the best way to proceed, as indicated earlier. The reason for instigating an insolvency regime

---

11 Mokal, R, 'An agency cost analysis of the wrongful trading provisions: redistribution, perverse incentives and the creditors' bargain' (2000) 59 CLJ 335 at 354.

is to prevent the dismembering of the company, as both administration and liquidation usher in a moratorium on claims.

It might be noted that just because directors continue to trade does not necessarily mean that they have not taken every step. As Vanessa Finch has said:

> If directors reasonably believe that creditors may fare worse in a premature forced sale of assets, and that this combined with the cost of liquidation proceedings may well be disastrous from unsecured creditors' point of view, the directors' duty under section 214 may well include a duty to attempt a company rescue or to stay at the helm.[12]

While what the learned commentator says is undoubtedly true, the comment was made well before administration became far easier to implement.

Miscellaneous options

If a director feels that resignation is not the most appropriate action to take, but he or she is alone in the opinion that is held about the company, the director should, amongst other things, ensure that his or her concern is minuted in board meetings and the director should call for action such as the seeking of professional advice, the compilation of up-to-date accounts and projections of profits and losses and ensure that these requests are minuted. In some situations it might be prudent for the director, himself or herself, to obtain information concerning the company's state and other records, rather than relying on others who might be either of the opinion that the director is 'over the top' with his or her concerns, or have secrets to keep. If a director protests against continued trading and does what he or she can to bring about the cessation of trading, it is more likely that no liability will attach to him or her (*Secretary of State for Trade and Industry v Taylor* [1997] 1 WLR 407 at 415; *sub nom Re CS Holidays Ltd* [1997] BCC 172 at 178 – dealing with an application for a director's disqualification). The Institute of Directors in its guidelines suggests that a director whose concerns are not being recognised might consider gaining the support of shareholders, although one wonders if most shareholders would be overly concerned, as they are not going to be liable and it might be better for them if the company carried on trading with the hope of pulling itself out of its malaise. The other recommendation of the Institute is for a director to talk to the auditors.[13] While the Insolvency Act 1986 permits the directors to petition for the winding up of their company

---

12 Finch, V, 'Directors' duties: insolvency and the unsecured creditor' in Clarke, A (ed), *Current Issues in Insolvency Law*, 1991, London: Stevens, p 96.

13 'IOD Guidelines for Directors' 1991, at paras 339–345 and referred to in Hicks, A, 'Advising on wrongful trading: Part 2' (1993) 14 Co Law 55 at 58.

(s 124(1)), a single director may neither do so (*Re Instrumentation Electrical Services Ltd* (1988) 4 BCC 301), nor petition for an administration order, unless he or she is a creditor, so these options are not available. Also, if a director disagrees with the board, he or she would not be wise to publicise his or her concerns as this could escalate the company's demise.[14]

What other steps could or should directors take to safeguard themselves? One or more of the following may be prudent:

(a) calling a creditors' meeting in order to advise them of the state of the company;

(b) convening regular board meetings to review the position of the company and ensure that discussions and processes are clearly documented, including an indication that creditor interests are taken into account in the decisions made;

(c) assessing the reasons for the company's financial woes and addressing them in some positive way(s);

(d) regularly assessing and monitoring the financial position of the company;

(e) ensuring that the company's accounts are properly kept up to date.

A possible option is for the directors to operate more cautiously and, in some cases, for the company to reduce the volume of its trading activities. In *Re Continental Assurance*, Park J was impressed with the fact that the directors 'reduced the scale of trading to minimal and cautious levels', and eventually ceased trading when they were advised that their company was insolvent (at 769). But conservative action, such as restricting trading to a cash basis, might not be sufficient, as overheads and recurrent expenses will continue to mount up.[15]

Directors should also consider the fees being paid to them. If these are excessive, in the circumstances, then that might lead a court hearing a subsequent wrongful trading case to the view that the directors did not take every step that they could have taken. For instance, in *Re Purpoint Ltd* (at 125; 495) the court was critical of one of the directors for the excessive remuneration that he received. Directors should also take into account the fact that it is probable that a court is more likely to hold a director not liable if he or she pursues orthodox business practices and evaluates the effect of actions on creditors.

Of course, it is prudent for a director to ensure that he or she keeps a detailed record of all that he or she has done to minimise the losses of creditors.

---

14 See *ibid.*   15 *Op. cit.* fn 6 above at 214.

Inability to take steps to minimise losses

The provision fails to cater for the position where a director is unable to take every step to minimise potential loss to creditors. For example, what if a director is ill or overseas? In the Australian case of *Androvin v Figliomeni* (1996) 14 ACLC 1461, a director was held not liable under the Australian equivalent of s 214 (Corporations Act 2001, s 588G), because the breach of the provision occurred while he was overseas. The director had indicated to the other directors, before his departure, that he would not be in a position to act as a director or accept any responsibilities during his absence. As a result there had been a fundamental change in the working operations of the company. It is very likely that British directors would not, in similar circumstances, be saved from liability, because directors might be thought to be irresponsible if they were to absent themselves from the country for a long period of time, and even then, in today's world, communications enable contact to be maintained. As far as illness goes, it would very much depend on the nature and length of the illness.

Concluding comments

While this discussion seems to be rather worrying for directors, they can at least take some comfort from the fact that when considering the steps taken, the courts will not use the benefits of hindsight (*Re Sherborne Associates Ltd* [1995] BCC 40 at 54; *Re Brian D Pierson (Contractors) Ltd* at 50; 303), and so when determining whether a director took every step, this determination should not be considered in light of later developments that could not reasonably have been foreseen by directors. Directors would have had more guidance and assurance if one of the Cork Report's original recommendations had been accepted, namely that any person who considered that he or she is or might become guilty of wrongful trading could apply to the courts for relief in advance ([1798–1802]). The proposal is discussed in the next chapter.

While the defence can be criticised, it is noteworthy that directors are only required to do that which would be expected of them.[16] Also, one would expect the courts to take the view that directors are not obliged to be responsible for outside factors that are not reasonably foreseeable.[17]

It is interesting to note that no other common law jurisdiction has invoked a defence in the same terms as s 214. The Australian provision sets out a number of defences. One comes close to that found in s 214(3), namely that the directors took 'all reasonable steps' to stop the incurring of debts

---

16 Mokal, R, *Corporate Insolvency: Theory and Application*, 2005, Oxford: Oxford University Press, p 298.
17 *Ibid.*

(s 588H(5)). It also gives some indication as to what the court can take into account in considering this defence (s 588H(6)). The defence to the Irish equivalent (Companies Act 1963, s 297A) is, in effect, that the officer acted honestly and responsibly in relation to the conduct of the affairs of the company and the court should, given the circumstances, relieve the officer of liability. It was acknowledged by Lynch J in *Re Hefferon Kearns Ltd (No 2)* (unreported, but noted in (1993) JIBL 93) that the provision was more widely drafted than the equivalent provision in s 214 of the UK Act. The Irish provision is similar to s 727 of the UK Companies Act, a provision that permits courts to relieve a director of liability where he or she is proved to be liable, and which is discussed next.

Relief from liability

Essentially s 214(3) is exhaustive of the defences available to a director. A director is not able to avail himself or herself of general defences.[18] In particular it has been held that a person cannot be excused for wrongful trading under s 727 of the Companies Act 1986. The provision permits a court to excuse a director from liability arising out of his or her negligence, breach of duty or breach of trust on the basis that he or she had acted honestly and reasonably, and, as a consequence of his or her actions, ought fairly to be excused from liability. The reason given for the fact that s 727 does not apply is that it is incompatible with the objective nature of the test found in s 214, namely that the action of the director could not be said to be reasonable (*Re Produce Marketing Consortium Ltd; Re Brian D Pierson (Contractors) Ltd*).[19]

Notwithstanding this, in *Re D'Jan of London Ltd* [1993] BCC 646 where Hoffmann LJ held that the test in s 214(4) was to be used in determining whether a director had breached his or her duty of care and skill, his Lordship said that a director found liable could be relieved under s 727. Hoffmann LJ acknowledged that it might 'seem odd that a person found to have been guilty of negligence, which involves failing to take reasonable care, can ever satisfy a court that he acted reasonably' (at 648). But, as his Lordship noted, (at 649), s 727 contemplates that a director may do so and 'it follows that conduct may be reasonable for the purposes of s 727 despite amounting to lack of reasonable care at common law'. In *Bairstow v Queens Moat Houses plc* [2000] BCC 1025 Nelson J, when determining whether directors were liable for paying unlawful dividends, said (at 1034) that:

> [E]ven if under the rules of negligence a director ought to have known of the facts which rendered the payments unlawful, the court may nevertheless relieve him from liability if considering his personal situation it was

---

18 *Op. cit.* fn 6 above at 214.
19 See the comments of Nelson J in *Bairstow v Queens Moat Houses plc* [2000] BCC 1025.

reasonable that he did not in fact know. It is a matter of discretion for the court on the individual facts of the case as to whether the director should escape the normal consequences of his breach of duty and be excused liability for his negligence.

The Court of Appeal subsequently reversed his Lordship's decision to excuse the directors under s 727 ([2001] 2 BCLC 531) on the basis that as the judge had found that the former directors were guilty of dishonestly preparing false accounts in order to deceive the market, it was not open to him to find that they had so acted. However, the court did not impugn the judge's comment quoted above. It is submitted that what Nelson J said could be applied to the area of wrongful trading, and so one could argue that s 727 is able to operate. Subsequently, in *Re MDA Investment Management Ltd* [2005] BCC 783 at 838 Park J said that the reasonableness of a director's conduct must be assessed objectively, and the issue of subjectivity is only relevant when assessing the honesty of a director. The judge made it clear that in *Re D'Jan* Hoffmann LJ did not intend to provide for a purely subjective test.

Also, while s 214 undoubtedly includes an objective approach, it also embraces the subjective, as was discussed in Chapter 8. Furthermore, s 727 'is not entirely free of subjective factors',[20] in that it requires consideration of the respondent's state of mind in examining the issue of honesty.

In *Re DKG Contractors Ltd* [1990] BCC 903 the judge said that the directors had not acted reasonably in that they failed to obtain, as they should have, some professional advice before trading in the way that they had, and they had not taken up what advice they were offered (at 912). The judge decided not to relieve the directors of liability under s 727 (at 913), but he did not espouse the view that s 727 was not available in wrongful trading cases.

It would appear that respondents to insolvent trading actions in Australia are able to be relieved from liability under the Corporations Act 2001 equivalent, s 1318 (*Kenna & Brown Pty Ltd v Kenna* (1999) 32 ACSR 430), but it is critical that the Australian provision does not refer to the need to act reasonably; it limits itself to providing that the respondent must have acted honestly.

Even if relief were possible under s 727, it is likely that it would be employed in few situations, for, as discussed in Chapter 8, the courts have tended to visit liability on directors only when they are irresponsible, and in such cases the courts are likely to refrain from excusing them from liability on the basis that the directors ought not to be excused. The possibility of the use of s 727 does allow judges to find directors liable under s 214 in cases short of irresponsibility, yet they can excuse them under s 727. This approach maintains the integrity of s 214, but permits courts to excuse those directors whose conduct is not completely irresponsible. Professors Robert Bradgate and Geraint Howells (as they are now), writing in 1990, gave the following

---

20 Bradgate, R, and Howells, G, 'No excuse for wrongful trading' [1990] JBL 249 at 251 fn 11.

instance of where s 727 might apply.[21] Say the directors of a company, which has no reasonable prospect of avoiding insolvency, decide to keep trading to permit their company to complete a contract that is vital for the other party to the contract in order to permit the latter to fulfil a valuable export contract. Whilst the directors are in breach of s 214 they might be regarded as acting reasonably. Of course, the riposte to this might be that the actions of the directors would not be regarded as reasonable by the general body of creditors.

But it is questionable whether s 727 needs to be relied on where a court is of the opinion that a director should be excused from liability. The reason is that a judge can achieve the same result as excusing liability under s 727, if he or she were to reduce or make no order for contribution against a director under s 214, for the judge has a discretion as to whether he or she thinks a contribution should be made.[22] The court could use this approach in circumstances where the respondent was found to be liable, but where he or she was ill or absent from the country.

21 *Ibid* at 253.　　22 *Ibid.*

10 An assessment of wrongful trading: pros, problems and prognoses

Introduction

Some assessment of the wrongful trading provision has been undertaken in earlier chapters in the natural course of discussing the provision, its scope and the relevant defence. However, to provide some detailed assessment of the provision would have derogated, in many places, from the general discussion. It is appropriate, now that we have examined s 214 and provided an exposition of the provision and its effect, that I endeavour to engage in an assessment. This chapter identifies some particular issues that need to be examined analytically, and this is followed by a more general assessment of the provision. The chapter culminates with some suggestions for reform and some concluding remarks. All of this is done in light of the fact that the Company Law Review Steering Group (CLRSG), established in 1998 to provide a comprehensive review of company law in the UK, declined to evaluate s 214, preferring to see it as an issue firmly within insolvency law, and in any event it saw no need for changing the provision.[1] The government in its Company Law Reform Bill did not address wrongful trading.[2]

Applicants

As explained in Chapter 8,[3] the UK is very much in the minority when it comes to determining who can initiate proceedings for wrongful trading. While only a liquidator is entitled to bring wrongful trading proceedings in the UK, in other common law jurisdictions various persons and bodies are able to initiate actions in relation to their equivalent of wrongful trading.

It is submitted, for the reasons expressed in Chapter 8, that at the very least, administrators should be empowered to commence proceedings. This

---

1 Company Law Review, *Modern Company Law for a Competitive Economy: Developing the Framework*, 2000, London, DTI at para 3.72.
2 Introduced into the House of Lords in November 2005.
3 See above at pp 79–81.

will reflect the fact that administration is becoming more and more popular, and might, in due course, overtake liquidation as the most frequently invoked formal regime for insolvent companies.[4]

In addition, it is contended that it is meritorious for a public official, probably the Secretary of State for Trade and Industry, also to be granted the right to bring proceedings. This is something that is permissible in both Ireland and Australia. In the latter country, action is able to be initiated by the corporate regulator, the Australian Securities and Investment Commission, and it is able to secure orders for compensation of creditors as well as civil penalty orders. Permitting a public official to take action would enable an action to be commenced where perhaps either the liquidator is having difficulty in securing financial support for litigation, and where it is thought that to foster the public interest of deterring directors from engaging in wrongful trading, action ought to be taken, or liquidators simply cannot be persuaded to launch proceedings for one reason or another. Also, as discussed later in this chapter, such a move would allow the Secretary of State to obtain a declaration in relation to wrongful trading and then seek a disqualification order. The court should, on an application by the public official, be able to make an award of compensation to the liquidator provided that it can be established that at least one creditor has suffered loss as a result of the illicit trading sponsored by the directors.

In Ireland s 297A of the Companies Act 1963 allows creditor action, as well as action by contributories, without the same restrictions imposed on creditors in Australia,[5] but it seems that few creditors have taken advantage of it, perhaps because of the cost of proceedings and the lack of certainty as far as outcome is concerned. It is unlikely that contributories would have any interest in issuing proceedings. As their liability is limited, they are not likely to be overly worried about their company falling into insolvency, which is usually the case when consideration is given to the bringing of wrongful trading type proceedings, and any award from an action commenced by a contributory is likely to go to the creditors and not benefit the contributories. Also, any action taken against directors might precipitate the company becoming subject to some insolvency regime, ending the trading of the company, and, hence, terminating the chance of the contributories making any further money out of the company.

Like the Irish provision, the Singaporean counterpart permits proceedings to be taken by creditors. However, unlike many jurisdictions, including the UK, these proceedings may be taken prior to the liquidation of the company

---

4   This appears to have occurred in Australia. In 2003 there were 2,235 compulsory windings up, 1,268 creditors' voluntary liquidations, and 2,699 administrations (see *Corporate Insolvency Laws: A Stocktake* (30 June 2004), a report of the Australian Parliament's Joint Committee on Corporations and Financial Services and accessible at www.aph.gov.au/ senate/committee/corporations_ctte/ail/report/ail.pdf> at p 73).

5   See above at p 80.

(Companies Act 1990, s 339(3)) and this is said to be attractive in that creditors can take action to prevent loss, in some cases, before the company collapses totally. Also, as Lee Suet Joyce states:

> If insolvent liquidation of the company had been a prerequisite to trigger the fraudulent and insolvent trading provisions, corporate managers would be given the incentive to take any risks so long as they are able to avoid insolvent liquidation at the end of the day.[6]

Should creditors be allowed in the UK to bring proceedings? There is some history of allowing creditors to bring similar proceedings. While the present fraudulent trading provision does not permit creditor actions, in the Companies Act 1948 the equivalent provision did permit creditors to bring proceedings, an example being *Re Cyona Distributors Ltd* [1967] 1 Ch 889. While it is upon liquidation that creditors will be most concerned about getting some compensation, being able to initiate proceedings before liquidation has advantages. First, if a creditor has evidence that the directors are engaging in wrongful trading, and he or she can see that if things continue on as they are the company will end up in liquidation, the ability to set in motion proceedings as a sort of pre-emptive strike is beneficial. Second, it might lead to better standards of corporate governance[7] as directors would be more concerned about actions being brought against them. Third, there is a potential benefit in creditors being able to take action in that the funds of the company in liquidation would not have to be employed, and this might benefit creditors in general.[8] Fourth, it has been argued that if creditors had the right to proceed they might be able to use this as a threat while the company is trading to convince a director to pay off the creditor, and this might mean that the company can keep out of liquidation and survive, to the betterment of creditors in general.[9] But, with respect, it seems unlikely that a director is going to pay out a creditor from his or her own funds in most cases. They might reason, quite adroitly, that the company could still fall into liquidation and his or her payment would be otiose.

The reality of the matter is that creditors would not be willing to bring proceedings unless they could be sure that they would get some benefit from them. Even if the award was to be distributed amongst all of the unsecured creditors, meaning that the applicant creditor would get a share, he or she might reason, with some justification, that it is not worth his or her while bringing proceedings and taking on considerable risk where the creditor has

---

6   Joyce, L, 'Fraudulent and Insolvent Trading in Singapore' (2000) 9 *International Insolvency Review* 121 at 125.
7   *Ibid* at 127.
8   Dabner, J, 'Trading whilst insolvent – a case for individual creditor rights against directors' (1994) 17 U NSW L J 546 at 567.
9   *Ibid*.

to share the fruits of the action with others who engage, in effect, using economic language, in freeriding. As discussed in Chapter 6, one could end up with the situation where all creditors seek to freeride, and no one actually commences proceedings.

There are a number of drawbacks with permitting creditors to initiate proceedings, and these are similar to those applying to permitting direct actions by creditors against directors for breach of duty to creditors.[10] One reason against it is that it might allow creditors to exert pressure on directors to have their own debts satisfied prior to insolvency, and this, if creditors were permitted to benefit solely from the fruits of any action, might lead to an avalanche of litigation. One or a few creditors might succeed in proceedings, but that could leave the directors impecunious and unable to pay any other creditors. The creditors likely to succeed would be the strong and well-informed ones.

The point of liability

Directors are liable for wrongful trading if they knew or ought to have concluded that there was no reasonable prospect of the company avoiding going into insolvent liquidation. Prima facie this appears to provide, in contrast with the time when directors become liable for breach of their duties to creditors (see Chapter 13), a defined point at which directors must take care. But the fact of the matter is that the provision fails to specify what sort of action constitutes wrongful trading, or, at least, what action breaches the provision, and thus there is a great deal of uncertainty surrounding what that point might be. What constitutes 'a reasonable prospect' is 'inherently elusive'.[11] This uncertainty causes potential problems not only for directors, but also for liquidators who are given little guidance in assessing whether a director has acted wrongly. The uncertainty would have been avoided to a large degree had the recommendations of the Cork Report been accepted, namely that liability would occur if the director continued to incur liabilities at a time when the director knew or ought or to have known that there was no reasonable prospect of the company being able to satisfy those liabilities. This is an issue that is discussed later in the Chapter.

As discussed in Chapter 8, for a successful action, there is a need to identify a point in time from which the company was conducting wrongful trading, and this entails liquidators specifying a date from which the director should have realised that insolvent liquidation was inevitable. The courts have been rather

---

10 See below at pp 249–252.
11 Prentice, D, 'Corporate personality, limited liability and the protection of creditors' in Rickett, C, and Grantham, R, *Corporate Personality in the 20th Century*, 1998, Oxford: Hart Publishing, p 119. See the comments in Cheffins, B, *Company Law: Theory, Structure and Operation*, 1997, Oxford: Clarendon Press, p 542.

conservative in deciding wrongful trading cases and have been reluctant to find that the date from which liability for wrongful trading begins was too far back from the advent of insolvent liquidation. In *Re Purpoint Ltd* [1991] BCC 491 Vinelott J stated (at 498) that:

> I have felt some doubt whether a reasonably prudent director would have allowed the company to commence trading at all. It had no capital base . . . However, I do not think that it would be right to conclude that [the respondent] ought to have known that the company was doomed to end in an insolvent winding up from the moment it started to trade. That would, I think, impose too high a test.

Cooke and Hicks have concluded that the courts may be inclined to give directors the benefit of the doubt and not to adopt too early a time from which liability should run.[12]

While wrongful trading cannot occur until there is an end to all reasonable hope of the company's recovery, liquidators are able to take action against directors for breach of duty to take into account the interests of creditors (discussed in Chapters 11–19), and claim for amounts lost at a time earlier than when wrongful trading commences. This could be when the company's solvency is questionable, there is a risk of insolvency or even if there is financial instability. These financial states are likely to precede that time when the director knew or ought to have concluded that there was no reasonable prospect of the company avoiding going into insolvent liquidation. It can be concluded that the liability of directors for breach of duty can be identified in many cases at an earlier point in time than the trigger which imposes liability for wrongful trading, so, with a breach of duty claim either there is a greater likelihood of succeeding, or else there is a chance of obtaining a larger sum from the court, because the period of the director's wrongdoing would be longer. Also, as there is no requirement for a liquidator to specify the exact point from which the director owed a duty to consider the creditors' interests, the liquidator is not so hamstrung in making out a case. This issue is discussed further in Chapter 13.

Wrongdoing

Section 214 is said to deal with wrongful trading, but this expression is not mentioned in the provision and it is highly debatable as to whether a breach of s 214 involves trading that is 'wrongful'. As Marion Simmons QC has noted,[13] the *Oxford Dictionary* definition of 'wrongful' is 'full of wrong, injustice, or injury; marked . . . by wrong, unfairness or violation of equity'.

---

12 'Wrongful trading – predicting insolvency' [1993] JBL 338 at 341.
13 'Wrongful trading' (2001) 14 *Insolvency Intelligence* 12.

This definition seems to suggest that there is a need to establish blame, something which does not seem to fit with the wording of the section, and certainly something which was never envisaged by the Cork Committee.

But there are indications in the cases that courts are going to consider issues of blameworthiness in determining liability. In *Re Continental Assurance* [2001] BPIR 733 (at 769–770 in particular) Park J made a lot of the fact that the directors were conscientious and that no wrong could be apportioned to them. As I asked in Chapter 8: is that an issue which the provision requires us to consider? My view is that the correct answer is negative. Now whether or not that is fair is another issue. But clearly the Cork Committee and the government were trying to get away from the need to prove some kind of subjective culpability. There are many comments in *Continental Assurance* where the judge talked about whether the directors were culpably wrong. Certainly, it would seem, given the case law, that the courts can take into account how culpable the respondent director(s) has been, and Vanessa Finch feels that this has diminished the effect of s 214.[14] As I stated in Chapter 8, blameworthiness should, at most, only be relevant when the court comes to determining the level of contribution to be paid by a director who is found liable. As the Court of Appeal stated in the fraudulent trading case of *Bank of India v Morris* [2005] EWCA (Civ) 693 at [103], wrongful trading is about negligence, and the court contrasted this with fraudulent trading which involves some subjective activity that was dishonest, that is, clearly wrong. Moral blame is reserved for fraudulent trading.

Every step – the defence

The previous chapter discussed the only defence that might be available to a respondent. It noted the potential severity of the wording of the defence. While it must be said that the courts do not appear to have interpreted the wording in s 214(3) in an overly restricted way, it is submitted that the defence is overly onerous on respondents, and it would appear that Parliament intended it that way. This is asserted on the basis that an attempt at amending the provision to 'every reasonable step' was rejected in Parliament.[15] It is submitted that it would be better to employ the expression used in one of the defences that is open to a director in Australia when the subject of insolvent trading proceedings, namely that he or she took 'all reasonable steps' (to stop the company incurring debts (Corporations Act 2001, s 588H(5)). The Australian statute also gives some indication as to what things the court may take into account in considering this defence. Section 588H(6) provides that

---

14 Finch, V, *Corporate Insolvency Law: Perspectives and Principles*, 2002, Cambridge: Cambridge University Press, p 515.
15 Sealy, L, *Disqualification and Personal Liability of Directors*, 5th edn, 2000, Bicester: CCH.New Law, p 72.

the issues that a court may take into account (and these are not to be seen as exhaustive) are: any action taken to appoint an administrator; when the relevant action was taken; and the results of the action. Placed in a British context the defence, based on this Australian defence, could be that the respondent satisfied a court that he or she took all reasonable steps to mini- mise the potential loss to the company's creditors. While it might be thought that the courts have applied the idea of reasonable steps, it would be good to have it clearly stated in the legislation, with, it is hoped, a consistent approach resulting. This issue is discussed further later in the chapter.

Funding

Andrew Hicks, writing in 1993, following a survey he conducted amongst insolvency practitioners and solicitors, said that the greatest inhibition to wrongful trading proceedings was the cost of investigating and then pursuing the action.[16] It is probable that this issue remains an important one for liquid- ators, but perhaps not quite so much of an obstacle as in 1993. However, after saying that, proceedings are clearly far from inexpensive. A solicitor, Peter Fidler, said in 2001 that anecdotal evidence suggested that a minimum of £50,000 was needed to run a wrongful trading case, even where the claim is relatively small.[17] Ensuring that the liquidator has sufficient funds behind him or her is critical, for cases can take a long time to be heard. For instance, the trial in *Re Continental Assurance* lasted for 72 days, three times as long as the estimated period (at 765).

Obviously, any liquidator has to be concerned about the costs and expenses of litigation in two respects. First, he or she must ensure that the funds of the company are not needlessly wasted, thereby reducing the dividend payable to creditors. Second, the liquidator will want to ensure that he or she is not liable to pay for litigation out of his or her own pocket. The latter is particularly relevant to s 214 actions because, as the action is endowed to the liquidator personally, he or she will need to initiate such an action in his or her own name and as a consequence will be personally liable for any costs incurred (*Van den Hurk v Martens & Co Ltd* [1920] 1 KB 850; *Re Wilson Lovatt & Sons Ltd* [1977] 1 All ER 274; *Re MC Bacon Ltd (No 2)* [1990] BCLC 607; [1990] BCC 430).

Rule 4.218(1)(a) of the Insolvency Rules 1986 provides that expenses or costs which are properly chargeable or incurred by the official receiver or the liquidator in preserving, realising or getting in any of the assets of the company or otherwise relating to the conduct of any legal proceedings which he has power to bring or defend whether in his own name or the name of the company, are payable out of company funds before any other sums. But this

16 'Wrongful trading – has it been a failure?' (1993) 8 I L & P 134 at 134.
17 'Wrongful trading after *Continental Assurance*' (2001) 17 I L & P 212 at 212.

wording of the provision has only existed since the enactment of r 23 of Insolvency (Amendment) (No 2) Rules 2002 (SI 2002/2712). Before the change, the provision was interpreted in such as way that the liquidator's own legal expenses in taking action under adjustment actions (such as preference claims) or wrongful trading proceedings could not be claimed out of the company's funds (*Re Floor Fourteen Ltd* [2002] BCC 198, CA). This is still the case for liquidations entered into prior to 1 January 2003. But for those occurring after this date, r 4.218(1)(a) of the Insolvency Rules 1986, as it now stands, is such that it certainly means that the liquidator's own expenses of running litigation rank with the liquidation costs and expenses, and can be claimed from company funds. Whether this is the case as far as an adverse costs order made in wrongful trading proceedings against the liquidator or the company, is not clear. Any expenses or costs awarded to a successful litigant against the company in liquidation or its liquidator were at common law to be paid in priority to the general expenses and costs of the liquidation and any subsequent priority claims, such as preferential creditor claims (*Re London Metallurgical Company* [1895] 1 Ch 758; *Re MT Realisations Ltd* [2003] EWHC 2895 (Ch); [2004] 1 BCLC 119; *Re Toshoku Finance (UK) plc* [2002] BCC 110, HL). The difficulty for liquidators is that adverse costs are not prima facie within r 4.218(1)(a) and it has been held by the House of Lords that if any expense claim is not covered by r 4.218 then it cannot be deducted under that provision (*Re Toshoku Finance*). It might be submitted that to include adverse costs orders within the general term of 'expenses' is unfair as far as the party who succeeds against the liquidator is concerned, as the company's funds might not be sufficient to pay out the costs order. Second, it might be notable that r 4.220(2) has not been amended in light of the changes to r 4.218(1)(a) in that it continues to state that nothing in the Rules (meaning rr 4.218 and 4.219) 'affect the rights of any person to whom such costs are ordered to be paid'. Further, it would seem that the amendment to the Rules was intended to overcome decisions like *Re MC Bacon Ltd (No 2)* [1991] Ch 127 and *Re Floor Fourteen Ltd*, where the liquidator was not entitled to recover *his own* legal expenses from company funds under this rule. An adverse costs order would not involve the liquidator's own expenses, but that of the respondent. Thus, it would seem that someone with an adverse costs order is entitled to be paid in priority to liquidation expenses,[18] and the liquidator will not be able to claim the costs as an expense under r 4.218(1)(a).[19] This is an issue that must surely concern a liquidator in contemplating the taking of wrongful trading proceedings. Certainly, despite

---

18 See the arguments mounted in Gleghorn, S, '*Re MT Realisations Ltd*: recovering costs from an insolvent company' (2004) 20 I L & P 105 against the amendment to the Rules covering adverse costs orders.

19 *Ibid*; Gregorian, R, and Butler, R, 'Liquidators' litigation expenses, funding arrangements and the amendment to rule 4.218' (2004) 20 I L & P 151 at 154.

the amendment to r 4.218(1) at the beginning of 2003, there does not appear to have been an increase in the number of actions brought under s 214, and this *might* mean that liquidators are still concerned about adverse costs orders.

While a liquidator has probably been aided with the change to r 4.218(1)(a), he or she faces another problem. As a result of the House of Lords' decision in *Buchler v Talbot* [2004] UKHL 9; [2004] 2 AC 298; [2004] 2 WLR 582; [2004] 1 BCLC 281 costs and expenses cannot be taken from company assets that are subject to a floating charge, because the charge removes the property that is subject to it into a separate fund and this is not company property for liquidation purposes.[20] The government is seeking to overcome the effect of this decision. The Company Law Reform Bill provided in clause 868 that a new provision (s 176A) will be introduced into the Insolvency Act.

It might be thought that if a liquidator has a particularly strong case, he or she should not be so worried about funding because a significant part of the liquidator's costs will usually have to be paid by the respondent. But, of course, all sorts of problems might ensue. The respondent might prevaricate in making payment, and the liquidator, therefore, may have to bear the cost until payment is forthcoming, if at all. Further, a respondent might disappear or might be impecunious and so the liquidator may recover little or nothing in terms of costs.

So, funding can be an issue that presents difficulties for liquidators. This is particularly so in all cases except where there is a significant amount of assets of value in the company's estate, and free from falling under a floating charge. Often, a liquidator will have to consider finding some way of financing the action, or at least safeguarding his or her own financial position. Realistically, funding will need to be sought from creditors or even outside sources. While a liquidator might be able to obtain funding through fighting funds or indemnities from creditors,[21] these are not favoured so much nowadays. There is little incentive for creditors to provide indemnities when any fruits obtained will be divided amongst all creditors. Contrast the situation in Australia where, under s 564 of the Corporations Act 2001, if a creditor provides an indemnity for a liquidator's proceedings, and property is recovered as a result of those proceedings, the court may make an order as to the distribution of that property with a view to giving an advantage to the indemnifying creditor, in addition to providing that the creditor be repaid any costs that have been incurred in supporting the proceedings.[22] The Cork Committee advocated

---

20 For a critique of the decision of the House of Lords, see Mokal, R, 'Liquidation expenses and floating charges – the separate funds fallacy' [2004] LMCLQ 387. Also, see Rajak, H, 'Liquidation expenses versus a claim secured by a floating charge' (2005) 18 *Insolvency Intelligence* 97.

21 For a discussion of this, see Keay, A, *McPherson's The Law of Company Liquidation*, 4th edn, 1999, Sydney: Law Book Co, pp 580–584; Keay, A, 'Pursuing the resolution of the funding problem in insolvency litigation' [2002] Insolv L 90.

22 For a discussion of this, see Keay, 'Pursuing the resolution' *ibid*.

something similar to the Australian scheme (at [1797]), but this has never been pursued.

More frequently liquidators are entering into arrangements with companies which specialise in funding actions, in exchange for either an assignment of the action or a portion of any successful claim. The problem for liquidators is that in securing funding in the manner just suggested, they are engaging in maintenance and/or champerty. The former is the assistance or encouragement of proceedings by someone who has no interest in the proceedings nor any motive recognised by the law as justifying interference in the proceedings. The latter is a form of maintenance[23] in that assistance or encouragement of proceedings is provided in exchange for a promise to provide a share of the proceeds of the action. While these doctrines may be archaic,[24] they are still relevant in several areas, such as in the assignment of causes of action. However, an inveterate exception to the application of these doctrines is the rule that a trustee in bankruptcy (and liquidators and administrators) is able to lawfully assign any of the bare causes of action of the bankrupt (being property of the bankrupt) that have vested in the trustee on the basis that the trustee is to receive a share of any proceeds of ensuing litigation (*Seear v Lawson* (1880) 15 Ch D 426; *Re Park Gate Waggon Works Co* (1881) 17 Ch D 234, CA; *Ramsey v Hartley* [1977] 1 WLR 686, CA; *Stein v Blake* [1996] 2 AC 243, HL; *Norglen Ltd v Reeds Rains Prudential* [1998] 1 All ER 218 at 232, HL). This exception (referred to here as 'the insolvency exception', as it applies to liquidation[25] and administration as well as bankruptcy) is based on the idea that the legislature has granted to the liquidator the power to realise the assets of the company and to the transfer of an action to an insurer in return for the financing of it, and the fact that an insurer funds proceedings in exchange for the payment of a part of the proceeds, has been treated as a sale by Lightman J in *Grovewood Holdings Plc v James Capel & Co Ltd* [1995] BCC 760 at 764. Liquidators have power to sell the company's property,[26] and this includes causes of action. Notwithstanding this, according to *Re Oasis Merchandising Services Ltd* [1995] BCC 911 at 919 it is not possible for a liquidator to assign a cause of action under s 214 to an insurer in exchange for a promise to pay the liquidator a part of the fruits of the claim. This is because actions commenced under provisions like s 214 are granted to the liquidator personally by legislation and not to the company; an action under s 214 is only given to the liquidator and involves the recovery of moneys to which the company never had any right (*Re Oasis Merchandising* at 918). The courts are most concerned that there is no interference in the action by a third party, and that there is no loss of control of the action by the liquidator.

---

23 Referred to as 'aggravated maintenance': *Guy v Churchill* (1888) 40 Ch D 481 at 489.
24 See the comments of Oliver LJ in *Trendtex Trading v Credit Suisse* [1980] QB 629 at 674, CA.
25 Causes of action are company property which can be dealt with by liquidators under Sched 4, para 6 to the Insolvency Act 1986.
26 See ss 165 and 167 and para 6 of Sched 4.

This will, undoubtedly occur where an insurer is covering the costs, for it will want to be involved in strategic decisions, particularly when it comes to settlement offers.

It is also highly debatable whether a liquidator could agree to assign only part of the fruits of a wrongful trading action to an insurer, thereby retaining control over the proceedings. This is because it was held by Lightman J in *Grovewood Holdings Plc v James Capel & Co Ltd* that a share of the proceeds of an action could not be assigned without falling foul of the rule against champerty. Unlike a bare cause of action, which can be assigned, as it comes within the insolvency exception (to the rules on champerty), a portion of the fruits of an action does not constitute property for these purposes and cannot be assigned without breaching the rules against champerty (*Grovewood Holdings; Re Oasis Merchandising* at 918). While Peter Gibson LJ in the Court of Appeal in *Re Oasis Merchandising Services Ltd* [1997] 1 All ER 1009 stated that there was much to be said for the idea of allowing the assignment of a right to a share in the fruits of an action by a liquidator provided that an outsider could not influence or interfere in the conduct of the proceedings (at 1002), the uncertainty that exists is likely to deter liquidators from seeking funding and, hence, taking action under s 214. Consequently, it has led one commentator to conclude that s 214 is little more than a 'paper tiger',[27] a view reflected in the business community.[28]

A possible way around the funding problem just identified is to adopt the approach of the Australian provision, s 588G. In Australia liquidators are able to avail themselves of funding by assigning the fruits of an action, as occurred in *Re Movitor Pty Ltd* (1995) 19 ACSR 440. This is because s 588G is drafted in such a way that a claim is deemed to be a debt recoverable by the company, and the debt is able to be regarded as part of the company's property and able to be sold by a liquidator.

Another method of funding actions is to instruct solicitors who are willing to operate on a conditional fee basis. This is permitted by the introduction of the Conditional Fee Agreements Order 1995.[29] Solicitors can agree that they will only be entitled to fees if the action succeeds. But, solicitors do not appear to be overly enthused about entering into an agreement with a liquidator where wrongful trading actions are involved.[30] It is highly likely that creditors and solicitors (operating on a conditional fee basis) are not going to be ready to undertake the risks that relate to wrongful trading litigation, especially in light of cases such as *Re Continental Assurance*.

27 Cook, C, 'Wrongful trading – is it a real threat to directors or a paper tiger?' [1999] Insolv L 99 at 100.

28 'Wrongful trading laws that directors ignore' *Accountancy Age*, 29 October 1992 at 8.

29 SI 1995/1674.

30 Hicks, A, *Disqualification of Directors: No Hiding Place for the Unfit*, Research Report No 59, 1998, London: Chartered Association of Certified Accountants, p 95; Arsalidou, D, 'The impact of section 214(4) of the Insolvency Act 1986 on directors' duties' (2001) 22 Co Law 19 at 21.

Perhaps it is time to consider other ways of funding actions, such as the creation of a central fund on which liquidators could draw, if they could establish a good case. This was a process that was used in Australia in relation to bankruptcies for many years and appeared to work well, particularly where bankruptcy trustees did not have sufficient funds to institute recovery proceedings or seek private examinations of the bankrupt and others. Such a fund could be financed by government or a levy on companies in general, with repayment to the fund if a liquidator were successful in proceedings issued. Another possible approach, mentioned above, is to give the courts discretion to give to any creditor who funds an action a prescribed amount out of the award pursuant to the s 214 proceedings, before the creditors are paid out, as well as any costs that they have expended, in order to give them an advantage as consideration for the risk that has been adopted.[31] The effect of this last proposal was achieved by a creditor in *Katz v McNally* [1997] 2 BCLC 579, CA, who indemnified the liquidator in exchange for a first charge over any sum recovered in the litigation. But it would seem that that strategy is not permissible, certainly in some situations, given the latest Court of Appeal decision in *Re R S & M Engineering Co Ltd* [2000] Ch 40; [1999] 2 BCLC 485. Legislation would have to be enacted to permit courts to benefit indemnifying creditors.

The public factor

As was discussed in Chapter 8, the fact that wrongful trading does not lead to criminal liability should not be seen as an indication that s 214 has no public role to play. On the contrary, it is intended to play a public as well as a private role. In *Re Oasis Merchandising Services Ltd* (at 918) Robert Walker J adverted to the public element in s 214 proceedings, which involves an attempt to prescribe a minimum standard of conduct of directors in managing the affairs of companies. The public function is marked by the fact that it is linked to directors' disqualification, and is a process intended to protect the public from reckless and/or dishonest directors. It is difficult for any provision to fulfil both private and public functions, and it is doubtful whether s 214 comes near to doing so.[32] It may be argued that the inclusion of a public function in s 214 attenuates its potency as a weapon in civil litigation; it is difficult to distinguish the private and public functions and the extent of improper behaviour needed to fulfil the latter function, which would be more stringent than in relation to the former, could be required before a court would be willing to hold that a civil action should succeed. Also, director disqualification might well depend on whether success can be secured in a

---

31 This is discussed in detail in Keay, 'Pursuing the resolution' *op. cit.* fn 21above.

32 See the comments in Schulte, R, 'Enforcing wrongful trading as a standard of conduct for directors and a remedy for creditors: the special case of corporate insolvency' (1999) 20 Co Law 80.

wrongful trading action, and it seems anomalous that a public function is dependent on success in a civil case, particularly where the civil action cannot be initiated by a public official.

Reality dictates that a liquidator is not going to initiate proceedings where the actions of the director merit such a process unless there is a good chance that the proceedings will be successful and lead to a decent contribution order. It seems unreasonable to expect a liquidator to pursue wrongful trading actions because of the unfitness of a director and to achieve public policy aims. It is arguable whether the Secretary of State could in fact pursue disqualification proceedings against a director under s 6 of the CDDA (unfitness ground) on the basis that he or she has engaged in wrongful trading. Richard Schulte has submitted that the Secretary of State cannot do so.[33] Perhaps this problem might be overcome by doing something that was advocated earlier in the chapter, namely granting to the Secretary of State for Trade and Industry the power to initiate wrongful trading proceedings with the aim of securing a disqualification order against the director. This would enable a public official to focus on the enforcement of the public aspect of wrongful trading. As explained earlier, in other common law jurisdictions public officers or bodies are able to commence proceedings for an equivalent of wrongful trading.

An assessment

The impact of the provision

Shortly after the enactment of the Insolvency Act, a number of academics regarded wrongful trading as a significant weapon in the arsenal of liquidators. Academics and practitioners alike saw s 214 as having a bright future in providing much-needed protection for creditors.[34] In the early days of the provision Professor Dan Prentice said that it was 'unquestionably one of the most important developments in company law this century'.[35] Dr Fidelis Oditah said that s 214 was a 'welcome additional weapon in the fight against abuse of the privilege of limited liability by directors of trading companies'.[36] This optimism might be seen as justified in light of the fact that liquidators won early cases (*Re Produce Marketing Consortium Ltd* (1989) 5 BCC 569; *Re DKG Contractors Ltd* [1990] BCC 903; *Re Purpoint Ltd* [1991] BCC 121; [1991] BCLC 491). However, since these statements were made, other commentators have been more circumspect and less optimistic about the potential, and impact, of the wrongful trading provision. It is not putting it too highly to say that s 214 has not lived up to its early promise. For example, Professor Steve Griffin states that:

33 *Ibid* at 82.   34 *Ibid*.
35 'Creditor's interests and director's duties' (1990) 10 OJLS 265 at 277.
36 'Wrongful trading' [1990] LMCLQ 205 at 222.

[D]espite the provision's potential to significantly displace the director's protective shield of limited liability, section 214 has, in reality, failed to fulfil its objective of achieving an efficient means by which the wrongful trading activities of directors can be successfully penalised.[37]

Arguably, the impact of s 214 has been disappointing.[38] First, there have only been a relatively small number of reported cases to date, with a number of cases that appear to deal with s 214, only addressing peripheral issues (such as *Re Farmizer (Products) Ltd* [1995] BCC 926; [1995] 2 BCLC 462 (appeal from this decision was dismissed in [1997] 1 BCLC 589; [1997] BCC 655) dealing with procedural issues; *Burgoine v London Borough of Waltham Forest* [1997] BCC 347; [1997] 2 BCLC 612; and *Re Oasis Merchandising Services Ltd* with its focus on champerty and funding arrangements), and while there have undoubtedly been claims either threatened by liquidators or commenced without going to trial, perhaps because the claim was settled prior to hearing, such as the claims against the finance director and one of the non-executive directors in *Re Continental Assurance*,[39] as well as unreported decisions, it would seem that s 214 has not been as regularly invoked as the Cork Committee would have hoped or expected.[40] As Griffin pointed out, when writing in 1999, there had been an average of 18,000 insolvent liquidations per year since 1986 (although this number has reduced in recent times, probably partly due to the increased use of administrations) and one would expect there to have been more actions brought.[41] So, the initial enthusiasm has waned considerably and there have been several negative assessments of the provision over the past ten years, including a concern that few proceedings have been initiated.[42] This appears to have empirical support from a survey of disqualified directors conducted by Hicks and reported in 1998.[43] Of those disqualified on the ground of unfitness, the learned commentator found that the most common basis for this was trading while insolvent, yet no proceedings were brought under s 214 against these directors.[44] An example appears to be *Official Receiver v Zwirn* [2002] BCC 760. One might think that

---

37 *Personal Liability and Disqualification of Company Directors*, 1999, Oxford: Hart Publishing, p 96.

38 *Op. cit.* fn 14 above at 513.   39 *Op. cit.* fn 16 above.

40 See the comments in Godfrey, P, and Nield, S, 'The wrongful trading provisions – all bark and no bite' (1995) 11 IL & P 139 at 140. However, note that Louis Doyle said that data up to 1993 suggested that proceedings for wrongful trading were regularly issued: 'Ten years of wrongful trading' (1996) 18 I L & P 10.

41 *Op. cit.* fn 37 above at 97. Between 1989 and 1993 there were 92,500 liquidations (Godfrey and Nield, *ibid* at 140), although these figures represent part of the fallout from the bad recession of the late 1980s.

42 For instance, see *ibid*; Walters, A, 'Enforcing wrongful trading – substantive problems and practical incentives' in Rider, B A K (ed), *The Corporate Dimension*, 1998, Bristol: Jordans; *op. cit.* fn 27 above.

43 *Op. cit.* Hicks, fn 30 above.   44 *Op. cit.* Arsalidou, fn 30 above at 20.

in light of cases such as *Re Continental Assurance*, the number of claims might well have diminished, or at least those that actually led to the initiation of court proceedings, as opposed to claims settled prior to proceedings. What is not in issue is that in many cases, with *Re Continental Assurance* being, perhaps, the *locus classicus*, there will be substantial difficulties that liquidators have to overcome, especially in terms of evidence. Clearly, establishing a case is frequently not going to be easy, and, courts are going to require some convincing evidence where the directors have not acted irresponsibly.

Hicks found[45] in a survey completed in the early 1990s that liquidators were not initiating proceedings for a number of reasons:

(a) the directors might be impecunious. It is to be noted that this is a real concern, and one mentioned specifically by Lightman J in *RBG Resources plc (in liquidation) v Rastogi* [2005] 2 BCLC 592 at 603, which liquidators should take into account;
(b) any award would go to a secured creditor;
(c) lack of funding;
(d) concern that if an action failed, they might be liable personally for costs and might not be able to indemnify themselves from company funds.

It would seem that all but the second reason still applies.

The problem with a lack of cases on wrongful trading is that an absence of visible enforcement might well derogate from the wrongful trading provision acting as a deterrent.[46] Directors might get the idea that liquidators are unlikely to take proceedings, except in the most clear-cut case.

A second indication that the impact of s 214 has been disappointing is that those liquidators who have taken proceedings have struggled to obtain judgments (notable examples are *Continental Assurance; The Liquidator of Marini Ltd v Dickensen* [2003] EWHC 334 (Ch); [2004] BCC 172). Rarely, it would seem, where directors have made an effort to understand the position of their company, and where they decided to continue doing business, will they be held liable (*Re Sherborne Associates Ltd* [1995] BCC 40; *Continental Assurance*). The courts do not appear readily to impose liability on directors, and this is particularly so where the directors have sought and obtained advice from professionals. In most cases where directors have been found liable they have been found to have acted irresponsibly, such as in *Re Purpoint Ltd* where the respondent director, after being advised of the rather parlous state of his company's affairs and that if he were to continue trading he ran the risk of being found liable of wrongful trading if the company went into liquidation, drew very large sums from the company (at 125, 495).

But Dr Rizwaan Mokal argues[47] that the efficacy of s 214 cannot be

---

45 *Op. cit.* fn 16 above.   46 *Op. cit.* Walters, fn 42 above at 159–160.
47 *Corporate Insolvency: Theory and Application*, 2005, Oxford: Oxford University Press, p 298.

determined by consideration of the number of proceedings or the number of successful claims. He opines that the provision could have been successful in bringing home to directors that they must consider the interests of creditors if their company is failing, and that a more accurate way of testing the section's effectiveness would be to compare the dividends paid to creditors before and after the introduction of the provision. The point that Mokal makes is a laudable one, but the problem with the approach suggested for testing efficacy is that it is unlikely that one could determine whether the outlawing of wrongful trading was the reason for any change in dividend levels. Also, if, as it appears is the case, wrongful trading is perceived as being a weak provision, it might cause directors to refrain from taking the action required by s 214 seriously. While the volume of proceedings probably cannot determine the efficacy of s 214, it might well be seen as an element in the aim of deterring wrongful trading, for, as we have established already, it is generally accepted that directors can be expected, when their companies are in difficulty, to embrace actions which involve more risk.[48]

Third, the provision has come under increasing attack from academics and practitioners alike.[49]

Fourth, besides the fact that s 214 actions appear to be few and far between, it has been asserted,[50] with some justification, that there is no evidence to suggest that directors' conduct has become more responsible in relation to their companies' affairs as a consequence of the advent of the provision. However, there is little or no empirical evidence that really supports that conclusion, although this seems to be the general anecdotal view pervading the legal and insolvency professions. While Hicks concluded in 1993 that the provision had led to directors closing down businesses for fear of proceedings under s 214, he felt that 'the scare factor' might be diminished due to the fact that directors were becoming aware that the chance of a successful claim was not more than a remote possibility.[51] This view, although not borne out by significant empirical evidence, certainly appears to be supported by subsequent events and comments. But Hicks said that the consensus amongst the respondents to his survey in 1993 was that it had encouraged directors to be responsible in making decisions in light of insolvency.[52] It is

---

48 Adler, B, 'A re-examination of near-bankruptcy investment incentives' (1995) 62 U Chi L Rev 575 at 590–598; Daigle, K, and Maloney, M, 'Residual claims in bankruptcy: an agency theory explanation' (1994) 37 *Journal of Law and Economics* 157. See Company Law Review Steering Group, *Modern Company Law for a Competitive Economy: Final Report* Vol 1 (DTI, London, 2001), at para 3.15.

49 For example, see Doyle, *op. cit.* fn 40 above; Godfrey and Nield, *op. cit.* fn 40 above; Walters, *op. cit.* fn 42 above; Griffin, *op. cit.* fn 37 above at 57–98; Simmons, M, 'Wrongful trading' (2001) 14 *Insolvency Intelligence* 12; Fidler, P, 'Wrongful trading after *Continental Assurance*' (2001) 17 I L & P 212, Keay, A, *McPherson's Law of Company Liquidation*, 2001, London: Sweet and Maxwell, pp 621–634.

50 *Op. cit.* fn 27 above at 104.   51 *Op. cit.* fn 16 above.   52 *Ibid.*

not possible to say whether this still remains the case. Hicks did not state whether his respondents made any distinctions between directors of large companies and those in closely held companies. Directors of closely held companies often commence the business carried on by the company and are sentimentally attached to their firms, often having sunk their life savings into them as well as a lot of effort. As a result they are frequently ready to try anything to keep their enterprise going,[53] and so one would intuitively think that the point made by Hicks might not be a major consideration as far as directors of closely held companies are concerned.

Fifth, Schulte has remarked that the provision has not achieved its public or private law role because of substantive and procedural problems.[54] He concludes in trenchant language that s 214 'is of no interest to a liquidator, no benefit to creditors, and for wrongdoers it is the impotent progeny of a fine legal theory'.[55] He calls for urgent reform.[56] As we have already noted, all that liquidators are really concerned about is recovering as much as possible for creditors, and they are not concerned about deterring directors from engaging in wrongful trading or any public aspects of the provision. Finch has taken the view that the judicial approaches to wrongful trading have not assisted in its use, and there has been confusion concerning the role of the provision.[57] She points out that while *Re Produce Marketing* said that any award is not to be seen as penal, other judges have regarded the remedy as a way of encouraging the enhancement of standards and to punish the errant.[58] Yet this has occurred in few cases.

Insolvent liquidation

The use of the balance sheet test to define 'insolvent liquidation' means that the situations where s 214 can be invoked might be limited. Including cash flow as well as balance sheet insolvency would appear to have the advantage of broadening the circumstances when liability might fall on directors. It might be argued that it would be unfair on non-executive directors who, while perhaps expecting to be presented with a copy of the balance sheet at a board meeting, are not involved in the day-to-day running of the business and might not know that the company is unable to pay its debts as they fall due. But there are usually signs that should alert all directors that the company is cash-flow insolvent or heading that way.

---

53 Mokal, R J, 'An agency cost analysis of the wrongful trading provisions: redistribution, perverse incentives and the creditors' bargain' (2000) 59 CLJ 335 at 353–354.
54 *Op. cit.* fn 32 above at 81.   55 *Ibid* at 88.   56 *Ibid.*
57 *Op. cit.* fn 14 above at 513.   58 *Ibid* at 514.

The conditions for liability

The main problems encountered with s 214 have surrounded the two main elements of the provision, one dealing with the primary condition for liability, and the other the defence, namely: when can it be said that there is no reasonable prospect of the company avoiding insolvent liquidation, and what can constitute 'every step' taken to minimise losses to creditors? This section of the chapter deals with the former.

Perhaps s 214 would have been more successful if it had been based on insolvency, namely directors would be liable if they traded (incurring debts) when the company was insolvent. This was the approach advocated by the Cork Committee and is the approach taken in Australia, which has amended its counterpart of s 214 on several occasions. The present section, s 588G of the Corporations Act 2001, while still producing some debates over interpretation and application, is credited with ensuring that companies in difficulty enter voluntary administration.[59] Section 588G states that directors will contravene the section if all of the following criteria apply:

(a) they are directors when the company incurs a debt;
(b) the company was insolvent at the time when the debt was incurred or became insolvent as a result of the incurring of the debt;
(c) at the time when the debt was incurred there were reasonable grounds for suspecting that the company was insolvent or would become insolvent as a result of the debt incurred; and
(d) the person was aware at the time of the incurring of the debt that there were grounds for suspecting the insolvency of the company or a reasonable person in a like position in a company that is in the company's circumstances would be aware of the company's insolvency.[60]

As adverted to above, the Cork Committee (at [1806]) had in fact recommended something akin to s 588G. It stated that directors should be liable if a company incurs liabilities with no reasonable prospect of satisfying them in full and the director knows or ought to have known that the trading was wrongful (at [1783]). It went on to define the action of 'wrongful trading' as:

> [A]t any time when the company is insolvent or unable to pay its debts as they fall due it incurs further debts or other liabilities to other persons without a reasonable prospect of meeting them in full.

59 Herzberg, A, 'Why are there so few insolvent trading cases?' (1998) 6 *Insolvency Law Journal* 77.
60 Like Australia, the Singaporean law (Companies Act, s 339) makes directors liable for causing their companies to incur debts when there is no reasonable expectation that the company will be able to repay the creditors.

The approach of the Committee was rejected by government with the end result that a person may be held liable for wrongful trading without incurring further debts. Conversely, directors will not be held liable necessarily if they continued to trade when their company was insolvent. But, the Cork Committee advocated (at [1786]) that 'if the directors at any time consider the company to be insolvent, they should have a duty to take immediate steps for the company to be placed in receivership, administration or liquidation'. This is not altogether radical or overly severe, as it is something that some other jurisdictions, such as France and Germany, require.[61] The use of insolvency as the trigger for liability was suggested by one of the respondents to Hicks when he conducted his 1993 survey.[62] Given the fact that administration may now be commenced extrajudicially, and without a lot of formality and cost, this approach has attractions. It is certainly the approach taken in Australia, where voluntary administration has been embraced frequently, and is posited as the reason for a reasonably low number of reported cases.[63]

The benefit of invoking the Australian-style approach is that one gets away from having to ascertain whether a director knew or ought to have known that there was no reasonable prospect of the company avoiding insolvent liquidation. This is replaced with having to determine if directors had reasonable grounds for suspecting that the company was insolvent or would become insolvent as a result of the debt incurred, when incurring a debt. While 'insolvency' is not a precisely defined expression[64] (although arguably it is now more so than in the past), it is more certain than considering whether a director ought to have known that the company was not going to be able to avoid insolvent liquidation (a future occurrence) involving prediction as well as assessment. Arguably, directors might be able to detect insolvency before they could be expected to conclude that there was no reasonable prospect of the company avoiding insolvent liquidation.[65] It is easier for a director, and perhaps fairer, to ascertain whether his or her company is solvent or not than to be expected to look into a crystal ball and determine whether the company will recover and avoid insolvent liquidation. Although it is acknowledged that insolvency may not be evaluated precisely at any one point in time, directors would only be liable, on the above proposal, if there were reasonable grounds for suspecting insolvency and they knew or suspected that the company was insolvent.

Perhaps the thing that is against this approach is the determining of insolvency. Companies can go in and out of insolvency and directors, while they

---

61 See above at pp 77–78 for a discussion of the factors that trigger the equivalent of wrongful trading in other jurisdictions.

62 *Op. cit.* fn 16 above at 136.   63 *Op. cit.* fn 59 above.

64 Keay, A, 'The insolvency factor in the avoidance of antecedent transactions in corporate liquidations' (1995) 21 *Monash University Law Review* 305.

65 But note the criticism of the Australian criteria of insolvency in Morrison, D, 'The Australian insolvent trading prohibition – why does it exist?' (2002) 11 *International Insolvency Review* 153 at 166–169.

might perceive that the company is technically insolvent, know that they will be paid a sum in a few days that will make them solvent again. Of course, if the latter was to occur the company should recover and not go into liquidation, with no possibility of wrongful trading proceedings being commenced. While using insolvency as the test might mean that more directors take action such as putting their companies into administration, when this might not be necessary, that is not a huge problem as it gives an administrator a chance to see whether the company can be restored to health. The only drawback could be that if administration were used and was not strictly necessary, it would mean the incurring of extra costs. But this is, it is submitted, preferable to companies continuing to trade, incurring more and more debts, and prejudicing creditors in the long run. Intuitively, one would say that creditors would rather see their dividend reduced in a small way in relation to a few companies who did not need to go into administration if they were to see their losses because of wrongful trading reduced significantly. The strategy of the Cork Committee to deal with the issue of directors not knowing whether they are going to be liable or not was to propose that a director could apply to the court by chambers application for relief in advance. It was recommended that the court would 'have power to declare that, however matters later turn out, future trading of the kind which it has sanctioned should not be capable of giving rise to any claim for wrongful trading' (at [1798]). The Committee then set out examples of the kinds of declarations that it envisaged could be made by a court (at [1798]). These included that trading would not be deemed wrongful:

(a)　where trading for a specific period of time was sanctioned;
(b)　until a set level of borrowing is attained;
(c)　where there was trading to complete particular existing or prospective contracts;
(d)　where trading was conducted on a cash basis.

This procedure would be particularly helpful for a director who considers that he or she might be at risk under s 214. It would go some way to solving the problem that faces directors when they are concerned about their position, but do not know what to do about it. We have noted that directors cannot presently know with any degree of certainty what is involved in taking 'every step' to ensure they are able to keep themselves from liability.

The above suggestions would not, however, overcome another problem with s 214, and that is the issue of funding. It seems that actions are not likely to be readily instigated by liquidators because of problems with funding. This chapter has already highlighted the difficulties that liquidators may experience in trying to make claims.[66] Of course, even if funding is available in

---

66 See above at pp 127–132.

relation to costs of the proceedings and a liquidator obtains an order from the court, the problem facing the liquidator, and this of course applies to any claim against a director personally, is that the directors may be impecunious, perhaps due to the fact that they guaranteed the debts of their company to a bank, rendering the proceedings possibly tantamount to useless. However, this is an issue that is pervasive in litigation, and particularly where one is dealing with insolvency issues.

One advantage of the wrongful trading provision over the Australian provision is that technically the former could apply before a company is actually insolvent and so this might be the spur to a board looking to turn around a company before it in fact falls into an insolvent state. However, it is submitted that the empirical evidence that we have thus far, namely the reported cases, does not bear that out. It seems that more often than not, the point at which wrongful trading is said to commence is when the company is insolvent. The Australian provision effectively encourages directors to embrace a formal insolvency regime and place the company in the hands of an insolvency practitioner, while the British provision allows the directors to remain in control, and in that sense it is reminiscent of Chapter 11 bankruptcy in the US, where, except in limited circumstances when a trustee is appointed over the company's affairs by the court, the board remains in control of the company, a phenomenon known as 'debtor in possession'.

Defences

As indicated earlier, one of the two main problems with s 214 has been determining what the defence in subs (3) actually means. It is a vague provision and has, consequently, led to academics and practitioners in the literature attempting to arrive at determining what 'every step' means. I think that it is fair to say that while such commentaries are of some help, they do not take things too far.

Section 214(3) could be made less severe, if s 214 were to remain in its present state, if it provided that a respondent had to establish that he or she took all reasonable steps to minimise loss to creditors.

However, it is submitted that it is preferable if s 214 were overhauled, as advocated under the section 'The conditions of liability', and if this occurred then the defences contained in the Australian section that covers defences, s 588H, could be pressed into service. The section provides that a respondent can successfully defend an action if he or she can prove *one* of the following:

(a) that when the debt was incurred the director had reasonable grounds to expect (not merely suspect) that the company was solvent and would remain solvent even if the debt was incurred;

(b) that when the debt was incurred the director had reasonable grounds to believe, and he or she did believe, that a subordinate was competent, reliable and responsible for providing adequate information about the company's solvency and the director expected, on the basis of this information, that the company was solvent and would remain solvent;

(c) that when the debt was incurred the director, because of illness or for some other good reason, did not take part in the management of the company at that time; or

(d) that the director took all reasonable steps to stop the company from incurring the debt. It is explained in s 588H(6) that the matters that can be taken into account in proving this defence are: any action taken by the respondent in view of appointing an administrator; when that action was taken; and the results of the action.

Such defences provide greater precision than the provision that presently exists in the UK. It should be noted that the only defence that the Cork Committee appeared to consider was that the directors took immediate steps to have the company placed in receivership, administration or liquidation (at [1786]). I think that that does not give reasonable scope for directors who have acted properly to defend an action, although if the suggestions in this chapter were implemented then in the majority of cases the placing of the company in some kind of formal insolvency regime, probably administration, would be the only way that directors might escape liability.

Blameworthiness

It might be thought that in tying wrongful trading to director disqualification and even using the word 'wrongful', there must be a degree of blameworthiness required before a person can be held liable for a breach of s 214. Certainly it might be argued that in several cases the courts have seemed to require an element of moral wrongdoing before finding against a director.[67] This is something that was not envisaged by the Cork Committee, which saw wrongful trading as effecting a balance between encouraging the growth of enterprises and discouraging downright irresponsibility (at [1805]). In fact the Committee referred to the action that was to be proscribed as 'insolvent trading' which is the expression used in Australia. The use of the expression 'insolvent trading' is more attractive, as it has no moral overtones. Moral blame is a concept that is more suited to a breach of the fraudulent trading provision, s 213 (*Re Patrick & Lyon Ltd* [1933] Ch 786).

There are indications in several cases, such as *Continental Assurance* and *Re Sherborne*, that the courts are focusing overly on the need for blameworthy actions of directors before attaching liability to directors. Section 214 is not about blameworthiness. It is about whether directors were aware or should have been aware of their company's inevitable slide into insolvent liquidation. As Simmons implies,[68] the use of the word 'wrongful' is wholly inappropriate.

---

67 *Op. cit.* Godfrey and Nield, fn 40 above at 140.   68 *Op. cit.* Simmons, fn 49.

It is unfortunate that s 214 has been known as dealing with wrongful trading. The use of the word 'wrongful' while not found in the actual section itself suggests the need for moral wrong. This was criticised earlier in this chapter.

One commentator has stated that s 214 'sets a commercially moral standard of conduct for directors'.[69] With respect, this seems to be correct, but the critical thing is the inclusion of the word 'commercially'. The provision is saying nothing about general blameworthiness. It requires directors to do things in commercial life that would safeguard creditors. Blameworthiness may have its place when the court comes to the point of deciding what contribution should be made, but in no other context.

Reforms

Throughout this chapter, as well as in other chapters in Part C, there have been suggestions for reform. This section of the chapter aims to summarise the reforms that I advocate. The first five reforms are not extensive, and are suggested with the assumption that s 214 is retained in the same basic format, while the other reform suggestions are more dramatic and are predicated on a significant change to the law.

First, administrators and the Secretary of State for Trade and Industry should be included as those who are permitted to initiate wrongful trading proceedings. Second, the title of 'wrongful trading' should be deleted. If a title is to be given to s 214, it should be 'irresponsible trading' or, even better, 'illicit trading.' Third, the defence should be amended to provide that the respondent has to establish that he or she took 'all reasonable steps' to minimise losses to creditors. Fourth, the definition of 'insolvent liquidation' should embrace cash-flow, as well as balance-sheet, insolvency. Fifth, to make it plain that the unsecured creditors should primarily benefit from a contribution order under s 214, a subsection could, in common with s 588Y of the Australian Corporations Act 2001, provide that any contribution is unable to be paid to satisfy a secured debt unless the unsecured creditors have been paid in full.

The following suggestions are more radical, and are predicated on the basis of a different foundation for the action, something which is advocated in this chapter. The reforms are based on the recommendations of the Cork Committee and the Australian insolvent trading provisions. First, it would be more definite if directors were liable if they failed to prevent the incurring of debts when there were reasonable grounds for suspecting that the company was insolvent or would become insolvent as a consequence of incurring a debt or a reasonable person in a like position in the company in similar circumstances would have been aware or ought to have been aware of the company's financial position. This would simplify the situation as there would only be an objective test, eliminating the two tests that prevail in s 214

---

69 *Ibid* at 13.

at the moment. This can be done because the condition does not require assessing whether there was a reasonable prospect of the company not avoiding insolvent liquidation. The condition focuses solely on insolvency. It is submitted that insolvency here should mean either balance-sheet or cash-flow insolvency. It might be argued that this test would hamstring directors as they could not deal with their company's financial situation in a flexible and entrepreneurial manner, and specifically they could not trade their way out of the company's problems, except on a cash basis, or else they would fall foul of the provision. The answer to that is that administration could be used as a refuge. Administration would provide a moratorium against claims and would offer a chance for the company to look for ways to get itself back on its feet, under the professional guidance of an independent insolvency practitioner. This seems to accord with the government's desire to foster realistic corporate rescue.[70] The earlier that a company realises its predicament, the more likely it is that it can be saved and rehabilitated. Including a cash flow test as well as a balance sheet would also contribute to making it easier for companies which are in financial difficulty to embrace administration. For if a company is to enter administration at its initiative, besides filing with the court a notice of intention to appoint an administrator, the directors have to provide a statutory declaration which states, *inter alia*, that the company is unable to pay its debts or is likely to enter that state (Insolvency Act 1986, Sched B1, para 27).

Theoretically, directors under the present wrongful trading provision are able to engage in some risk-taking and in fact are able to continue to trade while insolvent, carefully juggling their companies' competing liabilities. With financially intelligent directors, and some good luck, the regime might well work. The directors may properly and sensibly seek financial assistance and advice as they tread the fine lines set for them by s 214. But the reality may be that many directors will fail in this task, and this will be so for many because they will not be able to deal with the difficulties encountered. This contrasts with the reform position that is being suggested whereby often administration would have to be embraced and an insolvency practitioner put in charge of that financial juggling, bringing to bear on the company the benefit of his or her insolvency experience and expertise and in circumstances where creditors are required to stand back while a solution is examined.

We must recognise the fact that there are difficulties with this approach, but all approaches have their shortcomings. The primary difficulties experienced in Australia are that whether a company is insolvent or not at a particular point of time is not always able to be gauged with precision, and ascertaining when a debt is incurred is not always straightforward.

---

70 See Review Group, 'A review of company rescue and business reconstruction mechanisms,' Insolvency Service, May 2000 at para 17; *Productivity and Enterprise: A World Class Competition Regime*, 2001, Cm 5233, at para 5.10.

Second, the defence to a claim under s 214 must be less vague than it is at the moment. The defences provided for in the Australian provisions (s 588H) do that. They could be introduced if s 214 was amended to embrace insolvent trading rather than so-called wrongful trading, and these suggested defences have been set out earlier under 'Defences'.

Conclusion

A number of problems have dogged s 214 ever since its advent, including the difficulty experienced by liquidators in getting funds to run proceedings and determining from what date wrongful trading commenced, as well as lack of certainty in relation to the meaning of elements of the section, such as: what constitutes a director taking 'every step' so as to minimise potential loss to company creditors?[71] Writing in the early days of the provision, Oditah, after detailing some of the problems with s 214 and espousing the view that it was 'not happily drafted',[72] expressed the hope that 'some of the problems will be worked out as more cases of wrongful trading come before the courts'.[73] Unfortunately, that has not occurred. The view espoused in 1993 by Hicks that 'proving that the directors should have predicted insolvency, except in extreme cases, may be hit and miss'[74] appears still to be apposite. The cases suggest that the courts will not hold directors liable for wrongful trading, save where they have clearly acted irresponsibly. The courts have tended to give directors the benefit of the doubt and have not applied an overly strict approach, evident particularly in cases like *Continental Assurance*. The position might well be the same in Australia, where a review of the significant insolvent trading decisions shows that where the action is successful the directors have invariably blatantly breached the law to a significant financial degree, and for an extended period.[75] However, this could well mean that these are the only cases that are actionable in Australia as directors have employed the administration process.

There seem to be several shortcomings endemic to the wrongful trading provision, and that might be the reason why courts in recent years in the UK have tended to place a benevolent interpretation on what directors have done, with *Continental Assurance Co Ltd* and *The Liquidator of Marini Ltd v Dickensen* being possible examples.

Arguably, wrongful trading has not plugged the gaps that the Cork Committee saw in director conduct and which could not be covered by fraudulent trading with its tough requirements, and there is an urgent need for a reform of the provision. Some helpful changes could be made without revamping the whole provision, such as deleting the use of the title 'wrongful

---

71 See s 214(3).   72 *Op. cit.* fn 36 above at 222.   73 *Ibid.*
74 'Advising on wrongful trading: Part 1' (1993) 14 Co Law 16 at 16.
75 For example, see *Fryer v Powell* (2002) 139 *Federal Law Reports* 433.

trading', giving administrators the power to commence proceedings and changing 'every step' to 'all reasonable steps'. But it has been suggested in this chapter that the preferable approach is to amend s 214 significantly as indicated in the previous section of the chapter, with the emphasis being on requiring directors to take action when suspecting insolvency. This would, it is submitted, lead to far greater use of the administration process and would give companies more chance of being rescued, as well as reducing the incidence of illicit trading and producing better dividends to creditors.

Part D

A duty to consider the interests of creditors

11 The development of the duty to consider the interests of creditors

Introduction

Thus far we have considered two responsibilities that are imposed on directors as a result of statute. We now turn to a responsibility that has been developed, not by the legislature, but by the courts, and they have done this over the past 20 years or so. This is a duty imposed on directors to consider the interests of their companies' creditors in certain circumstances. There has been a substantial corpus of case law on this responsibility, and there has been a significant amount of debate as to whether the responsibility should exist. This latter issue is discussed in detail in Chapter 19. What this chapter and the following two chapters seek to do is to provide an exposition and analysis of the law as it has developed. This Chapter specifically charts the developments that have taken place since the responsibility was first raised in 1976. The focus is on the law in the UK, but the law is practically the same in Ireland, Australia and New Zealand, and some of the decisions in these jurisdictions are considered, particularly where they have contributed to the development of the jurisprudence in the area. The chapter includes some consideration of the law in these countries, together with Canada and the United States. The latter's law shares some commonality with the UK and the other countries mentioned above, although it has tended to develop in different ways to that in Ireland, Australia and New Zealand.[1]

It is trite law that in UK corporate law, directors of companies owe duties of loyalty to their companies as a whole.[2] What is meant by 'companies as a whole' is a vexed question, for it has been an extremely difficult phrase to interpret. However, it is fair to say that it has been traditionally interpreted as meaning that the duties are owed to present and future shareholders,[3] and

---

1 The American position is not helped by the fact that there are inconsistent approaches and differences between courts in different states.
2 *Percival v Wright* [1902] 2 Ch 421; *Multinational Gas and Petrochemical Co v Multinational Gas and Petrochemical Services Ltd* [1983] Ch 258.
3 Hannigan, B, *Company Law*, 2003, London: LexisNexis, p 203; Davies, P, *Gower and Davies' Principles of Modern Company Law*, 7th edn, 2003, London: Sweet and Maxwell, p 372; Hirt,

not, absent exceptional circumstances, to any individual members.[4] This approach involving maximising profits for shareholders is generally described in modern times as the shareholder primacy theory,[5] and regarded probably as the pre-eminent position in Anglo-American corporate law. Whether in fact UK case law actually historically supports shareholder primacy is a moot point and not within the scope of this book *per se*.[6] The principle is frequently justified on the basis that the shareholders 'own' the company and are, as a consequence, entitled to have it managed for their benefit.[7] However, there is significant commentary to the effect that the company is not to be regarded, just as the shareholders, but as an enterprise and that this includes others besides shareholders, such as creditors in certain cases.[8]

While directors do not have any obligation under statute to ensure that their company does not trade while insolvent or at a loss (*Secretary of State*

H, 'The company's decision to litigate against its directors: legal strategies to deal with the board of directors' conflict of interest' [2005] JBL 159 at 164–165. Section 309 of the Companies Act 1985 does require directors to take into account the interests of employees, but the section has been generally regarded as impotent.

4   *Percival v Wright* [1902] 2 Ch 421; *Multinational Gas and Petrochemical Co v Multinational Gas and Petrochemical Services Ltd* [1983] Ch 258, CA; *Peskin v Anderson* [2000] BCC 1110; [2000] 2 BCLC 1 (and affirmed on appeal by the Court of Appeal [2001] BCC 874). Also, see the comments of the UK's Jenkins Committee, Cmnd 1749 (1962) at para 89. For exceptional circumstances, see Hannigan, *ibid* at 200–202. The same approach is adopted in the United States: *Re Ben Franklin Retail Stores Inc* (1998) 225 BR 646 at 653 (Illinois).

5   Macey, J, 'An economic analysis of the various rationales for making shareholders the exclusive beneficiaries of corporate fiduciary duties' (1991) 21 *Stetson Law Review* 23; Bainbridge, S, 'In defense of the shareholder maximization norm: a reply to Professor Green' (1993) 50 *Washington and Lee Law Review* 1423; Black, B, and Kraakman, R, 'A self-enforcing model of corporate law' (1996) 109 *Harvard Law Review* 1911; Smith, D, 'The shareholder primacy norm' (1998) 23 *Journal of Corporation Law* 277; Bainbridge, S, 'The board of directors as nexus of contracts' (2002) 88 *Iowa Law Review* 1; Armour, J, Deakin, S, and Konzelmann, S, 'Shareholder primacy and the trajectory of UK corporate governance' (2003) *British Journal of Industrial Relations* 531.

6   See Keay, A, 'Shareholder primacy and the advent of enlightened shareholder value in the reform of directors' duties in the United Kingdom', a paper presented to the Corporate Law Teachers' Conference, Brisbane, Australia, 7 February 2006.

7   The view was made more (in)famous by the comments of the Noble laureate economist, Milton Friedman, in 'The social responsibility of business is to increase its profits', *New York Times*, September 13, 1970, Section 6 (Magazine). See, for instance, van der Weide, M, 'Against fiduciary duties to corporate stakeholders' (1996) 21 *Delaware Journal of Corporate Law* 27; Stout, L, 'Bad and not-so-bad arguments for shareholder primacy' (2002) 75 *Southern California Law Review* 1189 at 1190–1191. The view is criticised by Professor Stout.

8   Heydon, J, 'Directors' duties and the company's interests' in Finn, P (ed), *Equity and Commercial Relationships*, 1987, Sydney: Law Book Co, pp 134–135; Grantham, R, 'The judicial extension of directors' duties to creditors' [1991] JBL 1 at 6; Wishart, D, 'Models and theories of directors' duties to creditors' (1991) 14 *New Zealand Universities Law Review* 323 at 338–339; Crespi, G, 'Rethinking corporate fiduciary duties: the inefficiency of the shareholder primacy norm' (2002) *Southern Methodist University Law Review* 141. This is discussed in more detail in Chapter 14.

for Trade and Industry v Taylor [1997] 1 WLR 407 at 415; *sub nom Re CS Holidays Ltd* [1997] BCC 172 at 178, although this might later lead to a director's disqualification order being made (*Secretary of State for Trade and Industry v Creegan* [2002] 1 BCLC 99 at 101, CA), in the UK,[9] parts of the Commonwealth,[10] Ireland (*Re Frederick Inns Ltd* [1991] ILRM 582, Irish HC, and affirmed at [1994] ILRM 387, Irish SC; *Jones v Gunn* [1997] 3 IR 1; [1997] 2 ILRM 245) and the United States,[11] courts have held that as part of directors' duties to their companies, directors must, in their decision-making in relation to their company's affairs, where varying degrees of financial difficulty exist, take into account the interests of the creditors of their companies. The responsibility does not exist at all times, and the circumstances that will precipitate the advent of the responsibility are discussed in Chapter 13. In a situation where creditors' interests intrude, the shareholders cannot ratify any breach by directors,[12] as they can when creditors' interests are not to be taken into account, for they are not the only group who is interested in the company's funds. Hence, the directors cannot be sure, just because they have secured the ratification of their actions by the shareholders, that they are not going to be held liable.

In the ensuing discussion in this chapter and Chapters 12–19 I will talk about a duty to creditors. It is debatable whether the obligation owed by directors can be termed 'a duty', and even if it can be, that it is able to be regarded as a duty to creditors. The latter issue is discussed in detail in Chapter 15, but for ease of exposition, I will use the expression 'duty to creditors' from time to time.

The evolution of the duty

The duty owes its genesis in modern times to several decisions delivered in Australasia, although in the United States courts had found that directors

---

9 For example, see *Lonrho Ltd v Shell Petroleum Co Ltd* [1980] 1 WLR 627; *Re Horsley & Weight Ltd* [1982] 3 All ER 1045; *Winkworth v Edward Baron Development Ltd* [1986] 1 WLR 1512; [1987] 1 All ER 114; *Brady v Brady* (1988) 3 BCC 535; *Liquidator of West Mercia Safetywear v Dodd* (1988) 4 BCC 30; *Facia Footwear Ltd (in administration) v Hinchliffe* [1998] 1 BCLC 218; *Re Pantone 485 Ltd* [2002] 1 BCLC 266.

10 Most notably Australia (*Ring v Sutton* (1980) 5 ACLR 546; *Hooker Investments Pty Ltd v Email Ltd* (1986) 10 ACLR 443; *Grove v Flavel* (1986) 4 ACLC 654; 11 ACLR 161; *Kinsela v Russell Kinsela Pty Ltd* (1986) 4 ACLC 215; (1986) 10 ACLR 395; *Jeffree v NCSC* (1989) 7 ACLC 556; 15 ACLR 217; *Galladin Pty Ltd v Aimnorth Pty Ltd (in liq)* (1993) 11 ACSR 23) and New Zealand (*Nicholson v Permakraft (NZ) Ltd* (1985) 3 ACLC 453; *Hilton International Ltd (in liq) v Hilton* [1989] NZLR 442).

11 For example, *Geyer v Ingersoll Publications Co* 621 A 2d 784; *Credit Lyonnaise Bank Nederlander, NV v Pathe Communications Corp* 1991 Del Ch LEXIS 215; (1992) 17 *Delaware Journal of Corporate Law* 1099; *Re Kingston Square Assocs*, 1997 Bankr LEXIS 1514.

12 For instance, see *Re Horsley & Weight Ltd* [1982] 3 All ER 1045; *Kinsela v Russell Kinsela Pty Ltd* (1986) 4 ACLC 215; (1986) 10 ACLR 395; *Re DKG Contractors Ltd* [1990] BCC 903.

were liable to act in favour of creditors at certain times, for many years pursuant to the trust fund doctrine.[13] The starting point for any consideration of a duty to creditors is the judgment of the High Court of Australia in *Walker v Wimborne* (1976) 137 CLR 1; (1976) 3 ACLR 529. In that case a liquidator had brought misfeasance proceedings, under the equivalent of s 212 of the Insolvency Act 1986, against several directors of the company being liquidated, Asiatic Electric Co Pty Ltd ('A'). The claim was based on the fact that the directors had moved funds from A to other companies in which they held directorships. The relevant companies, including A, were treated by the directors as a group. The directors were accustomed to moving funds between companies and usually when this was done, no security was taken, and no interest charged or paid. At the time of the movement of funds that was the subject of the action, A was insolvent. A later entered liquidation. In his leading judgment, Mason J (whose judgment was approved by Barwick CJ) said (at 6–7; 531):

> In this respect it should be emphasised that the directors of a company in discharging their duty to the company must take into account the interests of its shareholders and its creditors. Any failure by the directors to take into account the interests of creditors will have adverse consequences for the company as well as for them.

His Honour went on to say that the transactions attacked by the liquidator were entered into pursuant to a course of conduct that involved a total disregard for the interests of A and its creditors (at 7; 532). The judge said that for there to be a misfeasance, there had to be a breach of duty, and in his view the actions of the directors constituted a breach of duty. His Honour was clearly accepting that directors had a positive obligation to creditors. The comments of Mason J were *obiter*, but it might be argued that what he said 'has taken on an authoritative status over the years'.[14]

It was not for some years that the approach propounded in *Walker v Wimborne* was followed in England. There were some statements made in the occasional case that indicated that the judges might favour this approach, but no direct application of the principle. For instance, in *Lonrho Ltd v Shell Petroleum Co Ltd* [1980] 1 WLR 627 (HL) Lord Diplock said (at 634), without any further elaboration, that the best interests of the company are not exclusively those of the shareholders, 'but may include those of its creditors'. It must be said that it is uncertain whether his Lordship was intending to

---

13 See below at pp 167–168 for a brief discussion of the doctrine.
14 McConvill, J, 'Directors' duties to creditors in Australia after *Spies v The Queen*' (2002) 20 *Company and Securities Law Journal* 4 at 12 and referring to Tomasic, R, Jackson, J, and Woellner, R, *Corporations Law: Principles, Policy and Process*, 1996, Sydney: Butterworths, pp 413–418.

make the statement in the context of directors' duties to creditors. But *Re Horsley & Weight Ltd* [1982] 1 Ch 442 was a case that examined the fact that the interests of a company could include those of the creditors. The case involved a claim by the liquidator of a company that the granting of a pension to a former director constituted a breach of duty, allowing for misfeasance proceedings to be brought. The liquidator failed in his claim, but Templeman LJ said (at 455) that:

> If the company had been doubtfully insolvent at the date of the grant [of the pension] to the knowledge of the directors, the grant would have been both a misfeasance and a fraud on the creditors for which the directors would remain liable.

Subsequently, in *Multinational Gas and Petrochemical Co v Multinational Gas and Petrochemical Services Ltd* [1983] Ch 258, a differently constituted Court of Appeal rejected the argument that the directors owed a duty to take into account creditors' interests after the directors made a bad decision and this led to the company becoming insolvent. Later in *Liquidator of West Mercia Safetwear Ltd v Dodd* (1988) 4 BCC 30, Dillon LJ said that the reason for the decision in *Multinational Gas* (his Lordship had been a member of the court in the earlier case) was the fact that the subject company was amply solvent and the decision of the directors was made in good faith. Christopher Riley asserted that the court in *Multinational Gas* was really only saying that directors owed no direct duty to creditors that was enforceable by creditors, as it went on to state that likewise there was no duty to individual shareholders, and 'it could hardly be suggested that their [shareholders'] interests need not be taken into account by directors'.[15]

A very influential decision, as far as Ireland and most Commonwealth jurisdictions are concerned, in the development of the responsibility, is the Australian case of *Kinsela v Russell Kinsela Pty Ltd* (1986) 4 ACLC 215; (1986) 10 ACLR 395. This was a decision given by the Court of Appeal in New South Wales. In that case the liquidator of a company, RK, which carried on business as a funeral director, brought proceedings to have a lease over premises granted by RK to directors of the company, set aside. The lease had been granted three months before the commencement of winding up, and at a time when the company's financial position was precarious. The company had sustained a significant loss during the previous year, had suffered less severe losses for several years and the accounts some six months before the lease was entered into showed that the company's liabilities exceeded its assets by nearly A$200,000. Also of importance, was the fact that the company had committed itself to performing services in relation to prepaid funerals. The lease involved the directors being given a term of three

---

15 'Directors' duties and the interests of creditors' (1989) 10 Co Law 87 at 91, fn 36.

years at a below market rental, there was no escalator clause to cover inflation and the directors were entitled, during the life of the lease, to purchase part of the premises for a sum which was well below true value. The court found that the intention of the directors was to put the assets of RK beyond the reach of its creditors, and to preserve what had been a family business for many years (at 219; 399). In delivering the leading judgment (with which the other members of the court concurred), Street CJ said that when a company is insolvent, the creditors' interests intrude (at 221; 401). His Honour went on to point out that in such a situation the shareholders are not entitled to ratify what would constitute a breach of duty (at 223; 404). As will be discussed in Chapter 13, his Honour refrained from formulating a test as to the degree of financial instability that is needed before directors are obliged to consider creditor interests, because the facts of the case did not require him to do so; as the company was clearly in a state of insolvency at the time of the relevant transactions, the duty arose.

The first major statement that indicated that the English courts would embrace any duty to creditors was given in the House of Lords in the case of *Winkworth v Edward Baron Development Co Ltd* [1986] 1 WLR 1512; [1987] 1 All ER 114. Here, X, and his wife, Y, were the directors and shareholders of a company, Z, having used company money to purchase their shares. Z bought a property that X and Y occupied as their home. As a consequence of this and other payments, the company was overdrawn on its bank account. The company's bank was given an undertaking by X that the deeds of the property purchased by Z would be held to the order of the bank. Y was unaware of this, as she did not take an active part in the company. X and Y sold their former marital home and paid part of the proceeds into Z's bank account. Then X, without the knowledge of Y, initiated the mortgage of Z's property to W in order to raise funds to discharge the indebtedness on the overdraft. Z subsequently became insolvent and went into liquidation. W commenced an action for possession against Z as it had defaulted on its mortgage payments. Y opposed these proceedings, on the basis that the payment of the funds from the former marital home gave her an equitable interest in the property. Ultimately the House of Lords held that Y did not have an equitable interest. Lord Templeman, in delivering a judgment unanimously supported by the other Lords, said that the equitable doctrine that a legal owner held in trust for those who contributed to the purchase of the property did not apply here because the payment made by X and Y to the bank account of Z was not referable to the acquisition of the property mortgaged to W as the property had been paid for before X and Y deposited their payment in Z's account. Also his Lordship said that X and Y had breached their duties to Z and Z's creditors when the company's funds were used for the purchase of their shares and when the company's overdraft was incurred and increased partly to benefit X and Y.

What is crucial in this case is the fact that Lord Templeman emitted a dictum which caused a significant amount of academic response, some of it

highly critical, and which constituted a development of what he had said in
Re Horsley & Weight Ltd [1982] 1 Ch 442. His Lordship said rather boldly
(at 1516; 118), without discussing any previous cases that either directly or
indirectly addressed the issue of directors' duties to creditors, that:

> [A] company owes a duty to its creditors, present and future. The com-
> pany is not bound to pay off every debt as soon as it is incurred and the
> company is not obliged to avoid all ventures which involve an element of
> risk, but the company owes a duty to its creditors to keep its property
> inviolate and available for the repayment of its debts . . . A duty is owed
> by the directors to the company and to the creditors of the company to
> ensure that the affairs of the company are properly administered and that
> its property is not dissipated or exploited for the benefit of the directors
> themselves to the prejudice of the creditors.

It has been suggested[16] that Lord Templeman *might* have been merely
restating the capital maintenance doctrine set out in *Re Exchange Banking
Company (Flitcroft's Case)* (1882) 21 Ch D 519, namely that the capital of a
company cannot be reduced save as provided for in statute, not even with the
sanction of a members' meeting, as 'there is a statement that the capital shall
be applied for the purposes of the business, and on the faith of that statement, which is sometimes said to be an implied contract with creditors,
people dealing with the company give it credit' (at 533 per Jessel MR). But
most have taken the comment of his Lordship to have been advocating a
direct duty to creditors and that the recipients of this duty included future
creditors. Perhaps the primary reason for taking this approach is that rather
than saying that the directors owed a duty to the company and this included
the creditors, his Lordship said that there was a duty owed to the company
and to creditors. We will return to a consideration of the issue in Chapter 16.
Certainly it appears that the latter view mentioned above was the one taken
by the Full Court of the Western Australian Supreme Court in *Jeffree v
NCSC* (1989) 7 ACLC 556. At a time when arbitration proceedings were
extant against a company, W, the controlling director, J, established a new
company and sold the assets of W to the new company for value but not
including anything for goodwill. When the person who initiated the arbitration proceedings succeeded, there were no assets held by W. Subsequently, the
then Australian corporate regulator, the National Companies and Securities
Commission, brought criminal proceedings against J on the basis that he
had breached his directorial duties (at the time, in Australia, both civil and
criminal proceedings could be brought against directors for breach of their

---

16 Farrar, J, 'The responsibility of directors and shareholders for a company's debts' (1989) 4
   Canta L R 12 at 14; Trethowan, I, 'Directors' personal liability to creditors for company
   debts' (1992) 20 ABLR 41 at 46.

duties). All three members of the court agreed with the views expressed by Lord Templeman and held J liable.

The dictum of Lord Templeman, which appeared to advocate a direct duty to creditors and that the recipients of this duty included future creditors, was met with some robust academic criticism.[17] Apart from one dictum in a Court of Appeal decision, the decision in *Jeffree v NCSC* and the decision of a couple of Canadian judges at first instance, the view that his Lordship expressed seems to have met with little agreement. Although in *Fulham Football Club Ltd v Cabra Estates plc* [1994] 1 BCLC 363 the Court of Appeal said that the duties of directors are to the company, and 'the company is more than just the sum total of its members. Creditors, both present and potential, are interested' (at 379).

The Court of Appeal, in *Liquidator of West Mercia Safetywear Ltd v Dodd* (1988) 4 BCC 30, the case that has probably become the leading case in England on the issue under discussion,[18] and cited and applied on many occasions, provided a more significant study of the area, and the usefulness of the duty became evident as a result. In this case, D was the director of two companies, X and Y. X was the parent company of Y. At the relevant time both companies were in financial difficulty. X had a large overdraft that D had guaranteed and it also had a charge over its book debts. One debt owed to X was £30,000, and this was owed by Y. A few days before there was a meeting of the members of Y, which was going to consider a motion that Y wind up, D transferred the sum of £4,000 that had been paid to Y by one of its debtors to X's overdrawn bank account. On liquidation of Y, the liquidator sought from the bank repayment to Y of the £4,000. The bank refused and so the liquidator sought both a declaration that D was guilty of misfeasance and breach of duty in relation to the transfer of the money to X, and repayment of the £4,000. At first instance, in the county court, the liquidator failed. He then appealed to the Court of Appeal. Dillon LJ, who gave the leading judgment with which the other members of the court (Croom-Johnson LJ and Caulfield J) concurred, found that the payment constituted a fraudulent preference (under the Bankruptcy Act 1914). As far as the claim that there had been a breach of duty was concerned, his Lordship approved of what Street CJ said in *Kinsela*, particularly in relation to the directors having a duty to consider creditor interests when a company is in financial difficulty, and came to the view that there was a breach of duty on the part of D.

---

17 Notably by Professor Len Sealy ('Directors' duties – an unnecessary gloss' [1988] CLJ 175). Professor Bob Baxt referred to the decision as 'remarkable' ('A senior australian court gives the "thumbs up" to the *Winkworth* principle' (1989) 7 *Companies and Securities Law Journal* 344).

18 Professor Paul Davies has said that the case provides the clearest recognition of the duty in English law: *Gower's Principles of Company Law*, 6th edn, 1997, London: Sweet and Maxwell, p 603.

Recent judicial opinion in the UK

As we have seen, the responsibility to creditors was developed in the 1980s. We now turn to see what decisions have been delivered in recent times. In reported cases those arguing for the duty have had mixed success. But perhaps in cases like *Kinsela* and *West Mercia Safetywear*, where the position of the companies was clearly such that what the directors did constituted a breach of duty, directors have been willing to settle any claims made.

The first case to consider is that of *Yukong Lines Ltd of Korea v Rendsburg Investments Corporation* [1998] BCC 870. Here the plaintiff was a shipping company (YL Ltd) which bought proceedings against two companies, R and L, and an individual, Y, for relief in relation to the repudiation of a charterparty by R. The charterparty involved the charter of a vessel for three years. The document was signed on behalf of R by Y, as a director of M, a broking company acting for R. A short time before the vessel was to be delivered by YL Ltd to R, Y wrote to YL Ltd advising it that R was unable to perform the charterparty because of matters beyond its control. YL Ltd issued proceedings against R. Subsequently YL Ltd added L and Y as defendants on the basis that they were undisclosed principals of R in relation to the charterparty. It was discovered that on the day that the charterparty was repudiated, a large sum was transferred from R's bank account to L. For our purposes, YL Ltd claimed damages from Y on the basis that he directed, at all material times, the affairs of R and L for himself and his family and the companies were his *alter ego* and that the transfer of assets from R to L was to put those assets beyond the reach of creditors. Leaving aside the arguments concerning the need to lift the corporate veil of R, we can focus on the claim by YL Ltd that it was injured by a conspiracy between R, L and Y. This conspiracy, according to the submission of YL Ltd, involved a breach of Y's fiduciary duty to R. The judge, Toulson J, accepted (at 884) that Y was a shadow director of R and that he owed a duty to R, and that the transfer of the funds from R to L was a clear breach of that duty. His Lordship relied on *Liquidator of West Mercia Safetywear v Dodd* in this regard. Toulson J denied that Y owed YL Ltd a direct fiduciary duty, but his Lordship did accept, following a reference to *West Mercia Safetywear* (which also included a reference to *Kinsela v Russell Kinsela Pty Ltd*), that where a director of an insolvent company acts in breach of a duty to the company by causing assets of the company to be transferred in disregard of the interests of its creditors, the director is answerable (at 885).

In *Facia Footwear Ltd (in administration) v Hinchliffe* [1998] 1 BCLC 218, FF Ltd was a company whose sole shareholder was X. X and Y were its directors. The company was party to certain arrangements with the F group of companies. The group had been assembled by X and Y. In June 1996 an administration order was made against FF Ltd. A few months later the administrators of FF Ltd commenced proceedings against X and Y for reimbursement of moneys alleged to have been paid improperly to third parties. The administrators alleged that because of the financial difficulties affecting the F group (including FF Ltd), X and Y had no realistic expectation that the payments, which had benefited the F group, could ever be repaid. X and Y argued that these payments had to be made or else the F group would have had to cease trading and that would have led to FF Ltd's demise. Also X and Y argued that they believed that the F group had a reasonable chance of surviving. The administrators sought summary judgment from the court. Sir Richard Scott V-C denied the application, but recognised that the administrators might succeed at a full hearing of the issues. His Lordship, importantly for our purposes, did find (at 228) that because of the parlous state of the finances of the F group, X and Y had to have regard for the interests of creditors. His Lordship acknowledged that the Australian case of *Kinsela v Russell Kinsela Pty Ltd*, the New Zealand case of *Nicholson v Permakraft (NZ) Ltd* (1985) 3 ACLC 453 and the English case of *West Mercia Safetywear* could be cited in support of the argument that the directors did owe a duty to take into account creditor interests.

In *Re Pantone 485 Ltd* [2002] 1 BCLC 266, the applicant liquidator failed before the High Court in a claim that the directors of the company in liquidation had disposed of company property without taking into account the interests of one of the creditors, an unsecured creditor entitled to priority in a distribution of the company's assets. However, Richard Field QC (sitting as a deputy High Court judge) acknowledged (at 286–287) that when a company was insolvent the directors had to have regard for the creditors' interests. The claim in this case was that the actions of the directors that were impugned failed to consider the priority creditor's interests. The judge's problem with the claim was that directors had a duty to make decisions, when their company was insolvent, while having regard for all of the general creditors, and not one, or a section, of the creditors. It was on this basis that the judge distinguished the case of *West Mercia Safetywear*.

Leslie Kosmin QC (sitting as a Deputy Judge of the High Court) in *Gwyer v London Wharf (Limehouse) Ltd* [2003] 2 BCLC 153; [2002] EWHC 2748 affirmed the principles laid down in *West Mercia Safetywear*, and said (at 181; [81]) that the directors of an insolvent company breached their duties to their company by not considering the interests of the creditors of the company when agreeing to a compromise over a legal action.

Most recently, the principles that have developed in the case law in England were applied in *Re MDA Investment Management Ltd* [2004] BPIR 75 at 102; [2003] EWHC 227 (Ch) at [70] by Park J.

Approaches in other jurisdictions

It is appropriate now to focus on what has happened in other jurisdictions where the duty has been held to exist, because it is clear from a study of the area that the Commonwealth and Irish courts have built upon earlier decisions in different jurisdictions. Some cases have been mentioned already.

Ireland

The first indications that Ireland might adopt a similar approach to that taken in the UK were given in the case of *Byrne v Shelbourne Football Club Ltd* (unreported, 8 February 1984, High Court and noted in Linnane, H, 'Directors' duties to creditors: the adoption of Kinsela in Irish law' (1995) 16 Co Law 319) when O'Hanlon J stated, in a dictum (and without approving of *Walker v Wimborne* or any other relevant judgments), that a company must consider what is best for its creditors before disposing of all of its property. In this case the company was insolvent, but the judge did not expressly limit what he had to say to insolvent companies.

The approach taken in Australia and England was openly embraced by both the Irish High Court and on appeal to the Supreme Court in the case of *Re Frederick Inns Ltd* [1991] ILRM 582, Irish HC, and affirmed at [1994] ILRM 387, Irish SC. In the former court, Lardner J said (at 589) that the approach taken in the cases of *Kinsela* and *West Mercia Safetywear* was 'consonant with the intent of Irish company legislation and . . . appropriate and applicable to insolvent companies in Irish law'. In the Supreme Court, Blayney J, in delivering the judgment of the court, said that when a company is insolvent, then the company has ceased to be the beneficial owner of the assets which it holds, and it cannot dispose of them without considering the interests of creditors ([1994] ILRM 387 at 396–397). The judges in both the High Court and the Supreme Court explicitly approved of the judgment in *Kinsela*. Subsequently, the High Court in *Jones v Gunn* [1997] 3 IR 1; [1997] 2 ILRM 245, after quoting parts of the judgments in *Re Frederick Inns Ltd*, adopted the same approach.

Australia

As discussed at the outset of the chapter, the responsibility under discussion has its genesis in Australia. And it is in this jurisdiction that the consideration and evaluation of the responsibility has equalled, or even exceeded, that conducted in the UK. So, some discussion of the most important Australian cases is worthwhile. I have already referred to perhaps the most important, namely *Kinsela v Russell Kinsela Pty Ltd*, because the comments of Street CJ have had a profound effect on the development of the case law generally in many jurisdictions, not least of all in the UK, and so apart from the occasional mention of it, I will not deal with it again. It is not intended to deal with all of the cases that have been decided on the issue.[19] In particular, reference will not be made to *Jeffree v NCSC* as that was discussed earlier.

19 Cases dealing with the issue that are not discussed in this context include: *Hooker Investments Pty Ltd v Email Ltd* (1986) 10 ACLR 443; *Grove v Flavel* (1986) 11 ACLR 161; *Galladin v Aimnorth Pty Ltd* (1993) 11 ACSR 23.

It was the 1980s before we saw Australian courts taking up the *Walker v Wimborne* dictum. Notwithstanding the success of proceedings against directors in *Kinsela*, in subsequent cases that have been reported while courts have recognised the existence of the duty, proceedings have not been successful on many occasions.[20] Perhaps this is due to the fact that where directors have clearly breached their duty they have not sought to defend actions to the point of trial. Certainly in the cases where directors have succeeded there has been some doubt about the financial stability of the company.

Perhaps one of the most important cases of the 1980s was the decision of the Full Court of the Supreme Court of South Australia in *Grove v Flavel* (1986) 11 ACLR 161. Importantly, for our purposes, Jacobs J, in giving the leading judgment, said that there was nothing in the comments of Mason J in *Walker* that limited the triggering of the duty to the insolvency of the company (at 167). It would seem that some have suggested that Jacobs J was advocating that directors owed a direct duty to creditors. With respect, it is submitted that the judgment does not suggest this, and the issue is taken up in Chapter 15.

In *Re New World Alliance Pty Ltd* (1994) 122 ALR 531; 51 FCR 425 the case was mainly based on an allegation that the directors against whom proceedings had been brought were in breach of s 592 of the Corporations Law, which outlawed insolvent trading, similar to wrongful trading under s 214 of the Insolvency Act 1986 in the UK or reckless trading in Ireland. However, the applicant had amended the pleadings to include a claim that the directors had breached their duties because they had not taken into account creditors' interests. This claim was the subject of only brief argument before the court. The judge, Gummow J, said (at 550; 444–445) that the duty owed to creditors provides for a limitation on the right of shareholders to ratify breaches of duties owed to the company, because when the duty to take into account creditor interests arises the creditors are regarded as having a direct interest in the company. His Honour noted (at 550; 445) that the duty is one of imperfect obligation owed to creditors and this cannot be enforced by creditors themselves. They have to rely upon a liquidator taking action.

In *Linton v Telnet Pty Ltd* (1999) 30 ACSR 465, the liquidator of T brought an action against L, the wife of one of the company's directors, claiming that she, L, held a house on trust for the company because some of the purchase price was paid with cheques drawn on T, in August 1992. The allegation was that L's husband who gave the cheques to L was, in doing so, in breach of his fiduciary duty to T. It had been agreed by the directors that the sum represented by the cheques was part of an interest-free loan to L's

---

20 There are instances of successes against directors in the following cases: *Ring v Sutton* (1980) 5 ACLR 546; *Jeffree v NCSC* (1989) 7 ACLC 556; 15 ACLR 217; *Galladin v Aimnorth Pty Ltd* (1993) 11 ACSR 23.

husband. At first instance, Hulme J of the New South Wales Supreme Court found for the liquidator on the basis, *inter alia*, that as L's husband was a bankrupt, he would have little prospect of repaying the loan, and the giving of an unsecured loan was a breach of duty. L appealed to the New South Wales Court of Appeal, which upheld the appeal. What seemed to be of significance for the Court of Appeal was the fact that the figures for the group of which T was a part were, at June 1992, reasonably healthy and sales and gross profits in fact increased in 1993 (at 475), so at the time of the giving of the cheques L's husband did not need to consider the interests of the creditors. Notwithstanding this decision, which was obviously based on the evidence that was before the court below, the court clearly accepted that directors owed a duty to their company to take into account creditor interests when their company is insolvent.

The only Australian High Court (the highest court in the Australian legal system) case that has considered the responsibility since *Walker v Wimborne* is *Spies v The Queen* (2000) 201 CLR 603; (2000) 173 ALR 529; [2000] HCA 43. The case did not turn on whether directors owed the responsibility that we are considering, but the High Court provided some helpful dicta. The court was called upon to consider a criminal charge laid against a director of an Australian company, namely that he was in breach of s 176A of the Crimes Act of New South Wales. This section provided that it was an offence for a director of a body corporate to intend to defraud or cheat the body corporate or any person in his or her dealings with the body corporate. Alternatively the director was charged with being in breach of s 229(4) of the Companies Code (NSW) because he was an officer of a corporation who made improper use of his position to gain an advantage for himself or cause detriment to the corporation. The greater part of the High Court judgment is not relevant to our purposes here. But in the course of the judgment the court considered whether the director could be in breach of a duty to creditors. The court denied (at [93]–[95]) that directors owe an independent duty to creditors, an issue taken up in Chapter 15. However, a majority of judges (Gaudron, McHugh, Gummow and Hayne JJ) appeared to approve of the comments of Gummow J, when he was a judge of the Federal Court, provided in *Re New World Alliance Pty Ltd*. While the comments of the judges of the High Court were clearly *obiter*, and they were very brief, it is most likely they will be of very persuasive force.[21]

Subsequent to *Spies*, two Western Australian cases, *The Bell Group Ltd (in liq) v Westpac Banking Corporation* [2001] WASC 315 and *Geneva Finance Ltd v Resource & Industry Ltd* (2002) 20 ACLC 1427, a Victorian case, *Johnson Matthey (Aust) Pty Ltd v Dascorp Pty Ltd* [2003] VSC 291 and a

---

21 One writer has argued that the comments of the judges were precipitated by the inappropriate use on the part of the prosecution of a submission that the director had breached his duty: *op. cit.* McConvill, fn 14 above at 9 and 11.

New South Wales case, *Emanuel Management Pty Ltd v Fosters Brewing Group* (2003) 178 *Federal Law Reports* 1, have followed the *obiter* comments in *Spies*.

New Zealand

The leading case in New Zealand is *Nicholson v Permakraft (NZ) Ltd* (1985) 3 ACLC 453, a decision of the Court of Appeal. In this case P Ltd held shares in two companies. The shares in P Ltd were nearly all held by three persons. P Ltd experienced liquidity problems and in mid-1975 a reconstruction plan that was proposed involved the incorporation of a new company that would acquire nearly all of the shares of P Ltd and the companies in which it held shares (X and Y). The new company, Z Ltd, was to purchase the land and buildings owned by P Ltd at valuation, as well as the shares P Ltd had in X and Y. The shareholders of P Ltd would be paid a dividend from the funds paid to P Ltd. Z Ltd would charge P Ltd rent for the use of its former buildings. This plan was put into effect. In mid-1976 P Ltd encountered difficulties, consistent with those experienced by the industry generally, and the bank put in receivers and eventually the company went into liquidation. The liquidator commenced an action against the shareholders of P Ltd in order to recover the dividend that was paid to them. At first instance, the directors were found to be in breach of duty. The shareholders successfully appealed. All three members of the Court of Appeal held that when a company is insolvent, the directors owe a duty to take into account creditor interests. The leading judgment was given by Cooke J, and his Lordship's comments were the most radical of all members of the court. Some of the judge's comments are mentioned, and discussed in detail, in later chapters. Suffice it to say at present that while his Lordship acknowledged that directors could owe duties to creditors, he did not think that at the time of the restructuring the directors in this case owed a duty to consider creditor interests. Richardson J agreed with the result that Cooke J came to, and while he agreed with the judgment of Cooke J, he preferred not to give any opinion on the nature and scope of duties owed to creditors (at 463).

In *Hilton International Ltd v Hilton* [1989] 1 NZLR 442, Tipping J had an opportunity of not only considering the judgments given in *Permakraft*, but also the comments of Lord Templeman in *Winkworth*. He clearly followed what Cooke J had to say (at 474) and stated that the actions of directors were, in this area, to be assessed on objective grounds (474–476).

Canada

Until quite recent times, directors in Canada have not had to be concerned about the responsibility under discussion here. Directors owed no duty to consider creditor interests. Claims by creditors against the actions of said companies to prejudice their interests have tended to rely on the oppression remedy found in s 241(2)(c) of the Canadian Business Corporations Act,[22] a provision discussed in detail in Chapter 16. This provides that the court is able to give a remedy if the directors' powers have been exercised 'in a manner that is oppressive or unfairly prejudicial to or unfairly disregards the interests of any security holder, *creditor*, director or officer' (my emphasis). Other Commonwealth jurisdictions provide for an oppression remedy, but do not permit creditors to invoke it; use of the remedy is generally limited to shareholders.[23]

So, notwithstanding the calls of some academics,[24] until the late 1990s Canadian cases did not impose on company directors obligations to creditors. Although Blair J in the Ontario Court of Justice (General Division) in the case of *Sidaplex-Plastic Supplies Inc v Elta Group Inc* (1998) 40 OR (3d) 563 suggested that the interests of creditors ought not to be disregarded in certain circumstances,[25] it was not until the decision of Greenberg J of the Quebec Superior Court (Bankruptcy and Insolvency Division) in *Peoples Department Stores v Wise* [1998] QJ No 3571, that a court accepted the fact that directors have a duty to creditors when their company is insolvent or in the vicinity of insolvency. In this case W company acquired P company from M company. Three brothers were the majority shareholders of W and the only directors of P. The brothers sought to run W and P jointly, but this caused significant problems for both companies, resulting in the companies' inventory records becoming more and more incorrect. On the recommendation of a senior manager who was employed by both P and W, the brothers embraced a joint stock procurement policy, involving the two companies dividing responsibility for purchasing stock. Within ten months both companies were insolvent and entered bankruptcy. The trustee of P filed proceedings against the brothers. One of the grounds for the trustee's claim was that the brothers had breached their duties by favouring the interests of W over those of P, and this action had ultimately prejudiced P's creditors. The judge, Greenberg J, found for the trustee and awarded C$4.4 million to the trustee. His Honour referred in detail to many of the Commonwealth cases that supported the fact that directors are required to take into account creditors' interests at certain times in the life of a company, and he was of the opinion (at [200]) that Canadian corporate law should follow the lead given elsewhere in the Commonwealth. In fact the judgment of Greenberg J could be seen as going further than decisions in other jurisdictions in that he accepted the notion that directors had a direct duty to creditors. This is not surprising when one notes that the judge quoted, with apparent approval

---

22 For a recent example, see *Re Sidaplex-Plastic Suppliers Inc* (1998) 40 OR (3d) 563, Ontario Court of Appeal.

23 For instance, see Companies Act 1985 (UK), s 459.

24 For example, Ziegel, J, 'Creditors as corporate stakeholders: the quiet revolution – an Anglo-Canadian perspective' (1993) 43 *University of Toronto Law Journal* 511.

25 But ultimately the judge relied on the oppression provision in s 241(2)(c) of the Canadian Business Corporations Act.

(at [197]), the dictum of Lord Templeman in *Winkworth v Edward Baron Development*.[26]

A year after *Peoples Department Stores* the Superior Court of Justice in Ontario decided *Canbook Distribution Corporation v Borins* (1999) 45 OR (3d) 565. In this case, Ground J quoted the judgment in *Peoples Department Stores* extensively and came to the same conclusion as Greenberg J. In *Canbook Distribution*, the learned judge was faced with an application for the dismissal of a claim by a creditor of a bankrupt company against the company's directors. The creditor sued in both its capacity as an assignee of the trustee in bankruptcy of the bankrupt company, and as a creditor of the company. The directors, who applied for dismissal of the claim, argued, *inter ali-*, that the creditor could not bring a claim in the capacities in which it purported to act. The creditor's argument was that it could bring a claim against the directors of its debtor company where the directors caused the company to enter into a transaction that was prejudicial to the interests of creditors (at [10]). Ground J accepted this argument and was of the opinion (at [16]) that: 'Canadian law was moving in the direction of recognizing such fiduciary duty, particularly in situations where the corporation was insolvent when it entered into the challenged transaction or the challenged transaction rendered the corporation insolvent.' In *Millgate Financial Corporation Ltd v BCED Holdings Ltd* 2003 CanLII 39497, Ontario SC, Cullity J of the Ontario Superior Court of Justice opined (at [89]) that directors had to consider creditors' interests when the company 'is insolvent, or near insolvent, or where the impugned transactions place the corporation's solvency in jeopardy'.

The Quebec Court of Appeal heard an appeal from the decision of Greenberg J in *Peoples Department Stores*. The court allowed the appeal of the directors. It doubted whether the duty discussed by Greenberg J did in fact apply ([2003] Q J No 505 (Montreal Registry) (5 February 2003) at [97]).[27] The court opined that one cannot equate the duty owed to the company, and to act in its best interests, with the interests of creditors, when the company is insolvent or in the vicinity of insolvency. The court said that directors are to have the interests of shareholders in view, and that it is for Parliament to change this and it was not the role of the courts.

The reaction of the trustee to the decision of the Quebec Court of Appeal was to appeal to the Supreme Court of Canada. The principal issue of the appeal, according to the Court, was whether the directors of a company owed a duty to creditors. The Court rejected the appeal and found for the directors on all grounds, including holding that the directors did not owe any duty to creditors ([2004] SCC 68; (2004) 244 DLR (4th) 564). Major and Deschamps

---

26 See above at pp 154–155.

27 For a discussion of the Court of Appeal's judgment, see Hemraj, M, 'Directors owe no duty to creditors: *Peoples Department Stores v Wise Stores Inc*' (2005) 26 Co Law 31.

JJ, in delivering the judgment of the Court, discussed the nature of fiduciary duties and said that in discharging their fiduciary duties, directors must act honestly and in good faith with a view to the best interests of the company (at [39]). And, because in this case there was no fraud or dishonesty in what the directors did, a point acknowledged by Greenberg J, they could not be said to have breached their fiduciary duty to the company (at [40]). The Court said that directors had a duty to act in the best interests of the corporation and that 'best interests of the corporation' meant acting to maximise the value of the corporation. Major and Deschamps JJ went on to say (at [42]–[43]):

> But if they [the directors] observe a decent respect for other interests lying beyond those of the company's shareholders in the strict sense, that will not . . . leave directors open to the charge that they have failed in their fiduciary duty to the company . . . We accept as an accurate state- ment of law that in determining whether they are acting with a view to the best interests of the corporation it may be legitimate, given all the circumstances of a given case, for the board of directors to consider, *inter ali- , the interests of the shareholders, employees, suppliers, creditors, consumers, governments and the environment . . . At all time, directors and officers owe their fiduciary duties to the corporation. The interests of the corporation are not to be confused with the interests of the creditors or those of any other stakeholders.

This statement indicates that in determining whether directors have acted in the best interests of the company, it might be appropriate for the directors to take into account the interests of creditors, but there is no duty owed exclusively to creditors, and this is even the case when a company is in the vicinity of insolvency (at [46]). Yet, the court did go on to say (at [47]) that when a company's financial position has deteriorated, directors should seek to act in such a way as to create a ' "better" corporation', which involves not favouring any one group of stakeholders. This decision is discussed further in Chapter 15.

At first blush the decision of the Supreme Court of Canada appears to deal a blow against the use of proceedings initiated against directors who allegedly fail in their responsibility to creditors. However, when looking more closely at the decision, that is not the case. On the contrary, it is contended that the decision is generally supportive of the line of case law that has developed in the UK and many other countries. Essentially, the Court was affirming that which is the prevailing approach in cases in other jurisdictions where dir- ectors are said to have an obligation to creditors where their company is in financial difficulty. It is to be recalled that the Court unequivocally held that directors have a fiduciary duty to their company. This, according to the judg- ment, meant that there could be no duty owed to the creditors. But such a view is not inconsistent with the leading English authorities, such as the Court of Appeal case of *West Mercia Safetywear Ltd v Dodd*. This latter case, and most of the cases decided on this issue[28] and either mentioned or discussed earlier in the chapter, have clearly stated that directors only owe a duty to the company, but that this involves taking into account creditor interests when the company is in some form of financial strife. What the Canadian decision has done, is simply to affirm the fact that no direct duty is owed to creditors by directors. The Court also found that, on the evidence, the directors had not failed to fulfil their fiduciary duty to the company.

The central aspect of the whole *Peoples Department Stores* litigation was based on an argument that the directors breached their duties to their company's creditors, that is, the directors owed a direct duty to creditors. It is regrettable that the Supreme Court did not, in its judgment, point out that the Commonwealth case law relied on by Greenberg J does not generally support the proposition that Greenberg J was willing to accept, namely that directors owe a fiduciary duty to creditors. If, however, the argument mounted in this litigation had been that the directors breached their duty to their company in failing to consider creditor interests, then while the Supreme Court would, it would seem, on the evidence still have found for the directors, it might have accepted the general argument as valid in law. As a result, it is submitted that Canadian trustees might still successfully argue a breach of duty to consider creditor interests in the future; *Peoples Department Stores* does not pre-empt that argument being legitimately put. More importantly, the decision does not cast doubts on the jurisprudence developed in the UK, other Commonwealth jurisdictions and Ireland. At its broadest, the decision merely puts a further nail in the coffin of the argument that directors owe direct duties to creditors when their company is in financial difficulty, a view expressly accepted by some courts (such as *Spies v The Queen*).

United States

Directors in the United States have been found to be liable when they have not considered creditor interests,[29] although it is fair to say that in the United States the jurisprudence has evolved in a different way than in the British Commonwealth and Ireland. Action has been able to be taken in the United States through two avenues. The first avenue that is available in some states,

---

28 Such as: *Nicholson v Permakraft (NZ) Ltd* (1985) 3 ACLC 453; *Kinsela v Russell Kinsela Pty Ltd* (1986) 4 ACLC 215; *Re Frederick Inns Ltd* [1991] ILRM 582, Irish HC, and affirmed at [1994] ILRM 387, Irish SC; *Yukong Lines Ltd of Korea v Rendsburg Investments Corporation* [1998] BCC 870; *Spies v The Queen* (2000) 201 CLR 603; (2000) 173 ALR 529; [2000] HCA 43; *Gwyer v London Wharf (Limehouse) Ltd* [2003] 2 BCLC 153; [2002] EWHC 2748; *Re MDA Investment Management Ltd* [2004] BPIR 75; [2003] EWHC 227 (Ch).

29 For example, *Revlon Inc v MacAndrews and Forbes Holdings Inc* 506 A 2d 173 at 179 (1986); *Polk v Good* 507 A 2d (1986); *Geyer v Ingersoll Publications Co* 621 A 2d 784 (1992); *Credit Lyonnais Bank Nederland NV v Pathe Communications Corp* 1991 (Delaware Chancery Court), LEXIS 215; (1992) 17 *Delaware Journal of Corporate Law* 1099.

such as New York,[30] is reliance on what is known as 'the trust fund doctrine'.[31] This was given birth to in the case of *Wood v Drummer* (1824) 30 F Cas 935 and provides that where a company is insolvent, the assets of a company represent a trust fund that must be retained for the creditors, who have the first claim on the assets. The Delaware Supreme Court said in *Bovay v H M Byllesby & Co* (1944) 38 A 2d 808, 813 that: 'An insolvent corporation is civilly dead in the sense that its property may be administered in equity as a trust fund for the benefit of creditors.' The notion is based on the idea that a fiduciary relationship exists between directors and creditors, and that a quasi-trust relationship arises.[32] The Delaware Chancery Court stated in *MacKenzie Oil Co v Omar Oil & Gas Co* (1923) 120 A 852 at 853: 'The assets of a corporation upon the event of insolvency may be regarded by creditors and stockholders as impressed with somewhat of the nature of a trust to be administered for their benefit.' What appears to be a modern application of the trust fund doctrine can be seen in the Florida case of *Miramar Resources Inc v Shultz* (1997) 208 BR 723, 729–730.

If company property is regarded as a trust fund, it could be followed into the hands of third parties who had notice of the trust.[33] The doctrine accords with the comments in a number of cases, as well as academic writings, to the effect that when a company is in financial difficulty the creditors are the residual claimants to the company's assets.[34] This principle is accepted in UK law in part, in that companies are not permitted to reduce capital without court approval, but the creditors are not said to be the beneficiaries of the fund of capital.

It must be said that the trust fund doctrine has sparked a reasonable amount of controversy and has led one commentator to say that 'perhaps no concept has created as much confusion in the field of corporate law'.[35] Others

---

30 For example, see *New York Credit Men's Adjustment Bureau Inc v Weiss* (1953) 110 NE 2d 397.

31 For a discussion of the doctrine, see Hunt, E, 'The trust fund theory and some substitutes for it' (1902) 12 Yale L J 63; Norton, J, 'Relationship of shareholders to corporate creditors upon dissolution: nature and implications of the "trust fund" doctrine of corporate assets' (1975) 30 *The Business Lawyer* 106; Shaffer, A, 'Corporate fiduciary – insolvent: the fiduciary relationship your corporate law professor (should have) warned you about' (2000) 8 ABI Law Rev 479 at 543–550.

32 *Whitfield v Kern* 192 A 48 (1937). The US Supreme Court affirmed the principle in *Pepper v Litton* 308 US 295 (1939). There is English authority to the effect that directors are not trustees for the creditors: *Re Wincham Shipbuilding Boiler & Salt Co* (1878) 9 Ch D 322.

33 *Wood v Drummer* (1824) 30 F Cas 935.

34 For example, Schwarcz, S, 'Rethinking a corporation's obligations to creditors' (1996) 17 *Cardozo Law Review* 647 at 668. This seems to be what was being said in the English case of *Brady v Brady* (1988) 3 BCC 535.

35 Beveridge, N, 'Does a corporation's board of directors owe a fiduciary duty to its creditors?' (1994) 25 *St Mary's Law Journal* 589 at 607.

have attacked it for its inconsistency,[36] and, generally speaking, the doctrine has not met with much academic support.[37] It is uncertain whether the doctrine applies in the foremost jurisdiction in the US, as far as corporate law is concerned, Delaware.[38]

Second, during the past ten years or so, some courts have been willing to find that directors have to consider creditors when their companies are either in the vicinity of insolvency or insolvent, and a trustee of a company that has entered Chapter 7 bankruptcy (liquidation) is allowed to bring suit against directors that did not consider creditors' interests at the appropriate time. *Credit Lyonnais Bank Nederland, NV v Pathe Communications Corp* 1991 Del Ch WL 277613; LEXIS 215; (1992) 17 *Delaware Journal of Corporate Law* 1099, is the classic case on this issue. It has similarities to many of the decisions decided in the UK and elsewhere in the Commonwealth. In *Credit Lyonnais*, Chancellor Allen of the Delaware Court of Chancery said that: 'At least where a corporation is operating in the vicinity of insolvency, a board of directors is not merely the agent of the residual risk bearers [the shareholders], but owes its duty to the corporate enterprise.' In referring to the enterprise the Chancellor appears to mean the community of interests that sustain the company. Also, the judge was moving the point of when duties arise to an earlier point, for previously the time when a duty arose was when insolvency occurred. In referring to the corporate enterprise the judge was meaning 'the corporation's long-term wealth creating capacity'. It was accepted that this included the creditors' interests. The case is discussed again in Chapter 14 when I consider how directors are to function when they are subject to the responsibility to creditors. Some United States' courts that have held that creditors are owed consideration by directors, and they have permitted creditors, on occasions, to take direct action against directors,[39] something which Commonwealth courts have generally not permitted.

We probably need to include in our general consideration of US law the fact that over half of the states have enacted what are known as 'constituency statutes'.[40] These provide that directors may consider the interests of

---

36 Varallo, G, and Finkelstein, J, 'Fiduciary obligations of directors of the financially troubled company' (1992) 48 *The Business Lawyer* 239 at 251.

37 For example, see Lipson, J, 'Directors' duties to creditors: volition, cognition, exit and the financially distressed corporation' (2003) 50 UCLA L Rev 1189 at 1206.

38 *Op. cit.* fn 36 above at 246.

39 For example, see *Geyer v Ingersoll Publications Co* 621 A 2d 784 (1992).

40 For example, Pennsylvania (the first to enact), New York, Wisconsin, Georgia, Illinois, Iowa, Massachusetts, Minnesota, Nebraska, New Jersey. A full list is set out by Miller, H, 'Corporate governance in Chapter 11: the fiduciary relationship between directors and stockholder of solvent and insolvent corporations' (1993) 23 *Seton Hall Law Review* 1466 at 1478, n 49 and Mitchell, L, 'A theoretical and practical framework for enforcing constituency statutes' (1992) 70 *Texas Law Review* 579 at 579, n 1.

constituencies (enumerated in the statutes[41]), other than shareholders, when they make corporate decisions. These statutes provide that management may consider the interests of a list of constituents in the company, and, effectively, they question whether directors should be considering shareholders' rights to the exclusion of the rights of other stakeholders. It should be added that these statutes apply, for the most part, only in takeover situations and other instances where control is at issue.

The American jurisprudence and the issues that it raises, while influencing the discussions in this book, are too complex to discuss here. But from time to time the American cases, and the theoretical debate that has emanated from that jurisdiction, will be adverted to and discussed.

The duty considered in the course of law reform in the UK

In the past eight or so years there has been significant discussion concerning wholesale amendment of the Companies Act, which culminated in the introduction of the Company Law Reform Bill into Parliament in November 2005. A prime issue in that discussion has been changes to the law as it affects the duties owed by directors.

The Company Law Review Steering Group

In March 1998 the Department of Trade and Industry commissioned a review that was to include proposals for the reform of UK company law in order to address a modern world.[42] This review was to be the most wide-ranging since the middle of the nineteenth century and was established to formulate a framework of company law which 'facilitates enterprise and promotes transparency and fair-dealing';[43] it was to be overseen by a Steering Group that has become known as the Company Law Review Steering Group (CLRSG). The CLRSG formulated the view that in legislation regulating companies there should be a statement of principles concerning duties of directors. The CLRSG rejected (provisionally), at one stage, the idea of including, in this statement of principles a requirement that directors must have regard for creditor interests.[44] One of the primary reasons for this view was that a statement of principles including mention of placing a responsibility on directors to creditors might 'cut across section 214 of the Insolvency

---

41 This is except for Arizona where directors are required simply to consider long-term as well as short-term interests of the company (Arizona Revised Statute Ann, s 10–1202(A) (1987)).

42 Company Law Review, *Modern Company Law For a Competitive Economy*, 1998, London: DTI, 1.

43 *Ibid*, Foreword.

44 *Modern Company Law for a Competitive Economy: Developing the Framework*, 2000, London: DTI, at para 3.73.

Act 1986' (the wrongful trading provision).[45] In Chapter 12 I seek to explain that a responsibility to creditors at common law does not cut across s 214, but merely supplements the provision to the advantage of liquidators and other office-holders. Nevertheless, by the time that the CLRSG published its Final Report on 26 July 2001, the majority of the group had changed its mind, certainly[46] in relation to the situation where insolvency threatens a company. In a relatively long discussion on the topic, the CLRSG said, *inter alia*, that:

> In providing a high level statement of directors' duties, it is important to draw to directors' attention that different factors may need to be taken into consideration where the company is insolvent or threatened by insolvency. To do so would risk misleading directors by omitting an important part of the overall picture.[47]

The CLRSG went on to observe, adroitly, it is respectfully submitted, that as a company's situation becomes more desperate financially:

> . . . the normal synergy between the interests of members, who seek the preservation and enhancement of the assets, and of creditors, whose interests are protected by that process [insolvency], progressively disappears. As the margin of assets reduces, so the incentive on directors to avoid risky strategies which endanger the assets of members also reduces; the worse the situation gets, the less members have to lose and the more one-sided the case becomes for supporting risky, perhaps desperate, strategies.[48]

The first White Paper

In July 2002 the government, in response to the Final Report of the CLRSG, published a White Paper, 'Modernising Company Law'.[49] In Volume 1 of the White Paper the government addressed the issue of directors having some responsibility to consider the interests of their companies' creditors when financial distress occurs. The White Paper stated that the government had concluded that the weight of the argument favoured the exclusion of any duties to creditors in the statutory statement envisaged by the CLRSG.[50] The government maintained that if there was a statement of duties to creditors in the statute then it would be incumbent on directors to make finely balanced judgments and they might err on the side of caution because of fear of

---

45 *Ibid* at para 3.72.
46 *Modern Company Law for a Competitive Economy: Final Report* Vol 1, 2001, London: DTI at para 3.13.
47 *Ibid* at para 3.12.   48 *Ibid* at para 3.15.   49 Cm 5553-1, TSO, July 2002.
50 *Op. cit.* fn 46 above at para 3.10.

personal liability, and this would be inconsistent with the rescue culture which the government was trying to foster.[51] It is respectfully submitted that this is not a convincing argument. First, directors might be as equally cautious because of fear of being held liable for wrongful trading as they would for fear of being held liable for failing to take into account creditor interests, and clearly the government is not contemplating the repeal of s 214 of the Insolvency Act.

Second, it is submitted that if directors were required to consider creditor interests, this could actually enhance the rescue culture. If a company is in some financial difficulty and its directors are aware of this and concerned that they might be held liable for creditor losses if they embraced certain actions, the prudent way out for them is to appoint an administrator. If this occurred, the directors would be safe from attack and a rescue strategy could be considered in the relative safety of administration if it was thought that the company could be saved. It is highly questionable whether companies which are in a state of needing to be rescued should continue to be run by the directors without some sort of professional and independent assistance. If directors, knowing that their company was embarrassed financially, ignored creditor interests and took risks this could well see the collapse of the company, and this would be counter to the government's desire for the strengthening of the rescue culture.

The second White Paper

Little or nothing happened following the publication of the White Paper in 2002. In March 2005 the government published a second White Paper, titled 'Company Law Reform',[52] that was said to build closely on the work of the CLRSG and the 2002 White Paper. *Inter alia*, as far as the changes to be effected in relation to directors, the new White Paper saw the duties of directors being included in the proposed sections of a new Act, rather than being placed in a Schedule, which had been the strategy employed by both the Final Report[53] of the CLRSG and the White Paper of 2002. Importantly, while the government did not propose to codify a duty to creditors, it did state in the draft Company Law Reform Bill that it put forward that the duty imposed on directors to promote the success of the company for the benefit of its members 'has effect subject to any enactment or rule of law requiring directors, in certain circumstances, to consider or act in the interests of creditors of the company' (cl B3(4)). In its explanatory notes the government stated that this provision 'preserves the current legal position that, when the company is insolvent or is nearing insolvency, the interests of the members should be supplemented, or even replaced, by those of the creditors' (cl B19).

---

51 *Ibid* at para 3.11.   52 Cm 6456.
53 Final Report, vol I, Annex C, 2001, cl 17 and Sched 2 of a draft Bill.

It is regrettable that the government has adopted the above view. If the government had supported the final proposal of the CLRSG, that would have reinforced the responsibility of directors to creditors. As it is at the moment, directors are not made clearly aware of their responsibilities which presently exist at common law. If they were then it might cause them to be more prudent when their company is confronted with financial difficulties. Also, any statement in legislation could give some indications when the responsibility of directors would arise, thereby dealing with one of the major problems facing directors at present (and addressed in Chapter 13). The government has not seen what the courts have seen, and that is that there is significant danger for creditors if directors of a company are able to externalise the cost of its debt.

Notwithstanding the fact that any responsibility of directors to creditors appears to be left to the common law, those who are suppliers and creditors of companies might find some solace from the fact that directors are required, in fulfilling their duty to act in such a way as to promote the success of the company for the benefit of its members as a whole, to take account, *inter alia*, of any need of the company to foster its business relationships with suppliers (cl B3(3)). However, this does not stop a company from running up debts with a supplier and then ditching the supplier and moving on to some other supplier to establish a new relationship. If this occurs then the original supplier has no alternative but to sue the company for the amount owed or petition for either administration or liquidation of the company. These actions are fraught with disadvantages, not least being that the company is wound up with few assets and the supplier gets little or nothing back.

Company Law Reform Bill

On 1 November 2005, the Company Law Reform Bill was introduced into the House of Lords. Clause B3 in the draft Bill included with the Second White Paper has now essentially become cl 156. Again, the government confirmed in the 'Guidance to Key Clauses', released with the Bill, that the law dealing with directors' duties to take into account creditors' interests should not be subject to legislation, but allowed to develop at common law (cl 70). Again, it is stated (in cl 156(4)) that the obligation to run the company in such a way as to benefit the members is excepted in cases where the law requires directors to take into account creditors' interests. The Bill was amended in the House of Lords and went to the House of Commons in May 2006. The Bill has been re-named as the Companies Bill 2006 and been subject to further amendment in the Commons. As it stood in July 2006 the Bill retains the provision excepting directors from running the business so as to benefit the members and for creditor interests to be considered in certain circumstances (Companies Bill 2006, clause 173(4)).

Conclusion

An examination of the recent case law demonstrates that while most courts have resisted the view that directors owe an independent duty to creditors of their companies, they have confirmed that directors do owe a duty to their companies to take into account the interests of creditors when companies are in some form of financial difficulty. A significant jurisprudence has developed in the UK, several Commonwealth jurisdictions and Ireland. The law is such that the corporate interest is identified with the particular interests of the corporate constituency most prejudiced by the action that is claimed to be a breach.[54]

It appears that liquidators, administrators and receivers who wish to proceed against directors for failing to consider creditor interests will continue to have to rely on this case law, as the government has stated clearly that it has significant reservations about including any reference to consider creditor interests in a revamped Companies Act. The fact that the government has taken this view is to be regretted, for while it is acknowledged that a responsibility of the kind we are considering here requires directors to make careful judgments, and there are difficulties with determining when a duty should arise, a duty to consider the interests of one's company's creditors is something that is warranted, an issue that is discussed in detail in Chapter 19, and, in the words of the CLRSG (expressing the views of some members of the Group), 'the common law rule is soundly based'.[55] In any event, as there is a responsibility imposed on creditors at common law to consider creditor interests, it might be appropriate, and arguably fairer, that it be brought to directors' attention in legislation.

The following chapters go on to define the duty and to examine its parameters.

---

54 *Op. cit.* Grantham, fn 8 above at 14.   55 *Op. cit.* fn 46 above at para 3.20.

12 The duty to creditors: nature, rationale and need

Introduction

This chapter first examines the nature of, and rationale for, the duty that directors have to consider the interests of creditors. But the largest part of the chapter is concerned with a consideration of whether, given the existence of the statutory claims of fraudulent trading and wrongful trading, as well as the existence of provisions in the Insolvency Act 1986 that allow for the adjustment of preferential transfers and transactions at an undervalue, and the avoidance of transactions intended to defraud creditors, there is any need for a duty to creditors.

The nature of the duty

There is a debate as to whether directors owe an independent duty to creditors when the duty is said to arise,[1] or the duty is owed to the company and as part of discharging that duty, the law requires directors to consider the interests of creditors. Whether the former is correct or not is a matter discussed in detail in Chapter 15. For the purposes of this chapter it matters not which of these positions is taken, although if the latter represents the state of the law, which I think that it does, then the duty might better be explained as an imperfect obligation[2] as creditors are unable, on this approach, to enforce a breach of the so-called duty.

In any event the duty is of a fiduciary nature. It is outside the scope of the book to consider what a fiduciary duty is and involves,[3] but briefly one can

---

1 See Chapter 13 for a discussion of the circumstances that lead to the duty arising.
2 See *Re New World Alliance Pty Ltd; Sycotex Pty Ltd v Baseler* (1994) 51 FCR 425 at 444–445; (1994) 122 ALR 531 at 550 (Aust Fed Ct); Heydon, J, 'Directors' duties and the company's interests' in Finn, P D (ed), *Equity and Commercial Relationships*, 1987, Sydney: Law Book Co, p 131.
3 See, for example, Hannigan, B, *Company Law*, 2003, London: LexisNexis, pp 225–295; Davies, P, *Gower and Davies' Principles of Modern Company Law*, 7th edn, 2003, London: Sweet and Maxwell, pp 380–423.

say that it is a duty of loyalty and good faith (*Bristol and West Building Society v Mothew* [1998] 1 Ch 1 at 18; [1996] 4 All ER 698, 711–712, CA). A duty of loyalty in the context of a company mandates that a director subordinates his or her interests to that of the company. According to Millett LJ in *Bristol and West Building Society v Mothew*, 'the principal is entitled to the single-minded loyalty of his fiduciary ... he may not act ... for the benefit of a third person without the informed consent of his principal' (at All ER 711–712). Cooke J of the New Zealand Court of Appeal in *Nicholson v Permakraft (NZ) Ltd* (1985) 3 ACLC 453 went as far as saying that if directors were to make payments that prejudiced the current or continuing creditors, when directors knew or ought to have known of the likelihood of prejudice, then this constitutes misfeasance (at 460), because the action would be a breach of duty and so proceedings could be commenced pursuant to s 212 of the Insolvency Act.

Unlike most protections given to creditors, but like the wrongful trading provision in the Insolvency Act 1986 (s 214), the duty imposes personal liability on the directors of the company. The benefit of this is, of course, if the company ends up in insolvent liquidation there is a chance that some money can be recouped from the directors. While the imposition of the duty places directors under the threat of legal proceedings in the future, it does permit them to exercise their discretion, if their company is financially distressed, to make decisions that favour, or at least do not prejudice, the creditors, without being open to the charge of not acting in the best interests of the members.

Perhaps the most controversial aspect of the duty is its *ex post* nature. At the time of entering into credit arrangements the directors are not subject to the duty. They only become subject to it at some time after the contracts have been finalised. It is fair to say that while creditors might have considered, and even raised the issue of management responsibilities, during the course of negotiations, few creditors will have required any terms in the credit contract, such as the inclusion of a negative pledge, to address what management does or does not do. It might be thought to be unfair for directors to be held liable for actions that are not covered by the credit contract,[4] and that their conduct could be reviewed by a court at some point down the track. Some commentators have even expressed doubts as to whether courts are capable of evaluating the conduct of directors.[5] This point warrants consideration and is addressed in Chapter 19. Suffice it to say at present, the law does not refrain, in other respects, from imposing responsibility *ex post*. For example, the

---

4   Some might argue that it also represents an illegitimate transfer of wealth from shareholders to creditors.

5   For example, see Easterbrook, F, and Fischel, D, *The Economic Structure of Company Law* 1991, Harvard University Press: Cambridge, Mass, p 98; Branson, D, *Corporate Governance*, 1993, Michie & Co: Charlottesville, p 339; Wishart, D, *Company Law in Context* 1994, OUP: Auckland, p 253.

power to adjust preferential transfers, under s 239 of the Insolvency Act 1986, when a company is in administration or liquidation, is one of a number of powers that invokes such a strategy.

The rationale for the duty

The duty is a form of creditor protection, inhibiting companies' externalising the cost of their debts at the time of financial distress, and arguably the duty is necessary because of the impotence of many of the other protections available.[6] The duty requires directors, at a time when the company is in some form of financial distress,[7] to take account of the interests of the company's creditors. The reason given for this is that if the company is insolvent, in the vicinity of solvency or embarking on a venture which it cannot sustain without relying totally on creditor funds, 'the interests of the company are in reality the interests of existing creditors alone' (*Brady v Brady* (1988) 3 BCC 535 at 552). At this time, the shareholders are no longer the owners of the residual value of the firm (the residual owners being those whose wealth directly rises or falls with changes in the value of the company)[8], having been, in effect, transplanted by the creditors, whose rights are transformed into equity-like rights.[9] Thus, the directors are effectively playing with the

---

6 For a discussion of the shortcomings of protections in the Companies Act, see, Armour, J, 'Share capital and creditor protection: efficient rules for a modern company law' (2000) 63 MLR 355, and for a discussion of the shortcomings of protections under the Insolvency Act, see below pp 180–188.

7 The point at which directors have to take into account creditor interests is not clear. The issue is considered in Chapter 13. The views stated in that chapter gain some support from the Company Law Review Steering Group in *Modern Company Law for a Competitive Economy: Final Report* Vol 1, 2001, London: DTI, at para 3.17–3.18.

8 Baird, D, 'The initiation problem in bankruptcy' (1991) 11 *International Review of Law and Economics* 223 at 228–229; Gilson, S, and Vetsuypens, M, 'Credit control in financially distressed firms: empirical evidence' (1994) 72 *Washington University Law Quarterly* 1005 at 1006. This seems to be what was being said in *Brady v Brady* (1988) 3 BCC 535. Professor Lynn LoPucki criticises the use of residual ownership: 'The myth of residual owner: an empirical study' (2004) 82 Wash ULQ 1341. Mr Leslie Kosmin QC (sitting as a Deputy Judge of the Chancery Division in *Gwyer v London Wharf (Limehouse) Ltd* [2003] 2 BCLC 153; [2002] EWHC 2748 (Ch) specifically stated that creditors' interests should be paramount at the time of insolvency (at [74]). Overall the cases provide little guidance.

9 Schwarcz, S, 'Rethinking a corporation's obligations to creditors' (1996) 17 *Cardozo Law Review* 647 at 668; Millner, R, 'What does it mean for directors of financially troubled corporations to have fiduciary duties to creditors?' (2000) 9 *Journal of Bankruptcy Law and Practice* 201 at 206–207. See Baird, *op. cit.* fn 8 above. Whether this gives creditors a proprietary interest in the assets of the company is a matter for debate. It is suggested in *Kinsela v Russell Kinsela Pty Ltd* (1986) 4 ACLC 215 at 221 that they do, but compare the discussion in Worthington, S, 'Directors' duties, creditors' rights and shareholder intervention' (1991) 18 MULR 121 at 141. For the view that several groups could be regarded as exposed to residual risk, see, Kelly, G, and Parkinson, J, 'The conceptual foundations of the company: a pluralist approach' (1998) 2 CfiLR 174.

creditors' money (*Brady* at 552),[10] and so the creditors may be seen as the major stakeholders in the company (*Kinsela v Russell Kinsela Pty Ltd* (1986) 4 ACLC 215 at 221). The result is that the directors have an obligation not to sacrifice creditor interests (at 221).[11] It might be said that technically the creditors are not the residual owners of the company unless the company is insolvent, because the creditors will end up not receiving full payment of the debts owed to them. But even those who are critical of responsibilities to creditors do accept that when a company is in financial strife the creditors are more worthy of duties being owed to them, compared with shareholders, as they lack control powers.[12] While a company is solvent, even if marginally so, there should, by definition, be sufficient assets to discharge liabilities to creditors and there will be something left over for the shareholders. But we need to look at this more practically. As is mentioned in Chapter 13,[13] determining insolvency is not always easily done, so directors who think that their company is just solvent could be wrong, because perhaps assets are not as valuable as they think[14] or the directors are basing their conclusion on outdated information, and, also, even if a company is solvent, but struggling, it might not be long before the company falls into an insolvent position. With the cash flow test of insolvency, namely looking at whether the company can pay its debts as they fall due, directors are more likely to be aware of their company's insolvency or that the company is in the vicinity of insolvency.

According to the views of financial economists, directors could be expected, when their companies are in difficulty, to embrace actions which involve more risk;[15] a position embraced by the Company Law Steering

---

10 Millner *ibid* at 207; Hartman, R, 'Situation-specific fiduciary duties for corporate directors: enforceable obligations or toothless ideals' (1993) 50 *Washington and Lee Law Review* 1761 at 1771; Lipson, R, 'Directors' duties to creditors: volition, cognition, exit and the financially distressed corporation' (2003) 50 *University of California at Los Angeles Law Review* 1189 at 1212.

11 Sarra, J, 'Taking the corporation past the "Plimsoll line" – director and officer liability when the corporation founders' (2001) 10 *International Insolvency Review* 229 at 235. See, Moffat, M, 'Directors' dilemma – an economic evaluation of directors' liability for environmental damages and unpaid wages' (1996) 54 *University of Toronto Faculty of Law Review* 293 at 302. This was the view of the Delaware District Court in *Official Committee of Unsecured Creditors of Hechinger Inv Co of Delaware Inc v Fleet Retail Finance Group* 274 BR 71 at 89 (2002).

12 Ribstein, L, and Alces, K, 'Directors' duties in failing firms', University of Illinois College of Law, Law and Economics Working Papers, Paper 50, 2006, accessible at www.law.bepress.com/uiuclwps/papers/art50.

13 Below at pp 197–199.

14 This could be an issue on both the balance sheet and cash flow tests of insolvency, either or both tests applying in most jurisdictions. See Goode, R, *Principles of Corporate Insolvency Law*, 2nd edn, 1997, London: Sweet & Maxwell, Chapter 4; Keay, A, 'The insolvency factor in the avoidance of antecedent transactions in corporate liquidations' (1995) 21 *Monash University Law Review* 305.

15 See *Credit Lyonnais Bank Nederland NV v Pathe Communications Corp* 1991 Del Ch WL 277613; LEXIS 215; (1992) 17 *Delaware Journal of Corporate Law* 1099 (Delaware Chancery

Group in its review of UK company law.[16] If, because the directors have little to lose where their company is in financial distress, they engage in excessive risk-taking,[17] then the creditors will be the ones to lose out if the risk does not bear fruit. Professor Robert Scott puts it this way:

> As long as the debtor's business prospects remain good, a strong reputational incentive deters misbehaviour. But once the business environment deteriorates, the [company's manager] is increasingly influenced by a 'high-roller' strategy. The poorer the prospects for a profitable conclusion to the venture, the less the entrepreneur has to risk and the more he stands to gain from imprudent or wrongful conduct.[18]

There is empirical evidence to support the fact that this tends to occur,[19] and it has become axiomatic that this risk-taking will take place,[20] particularly where the directors are also the 'owners'[21] in the context of closed companies, that is those companies with few shareholders and where the shareholders are managing the company. The unsecured creditors are protected only by contractual rights, but when companies are financially stressed there are, arguably, cogent arguments that their position warrants some form of fiduciary protection,[22] whereby the directors become accountable principally to the

Court). Also, see Nicolls, C C, 'Liability of corporate officers and directors to third parties' (2001) 35 Can Bus L J 1 at 35; Hartman, R, 'Situation-specific fiduciary duties for corporate directors: enforceable obligations or toothless ideals' (1993) 50 *Washington and Lee Law Review* 1761 at 1771; de R Barondes, R, 'Fiduciary duties of officers and directors of distressed corporations' (1998) 7 *George Mason Law Review* 45 at 46; Armour, J, 'The law and economics of corporate insolvency: a review' (2001) ESRC Centre for Business Research, University of Cambridge, Working Paper No 197, p 1.

16 *Modern Company Law for a Competitive Economy: Final Report* Vol 1, 2001, London: DTI at para 3.15.

17 See *op. cit.* Easterbrook and Fischel, fn 5 above at 60; Jelisavcic, V, 'A safe harbour proposal to define the limits of directors' fiduciary duty to creditors in the "vicinity of insolvency" ' [1992] *Journal of Corporation Law* 145 at 148.

18 'A relational theory of default rules for commercial contracts' (1990) 19 *Journal of Legal Studies* 597 at 624.

19 Daniels, R, 'Must boards go overboard? An economic analysis of the effects of burgeoning statutory liability on the role of directors in corporate governance' in Ziegel, J (ed), *Current Developments in International and Comparative Corporate Insolvency Law*, 1994, Oxford: Clarendon Press, p 549. However, de R Barondes, R, 'Fiduciary duties of officers and directors of distressed corporations' (1998) 7 *George Mason Law Review* 45 at 62 challenges this view.

20 Adler, R, 'A re-examination of near-bankruptcy investment incentives' (1995) 62 *University of Chicago Law Review* 575 at 590–598; de R Barondes, *ibid* at 46, 49.

21 Mokal, R, 'An agency cost analysis of the wrongful trading provisions: redistribution, perverse incentives and the creditors' bargain' (2000) 59 CLJ 335 at 353–354.

22 Van der Weide, M, 'Against fiduciary duties to corporate stakeholders' (1996) 21 *Delaware Journal of Corporate Law* 27 at 43; Rao, R, Sokolow, D, and White, D, 'Fiduciary duty à la Lyonnais: an economic perspective on corporate governance in a financially distressed firm' (1996) 22 *The Journal of Corporation Law* 53 at 64.

creditors.[23] Unless this occurs then the directors have every reason, at this time, to externalise the cost of the company's debt and to engage in risky ventures that could bring in substantial benefits, but could, if they fail, imperil the company. Allied to this reason is that managers of the company might, in order to sustain the company's business, offer higher priority to new creditors, thereby weakening the position of existing creditors.[24]

A second reason for the duty is that the level of risk upon which credit was calculated and extended by creditors has changed, and the duty compensates the creditor accordingly. The duty provides 'the greatest protection at the time of the greatest risk, and, by changing what the board can reasonably justify as being in the corporate interest'[25] prevents misuse of the corporate power to incur liabilities. So, the issue in this area is not one of mismanagement but one of creditors being exposed to risks that they did not agree to accept.[26]

As a result of the above, where companies are in financial straits, the courts have seen fit to provide some protection to creditors, over and above to what they have obtained contractually when extending credit to companies.

Is the duty needed?

The need for the shifting of the duty of directors to take into account the interests of creditors has been questioned by some commentators.[27] One reason for taking this position is that other claims available to liquidators, who will usually ultimately seek to enforce the duty, given that the predominance of authority denies that the directors owe an independent duty to creditors, are adequate for protecting creditors. In order to ascertain whether there is any need for actions in relation to breach of duties to creditors, this part of the chapter examines the claims that could conceivably be available to liquidators.[28]

---

23 See the comments in the recent case of *Re Pantone 485 Ltd* [2002] 1 BCLC 266 at 285–286.
24 Keay, A, 'Directors' duties to creditors: contractarian concerns relating to efficiency and over-protection of creditors' (2003) 66 MLR 665 at 669.
25 Grantham, R, 'The judicial extension of directors' duties to creditors' [1991] JBL 1 at 15.
26 Wishart, D, 'Models and theories of directors' duties to creditors' (1991) 14 *New Zealand Universities Law Review* 323 at 354.
27 For example, see Sealy, L, 'Directors' duties – an unnecessary gloss' [1988] CLJ 175 at 177; Sealy, L, 'Personal liability of directors and officers for debts of insolvent corporations: a jurisdictional perspective (England)' in Ziegel, J, above n 19 at 488. For an American writer in support of the general view put forward by Professor Sealy, see Tomkins, A, 'Directors' duties to corporate creditors: delaware and the insolvency exception' (1993) 47 SMU L Rev 165 at 183.
28 The focus is on the primary claims which could be brought by a liquidator. Claims, such as under s 263 of the Companies Act 1985, namely that distributions, except out of profits, are prohibited, are not considered.

Wrongful trading

The main argument that has been mounted by those who believe that there is no need for a duty to creditors is that liquidators can adequately protect and recompense creditors by bringing proceedings for wrongful trading under s 214 of the Insolvency Act.[29] It is certainly true that wrongful trading covers some of the ground which a duty to creditors is said, by the courts, to cover. But, in enacting the wrongful trading provision, Parliament cannot be seen to have intended to exclude the use of the breach of duty claim, because when the Cork Committee recommended it, and even when the Parliament passed the Insolvency Act 1986, there had been no real development of principles dealing with the interests of creditors.

The book has examined wrongful trading in depth in Chapters 7–10 and it is not intended to repeat what was written in those chapters. Suffice it to say, in Chapter 10, in particular, I identified some significant weaknesses with wrongful trading actions. As a consequence of these weaknesses, it is submitted that in certain cases a liquidator would be better served pursuing an action for breach of duty rather than wrongful trading.[30] In other cases it may be worthwhile for a liquidator to couple a breach of duty claim with a claim under s 214. Also, it is worth noting that only liquidators are able to initiate action under s 214, therefore administrators and administrative receivers must consider other actions, such as proceedings for breach of duty.[31]

One other important issue relates to funding. In Chapter 10 I identified the funding problems that confront liquidators who wish to take proceedings for wrongful trading, and I explained that liquidators have difficulty in obtaining outside funding as they are unable to assign the action because it is granted personally by s 214 to them. If a liquidator initiates proceedings for breach of duty there will not be the same funding problems. A liquidator is able to seek and obtain funding for a breach of duty action, and as such an action is able to be categorised as company property. The liquidator is entitled to agree to assign the action to an insurer in exchange for a share of any proceeds of the suit, thereby coming within the insolvency exception (*Grovewood Holdings Plc v James Capel & Co Ltd* [1995] BCC 760). Also, with a breach of duty action the liquidator will bring the action in the name of the company, hence any costs, the liquidator's and those incurred by the respondent if the liquidator's case fails, will be paid as a priority debt out of company assets. While an order for security for costs may be made against the company on the

---

29 For example, see Sealy, 'Gloss', *op. cit.* fn 27 above at 177; Sealy, 'Personal liability' *op. cit.* fn 27 above at 488.

30 A view taken in Hicks, A, 'Advising on wrongful trading – Part 1' (1993) 14 Co Law 16 at 20. Since then, drawbacks in relation to the usefulness of s 214 have become apparent.

31 For instance, in the Western Australian case of *Geneva Finance Ltd v Resource & Industry Ltd* (2002) 20 ACLC 1427 a receiver had brought proceedings that were based partly on a claim of a breach of a duty to creditors.

application of the respondent, no liability, generally, attaches to the liquidator for costs of those proceedings (*Re Wilson Lovatt & Sons Ltd* [1977] 1 All ER 274), because the liquidator is carrying out a public function on the part of all creditors and contributories (*Re Pavelic Investments Pty Ltd* (1982) 1 ACLC 1207), and provided that the liquidator has sought and obtained legal advice which indicates that he or she has good prospects of success, then the liquidator would be failing in his or her duty not to instigate proceedings. Admittedly it is possible for courts, under s 51(1) and (3) of the Supreme Court Act 1981, to order liquidators to pay the costs even though they are non-parties to the proceedings.[32] But this power is not overly exercised and on occasions its exercise has been said to be exceptional.[33] It appears that there is only one occasion on which it has been employed in a UK liquidation case, by the judge at first instance in *Metalloy Supplies Ltd v M A (UK) Ltd* [1997] 1 BCLC 165. The decision of the judge was appealed successfully by the liquidator in that case. So, a liquidator who brings a breach of duty action is not in such a vulnerable position as would be the case with a claim under s 214.

Adjustment provisions

Rather than focusing on the improper decisions of directors, something that is required if one pursues the idea of a duty to creditors, is it adequate to focus on a scheme of impugned transactions, as is the case in the United States? There are two kinds of transactions that might be impugned in UK law, namely those that should be adjusted under the Insolvency Act, and those that are regarded as defrauding creditors.

In performing their duties, liquidators will examine transactions entered into prior to winding up in order to assess whether they are able to apply for an adjustment of the transactions in order to swell the assets available to creditors. Parliament has taken the view, and it is a long-established one, that transactions by which an insolvent disposed of property within a certain time zone prior to the commencement of winding up, in circumstances which are unfair to the creditors, should be subject to adjustment.[34]

The adjustment provisions are set out in Part VI of the Insolvency Act

---

32 For example, see *Aiden Shipping Co Ltd v Interbulk Ltd* [1986] AC 965, HL; *Globe Equities Ltd v Globe Legal Services Ltd, The Times*, 14 April 1999, CA; *National Justice Compania Naviera SA v Prudential Assurance Co Ltd (No 2), The Times*, 15 October 1999, CA.

33 *Symphony Group v Hodgson* [1994] QB 179, CA; *Metalloy Supplies Ltd v MA (UK) Ltd* [1997] 1 BCLC 165 at 169, CA; *Locabail (UK) Ltd v Bayfield Properties Ltd, The Times*, February 29, 2000. See the discussion in de Kerloy, R, 'The personal liability of liquidators and administrative receivers for the costs of an unsuccessful action' (2000) 4 RALQ 13 at 17–18 as to what might be deemed exceptional circumstances.

34 The policy is consistent with that which exists in most advanced systems of law: Report of the Insolvency Law Review Committee, *Insolvency Law and Practice*, Cmnd 858 (1982), para 1200.

1986. A number of provisions may be relevant, but because of constraints of space I will restrict myself to consideration of the two most important adjustment provisions.

Preferences

One of the kinds of pre-liquidation transaction which a liquidator will be looking for is the giving of preferences. A preference involves a transfer of money or of some interest in property by a debtor to a creditor to settle an antecedent debt and it benefits that creditor to the prejudice of other creditors by granting the favoured creditor a greater share of the diminished assets of the debtor than that creditor would enjoy in liquidation.

Section 239 of the Insolvency Act 1986 provides that a liquidator might seek the adjustment of a pre-liquidation transaction on the basis that it is a preference. The most frequent adjustment order made by courts is akin to the old avoidance orders made under previous legislation (such as Bankruptcy Act 1914, s 44) namely the transaction is set aside and the position that existed prior to the entering into of the transaction is restored.

In order for a liquidator successfully to attack a transaction as a preference, the liquidator has to prove[35] a number of elements, including:

(a) the transaction was entered into within the six months before the onset of insolvency[36] or, if the respondent is a person connected with the company, within the two years prior to the onset of insolvency (s 239(2) of the Insolvency Act 1986);

(b) the company has done anything which has the effect of putting the recipient of the preference into a position which, in the event of the company entering insolvent liquidation, will be better than the position he or she would have been in had the thing not been done (s 239(4)(b) of the Insolvency Act 1986);

(c) the company was influenced in deciding to enter into the impugned transaction by a desire to enable the recipient to have a preference (s 239(5) of the Insolvency Act 1986);

(d) at the time of, or as a result of, the giving of the preference the company was unable to pay its debts within the meaning of s 123, in other words insolvent (s 240(2) of the Insolvency Act 1986).

---

35 Morritt J, in *Re Ledingham-Smith* ([1993] BCLC 635 at 639), discusses the issues which confront a court in a preference case.

36 This term is defined in s 240(3) of the Insolvency Act 1986 in relation to straight liquidations, the date of the commencement of winding up. According to s 129 of the said Act, this date is, in relation to compulsory liquidations, the date of the presentation of the petition to wind up; in voluntary liquidations it is the date of the resolution to wind up. Where there is an administration the relevant date is the date on which the petition seeking an administration order was presented (s 240(3)(a)).

Usually, the most difficult elements for a liquidator to establish are the last two mentioned. In particular, liquidators have found it difficult to succeed because they have not been able to prove that the company was influenced in deciding to enter into the transaction under challenge by a desire to enable the recipient to have a preference. This is well illustrated in the seminal case of *Re M C Bacon Ltd* [1990] BCLC 324. In that case a classic situation for a preference claim emerged. A bank had provided an unsecured overdraft facility to a company, B. B's fortunes plummeted during late 1986 and early 1987 and B was operating by using its overdraft facility to the full. The bank became aware of B's misfortunes and demanded security. In May 1987 a report by officers of the bank stated that B was insolvent, but it was reasonable to conclude that it could trade out of its problems. Shortly thereafter, a debenture was executed by B giving the bank a fixed and floating charge over B's assets. Subsequently, on 4 September 1987 B appointed an administrative receiver. On 7 September 1987 a liquidator was appointed. In due course the liquidator applied to have the debenture given to the bank set aside on the basis that it was a preference under s 239. In this case the main issue confronting Millett J (as he then was) was whether the company had been influenced by a desire to provide a preference for the bank. Millett J was of the opinion that B held the genuine belief that it could survive its financial problems and that it had no choice but to grant the debenture demanded by the bank. His Lordship went on to find that there was no reason why the directors of B would want to improve the bank's position in the event of an insolvent liquidation and that there was no motive other than a desire to avoid the calling in of the overdraft and to continue the carrying on of business (at 337). While it was accepted that the directors had the desire to make a payment to the bank, they did not have the desire to produce the effect mentioned in s 239(5), namely to improve the bank's position in the event of an insolvent liquidation (at 335). In most cases where preferences have been given, certainly where the recipient is not a person connected with the company, the company is not going to fulfil s 239(5). In cases where the recipient was a connected person, such as a director or a relative of a director of the company, there is a presumption that the company had the requisite desire of wanting to see the creditor's lot improved (s 239(6) of the Insolvency Act 1986). More often than not, payments are made to creditors to allow the company to keep trading, as in *Re M C Bacon Ltd*, by securing a credit line or the continued supply of goods needed by the company, and no connected person is involved.

Cases decided subsequent to the decision in *Re M C Bacon Ltd* have not taken the law much further; in most of the cases judges were preoccupied with the individual facts which were before them. In these cases the views of Millett J have been referred to widely, and generally approved.[37] In all of the

---

37 For example, see *Re DKG Contractors Ltd* [1990] BCC 903 at 909–910; *Re Lewis's of Leicester Ltd* [1995] BCC 514 at 523; *Re Living Images Ltd* [1996] BCC 112, 117; *Wills v*

cases dealing with preferences given by companies, the recipient of the prefer-ence has been a person who is able to be classified as a connected person. This is, it is submitted, an indication of the difficulty which a liquidator has in establishing that the company had the requisite desire. Where the creditor is a connected person the liquidator has a much greater chance of succeeding, especially when one also takes into account the fact that the liquidator can attack transactions entered into as far back as two years before the com-mencement of winding up. But where non-connected persons are concerned, the preference provisions seem to be close to impotent.[38] Not one reported case deals with the giving of a preference to a non-connected person, and in their copious study of the adjustment provisions, Professor David Milman and Dr Rebecca Parry found, in answer to their questioning of licensed insolvency practitioners who act as liquidators, that in excess of one third of respondents said that rarely are proceedings instituted against preferences.[39] In cases where directors have permitted their company to pay certain creditors and not others, but a liquidator is unable to make out a s 239 claim against the preferred creditors, it does not seem unreasonable that a liquid-ator should consider turning his or her attention to the directors and initiat-ing a claim for breach of duty. In fact in some of the cases already considered in this book, actions of directors in disposing of assets or giving preferences have simply been attacked on the basis that they constitute a breach of dir-ectors' duties, i.e., in granting a preference to one creditor the directors did not take into account the interests of all creditors.[40]

Insolvency is not a state that can always be established easily. In addition, if all of the elements for a preference can be established, it must be remem-bered that the time zone which applies is only six months (for non-connected parties) and that is not a substantial period of time. However, a breach of duty action might overcome these potential problems. First, there is a signifi-cant amount of authority to indicate that for a successful claim for breach of duty, proof of insolvency is not required. There may be occasions where a liquidator is unable to establish insolvency but can demonstrate that the actions of the directors in paying one or more creditors preferentially

Corfe Joinery Ltd (in liq) [1997] BCC 511 at 512; *Re Agriplant Services Ltd* [1997] BCC 842 at 848–849.

38 See Keay, A, 'Preferences in liquidation law: a time for a change' (1998) 2 CfiLR 198.

39 Milman, D, and Parry, R, 'A study of the operation of transactional avoidance mechanisms in corporate insolvency practice,' 1998, Oxford: GTI Specialist Publishers, Chapter 3.

40 For example, *Liquidator of West Mercia Safetywear Ltd v Dodd* (1988) 4 BCC 30; *Grove v Flavel* (1986) 43 SASR 410; 11 ACLR 161; *Kinsela v Russell Kinsela Pty Ltd (in liq)* [1986] 1 NSWLR 722; (1985) 10 ACLR 395. See Fisher, R, 'Preferences and other antecedent tran-sactions: do directors owe a duty to creditors?' (1995) 8 *Corporate & Business Law Journal* 203. This has also been the case in the United States. In *Asmussen v Quaker City Corp* 156 A 180 (1931) the directors of a corporation were held liable for allowing the distribution of company assets to specific creditors.

prejudiced the interests of the balance of the body of creditors. Second, where a transaction occurred outside of the time zone and s 239 is not available to the liquidator, a claim on the basis that entering into the preferential transaction constituted a breach of duty is not circumscribed by any time zone and may be available.

Another situation where a claim for a breach of duty might be preferable is where it is clear that the creditor who received a preference is impecunious and the directors of the company are not. This seemed to be the strategy in *Liquidator of West Mercia Safetywear Ltd v Dodd* (1988) 4 BCC 30 where the director of the company in liquidation had, prior to winding up, given a preference to the company's parent company. The parent had no assets to pay a judgment. So, the liquidator proceeded successfully against the director for breach of duty.

One final issue worth noting is that, like wrongful trading, a liquidator has problems in funding proceedings under s 239 because preference actions, as with wrongful trading proceedings, are personal actions given to the liquidator (*Re MC Bacon Ltd (No2)* [1990] BCC 430 at 434).[41] Therefore, many of the funding problems discussed earlier in relation to s 214 actions apply equally to actions commenced in order to attack preferences.

Transactions at an undervalue

Section 238 provides another option for liquidators (and administrators) to attack certain pre-liquidation transactions, this time on the basis that they are transactions at an undervalue. However, the fact that again there is a paucity of case law on the provision is, it is submitted, indicative of the problematic nature of the provision.[42] A liquidator or administrator must establish the following:

(a) the company is in liquidation or administration (s 238(1));
(b) the company entered into a transaction at an undervalue in the two years preceding the onset of insolvency (ss 238(2), 240(3));[43]
(c) at the time when the transaction was entered into the company was unable to pay its debts or the company was unable to pay its debts as a result of entering into the transaction (s 240(2));
(d) the transaction on the one hand was a gift or involved the company receiving no consideration, or on the other hand the consideration

---

41 In their study of transactional avoidance Professor Milman and Dr Parry found that the predominant reason for not pursuing proceedings is the lack of funding. This reason accounted for the failure to proceed in over 60 per cent of cases (*op. cit.* fn 39 above).

42 See above n 39.

43 See *Clarkson v Clarkson* [1994] BCC 921 for a case where a claim failed because the transaction did not occur within the relevant time period.

which the company received under the transaction was significantly less, in money or money's worth, than the consideration provided by the company (s 238(4)).

The establishment of the last condition can constitute a problem for a liquidator or an administrator, and although the onus of proving insolvency is removed in circumstances where the respondent is a connected person, as there is a rebuttable presumption that the company was insolvent at the time of the transaction (s 240(2)), in some cases, particularly where the recipient of the benefit is not a connected person, it may be better to pursue a claim for a breach of duty rather than a claim under s 238.

Like preferences, transactions at an undervalue are only able to be impugned where they occur within a set time period prior to liquidation or administration – two years in all cases under s 238. There may be cases where the directors have transferred property at an undervalue but this occurred more than two years before liquidation or administration. In such a situation an attack may be made on the transaction on the basis that it constituted a breach of duty to creditors.

Whether a transaction is a transaction at an undervalue pursuant to s 238(4)(b) will depend, it appears, on the question of value. In the typical case litigated under this section, the main issue is likely to be whether the company received significantly less consideration than it gave. Resolving this issue will entail a valuation in money terms of the consideration provided both by the company and by the other party to the transaction. It has been held that the liquidator must establish the respective values in money or money terms of the consideration given and received by the company and, also, demonstrate that what it received was significantly less than what it provided.[44] A liquidator cannot, it would seem, point to other non-financial benefits received by the other party to the transaction in order to establish the fact that the transaction falls within s 238. It is impossible to say what will constitute 'significantly less'. The expression has not been interpreted by the courts as yet.[45] If a liquidator or administrator were to rely on a breach of duty he or she would not be required to establish that the company received significantly less consideration than it gave, whatever that might mean, but simply that at a time when the directors should have been considering the creditors' interests they failed to do so in entering into the relevant transaction. This could be achieved by demonstrating that the creditors were prejudiced by the transaction.

As with s 239, Milman and Parry found in their study that s 238 actions

---

44 See *Re M C Bacon Ltd* [1990] BCLC 324 at 340–341 and approved of in *Phillips v Brewin Dolphin Bell Lawrie Ltd* [1999] BCC 557 at 566, CA.

45 Snaith, I, *The Law of Corporate Insolvency*, 1990, London: Waterlow Publishers, p 648, argues that a *de minimus* rule must apply.

were not initiated frequently, due, it would seem, to some of the reasons mentioned earlier in relation to preferences.[46]

Transactions defrauding creditors

Besides using the adjustment provisions to impugn transactions, which can only be done where there is a liquidation or an administration, it is possible to impugn transactions, whether before or during administration or liquidation, as fraudulent conveyances, on the basis that they defraud creditors. It is this latter base that is often used in the United States in circumstances where British and Commonwealth liquidators have looked to a breach of a duty to creditors.

Ever since the Statute of Elizabeth was enacted in 1571, fraudulent conveyances have been proscribed. Fraudulent conveyances involve transactions whereby debtors put assets out of the reach of creditors, often by transferring the assets to friendly parties. The present provision which embodies the fraudulent conveyance provision contained in the Statute of Elizabeth is s 423 of the Insolvency Act. Section 423 does not, unlike ss 238 and 239, operate solely in an insolvency situation. The employment of the provision is not limited to liquidators, administrators and bankruptcy trustees; it may be used by any creditor. As with s 238, s 423 seeks to allow transactions at an undervalue to be impugned. An applicant under s 423 must prove one of the following:

(a) the debtor makes a gift or enters into a transaction which does not provide the debtor with any consideration;
(b) the debtor enters into a transaction for which marriage is the consideration; or
(c) the transaction entered into by the debtor is for a consideration the value of which, in money or money's worth, is significantly less than the value, in money or money's worth, of the consideration provided by the debtor.

In addition, and this is the critical element which must be proved, the applicant under s 423 must establish (s 423(3)) that the person entering into the impugned transaction (this will be the debtor ordinarily) had the purpose of either putting assets beyond the reach of a person who is making, or who may make at some time a claim against the debtor, or otherwise prejudicing the interests of such a person (a creditor or potential creditor) in relation to the claim.[47]

---

46 Some 38.6 per cent of the authors' respondents said that they rarely issued proceedings under s 238 (*op. cit.* fn 39 above).
47 Evans-Lombe J specifically held in *Jyske Bank (Gibraltar) Ltd v Spjeldnaes (No2)* [1999] 2 BCLC 101; [1999] BPIR 525, that all that an applicant has to do is to prove that the purpose of the debtor was to put the assets beyond the reach of the applicant. It was not necessary to prove that the purpose was specifically designed to defeat the applicant's claim against the debtor.

Proving that something was done with a particular purpose in mind is never easy. The problem with the use of 'purpose' in s 423 is exacerbated by the fact that anyone taking proceedings under that section is required to demonstrate that the company's purpose either to put assets beyond the reach of claimants, or to prejudice claimants, was the company's substantial purpose (*IRC v Hashmi* [2002] 2 BCLC 489, CA). While this is easier to establish, on the whole, compared with the fact that the debtor had a dominant purpose, which was the state of the law prior to *Hashmi* (*Chohan v Sagar* [1992] BCC 306; affirmed on appeal [1994] 1 BCLC 706; [1994] BCC 134), this is still likely to thwart a significant number of applications under s 423.[48]

In the United States claims against directors for breach of their duties have been used where reliance on the fraudulent conveyance provisions has not been possible for one reason or another,[49] and there seems to be no reason why this cannot be the case in the UK, Ireland and Commonwealth jurisdictions. Of course, the attraction for a liquidator in proceeding on the basis of a breach of duty is that there needs to be no proof of subjective intention as there is with s 423 actions.

Fraudulent trading

One last action which may be relied upon by a liquidator in order to recover assets and/or money disposed of prior to liquidation, and which may be said to obviate the need for a duty to creditors, is a claim under s 213 of the Insolvency Act for fraudulent trading. I have already examined fraudulent trading in Chapters 3–6 and it is not intended to repeat what was said there. Suffice it to say that there are problems with initiating a fraudulent trading action, not least being that uncertainty exists concerning the meaning of 'intent to defraud' in s 213 and whether a respondent can be said to have *knowingly* participated in carrying on the business for a fraudulent purpose. This uncertainty might mean that a liquidator would be more inclined, where possible, to initiate proceedings based on other provisions or causes of action.

As with wrongful trading, only liquidators are able to initiate action under s 213, therefore administrators and administrative receivers must consider other actions.

A further issue which is a potential difficulty for liquidators is that, like s 214 claims, they may not be able to secure sufficient or any funding, for they are not permitted to assign the cause of action as it is personal to the liquidator (*Re Oasis Merchandising Services Ltd* [1995] BCC 911).

---

48 See Keay, A, 'Transactions defrauding creditors: the problem of purpose under section 423 of the Insolvency Act' [2003] Conv 272.
49 For example, *Snyder Electric Co v Fleming* 305 NW 2d 863 (1981).

Summary

It is submitted that there are deficiencies and weaknesses in all of the claims available to a liquidator and an administrator and, hence, every consideration should be given to a claim of breach of duty of directors of the company. In particular, the actions discussed here do not apply until there is proof of insolvency (or, with wrongful trading, where a director knew or ought to have concluded that there was no reasonable prospect of the company avoiding going into insolvent liquidation) or proof of improper purpose. The threshold for a breach of duty action seems to be set somewhat lower in terms of what has to be established by a liquidator because directors do not need to have an improper purpose and there is a significant amount of authority to suggest that the duty can be triggered before the onset of insolvency.

There is nothing prohibiting a liquidator from coupling a claim against a director for breach of the duty to take into account the interests of creditors with any of the kinds of proceedings considered here. There is no need for the liquidator to have to decide whether he or she is going to rely on this duty alone. Coupling a claim for breach of duty with one or more other claims could well be the most prudent course of action to adopt. The fact of the matter is that if one excludes the breach of duty action then there have been (and will continue to be) cases, such as *Ring v Sutton* (1980) 5 ACLR 546, *Kinsela v Russell Kinsela Pty Ltd* (1986) 4 ACLC 215; 10 ACLR 395, *Liquidator of West Mercia Safetywear v Dodd* and *Facia Footwear Ltd (in administration) v Hinchliffe* [1998] 1 BCLC 218, where liquidators would not have succeeded, and creditors would have been prejudiced.

Disadvantages of bringing proceedings for breach of duty to creditors

Undoubtedly there are disadvantages in pursuing a claim for a breach of duty. But, as we have seen, this is the case with any claim which is prosecuted in relation to the affairs of an insolvent company. What are the disadvantages with a breach of duty action compared with other possible actions? Unlike in a wrongful trading claim (*Re D'Jan of London Ltd* [1993] BCC 646), a court is able where the claim is for breach of duty to grant relief to the respondent director under s 727 of the Companies Act 1985. This provision permits a court to relieve, wholly or in part, officers from liability in relation to proceedings for negligence, default, breach of duty, or breach of trust. The defence does not have to be specifically pleaded (*Re Kirby's Coaches Ltd* [1991] BCC 130). Jurisdiction under s 727 can be exercised only if the court is satisfied that the person who sought relief had acted honestly, and reasonably, and that, having regard to all the circumstances of the case, he or she ought fairly to be excused (*Re J Franklin & Sons Ltd* [1937] 4 All ER 43). It is probably fair to say that as the law develops in relation to the duties of directors, and their required competence increases, that it may become more and more difficult to argue for the employment of s 727.[50]

On some occasions the respondent to a misfeasance proceeding (under s 212 of the Insolvency Act) has been relieved, under s 727, either wholly or in part, only if the obligation to make good the full amount for which prima facie he or she was liable,[51] and only if the interests of creditors were unlikely to be affected and the members themselves had acquiesced in the wrongful act. Given this, it is likely to be rare cases when s 727 can be invoked, and especially where a breach of duty claim is based primarily on the prejudice to creditors.[52]

With an action for breach of duty the liquidator will issue proceedings in the name of the company. It is likely that the respondent will apply for an order for security of costs pursuant to s 726 of the Companies Act 1985.[53] If the company is insolvent, as it will be in most situations, that may lead a court to making the order requested. But it cannot be said that there is a presumption that security will be ordered against a company in liquidation. It is submitted that while the fact that a company is in insolvent liquidation must constitute a significant factor in favour of ordering security, it is not conclusive. It has been said that insolvency is only regarded as prima facie evidence that a company is unable to pay costs unless contrary evidence is adduced (*Pure Spirit Co v Fowler* (1890) 25 QBD 235). However, it cannot be put more strongly than that and may be not as strong as that. In the Court of Appeal in *Sir Lindsay Parkinson & Co Ltd v Triplan Ltd* [1973] 1 QB 609 Lord Denning MR said that the court has a complete discretion whether or not to order security even where it is clear that if found liable to pay costs the company would not be able to do so (at 626). Subsequently, the Court of Appeal in *BJ Crabtree (Insulation) Ltd v GPT Communications Systems*[54] emphasised the fact that the discretion of the court was to be kept flexible and not to be limited by applying strict rules. In line with this view Maugham LJ in *Ebury Garages Ltd v Agard* (1907) L J 204 said that there may be many cases where a company could be insolvent and the court would not order security to be lodged.

Of course, even if a liquidator or administrator obtains an order from the

---

50 Oditah, F, 'Misfeasance proceedings against company directors' [1992] LMCLQ 207 at 213 and 219.

51 See *Re Sunlight Incandescent Gas Lamp Co* (1900) 16 TLR 535; *Re Home & Colonial Insurance Co* [1930] 1 Ch 102. For a recent case where the section was not applied, see *Re Westlowe Storage and Distribution Ltd* [2000] BCC 851.

52 In any case it is for the party in default to show that he or she is entitled to relief: *Re International Vending Machines Ltd* (1961) 80 WN (NSW) 465 at 474–475.

53 For an admirable treatment of security for costs in relation to company law, see Milman, D, 'Security for costs: principles and pragmatism in corporate litigation' in Rider, B A K (ed), *The Realm of Company Law*, 1998, London: Kluwer Law International, p 167.

54 (1990) 59 Build L R 43 and cited by Milman, *ibid* at 177.

court based on a breach of duty, the problem facing the liquidator/ administrator is that the order has to be enforced and at the end of the day the director(s) may be impecunious, rendering the proceedings tantamount to useless. However, this point must be put into perspective, for it applies equally to any claim against a director personally.

Probably the biggest drawback with pursuing a claim for breach of duty is the fact that the fruits of a successful claim will be available to any secured creditor who has a floating charge over all present and future company property, because, unlike property and money recovered under the other actions considered in this chapter, anything recovered is regarded as company property. Recoveries pursuant to actions for wrongful trading (*Re Oasis Merchandising Services Ltd* [1995] BCC 911) and preferences (*Re Yagerphone Ltd* [1935] 1 Ch 392; *Re MC Bacon Ltd (No2)* [1990] BCLC 607; [1990] BCC 430; *Katz v McNally* [1997] BCC 784; *sub nom Re Exchange Travel (Holdings) Ltd* [1998] BPIR 30) are not available to satisfy a chargeholder. Although courts have not expressed a specific view on the fate of recoveries from proceedings for fraudulent trading and transactions at an undervalue, it is accepted that they are analogous to wrongful trading and preferences respectively as far as the kinds of actions involved and courts are likely to hold that recoveries are to go to the unsecured creditors. Also, such actions, whether commenced by liquidators or administrators, are not actions owned by the company (and therefore available to chargeholders); rather they are actions which are bestowed on the office-holder by legislation. Of course where an administrative receiver is the one taking action for breach of duty this is not a drawback as the receiver is usually acting for the chargeholder who is entitled to be paid out of the amount recovered if his or her security does not cover what is owed.

Uses for breach of duty actions

Actions for breach of duty have been and can, it is submitted, continue to be used to enable liquidators to swell the assets available to creditors on an insolvent liquidation. They may also be used to thwart directors from proving in the winding up.[55] Perhaps one of the most significant roles that the duty to take into account creditors' interests is that it circumscribes the power of the shareholders to ratify a breach of duty,[56] for where the duty arises the law is clear that shareholders are unable to ratify directors' actions (*Liquidator of West Mercia Safetywear v Dodd* (1988) 4 BCC 30; *Re New World Alliance Pty Ltd; Sycotex Pty Ltd v Baseler* (1994) 122 ALR 531 at 550).

---

55 Prentice, D, 'Directors, creditors and shareholders' in McKendrick, E (ed), *Commercial Aspects of Trusts and Fiduciary Obligations*, 1992, Oxford: Oxford University Press, p 79.

56 *Nicholson v Permakraft (NZ) Ltd* (1985) 3 ACLC 453 at 460. See Prentice, D, 'Creditors' interests and director's duties' (1990) 10 OJLS 265 at 277.

Besides the benefit to liquidators, proceedings for breach of duty could be employed by an administrative receiver who is able to initiate proceedings as the agent of the company (*Gomba Holdings Ltd v Homan* [1986] 1 WLR 1301). As discussed previously, receivers have no right to use any of the other actions referred to earlier.[57]

Finally, the existence of the duty to consider the interests of creditors means that there is the possibility, because of potential personal liability, that it will act as a deterrent as far as unscrupulous and reckless directors are concerned so that they do not take actions, such as occurred in *Kinsela v Russell Kinsela Pty Ltd* (1986) 4 ACLC 215; (1986) 10 ACLR 395, which may well affect creditors' rights. In addition, it would be an incentive for directors to keep themselves apprised of what is going on in their companies and monitor activities.[58] These are issues that are traversed in more detail in Chapter 19.

Conclusion

This chapter has discussed the nature of and rationale for the duty under discussion. The duty is a fiduciary one and is *ex post* in nature. The duty exists because at a time when it applies, namely when a company is in financial difficulty, the shareholders are no longer the residual owners of the company; the creditors have effectively taken that position. If the company was run without consideration of the creditors' interests then they are the ones likely to lose out.

The Chapter has explored whether the duty is necessary, or whether creditors have adequate legislative protections. While significant provisions, such as s 214 of the Insolvency Act 1986, mean that the ambit of the duty does not have to be as broad as was once thought, the duty is not irrelevant and has not been relegated to the role of a 'bit part.' On the contrary, the duty, when the basis for the taking of misfeasance proceedings, can play an important part in curbing the abuses of trust of directors and compensating creditors of insolvent companies for whom liquidation is often 'an empty formality'.[59] In fact it may be a useful weapon in the arsenals of liquidators, administrators and administrative receivers. And there is a need to arm liquidators with as much ammunition as possible, especially where some of their weapons, such as the right to claim under the wrongful trading and preference provisions, have been partially, and in the case of the latter, substantially, spiked.

---

57 It is acknowledged that as a result of the enactment of the Enterprise Act 2002, the appointment of receivers is likely to fall off considerably over the next few years.

58 Lin, L, 'Shift of fiduciary duty upon corporate insolvency: proper scope of directors' duty to creditors' (1993) 46 Vanderbilt L Rev 1485 at 1516.

59 Finch, V, 'Directors' duties: insolvency and the unsecured creditor' in Clarke, A (ed), *Current Issues in Insolvency Law*, 1991, London: Stevens, p 91.

If it can be argued from the authorities, that directors owe a duty to creditors even outside of insolvency, an issue discussed in the next chapter, then this provides liquidators and administrators with a useful claim where other claims may be found wanting, either because they require difficult elements to be proved or else the elements just do not exist in the particular case. Also, one must not overlook the fact that administrative receivers, who lack the right to bring proceedings under legislative provisions discussed in this chapter, may be able to take action for breach of duty.

This chapter leads to the conclusion that while the duty of directors to take the interests of creditors into account can only go so far in protecting creditors, and that it is in need of further development and clarification to produce greater certainty, it can be useful to a number of insolvency office-holders and does not deserve to be cast aside as unnecessary; it is worthy of further exploration and use.

13 When does the duty arise?

Introduction

Thus far we have seen that while directors do not owe a duty to creditors at all times, there are circumstances when they do. What are those circumstances? This chapter seeks to provide some answers to that question. The chapter identifies and then examines the circumstances that the courts have identified as causing the duty to take into account creditors' interests to arise. Next, the Chapter assesses the positions taken in the various cases and considers what circumstances should exist before directors are obliged to consider creditors' interests. It is asserted in this chapter that there is a clear relationship between the extent of the risk of insolvency and the extent of the permissible risk to which directors can expose the assets of the company. Hence, the duty considered here is designed to protect the assets of the company when they are at risk of being lost. The assets may well be at risk because the directors are tempted to embrace a lucrative deal from which the shareholders will gain (and, if they are shareholders, from which the directors themselves will gain), but which will cause loss to the creditors if the deal is not successful.

It is critical to consider this issue as the elements of the duty need to be known precisely, so that directors are aware, as a matter of fairness, at what time they must begin to take into account the interests of the creditors, and when they might be held liable.

The point when the duty arises

First, while the dicta of Mason J in *Walker v Wimborne* (1976) 137 CLR 1; (1976) 3 ACLR 529) and Diplock LJ in *Lonrho Ltd v Shell Petroleum Co Ltd* [1980] 1 WLR 627 can be interpreted as suggesting a continuing duty owed to take creditors' interests into account, the mainstream of authority suggests that the duty does not arise where a company is clearly solvent. This point was made patent in *Multinational Gas and Petrochemical Co v Multinational Gas and Petrochemical Services Ltd* [1983] Ch 258 where Dillon LJ said that provided that a company is solvent, the shareholders are in substance the company, and the directors, therefore, do not owe duties to creditors, or, arguably to any other constituency of the company. His Lordship amplified his decision when giving his judgment in *Liquidator of West Mercia Safety-wear Ltd v Dodd* (1988) 4 BCC 30 and this is discussed later in the chapter. The New South Wales Court of Appeal in *Equiticorp Finance Ltd (in liq) v BNZ* (1993) 11 ACLC 952 also indicated (at 1016) that where there was no question about the solvency of a company, there was no need to consider the idea of a duty to creditors, and more recent cases have taken the same view.[1] The same approach has been taken in the United States.[2] This position would be congruent with the shareholder primacy approach generally followed in common law countries. This approach provides that the directors are to manage the company for the benefit of the shareholders and the shareholders alone. Whether the interests of creditors and other stakeholders should be considered by directors when a company is clearly solvent is an issue that needs to be left to another day.

Insolvency

It is almost non-contentious to say that the directors owe a duty to have regard for the interests of creditors when the company is insolvent.[3] While Mason J in the seminal case of *Walker v Wimborne* did not limit the duty to cases of insolvency or even of financial distress,[4] notwithstanding the fact that the case before him involved directors moving funds from their company, which was insolvent, to other companies, several of the cases in the 1980s introduced insolvency as a requirement.[5]

In one of the leading cases in the area, *Kinsela v Russell Kinsela Pty Ltd* (1986) 4 ACLC 215; (1986) 10 ACLR 395, the New South Wales Court of Appeal was faced with a claim against directors who, on behalf of their company, entered into a lease of the company's premises in favour of themselves for a three-year period with a three-year option at a rental which was well below the current market rental. At the time, the company was in a

---

1   For instance, see *Re Pantone 485 Ltd* [2002] 1 BCLC 266 at 285. Compare the decision of the New South Wales Court of Appeal in *Ring v Sutton* (1980) 5 ACLR 546, although that decision has been the subject of significant criticism, and has not been followed in Australia.

2   For example, see *Lorenz v CSX Corp* 1 F 3d 1406 at 1417 (Third Circuit, 1993).

3   For instance, see *Re Pantone 485 Ltd* [2002] 1 BCLC 266 at 285; *Gwyer v London Wharf (Limehouse) Ltd* [2003] 2 BCLC 153 at 178; [2002] EWHC 2748 at [74]. This is the case in the United States: *Bovay v HM Byllesby & Co* 38 A 2d 808 (1944); Miller, H, 'Corporate governance in Chapter 11: the fiduciary relationship between directors and stockholder of solvent and insolvent corporations' (1993) 23 *Seton Hall Law Review* 1466 at 1485.

4   It has been submitted that one can infer that Mason J was saying that creditors' interests must be taken into account before the advent of insolvency: Barrett, R, 'Directors' duties to creditors' (1977) 40 MLR 226 at 229.

5   For example, see the comments of Clarke and Cripps JJA of the New South Wales Court of Appeal in *Equiticorp Finance Ltd (in liq) v BNZ* (1993) 11 ACLC 952 at 1016. Their Honours did not appear to favour the duty arising at any time, other than on insolvency.

financially precarious state. Shortly after the lease was given the company entered liquidation pursuant to a winding-up order. Subsequently, the liquidator sought a declaration that the lease was voidable. Street CJ, in delivering the leading judgment, found against the directors of the company because of the fact that the company was clearly insolvent when the lease was executed. His Honour left open the door to the extension of the scope of the duty to encompass other states of financial distress short of insolvency, preferring not to comment on the degree of financial instability required before a duty was imposed on directors as he was not required to do so given the facts of the case (at 223; 404). But his Honour did say (at 223; 404) that: 'The plainer it is that it is the creditors' money that is at risk, the lower may be the risk to which the directors, regardless of the unanimous support of all of the shareholders, can justifiably expose the company.'

The views of Street CJ have been case cited with approval in a number of jurisdictions, including in England and Wales by the Court of Appeal in both *West Mercia Safetywear Ltd v Dodd* (at 33) and *Official Receiver v Stern* [2001] EWCA Civ 1787 at para 32; [2002] 1 BCLC 119 at 129–130. In very recent times we have seen a majority of the highest court in Australia (the High Court) in *Spies v The Queen* [2000] HCA 43; (2000) 201 CLR 603; (2000) 173 ALR 529; [2000] 74 ALJR 1263 accept that when a company is insolvent the directors must consider creditor interests. In the course of doing so the High Court approved of the comments of Gummow J (when he was a Federal Court judge) in *Re New World Alliance Pty Ltd* (1994) 122 ALR 531 at 550 when his Honour said that insolvency created a duty to creditors (*Spies* at [94]).

Certainly it is possible to say that when insolvency exists, the notions of corporate ownership and creditors' rights converge.[6] The creditors then are the real owners of the company (*Brady v Brady* (1987) 3 BCC 535 at 552, CA; *Kinsela* at 221);[7] the ownership rights of the shareholders having been expunged as there is nothing over which they have a claim.[8] Hence, if a company is insolvent, directors act improperly if they employ funds that are payable to creditors in order to continue the activities of the company,[9] save

---

6   Schwarcz, S, 'Rethinking a corporation's obligations to creditors' (1996) 17 *Cardozo Law Review* 647 at 666. The learned author sees the creditors' rights being transformed into equity-type rights with the advent of insolvency (*ibid* at 668).

7   Goode, R, *Principles of Corporate Insolvency Law*, 2nd edn, 1997, London: Sweet and Maxwell, p 455; McDonnell, S, '*Geyer v Ingersoll Publications Co*: Insolvency shifts directors' burden from shareholders to creditors' (1994) 19 *Delaware Journal of Corporate Law* 177 at 185.

8   Ferran, E, 'Creditors' interests and "core" company law' (1999) 20 Co Law 314 at 316.

9   Ross, M, 'Directors' liability on corporate restructuring' in Ricketts, C (ed), *Essays on Corporate Restructuring and Insolvency*, 1996, Wellington: Brooker's, pp 176–177. Some courts in the United States have gone as far as to say that in certain circumstances, directors owe a duty to creditors (Davis, L, McCullough, M, McNulty, E, and Schuler, R, 'Corporate reorganizations in the 1990s: guiding directors of troubled corporations through uncertain

where they will ameliorate creditor interests. The Supreme Court of Ireland in *Re Frederick Inns Ltd* [1994] ILRM 387; [1993] IESC 1 took the view that if companies are insolvent then creditors have the right to petition for their winding up, and if that is the case, the directors should not be dealing with company property in any way other than for the betterment of the creditors (at [38]). The Court said that such companies were no longer the beneficial owners of the assets that they held (at [38]).

If the trigger for the liability of directors to creditors is insolvency, one major problem is: what definition of insolvency applies? Some have said that insolvency is a broad and ambiguous term,[10] while others have focused on the indefinite nature of the concept.[11] Accounting details are often critical in assessing whether a company is insolvent or not and, in this regard, David Wishart is concerned that accounting practice is bedevilled by lack of definitions and difficulties with valuations.[12] He has stated that:

> [A]ccounting information is being called on to draw a definite line on which liability hangs yet which in many ways does not yield certain results. In emphasising legal form through the definition of status, consideration of the ambivalence of the position of creditors in insolvent companies is shifted from directors' duties to accounting requirements.[13]

All of these criticisms are fair, certainly in relation to the past, when there was no statutory definition of 'insolvency'. But now in the Insolvency Act 1986 there are definitions. 'Insolvency' can mean different things in different provisions, but generally the state of insolvency is defined in one of two ways. First, where 'it is proved to the satisfaction of the court that the company is unable to pay its debts as they fall due'.[14] Second, 'if it is proved to the satisfaction of the court that value of the company's assets is less than the

---

territory' (1991) 47 *The Business Lawyer* 1 at 3; Lo Pucki, L, and Whitford, W, 'Corporate governance in the bankruptcy reorganization of large, publicly held companies' (1993) 141 *University of Pennsylvania Law Review* 669 at 707.

10 Stilson, A, 'Re-examining the fiduciary paradigm at corporate insolvency and dissolution: defining directors' duties to creditors' (1995) 20 *Delaware Journal of Corporate Law* 1 at 113; Rao, R, Sokolow, D, and White, D, 'Fiduciary duty à la Lyonnais: an economic perspective on corporate governance in a financially distressed firm' (1996) 22 *The Journal of Corporation Law* 53 at 62.

11 Sealy, L, 'Director's wider responsibilities – problems conceptual practical and procedural' (1987) 13 *Monash University Law Review* 164 at 179.

12 Wishart, D, 'Models and theories of directors' duties to creditors' (1991) 14 *New Zealand Universities Law Review* 323 at 344.

13 *Ibid* at 345.

14 Section 123(1)(e) of the Insolvency Act. This is called 'equity insolvency' in the United States: Millner, R, 'What does it mean for directors of financially troubled corporations to have fiduciary duties to creditors?' (2000) 9 *Journal of Bankruptcy Law and Practice* 201 at 218.

amount of its liabilities, taking into account its contingent and prospective liabilities'.[15] The first definition provides for commercial or, as it is more frequently known, cash-flow insolvency. It is clear that the test is not without its problems.[16] The main difficulties with the cash flow test have been said to be that it is vague in meaning,[17] and the decision about whether a company, on a particular day, is insolvent, is often a difficult and imprecise one.[18] While these comments continue to hold some water, it is fair to say that in recent years there has been greater certainty in assessing whether or not a company was insolvent (on the cash-flow basis) at a particular point of time. To be sure, some reliance has to be placed on decisions from other jurisdictions, particularly Australia, in ascertaining the meaning of the definition.[19] The second definition provides for what is known as balance-sheet insolvency. In *Yukong Lines Ltd of Korea v Rendsburg Investments Corporation* [1998] BCC 870 Toulson J in High Court applied the balance sheet test and said (at 884) that in the case before him there was a clear breach of duty because the liability to a creditor was well in excess of the company's assets. While the UK applies either of the two definitions of insolvency mentioned above, as do Australia and other jurisdictions, some jurisdictions only employ one of the definitions. For instance, the United States invokes the balance sheet test as a formal test of insolvency (*Geyer v Ingersoll Publications Co* 621 A 2d 784 at 787, 789 (1992)).

Professor Len Sealy raises, in his attack on the use of insolvency as being the trigger for the advent of the duty, the fact that a company may move in and out of insolvency as its fortunes fluctuate, and that the duties of directors should be evaluated from a broad perspective and not on the basis of technicalities.[20] A riposte to this view is that if a company does move in and out of insolvency, obviously indicating that it is highly unstable from a financial point of view, then it is exactly the type of company whose affairs should be run with consideration for the creditors' interests; it is likely to collapse without much warning.[21] In fact, the point Sealy makes may well be a good reason for having a less definite point at which the duty is triggered. Professor Ross Grantham has made a similar point when he says that:

15 Section 123(2) of the Insolvency Act. This is called 'bankruptcy insolvency' in the United States: Millner, *ibid.*

16 For example, see Keay, A, 'The insolvency factor in the avoidance of antecedent transactions in corporate liquidations' (1995) 21 *Monash University Law Review* 305; Duns, J, 'Insolvency: problems of concept, definitions and proof' (2000) 28 ABLR 22.

17 Milman, D, 'Test of commercial insolvency rejected', (1983) 4 Co Law 231 at 232; *op. cit.* Stilson, fn 10 above at 113.

18 Chiah, K, 'Voidable preference' (1986) 12 *New Zealand Universities Law Review* 1 at 6; Riley, C, 'Directors' duties and the interests of creditors' (1989) 10 Co Law 87 at 88–89.

19 See Keay, A, *McPherson's Law of Company Liquidation*, 2001, London: Sweet and Maxwell, pp 84–91.

20 *Op. cit.* fn 11 above.

21 See the comments of Cooke J in *Nicholson v Permakraft (NZ) Ltd* (1985) 3 ACLC 453 at 459.

[I]nsolvency is the most obvious indication that the residual risk is no longer borne by the shareholders. Thus the question posed by the court is not simply whether the company is insolvent, but that given the distribution of risk does it continue to be appropriate to regard the interests of shareholders as exclusively reflecting the corporate interest.[22]

It is not unusual to find that insolvency is the point from which liability falls on someone. For instance, s 239 of the Insolvency Act 1986 provides that a transaction may only be regarded as a preference, and perhaps adjusted, if either the company was insolvent when the transaction that is impugned as a preference was entered into or the entering into of the transaction caused the company to become insolvent.[23] The difficulties which can exist with the notion of insolvency have not prevented the UK Parliament from using the idea of insolvent liquidation in relation to wrongful trading proceedings. Further, the Australian Parliament has been content to use the concept in s 588G of its Corporations Act 2001 in relation to insolvent trading, its equivalent of wrongful trading. It is submitted that many of the concerns over the issue of insolvency are illusory. Another important point to note is that insolvency rarely occurs overnight, and there are telltale signs of a company's demise well before the point that technical insolvency occurs. Often the directors of companies, particularly closely held ones, are just too proud or overly optimistic to recognise that the company is in trouble.[24]

If the trigger for the duty to creditors is insolvency, should the duty apply strictly, or only when it is, or should have been, clear to the directors that the company is insolvent? In *West Mercia Safetywear* Dillon LJ found against the director who was being pursued for breach of duty because that director knew that his company was insolvent when he gave a preference payment to a related company (at 33). While his Lordship did not specify knowledge of insolvency as a prerequisite for the duty to arise, it is worth considering whether knowledge should be taken into account. There is, it is submitted, a grave danger in introducing any notion of knowledge. Establishing a person's knowledge is, like intention, never very easy to ascertain. If there is a need for knowledge, the duty may well be tantamount to useless on many occasions because of the difficulty of proving knowledge. Perhaps it would be fairer to introduce, in addition to knowledge, an objective element, that is, ought the director have known that the company was insolvent? This is the approach employed in relation to wrongful trading, for a director is liable if he or she ought to have concluded that there was no reasonable prospect of the

---

22 Grantham, R, 'The judicial extension of directors' duties to creditors' [1991] JBL 1 at 15.
23 See s 239(2) and s 240(1) ('relevant time').
24 See, for instance, Mokal, R, 'An agency cost analysis of the wrongful trading provisions: redistribution, perverse incentives and the creditors' bargain' (2000) 59 CLJ 335 at 354.

company avoiding insolvent liquidation. Taking an approach like this would be the most equitable standard for creditors and directors alike.[25] All reported cases in the UK, Australia and New Zealand where directors have been held liable for breach of duty, appear to have been concerned with what may loosely be called 'closely held companies',[26] and if this is indicative, as it probably is, of the kind of cases which will be pursued, one might think that all directors sued ought to have known that their companies were insolvent, if in fact they were. This sort of requirement might have the added benefit of coercing directors into taking time, and obtaining assistance, in ascertaining what is the state of the finances of their companies. The consequence could be that directors will discover the plight of the company early enough to be able to do something to save it, such as taking their company into administration under Schedule B1 of the Insolvency Act.

Some cases have, however, given indications that a duty to take into account creditors' interests arises before the company enters an insolvent state. The next sections of the Chapter address this matter.

Near or in the vicinity of insolvency

While the state of insolvency is the most obvious case where a duty to creditors will arise because the creditors have clearly become the residual risk-bearers, an issue discussed in Chapter 12,[27] there will be other situations where the duty is triggered. As mentioned earlier, a majority of the High Court in *Spies* approved of the comments of Gummow J in *Re New World Alliance* when his Honour said (at [94]) that if a company is nearing insolvency directors have a duty to creditors. In New Zealand in *Nicholson v Permakraft (NZ) Ltd* (1985) 3 ACLC 453, 459 Cooke J included near-insolvency, along with insolvency or doubtful insolvency, as the trigger for the imposition on directors of a duty to creditors, although the other judges, Richardson and Somers JJ in the same case, were more circumspect and did not commit themselves (at 463, 464). Most recently EM Heenan J in the Supreme Court of Western Australia in the case of *Geneva Finance Ltd v Resource & Industry Ltd* (2002) 20 ACLC 1427 accepted that the duty applied where the company was insolvent or approaching insolvency. But perhaps the most important developments in this regard have occurred in the United States, and particularly in *Credit Lyonnaise Bank Nederlander, NV v Pathe Communications Corp* (1991) Del Ch WL 277613; LEXIS 215; (1992) 17 *Delaware Journal of Corporate Law* 1099. In this case Chancellor Allen of the Delaware Court of Chancery stated that:

---

25 *Op. cit.* McDonnell, fn 7 above at 208.

26 This for the most part appears to be the situation in the United States as well: Lin, L, 'Shift of fiduciary duty upon corporate insolvency: proper scope of directors' duty to creditors' (1993) 46 Vanderbilt L Rev 1485 at 1518.

27 Above, pp 176–177.

> At least where a corporation is operating in *the vicinity of insolvency*, a board of directors is not merely the agent of the residual risk-bearers [the shareholders], but owes its duty to the corporate enterprise. [My emphasis.]

The corporate enterprise to which the learned judge refers clearly comprises both shareholders and creditors,[28] and is an issue that is taken up in the next chapter. While Chancellor Allen failed to explain exactly what he meant by 'in the vicinity of insolvency' he seemed to be suggesting that the duty to creditors arises when the company is nearing insolvency.[29] Likewise in *Gwyer v London Wharf (Limehouse) Ltd* [2003] 2 BCLC 153 at 178; [2002] EWHC 2748 at [74], Leslie Kosmin QC (sitting as a deputy judge of the High Court) said that the duty arose where the company was on the verge of insolvency and that is probably close or near to insolvency.

This requirement means that if a company is in the vicinity of insolvency, directors should take stock of the company's position to ascertain whether the company will remain solvent after the action which is contemplated.

While insolvency may suffer from imprecision, prescribing the triggering of the duty when the company is near to insolvency suffers even more from that problem,[30] for it is impossible in many situations to say from what point a company is nearing insolvency, except where one is viewing the company's dealings *ex post*.

Doubtful solvency

While some commentators have been concerned about prescribing insolvency as the trigger for the duty to creditors because, *inter alia*, the company may move in and out of technical insolvency and the directors may not be aware of the company's insolvent state, legislating that the duty arises where it is doubtful whether the company is solvent allows for more leeway for liquidators in proving cases and means that directors do not have to ascertain whether their companies are in fact insolvent. Several cases, including the

---

28 Tompkins, A, 'Directors' duties to corporate creditors: Delaware and the insolvency exception' (1993) 47 SMU L Rev 165 at 168; Beveridge, N, 'Does a corporation's board of directors owe a fiduciary duty to its creditors' (1994) 25 *St Mary's Law Journal* 589 at 590.

29 *Geyer v Ingersoll Publications Co* 621 A 2d 784; *op. cit.* Rao *et al*, fn 10 above at 65. The duty is owed, in the US, to creditors, and not, as in Commonwealth jurisdictions, to the company to take into account creditor interests. Interestingly, a Minnesota court in *Snyder Elec Co v Fleming* (305 NW 2d 863 at 869 (1981)) referred to directors owing duties to creditors when a company was on the verge of insolvency.

30 See the comments of Richardson J in *Nicholson v Permakraft (NZ) Ltd* (1985) 3 ACLC 453 at 463. It has been suggested that 'in the vicinity of insolvency' may, like 'obscenity', be difficult to define, but a reasonable director can be expected to know it when he or she sees it (*op. cit.* Rao *et al*, fn 10 above at 64 fn 78).

Court of Appeal in *Brady v Brady* (at 552), have held that directors may be under a duty when a company's solvency is doubtful.[31]

The argument that may be levelled at this as the trigger-point for the duty is that it is also imprecise. Unlike insolvency, which is now defined in the insolvency legislation of most common law countries, there is no definition of doubtful solvency. Who must doubt the solvency of the company? Directors could probably ascertain when the solvency of their company is doubtful more easily than when insolvency has occurred. Insolvency occurs at one point. Doubtful solvency is broader. Yet, as with 'near-insolvency', from what point is a court going to say that a company was doubtfully solvent?

Risk of insolvency

Moving further away from the point of insolvency, some cases support either expressly or implicitly the fact that directors have a duty to creditors once there is a risk of insolvency.[32] In *West Mercia Safetywear* Dillon LJ referred to his earlier judgment in *Multinational Gas and Petrochemical Co v Multinational Gas and Petrochemical Services Co*, a case in which the Court of Appeal rejected the argument that the directors owed a duty to take into account creditors' interests following the fact that directors made a bad decision and this led to the company becoming insolvent (at 33). His Lordship said that the reason for his decision in *Multinational Gas* was the fact that the subject company was amply solvent and the decision of the directors was made in good faith (at 33). His Lordship implies in *West Mercia Safetywear* that if the company in *Multinational Gas* had not been amply solvent and there was a risk of insolvency as a result of the directors' decision, then he would have held there to have been a duty.

In *Nicholson v Permakraft* Cook J also indicated that directors might be under a responsibility to creditors where the company was risking insolvency. His Lordship said that directors owed a duty where a 'contemplated payment or other course of action would jeopardise solvency' (at 459), and similar language is used by Giles JA in *Linton v Telnet Pty Ltd* (1999) 30 ACSR 465 at 478.

Taking up what Cooke J had to say, one is moved to ask whether the directors must know either that there is a risk of insolvency, or that the action

---

31 For instance, see *Nicholson v Permakraft (NZ) Ltd* (1985) 3 ACLC 453 at 459, 463, 464 (NZCA); *Gwyer v London Wharf (Limehouse) Ltd* [2003] 2 BCLC 153 at 178; [2002] EWHC 2748 at para 74. Also, see the comments of Templeman LJ in *Re Horsley & Weight Ltd* [1982] 1 Ch 442 at 455; *Geyer v Ingersoll Publications Co* 621 A 2d 784 (1992).

32 For example, see *Wright v Frisina* (1983) 1 ACLC 716; *Grove v Flavel* (1986) 11 ACLR 161, 170; *Kinsela v Russell Kinsela Pty Ltd* (1986) 4 ACLC 215, 223 (agreeing with Cooke J in *Nicholson v Permakraft*); *Winkworth v Edward Baron Development Ltd* [1986] 1 WLR 1512; *Hilton International Ltd (in liq) v Hilton* [1989] NZLR 442.

could lead to insolvency. Again, as with the case where insolvency is the trigger, requiring knowledge is leaving the creditors too exposed. Such a requirement could too easily favour the indigent director who has not sought to apprise himself or herself of the state of the company's affairs and, consequently, did not know that there was a risk of the company becoming insolvent. Consequently, in addition to prescribing knowledge of the risk of insolvency, an objective test has to be employed. Therefore, the trigger for the duty would be either where the directors knew of the risk of insolvency, or where they ought to have known of the risk of insolvency or that one of the reasonably expected consequences of their action could be insolvency. This is favoured by Cooke J in *Permakraft* (at 460).

Financial instability

Other cases have not sought to identify with any precision how close to insolvency the company must be before the duty arises. They have been content to say that the company must be in a dangerous financial position (*Facia Footwear Ltd (in administration) v Hinchliffe*), financially unstable (*Linton v Telnet Pty Ltd*), or in financial difficulties (*Re MDA Investment Management Ltd* [2004] BPIR 75 at 102; [2003] EWHC 227 (Ch) at [70]). These phrases can mean a number of things and can be regarded as indefinite, but it is fair to say that for the most part, from a financial economist's viewpoint, they mean that the company is facing insolvency,[33] and this appears to have been the meaning given in the cases. Therefore, the trigger point is probably close to 'doubtful solvency' or a 'risk of insolvency'.

In the Australian case of *Grove v Flavel* (1986) 11 ACLR 161, the Full Court of the Supreme Court of South Australia said that it was not persuaded that any duty could be owed save where there is 'insolvency *or* financial instability' (at 169), thereby clearly indicating that insolvency is not the only factor that will cause the duty to arise, but making it equally clear that there had to be some feature of financial instability in existence. What that actually means, however, was not considered by the court.

In the United States case of *Re Healthco International Inc* 208 BR 288 (1999) (Ma) the court said (at 302) that directors had a duty in relation to creditors when the company is suffering from a 'condition of financial debility short of insolvency but which makes the insolvency reasonably foreseeable'.

An assessment

Perhaps the first thing to note is that the preponderance of authority favours the view that a duty to take into account the interests of creditors does not

---

33 *Op. cit.* Rao *et al*, fn 10 above at 62.

arise where a company is clearly solvent.[34] But as already noted in this chapter, there is a significant amount of judicial opinion that supports the view that the duty is triggered before a company actually becomes technically insolvent. After saying that, it is plain, as indicated at the outset of the Chapter, that, while there is significant agreement amongst judges both as to the need for a duty to creditors, and the fact that the duty should not arise until the company is suffering some degree of financial difficulty, there is no unanimity on the question of when the duty is triggered.

At the outset one can say that Mason J did not expressly limit the taking of the interests of creditors into account to the time when the company is insolvent, a point affirmed by Jacob J in his leading judgment in *Grove v Flavel* (at 167). It has been asserted by Reginald Barrett that:[35]

> In fact, Mason J seems to infer that creditors' interests must be taken into account even before insolvency, since those interests 'may be prejudiced by the movement of funds between companies in the event that the companies become insolvent'. This suggests that the theoretical possibility of future insolvency is sufficient to require directors to give continuing attention to creditors' interests.

If the duty is imposed at one extreme of the financial spectrum, namely insolvency, there is the significant danger that creditors will not benefit, for the reasons to be outlined shortly. If the duty was to apply at the other extreme, namely when the company is clearly solvent,[36] then it would have the effect of unreasonably interfering with the decision-making of directors, hamper the business of the company and would be likely to lead to directors being over-cautious.

The New South Wales Court of Appeal in *Linton v Telnet Pty Ltd* said that when directors should pay attention to the interests of creditors was dependent on the facts (at 626). In *Kinsela* (at 223) Street CJ said:

> I hesitate to attempt to formulate a general test of the degree of financial

---

34 For example, see *Mutlinational Gas and Petrochemical Co v Mutlinational Gas and Petrochemical Services Ltd* [1983] Ch 258; *Nicholson v Permakraft (NZ) Ltd* (1985) 3 ACLC 453; *Brady v Brady* (1988) 3 BCC 535; *Kinsela v Russell Kinsela Pty Ltd* (1986) 4 ACLC 215; *Liquidator of West Mercia Safetywear v Dodd* (1988) 4 BCC 30; *Equiticorp Finance Ltd (in liq) v BNZ* (1993) 11 ACLC 952. In this last case the New South Wales Court of Appeal said that Mason J's comments in *Walker v Wimborne* (1976) 137 CLR 1 were made in the context of an insolvent company (at 1016).

35 *Op. cit.* fn 4 above at 229.

36 The controversial dictum of Lord Templeman in *Winkworth v Edward Baron Development Ltd* [1986] 1 WLR 1512 at 1517, seems to provide that directors of companies which are solvent are under the duty. But, save for the decision in *Jeffree v NCSC* (1989) 7 ACLC 556, no court seems to have followed that view.

instability which would impose upon directors an obligation to consider the interests of creditors.

While the comment in *Linton v Telnet Pty Ltd* is undoubtedly true, and the latter comment in *Kinsela* understandable, we must arrive at some guidelines to be fair to directors so that they can plan and know when they must exhibit some loyalty to creditors. Also, guidelines must be identified if this development of the law is not to suffer further criticism on the basis that it is imprecise and produces uncertainty.

Some of the cases that have been decided are of limited assistance as they involve situations that are relatively clear cut, and because of that fact they failed to establish any specific guidelines to assist in more difficult and marginal cases. Instances are the cases of *Kinsela* and *West Mercia Safetywear* where all would probably agree that the directors should have been held liable for breach of duty. While these cases were discussed in Chapter 11, it might be worthwhile recapping their facts. In the former case the liquidator of RK, carrying business as a funeral director, brought proceedings to have a lease over premises granted by RK to directors of the company, three months before the commencement of winding up, set aside. The lease had been granted at a time when the company's financial position was precarious. The company had sustained a significant loss during the previous year, had suffered less severe losses for several years and the accounts some six months before the lease was entered into showed that he company's liabilities exceeded its assets by nearly A$200,000. Also of importance was the fact that the company had committed itself to performing services in relation to pre-paid funerals. The lease involved the directors being given a term of three years at a below market rental, there was no escalator clause to cover inflation and the directors were entitled, during the life of the lease, to purchase part of the premises for a sum which was well below true value. As Street CJ said (at 219), in delivering his leading judgment:

> [T]his insolvent company [RK], in a state of imminent and foreseen collapse, entered into a transaction which plainly had the effect, and was intended to have the effect, of placing its assets beyond the reach of its creditors . . . by means of . . . the terms of a lease [which] were, to say the least, commercially questionable.

In *West Mercia Safetywear*, D, a director of WMS, transferred £4,000 to WMS's parent company on 21 May 1984. WMS entered liquidation on 4 June 1984. The liquidator of WMS brought misfeasance proceedings against D, seeking the recovery of the £4,000, on the basis that D breached his duty to WMS. Although the payment was clearly a voidable preference, preference proceedings against the parent company, under the then-equivalent of s 239 of the Act, were not issued, because, one assumes, the parent company was insolvent. D had paid the money to the parent company because he had guaranteed the parent's debts and he wanted to reduce his financial exposure. Of critical importance to Dillon LJ in delivering the leading judgment of the Court of Appeal was that D knew that WMS, at the time of the payment, was insolvent (at 33).

At the other extreme, but equally clear cut, are cases like *Multinational Gas and Petrochemical Co v Multinational Gas and Petrochemical Services Ltd*. In that case three oil companies agreed to a joint venture in relation to liquefied petroleum gas and liquefied natural gas. This involved forming X company in Liberia. Another company, S, was registered in England to act as the adviser and agent of X. The directors of X made a number of decisions which resulted in X chartering or acquiring some 20 tankers. This led to the incurring of future financial liabilities. A downturn in the market caused X financial difficulties and it halted trading. Both X and S went into liquidation. X sued, amongst others, S and those exercising powers of management in relation to S, for breach of duty, namely making decisions which resulted in X becoming insolvent. As mentioned earlier, in that case, according to Dillon LJ in *West Mercia Safetywear* (at 33), a member of the Court of Appeal bench in *Multinational Gas*, X was amply solvent at the time of the impugned transactions and the directors made business decisions in good faith and were not liable for breach of duty.

Factors to be considered

The need for risk-taking

In determining the circumstances that should exist before the duty arises, one must take into account a number of factors. First, undoubtedly companies need, at times, to take risks to prosper.[37] One can even say that without risks being taken, we would not enjoy some of the things that we do enjoy in society today.[38] The corollary of this, certainly from a theoretical perspective, is that one of the functions of the directors, being the persons who manage a risk-taking enterprise, is to engage in overseeing the very action of risk-taking.[39] One of the arguments of those who question the existence of a duty to creditors is, *inter alia*, that directors are placed under greater pressure when making decisions and the company's development might be stifled as

37 Allen, W, 'Ambiguity in corporation law' (1997) 22 *Delaware Journal of Corporate Law* 894 at 896.

38 *Op. cit.* Sealy, fn 11 above at 181. Also, see Easterbrook, F, and Fischel, D, *The Economic Structure of Company Law*, 1991, Cambridge, Mass: Harvard University Press, pp 41–44, referred to in Telfer, T, 'Risk and insolvent trading' in Rickett, C, and Grantham, R (eds), *Corporate Personality in the 20th Century*, 1998, Oxford: Hart Publishing, pp 127–128.

39 See Whincop, M, 'Taking the corporate contract more seriously: the economic cases against, and a transaction cost rationale for, the insolvent trading provisions' (1996) 5 *Griffith Law Review* 1 at 13.

directors become extremely cautious and refuse to take risks. This is the point on which Vladimir Jelisavcic focuses when discussing the Delaware decision of *Credit Lyonnais Bank Nederland NV v Pathe Communications Corp.* The learned commentator states in relation to the 'in the vicinity of insolvency' test that it:

> ... exposes directors to liability for breach of fiduciary duty to creditors without clearly defining the point at which this new duty springs forth. This poorly defined, potentially large personal liability could chill directors' exercise of their business judgment when confronted with difficult choices. Directors may feel constrained to make overly conservative decisions when they are unsure whether their corporation is in the 'vicinity of insolvency'.[40] [Footnote omitted.]

This is an issue that is discussed in more detail in Chapter 19 when we consider the duty from a theoretical perspective, but suffice to say at this point, it has been said that the duty 'results in the inability of directors to take risks with corporate assets for the purposes of extinguishing or minimising the firm's temporary financial distress'[41] and changes the role of directors from an 'active management mode to one of passive asset-preservation'.[42]

There is a time to take high risks[43] (where the success rate is low), such as marketing a new untried product, there are times to take calculated risks, and there are times when few or no risks should be taken. The degree of the risk permitted will depend on the actual level of financial difficulty. If the company is financially embarrassed, the shareholders and directors may have nothing to lose by embracing a high-risk strategy;[44] the taking of significant risks could be highly profitable and 'make the company'. But if the gamble does fail then the ones 'picking up the tab' are the creditors. The directors do not have the right to gamble with the creditors' money. This does not mean that directors must sit on their hands or refrain from seeking to take the company forward; their only obligation is to refrain from taking action that cannot be calculated overall to be in the interests of the creditors. The degree of financial instability and the degree of risk are interrelated[45] and the

---

40 'A safe harbour proposal to define the limits of directors' fiduciary duty to creditors in the "vicinity of insolvency" ' [1992] *Journal of Corporation Law* 145 at 159.

41 *Op. cit.* Stilson, fn 10 above at 91. Also, see Yeo, V, and Lin, J, 'Insolvent trading – a comparative and economic approach' (1996) 10 *Australian Journal of Corporate Law* 216.

42 Yeo and Lin, *ibid* at 216.

43 For instance, in *Mutlinational Gas and Petrochemical Co v Mutlinational Gas and Petrochemical Services Ltd* [1983] Ch 258. In that case it was acceptable as the company was plainly solvent.

44 Ironically directors might in such circumstances, absent any duty to take creditors' interests into account, not be liable in taking such action even though the action is close to reckless because the shareholders would not complain.

45 See *Kinsela v Russell Kinsela Pty Ltd* (1986) 4 ACLC 215 at 223; *Equiticorp Finance Ltd (in liq) v BNZ* (1993) 11 ACLC 952 at 1017.

latter must be determined by the former. As Clark and Cripps JJA in the New South Wales Court of Appeal in *Equiticorp Finance Ltd (in liq) v BNZ* ((1993) 11 ACLC 952) said (at 1007):

> [T]he question whether directors are required to consider the interests of creditors in determining whether particular action is or is not for the benefit of the company depends upon the state of solvency of the company at the time of the contemplated action.

Hence, the more obvious it is that the creditors' interests are at risk, the lower must be the risk to which directors should expose the company (at 1007).[46] So, providing that a director must, in certain cases, have concern for the interests of creditors does not mean that risk-taking is to be totally proscribed.[47]

Also, it is submitted that too much is often made of the argument that the duty will stifle the development of a company's business. This is discussed in detail in Chapter 19.

An increase in costs

It must be acknowledged that the existence of a duty to creditors might, in some cases, produce an increase in a company's costs as directors might well have to undertake investigations to ascertain whether their contemplated actions could precipitate insolvency and these investigations, it may be argued, could occupy inordinate periods of time and perhaps even limit the company's profitability. This might entail, by way of protection for the directors, the securing of more expert opinions than is normal, undertaking copious checks and even some valuations of the company's assets, all of which would add to the company's operating costs. This, again, is discussed in more detail in Chapter 19.

The need for precision

A third factor to consider is that concern has been voiced about the difficulty of stating with precision when the shift in duty is to occur. It is submitted that there must be a balance. On one side the law must not unduly hamper directors and must allow companies to be governed in a commercial manner, for as Lockhart J said in the Australian case of *Australian Innovation Ltd v Paul Andrew Petrovsky* (1996) 14 ACLC 1357 at 1361:

---

46 See the view of Rao *et al*, *op. cit.* fn 10 above at 65.
47 Even Lord Templeman in *Winkworth v Edward Baron Development Ltd* [1986] 1 WLR 1512, perhaps the high-water mark as far as decisions go in this area, did not suggest that the taking of a risk should be prohibited.

It is important that the courts do not impose burdens upon directors which make their task so onerous that capable people will be deterred from serving as directors.

But on the other side of the coin, the law must ensure that it does not permit directors to do whatever they like so that the position of the creditors is ignored. Limited liability is a privilege and it must not be forgotten that it can work to the disadvantage of creditors. As Cooke J stated in *Permakraft* (at 459):

> It [limited liability] is a privilege healthy as tending to the expansion of opportunities and commerce, but it is open to abuse. Irresponsible structural engineering – involving the creating, dissolving and transforming of incorporated companies to the prejudice of creditors – is a mischief to which the courts should be alive.

If a duty is imposed on directors before the advent of insolvency then they will have the task of reconciling the interests of the creditors on the one hand and the shareholders on the other. It is submitted that directors are often seeking to balance interests in the decisions which they make. Directors are presently required by s 309 of the Companies Act 1985 to have regard for company employees as well as members in carrying out their functions. If the Company Law Reform Bill, discussed in Chapter 11, becomes law, directors will need to take into account certain material factors, such as the interests of its employees, the need to foster its business relationships with suppliers, customers and others, the need to consider the impact of its operations on the community and the environment, and the need to maintain a reputation for high standards of business conduct.[48] This issue is discussed further in the next chapter.

Even when subject to the duty directors may still take action to serve the interests of members provided that that action does not prejudice the interests of creditors. This is an important issue and is discussed in the next chapter in some depth.

A cause for panic?

Is the existence of a duty, when a company is subject to financial distress, likely to make directors panic and place their company into administration or even liquidation prematurely, thereby ensuring that all stakeholders lose out? There is no indication in the empirical studies conducted in relation to administration that this is the case. It is more likely that directors will take the decision to appoint an administrator or liquidate because of fear

---

48 Clause 156 of the bill. This clause had become cl 158 when the bill was taken to the House of Commons.

of liability for wrongful trading. This issue is discussed in more detail in Chapter 19.

A suggested trigger for the duty

There is adequate authority for us to say that directors owe a duty where they are aware or ought to be aware that their company is insolvent, near insolvent, at a risk of insolvency or in financial difficulties. But this does not tell us what is the earliest point when the duty will arise. Directors are still 'in the dark' on this issue. It is submitted here that the earliest point at which the duty is triggered is where the circumstances of a company are such that its directors know, or can reasonably expect, that the action upon which they are going to embark could lead to the insolvency of the company.[49] The reason for taking this point is that companies that are not insolvent, or even close to it, can fall into that state quickly in some situations, and the suggested trigger is merely an attempt to cause directors to think through the consequences of their decision-making. Directors might see their company's financial state as not parlous and that might cause them not to consider adequately, or at all, the actions that they are proposing for the company's business.

If the point suggested were adopted, then the point of liability would not be the same across the board as the court would have to take into account the circumstances of each company, so that the more obvious it is that the creditors' money is at risk, the lower the risk to which directors are justified in exposing the company (*Kinsela* at 223). So, while a company will usually be experiencing some significant financial problems before the duty arises, at one extreme the duty could conceivably be triggered where a company, while not financially strong, has no obvious major financial concerns, but the company is contemplating action which constitutes a very substantial risk, and if the venture fails, the company may well fall into insolvency, as was the case with the company in the United States case of *Re Healthco International Inc* (1999) 208 BR 288 (Ma).

If the test posited here is implemented as the trigger for the duty, the action that directors would have to take is discussed in the next chapter. It might well include, before directors take any action which might conceivably have a substantially negative effect on creditors' interests, inquiring into the affairs of their company[50] and reviewing all material information relative to the financial standing of the company as well as taking advice on the extent of the effects of the action being proposed.

---

49 See the comments of Schwarcz, *op. cit.* fn 6 above at 671–672; Finch, V, 'Directors' duties: insolvency and the unsecured creditor' in Clarke, A (ed), *Current Issues in Insolvency Law*, 1991, London: Stevens, p 106.
50 See the comments of Tipping J in *Hilton International Ltd (in liq) v Hilton* [1989] NZLR 442 at 476.

While what is being suggested is more developed and elaborate than is indicated by the comments of Cooke J in *Permakraft* (at 449), what his Lordship had to say in that case provides some foundation for the trigger put forward here. In *Permakraft* Cooke J said (at 449) that a duty to creditors existed where the company is insolvent, near insolvent, of doubtful solvency or 'if a contemplated payment or other course of action would jeopardise solvency'. His Lordship went on to say (at 449) that as a matter of business ethics, it is proper that directors take into account whether any course of action will deleteriously affect their company's ability to discharge promptly debts owed to creditors. Also, in *obiter* comments in *Re Horsley & Weight Ltd* [1982] 1 Ch 442; [1982] 3 All ER 1045, Cumming-Bruce LJ said (at 455; 1055) that the liquidator could not succeed in that case for misfeasance, because 'the evidence fell short of proof that the directors should at the time have appreciated that the payment was likely to cause loss to creditors'. This suggests that if directors did appreciate that what they were going to do might cause loss to creditors, they would be in breach if they did take the action and creditors lost out.

The test that has been suggested is objective. Is this fair? Objective tests have been invoked in relation to other responsibilities of directors. For instance, the duty of care and skill involves an objective test (*Re D'Jan of London Ltd* [1993] BCC 646), as does the test for wrongful trading. Unless one provides for an objective test one can have directors, like the defendants in the Australian case of *Wright v Frisina* (1983) 1 ACLC 716 at 717, claiming that it is easy to be wise after the event and at the time of the alleged shift they were not aware of the company's predicament. Also, as indicated earlier, if a subjective test is applied it could make the directors' position close to impregnable. Cooke J in *Permakraft* clearly favoured an objective test when assessing the actions of the directors (at 460). In that case his Lordship applied a test similar to that proposed here and concluded that the directors could not be held to have been able to foresee, or ought to have foreseen, the action that they were going to adopt as likely to cause creditors harm (at 462). Also in New Zealand, Tipping J in *Hilton International Ltd v Hilton* [1989] 1 NZLR 442, said (at 474–475) that when paying out money, the directors are liable if they do not reasonably believe that the company's financial health and its creditors will not be jeopardised. His Lordship went on to say (at 475) that this involved taking 'reasonable steps to ensure that the company's financial position would not be jeopardised' by the action that the directors proposed to take.

Can courts undertake this inquiry into the state of a company and the investigations made by directors, and then make the necessary determination? Wishart has questioned[51] the expertise of judges to 'determine the limits of acceptable business decisions'. He also points out that it is because of this fact that judges have not interfered in the internal workings of companies.

---

51 *Op. cit.* fn 12 above at 341.

But he relies on a very old case,[52] and while Street CJ in *Kinsela* (at 223) accepted that courts have traditionally and properly been cautious about entering boardrooms when deciding the commercial justification of executive actions, his Honour approved (at 223) of the opinion of Cooke J in *Permakraft* who said (at 457) that, *inter alia*, creditors' interests were to be considered 'if a contemplated payment or other course of action would jeopardise its solvency', and this requires, as a matter of necessity, an examination of the decision of a board. Also, there are indications in recent cases that many judges no longer see the boardroom as sacrosanct and there are examples of courts in the past 20 years demonstrating a readiness to review the way in which companies operate and the merits of decisions which have been made at a managerial level.[53] Admittedly there is a potential danger that courts will see everything with hindsight, always a most wonderful thing (*Linton v Telnet Pty Ltd* at 475), and allow that unreasonably to influence them in the final outcome of a case. But courts have indicated that they are wary of employing hindsight. When dealing with a wrongful trading case, the judge in *Re Sherborne Associates Ltd* [1995] BCC 40 expressed the view (at 54) that it is dangerous to assume that 'what has in fact happened was always bound to happen and was apparent'.[54] The fact of the matter is that UK courts have refused to second-guess directors in their commercial dealings.[55] Dillon LJ made this reasonably plain in *West Mercia Safetywear* (at 33), when he discussed the decision in *Mutlinational Gas*. His Lordship said (at 33) that in the latter case at the time of the transaction that led to the claim under consideration:

> [T]he company was amply solvent, and what the directors had done at the bidding of the shareholders had merely been to make a business decision in good faith, and act on that decision. It subsequently turned out to be a bad decision, but the position had to be decided on the facts at the earlier stage where the company was amply solvent and the parties were acting in good faith.

Obviously courts must take into account all relevant factors at the time of the director's decision. Decisions like *Permakraft, Re Welfab Engineers Ltd* [1990] BCC 600, *Linton v Telnet* and *Brady v Brady* indicate that they have done so. For instance, in *Linton v Telnet* the liquidator of T brought an action

---

52 *Burland v Earle* [1902] AC 83. Also, see *Carlen v Drury* (1812) 35 ER 61; *Dovey v Corey* [1901] AC 477 at 488.

53 For example *AWA Ltd v Daniels* (1992) 7 ACSR 759.

54 Lewison J in *Secretary of State for Trade and Industry v Goldberg* [2004] 1 BCLC 597 at 613 made the same point in relation to an assessment of a director's conduct when hearing an application under the Company Directors' Disqualification Act 1986.

55 Law Commission, *Company Directors: Regulating Conflicts of Interests and Formulating a Statement of Duties* (Law Commission Consultation Paper No 153, 1998) at para 15.30.

against L, the wife of one of the company's directors, claiming that she, L, held a house on trust for the company because some of the purchase price was paid with cheques drawn on T. The allegation was that L's husband who gave the cheques to L, was, in doing so, in breach of his fiduciary duty to T. It had been agreed by the directors that the sums represented by the cheques were part of an interest-free loan to L's husband. At first instance, Hulme J of the New South Wales Supreme Court found for the liquidator on the basis, *inter alia*, that as L's husband was a bankrupt, he would have little prospect of repaying the loan, and the giving of an unsecured loan was a breach of duty. L appealed to the Court of Appeal, which upheld the appeal. The cheques had been given to L in August 1992 and Giles JA, in delivering the leading judgment (with Beazley JA and Sheppard AJA concurring), noted (at 475) that the figures for the group of which T was a part were, at June 1992, reasonably healthy and sales and gross profits in fact increased in 1993. His Honour went on to say (at 475), most poignantly, that:

> While the net loss for the year ended 30 June 1993 *could later be seen* as the beginning of its decline, peril to creditors on a group basis as at August 1992 did not leap out from the figures. [My emphasis.]

In *Re Welfab Engineers Ltd* Hoffmann J (as was then) had to decide whether or not directors had breached their duty to the company (by not taking into account the interests of creditors) in accepting one bid for the company's property and not others at a time when the company was in desperate financial straits. The learned judge, in coming to his decision, took into account the commercial environment at the time of the making of the transaction alleged to constitute the breach, even though it occurred some seven years in the past. At the time of the alleged breach the region in which the company's business operated was suffering a harsh recession and this impacted markedly on the decision made.

In fact a perusal of the cases in the UK, Australia and New Zealand suggests that courts have erred on the side of magnanimity when confronted with the evidence allegedly against directors who are sued for breach of duty. Arguably the only occasions on which courts have found directors liable in the jurisdictions just referred to is when the directors have done something either commercially improper or verging on the improper.[56] Where directors have made decisions that have turned out to be bad ones, but they acted in good faith, the courts have refrained from holding them liable.[57] This latter

---

56 For example, see *Grove v Flavel* (1986) 4 ACLC 654; *Kinsela v Russell Kinsela Pty Ltd* (1986) 4 ACLC 215; *Liquidator of West Mercia Safetywear v Dodd* (1988) 4 BCC 30; *Hilton International Ltd (in liq) v Hilton* [1989] NZLR 442; *Jeffree v NCSC* (1989) 7 ACLC 556; *Galladin Pty Ltd v Aimnorth Pty Ltd (in liq)* (1993) 11 ACSR 23

57 For example, see *Nicholson v Permakraft (NZ) Ltd* (1985) 3 ACLC 453; *Re Welfab Engineers Ltd* [1990] BCC 600; *Linton v Telnet Pty Ltd* (1999) 30 ACSR 465.

trend may be as a result of the courts' concern that there is little guidance for directors as to when they are to take into account creditors' interests, and they have not felt it proper to hold them liable under this ground except where there is impropriety or a complete disregard for the solvency of the company. Interestingly, the courts have tended to take the same approach when hearing claims of wrongful trading against directors.

In sum, while judges will, it is acknowledged, often have to wrestle with difficult questions flowing from differing views of what constitutes right action in the circumstances in which companies are to be found,[58] they are able to make the necessary assessment of the actions of creditors.

Whether the decision in *Multinational Gas* where the Court of Appeal said that directors have no responsibility to any persons other than shareholders when the company is solvent, is opposed to the suggested trigger is an issue that needs to be addressed. Clearly, in this case Dillon LJ, in his judgment, was not envisaging the kind of situation that I am positing in this section of the chapter. His Lordship did say that the duties owed by a director may depend, *inter alia*, on the particular knowledge of the individual director (at 288). What I am suggesting here is that if a director knew or ought to have expected that the action to which he or she is committing the company could cause the company to become insolvent, then the duty should exist. In *Multinational Gas* there was not a suggestion that the directors knew or ought to have expected that insolvency could result from the venture undertaken. So the suggestion put forward here is not inconsistent with what Dillon LJ said. His Lordship seemed to be at pains to say that the directors could not owe a duty to future creditors, whereas what I am suggesting relates to a responsibility to existing creditors at the time of the venture which leads to the financial malaise of the company.

Finally, providing that the duty to take into account the interests of creditors is triggered where the circumstances of a company are such that its directors know, or can reasonably expect, that the action upon which they are going to embark could lead to the insolvency of the company, could be advantageous for interests other than the creditors. If directors are required to have consideration for creditors' interests they are less likely to set in train a course of action that could precipitate the collapse of their companies, which in turn could lead to redundancies for employees. Furthermore, if a company has a large workforce or is an important part of a community, its collapse would have a deleterious impact on the local community, including schools and shops.[59]

---

58 *Op. cit.* Allen fn 37 above at 899.

59 See Veach, J, 'On considering the public interest in bankruptcy: looking to the railroads for answers' (1997) 72 *Indiana Law Journal* 1211 at 1225; Keay, A, 'Insolvency law: a matter of public interest?' (2000) 51 NILQ 509 at 517–518.

Conclusion

The duty to take into account creditor interests cannot be, according to the preponderance of authority, a continuing one. It clearly arises when a company is insolvent, near to it or at a risk of falling into insolvency. The duty is triggered if the directors know or ought to know that their company is in one of the states just mentioned. It has also been indicated that the duty is triggered even where companies are merely in financial difficulties. It has been argued here that the duty may arise at a point before a company can be said to be in financial difficulties. There is concern that the courts have failed to arrive at a consistent approach as far as the point in time from which the duty operates. This is problematic for both directors and liquidators. The former, who probably feel that they have been the target of several attacks from both the legislature and the courts in recent years, need to know what is able to trigger the duty. Also, a failure to provide a defined standard affects directors in the making of business decisions and this can be prejudicial for the performance of their companies, as the directors may well be inclined to make decisions on the basis of avoiding liability rather than what is commercially appropriate.[60] Liquidators and administrators need to know in what kind of situations they are at liberty to pursue directors of failed companies for breach of duty.

Hitherto, while a little disconcerting for those who require certainty in the law at all times, the uncertainty as to the circumstances which will provoke the duty is not an unusual situation for a developing area of law. As Justin Dabner has said:

> Whenever the judiciary embarks upon new developments a degree of uncertainty must eventuate. This is the price of a dynamic legal system which recognises current social attitudes and attempts to update the law accordingly.[61]

What has been argued for in this chapter is that the earliest point at which the duty is triggered is where the circumstances of a company are such that its directors know, or can reasonably expect, that the action upon which they are going to embark could lead to the insolvency of the company.

---

60 *Op. cit.* Rao *et al*, fn 10 above at 65.
61 'Directors' duties – the schizoid company' (1988) 6 *Company and Securities Law Journal* 105 at 112.

14 How are the directors to function when subject to a duty to creditors?

Introduction

The previous chapter dealt with one of the two critical issues that really has not been resolved by the case law, namely when do directors have to take into account creditor interests? This chapter addresses the other major issue that the courts have not resolved: how are the directors to act if they are subject to the responsibility to consider creditor interests? The reason for this is because there has not been a clearly articulated formulation of the director's duty in this regard, and this is the case not only in the UK, but also in the United States, Ireland and the British Commonwealth.

What does it mean to say that directors are to consider creditor interests? The problem is that, hitherto, directors have been given few signposts by the courts. This is recognised by one commentator, who has said that the nature of the duties of directors, when subject to an obligation to consider creditor interests, are 'vague and diaphanous'.[1] In this chapter I seek to wrestle with how directors are to function if they are subject to the duty. In particular, the Chapter is concerned with considering how are directors to act, given that the traditional position in Anglo-American jurisdictions is that directors are obliged to focus on shareholders' needs, and how are directors to fulfil their duty to creditors when there are different kinds of creditors with different interests?

The concept of directors having to consider creditors' interests has been criticised by some commentators, although not by the courts, for several reasons. One major concern (others are canvassed in Chapter 19) is that there are profound difficulties in working out how such a responsibility would operate. Professor Len Sealy has stated that when you have a position where duties are owed to different persons, 'with potentially opposed interests, the duty bifurcates and fragments so that it amounts ultimately to no more than

---

1 Miller, H, 'Corporate governance in Chapter 11: the fiduciary relationship between directors and stockholders of solvent and insolvent corporations' (1993) 23 *Seton Hall Law Review* 1467.

a vague obligation to be fair'.[2] In similar vein, as far back as the 1930s, Professor Adolf Berle said that:[3]

> When the fiduciary obligation of the corporate management and 'control' to stockholders is weakened or eliminated, the management and 'control' become for all purposes absolute ... The only thing that can come out of it, in any long view, is the massing of group after group to assert their private claims by force or threat ... This is an invitation not to law or orderly government, but to a process of economic civil war.

The main concern of those directors who are aware of their responsibilities, and that may not, admittedly, be a large portion of all directors, is that there is no certainty for them. These directors know that at some stage in the future their actions *might* be reviewed by a court. This issue is a governance issue that follows from the fact that directors' duty is not, according to the volume of authority, one owed to creditors, but to the company, so it is not creditors alone whom directors have to consider when subject to the responsibility to creditors. This chapter examines the issues raised above, elaborating on the problems encountered by directors, and it formulates a framework for determining how the actions of directors should be evaluated. This should go some way to enabling directors to know what to do or what not to do in order to avoid liability.

In what ways are directors to function?

The issues

The central question in this chapter is: how are directors to discharge their duty when circumstances are such that they are required to take into account creditor interests? Or, as Chris Riley has put it: 'Are the interests of the creditors merely one competing interest to be borne in mind by directors in their running of the company, and if so, how much prominence are they to be given?'[4] The question might be put in more economic terms as: how do directors fairly allocate company resources?

The simple fact is that the case law gives little indication as to what directors are to do. One of the main drawbacks with the case law as it presently stands is that it fails to address how the obligation imposed on directors to take into account creditor interests fits in with the traditional duties that

---

2 'Directors' wider responsibilities – problems conceptual practical and procedural' (1987) 13 *Monash University Law Review* 164 at 175.
3 'For whom corporate managers are trustees' (1931) 45 Harv L R 1365 at 1367–1369.
4 Riley, C, 'Directors' duties and the interests of creditors' (1989) 10 Co Law 87 at 89.

directors have in relation to shareholders.[5] For the most part, the cases have merely said that directors must take into account the creditors' interests in making their decisions.[6] In the recent decision of *Gwyer v London Wharf (Limehouse) Ltd* [2003] 2 BCLC 153; [2002] EWHC 2748, the court was a little more forthcoming when it said (at 181; [81]) that in considering the interests of creditors, directors are to take into account the impact of their decision on the ability of the creditors to recover the sums due to them from the company, but this is as far as any court has really gone.

The problem facing us is not unique. For instance, s 214 of the Insolvency Act, which, as we have seen, proscribes what is known as 'wrongful trading', merely prescribes the conditions for wrongful trading; it fails to set out how directors are to act to avoid it, save stating that they are to take every step with a view to minimising losses to the creditors at a time when they knew or ought to have concluded that there was no reasonable prospect of the company avoiding insolvent liquidation.

As the duty is usually regarded as being owed to the company, and not to the creditors, it means that it does not simply entail directors refraining from disposing of assets improperly or diverting property to insiders in the company, but extends to all of the duties that are owed by directors to companies, including duties of loyalty.

The financial state of the company

Whether or not directors are obliged to consider creditor interests all depends on the financial state of their company, as considered in the last chapter.

Solvency

Where companies are solvent and suffering no financial difficulty, it is often regarded as being axiomatic that directors must seek the maximisation of shareholder value,[7] the so-called 'shareholder primacy principle' referred to earlier. As we saw in the previous chapter, the directors of companies that are solvent generally have no responsibility to take into account creditor interests.[8]

---

5   This is also the case in the United States, where the position is still uncertain and developing: Cieri, R, Sullivan, P, and Lennox, H, 'The fiduciary duties of directors of financially troubled companies' (1994) 3 *Journal of Bankruptcy Law and Practice* 405 at 405.

6   The same has been held in the Delaware courts in the United States: see *Credit Lyonnais Bank Nederland NV v Pathe Communications Corp* (1991) WL 277613; LEXIS 215; (1992) 17 *Delaware Journal of Corporate Law* 1099 (Delaware Chancery Court).

7   *Op. cit.* fn 5 above at 406.

8   For example, see *Brady v Brady* (1987) 3 BCC 535, CA.

Insolvency

In contrast, as was discussed in Chapter 13, the courts have held unequivocally that where a company is insolvent, its directors must consider the interests of creditors.[9] In perhaps the leading English case on this topic, *Liquidator of West Mercia Safetywear Ltd v Dodd* (1988) 4 BCC 30, the Court of Appeal stated what seems to be an accepted view in the UK and elsewhere as far as the role of directors is concerned when their companies are insolvent (at 33). The court said that where a company is insolvent, the creditors' interests overrode the interests of the shareholders.[10] More recently, *Re Pantone 485 Ltd* [2002] 1 BCLC 266 at [69] and *Gwyer v London Wharf (Limehouse) Ltd* (at [74]), have indicated that when a company is insolvent then the creditors' interests are paramount.[11] This approach was also advocated by Street CJ in the New South Wales Court of Appeal in *Kinsela v Russell Kinsela Pty Ltd (in liq)* (1986) 4 ACLC 215 at 221; 10 ACLR 395 at 401. Likewise, the Irish Supreme Court in *Re Frederick Inns Ltd* [1993] IESC 1 at [47] said that:

> Because of the insolvency of the companies the shareholders no longer had any interest. The only parties with an interest were the creditors. The payments made could not have been lawful because they were made in total disregard of their interests.[12]

In the United States in the recent Massachusetts case of *Re Healthco International Inc* (1997) 208 BR 288 the Bankruptcy Court held, in common with many US cases,[13] that when a company is insolvent the creditors' interests are pre-eminent.[14]

---

9 For instance, see *Liquidator of West Mercia Safetywear Ltd v Dodd* (1988) 4 BCC 30.

10 Also, see the earlier Court of Appeal case of *Brady v Brady* (1987) 3 BCC 535 at 552.

11 Professors L Lo Pucki and W Whitford, ('Corporate governance in the bankruptcy reorganization of large publicly held companies' (1993) 141 U Pa L Rev 669 at 709) disagree, taking the view that management owes duties to both creditors and shareholders of an insolvent company until a bankruptcy reorganisation occurs. But from their empirical research Lo Pucki and Whitford found that the managers of large public companies that are insolvent aligned with creditors more frequently than shareholders (at 745).

12 There is a divergence of opinion in the courts in the United States as to whether duties are still owed to shareholders when a company is insolvent. See Millner, R, 'What does it mean for directors of financially troubled corporations to have fiduciary duties to creditors?' (2000) 9 *Journal of Bankruptcy Law and Practice* 201 at 217.

13 See, for example, *Snyder Electric Co v Fleming* 305 NW 2d 863 (1981) (MN); *Hixson v Pride of Texas Distribution Co Inc* 683 SW 2d 173 (1985) (TX); *Geyer v Ingersoll Publications Co* 621 A 2d 784 (1992) (DE).

14 The court in *Re Healthco International Inc* (1997) 208 BR 288 at 300 cited a number of American cases for the proposition. Some are: *Pepper v Litton*, 308 US 295, 60 S Ct 238, 84 L Ed 281 (1939); *McCandless v Furlaud*, 296 US 140, 56 S Ct 41, 80 L Ed 121 (1935); *Clarkson Co Ltd v Shaheen*, 660 F 2d 506 (2d Cir 1981); *Automatic Canteen Co of Am v Wharton* 358

The government appears to accept that this approach is correct as it stated in the 'Guidance to Key Clauses', published at the same time as the Company Law Reform Bill in November 2005 that cl 156(4) of the bill recognises that the duty to promote the success of the company for the benefit of the members is displaced when the company is insolvent.[15]

So, if creditors' interests are paramount, directors have to put aside the shareholder primacy principle and, rather than seeking to maximise shareholder wealth, the directors should maximise creditor wealth. Directors will do so by eliminating the high-risk policies that they might have followed when implementing shareholder primacy. The company's affairs are to be administered in such a way as to ensure that actions will enhance the wealth of creditors, that is, the creditors will be repaid more of the funds that are owed to them.

It has been said that if directors must engage in creditor maximisation, then that produces an inefficient result in that directors will ignore potentially lucrative but risky investments.[16] But, of course, if one limits creditor maximisation to the time when the company is insolvent, then arguably the company should not be indulging in risky activities in any event. What will creditor maximisation involve? Directors know that the primary interest of creditors is to get repaid in full, or as far as possible. So, essentially, directors can keep this at the backs of their minds. Anything that makes repayment less likely, harms creditor interests and should be eschewed as a valid action.

Therefore, once a company is insolvent, the task of the directors is, relatively speaking, a little easier in that they must focus on the creditors' interests. Consequently, it is the period of time before insolvency occurs, but when the directors are obliged to take into account the interests of creditors, that is more of a concern as far as ascertaining how directors are to function. It would seem that the predominance of case law supports the view that while directors must consider creditor interests, they are not obliged to focus solely on those interests. But what are they are to do?

The balancing of interests

One approach that could be invoked when directors are bound to consider creditor interests, is to say that the directors, in determining what to do, must

---

F 2d 587, 590 (2d Cir 1966); *New York Credit Men's Adjustment Bureau, Inc v Weiss*, 305 NY 1, 110 NE 2d 397 (1953); *The Official Comm of Unsecured Creditors of Buckhead America Corp v Reliance Capital Group, Inc (Re Buckhead Am Corp)* 178 BR 956 at 968 (De, 1994).

15 Paragraphs 69–70. The Guidance can be accessed at www.dti.gov.uk/cld/guidancekey.doc.

16 Lipson, J, 'Directors' duties to creditors: volition, cognition, exit and the financially distressed corporation' (2003) 50 *University of California at Los Angeles Law Review* 1189 at 1225.

balance the interests of creditors and shareholders. The latter's interests are not to be forgotten, certainly outside of insolvency, as the traditional view is that their interests must be taken into account by directors. In *Re MDA Investment Management Ltd* [2004] 1 BCLC 217 at 245; [2004] BPIR 75 at 102 Park J indicated that when a company is in financial difficulties, although not insolvent, 'the duties which the directors owe to the company are extended so as to encompass the interests of the company's creditors as a whole, *as well as those of the shareholders*' (my emphasis). Reginald Barrett assumes that there must be a balancing between the interests of shareholders and creditors if creditors' interests are to intrude. He has said that 'there will be insoluble problems of reconciling conflicting interests' of shareholders and creditors if a duty to creditors applied other than where insolvency exists.[17] The conflict between the interests of shareholders and creditors is likely to be more manifest when it comes to the issue of risk. As Riley puts it: 'How are directors to balance such competing interests when deciding whether to embark upon some speculative ventures?'[18] The following comment of Lord Templeman in *Winkworth* [1986] 1 WLR 1512 at 1516; [1987] 1 All ER 114 at 118 sounds sensible, yet what does it actually mean as far as a director is concerned when he or she is trying to run the company's business?

> The company is not bound to pay off every debt as soon as it is incurred, and the company is not obliged to avoid all ventures which involve an element of risk – but it owes a duty to its creditors to keep its property inviolable and available for the repayment of its debts.

As one American court put it in relation to the law as it applied, at least in the state of Delaware: 'The extent to which directors of putatively insolvent corporations can continue to advance the interests of stockholders without violating their fiduciary duty to the corporate entity or to creditors remains hazy . . .' (See *Jewel Recovery LP v Gordon* (1996) 196 BR 348 at 355.)

The next section of the Chapter identifies and then considers the issues that arise if directors are to balance the interests of shareholders and creditors in making appropriate decisions.

Shareholders v creditors

Shareholders and creditors alike supply capital to companies, with each contributing 'funds in exchange for claims on cash flows generated by the entity's [company's] operations'.[19] While in a wide range of issues the interests of

---

17 'Directors' duties to creditors' (1977) 40 MLR 226 at 231.
18 *Op. cit.* fn 4 above at 90.
19 Lin, L, 'Shift of fiduciary duty upon corporate insolvency: proper scope of directors' duty to creditors' (1993) 46 *Vanderbilt Law Review* 1485 at 1488.

shareholders and creditors will be aligned,[20] it cannot be doubted that there is likely to be some conflict between the interests of the two groups at some point,[21] with the conflict increasing as 'the financial condition of the firm deteriorates and its debt-equity ratio increases'.[22]

It is likely, particularly when a company is in financial difficulty, that it is in the shareholders' interests to embrace greater risks,[23] for they have little to lose if a venture is not successful, while if it is successful the company 'could be made', and not only will creditors be paid, but the shareholders will make a substantial amount. Of course, if the venture is unsuccessful the share-holders, because of the concept of limited liability, will not lose any more than they would if the company took no action. By way of illustration, let us say that there are two projects, both costing £100,000. Project A offers a safe return of £110,000 (the initial outlay together with a clear profit). Project B offers a 50:50 chance of success, whereby if it does not succeed the company will only have returned to it the sum of £50,000, but if it succeeds the com-pany will get £150,000. The shareholders will generally prefer B to A and the creditors, if the sum total owed to them exceeds £50,000, will favour A over B. If B succeeds then the shareholders will gain most from it. If, however, B fails, the creditors will absorb most of the loss.

While it is axiomatic that shareholders and creditors have divergent views about risk and returns, so that conflict between the two constituencies is unavoidable in some cases, there are a number of substantial points that have been made for advocating a balancing exercise. First, it has been argued that resolving conflicts is part and parcel of being a director. Some management specialists have even said that managing competing interests is a primary function of management.[24] The fact that the balancing of diverse interests is

---

20 Leung, W, 'The inadequacy of shareholder primacy: a proposed corporate regime that recognizes non-shareholder interests' (1997) 30 *Columbia Journal of Law and Social Problems* 589 at 590 fn 8; Macey, J and Miller, G, 'Corporate stakeholders: a contractual perspective' (1993) 43 *University of Toronto Law Review* 401 at 415.

21 Coffee, J, and Schwartz, A, 'The survival of the derivative suit: an evaluation and a proposal for legislative reform' (1981) 21 Colum L Rev 261 at 313; Harvey, D, 'Bondholders' rights and the case for a fiduciary duty' (1991) 65 *St John's Law Review* 1023 at 1040, fn 86; Whincop, M, 'Taking the corporate contract more seriously: the economic cases against, and a transaction cost rationale for, the insolvent trading provisions' (1996) 5 *Griffith Law Review* 1 at 10–11; *op. cit.* fn 5 above at 414.

22 *Op. cit.* fn 19 above.

23 Scott, R, 'A relational theory of default rules for commercial contracts' (1990) 19 *Journal of Legal Studies* 597 at 624; *op. cit.* fn 11 above at 768; Adler, B, 'A re-examination of near-bankruptcy investment incentives' (1995) 62 U Chi L Rev 575 at 590–598; de R Barondes, R, 'Fiduciary duties of officers and directors of distressed corporations' (1998) 7 *George Mason Law Review* 45 at 46, 49.

24 Ansoff, H, *Strategic Management* 1984, Englewood Cliffs: Prentice-Hall and referred to in Harrison, J, and Freeman, R, 'Stakeholders, social responsibility and performance: empirical evidence and theoretical perspectives' (1999) 42 *Academy of Management Journal* 479 at 479. Management commentators have asserted that directors are in effect to act as referees

within directors' abilities and skills is something that has been recognised as far back as 1973 by a UK Department of Trade and Industry Report,[25] and by some American courts. For example, in the American decision of *Re Healthco International Inc* 208 BR 288 at 301 (1997), the Delaware court played down the conflict between shareholders and creditors, saying that there were not irreconcilable conflicts and the action of looking out for creditors' and shareholders' interests was merely an incident of a director's fiduciary obligations. It has been contended that it is not unmanageable or unreasonable for persons occupying positions like directors, to make allocative decisions. Directors have been classified as fiduciaries and society regularly requires those who are fiduciaries to make balanced decisions that can be quite difficult.[26] Proponents of the view might point to another kind of fiduciary, the trustee. Trustees have to make investment decisions sometimes with various categories of beneficiaries in mind. This can involve weighing up risk in a similar manner that is required by a director under a duty to consider creditor interests. It usually involves the steering of a middle course.

Second, while it is argued that it is easier to police how directors are acting when directors are only to act for shareholders and no one else,[27] it must not be forgotten that, once all is said and done, it is not always easy to perceive what is in the best interests of the shareholders, and directors have to balance various elements. For example, a particular action might boost the share prices of a company, but it will also reduce the likelihood of dividends for a year or so.

Third, there is evidence that directors are often seeking to balance interests in the decisions which they make.[28] A corporate reputation survey of Fortune 500 companies (the largest listed companies in the US) found that satisfying the interests of one stakeholder does not automatically occur at the expense of other stakeholders.[29] It might be concluded, it is argued, that if the interests of creditors are considered, then it does not necessarily mean that shareholders'

---

between two stakeholder groups (Aoki, M, *The Co-operative Game Theory of the Firm*, 1984, Oxford: Clarendon Press, and referred to in Donaldson, T, and Preston, L, 'The stakeholder theory of the corporation concepts, evidence, and implications' (1995) 20 *The Academy of Management Review* 65 at 86).

25 *Company Law Reform*, Cmnd 5391 at paras 55–59.

26 Campbell, R, 'Corporate fiduciary principles for the post-contractarian era' (1996) 23 *Florida State University Law Review* 561 at 593.

27 For example, Clark, R, *Corporate Law* (1986) at 20 and referred to in Committee on Corporate Laws, 'Other constituency statutes: potential for confusion' (1990) 45 Bus Law 2253 at 2270.

28 It has been noted that directors do already consider the interests of various constituents: *Report of the Committee on Corporate Governance* (chair, Sir Ronald Hampel) (1998) and referred to by Dine, J, 'Implementation of European initiatives in the UK: the role of fiduciary duties' (1999) 3 CfiLR 218 at 223.

29 Preston, L, and Sapienza, H, 'Stakeholder management and corporate performance' (1990) 19 *Journal of Behavioral Economics* 361.

interests will be prejudiced. It has been found empirically, in a study of UK private water companies, that the requirement that directors must consider customer interests as well as that of shareholders, can result in 'mutual benefits for different stakeholder groups with apparently conflicting economic interests'.[30] For instance, in taking into account creditor interests by reviewing all available material information relating to the financial standing of the company before embarking on any actions, shareholders might well benefit in that the company might be spared from pursuing an inappropriate strategy. Further, in undertaking the necessary monitoring to protect creditors, directors might identify improvements that could be made in the company's procedures and profit-making processes that could lower costs and increase profits, thereby promoting overall benefits for the company. Other empirical evidence, obtained in a study by the *Financial Times* of Europe's most respected companies, indicated that chief executive officers were of the view that one of the features of a good company was the ability to balance the interests of stakeholder groups.[31]

Fourth, shares come in different shapes and sizes and companies often have different kinds of shares, such as ordinary and preference, and it is incumbent on directors to balance the interests of different kinds of shareholders, so that they act fairly between them (*Mills v Mills* (1938) 60 CLR 150 at 164; *Re BSB Holdings Ltd (No2)* [1996] 1 BCLC 155 at 246–249) for, on occasions, these different classes of shareholder have opposing interests.[32] Professors Jonathan Macey and Geoffrey Miller[33] point out that some preferred shareholders may have interests that resemble those of fixed claimants, such as creditors, more than those associated with common shareholders. Some shareholders intend only to retain shares for a short term, while others are in for the long haul. Other shareholders hold a diversified portfolio, with their investment spread around a number of companies, and still others might have all their investment concentrated in the one company. In companies that are closely held, one sometimes has the problem of controlling and minority shareholders having conflicting interests. Notwithstanding this, no concerns are voiced about the stresses of decision-making for directors in this latter respect, nor is it argued that directors, in balancing interests, are too burdened. Although it has been noted how divergent are the interests of preference shareholders as against ordinary shareholders, it is explained away on

30 Ogden, S, and Watson, R, 'Corporate performance and stakeholder management: balancing shareholder and customer interests in the UK privatized water industry' (1999) 42 *Academy of Management Journal* 526 at 536.
31 Referred to in Scholes, E, and Clutterbuck, D, 'Communication with stakeholders: an integrated approach' (1998) 31 *Long Range Planning* 227 at 230.
32 McDaniel, M, 'Bondholders and stockholders' (1988) 13 *Journal of Corporation Law* 205, 273; *op. cit.* fn 26 above at 593; de R Barondes, *op. cit.* fn 23 above at 78.
33 'Corporate stakeholders: a contractual perspective' (1993) 43 *University of Toronto Law Review* 401 at 433.

the basis that while such creditors are 'not perfectly homogenous, nor are they a motley crew'.[34]

Furthermore, as indicated earlier in the book,[35] it has been held in UK law that directors are obliged to conduct the affairs of their company for the benefit of the company as a whole, and that has been interpreted to mean the interests of both the present and future shareholders of the company.[36] So, in some of their decision-making, it is likely that directors will have to balance the interests of present shareholders as against the interests of future shareholders. In other words, directors will have to balance short-term considerations as against long-term considerations, so that they are not unfair to either present shareholders or future shareholders.[37]

So, there are significant points that favour the idea that directors should balance the interests of creditors and shareholders when directors are subject to a responsibility to take into account creditor interests. However, it is submitted that they are outweighed by the many problems involved in endeavouring to strike a balance between interests. Clearly, most commentators, whatever view they take, accept that the balancing of shareholders' and creditors' interests is a tricky issue. It means that directors have to solve what some commentators see as impossible conflicts of interest.[38] Specifically, directors have to cope with the following.

First, it might be difficult for directors to take into account creditor interests as they are so accustomed to focusing on the interests of shareholders alone. It has been argued that directors will not understand the interests of creditors as they are usually involved in exercising entrepreneurial skills.[39] With respect, directors are not just pure entrepreneurs, they have responsibilities in relation to the finances of the company and they have to be financial managers. But, notwithstanding this, it must be acknowledged that directors will rarely align themselves with creditor interests. This is demonstrated by an empirical study, conducted by Professors Lyn Lo Pucki and William Whitford, of

---

34 For instance. van der Weide, M, 'Against fiduciary duties to corporate stakeholders' (1996) 21 *Delaware Journal of Corporate Law* 27 at 38–39.

35 See pp 149–150.

36 See *Re Smith & Fawcett Ltd* [1942] Ch 304; *Ganmain v National Association for Mental Health* [1971] Ch 317.

37 This is affirmed as a proper approach by the Company Law Reform Bill (cl 156) presently before Parliament.

38 There are many American commentators who take this view. For example, Macey, J, 'An economic analysis of the various rationales for making shareholders the exclusive beneficiaries of corporate fiduciary duties' (1991) 21 *Stetson Law Review* 23 at 31; Jelisavcic, V, 'A safe harbour proposal to define the limits of directors' fiduciary duty to creditors in the "vicinity of insolvency" '(1992) 17 *Journal of Corporation Law* 145 at 148; Beveridge, N, 'Does a corporation's board of directors owe a fiduciary duty to its creditors?' (1994) 25 *St Mary's Law Journal* 589 at 621. This view gains some support from the Ontario High Court of Justice in *Royal Bank of Canada v First Pioneer Investments Ltd* (1980) 20 OR (2d) 352.

39 *Op. cit.* fn 34 above at 60.

large companies in the United States that have entered bankruptcy under Chapter 11 of the Bankruptcy Reform Act 1978.[40] The learned writers found that directors of solvent companies never aligned with creditors.[41] Hence, for directors to take into account creditors' interests will necessitate something of a culture change.

Second, it has been argued that requiring the balancing of interests, means that directors have to serve two masters.[42] Many commentators argue against the idea of directors being required to have regard for a number of constituencies, on the basis that directors cannot manage companies properly in such circumstances. An example of the predicament in which directors could find themselves, according to Professor Dale Tauke, is where the company has excess funds and has to decide whether to pay a dividend to shareholders or retain the funds.[43] In this situation, the learned commentator asserts, the shareholders will prefer the former decision and the creditors the latter. Which constituency do the directors favour?

Third, the agency theory,[44] the theory that directors act as the agents of shareholders, has, as one of its elements, the notion that directors will be opportunistic and engage in self-serving activity known as shirking. Consistent with that, it might well be that directors will use the requirement to balance between conflicting interests as an opportunity to foster their own self-interest.[45] In their empirical study, Lo Pucki and Whitford found that this occurs with respect to companies that are subject to Chapter 11 bankruptcy.[46] Directors might consider that if they favour the shareholders, their position might be enhanced, especially if they own shares in the company, or if their compensation packages are tied to share prices.[47] On the other hand, executive directors who are concerned about their reputation and the need to find posts elsewhere in the future, might, under the guise of effecting a balance, favour creditor interests in an effort to keep a company operating and being able to satisfy creditors so that they are not, personally, tainted by a financial collapse of the company.

In this regard a word about what are called, in the United States,

40 *Op. cit.* fn 11 above at 751.   41 *Ibid.*
42 Hurst, T, and McGuiness, L, 'The corporation, the bondholder and fiduciary duties' (1991) 10 *Journal of Law and Commerce* 187 at 205
43 Tauke, D, 'Should bondholders have more fun? A re-examination of the debate over corporate bondholders' rights' (1989) *Columbia Business Law Review* 1 at 60.
44 This is based on a large number of works, but the most influential are: Jensen, M, and Meckling, W, 'Theory of the firm: managerial behavior, agency costs and ownership structure' (1976) 3 *Journal of Financial Economics* 305; Fama, E, 'Agency problems and the theory of the firm' (1980) 88 J Pol Econ 288; Fama, E, and Jensen, M, 'Separation of ownership and control' (1983) 26 *Journal of Law and Economics* 301; Easterbrook, F, and Fischel, D, *The Economic Structure of the Corporate Law*, 1991, Cambridge, Mass: Harvard University Press.
45 Roe, M, 'The shareholder wealth maximization norm and industrial organization' (2001) 149 U Pa L Rev 2063 at 2065.
46 *Op. cit.* fn 11 above at 710   47 *Op. cit.* fn 43 above at 65

'constituency statutes' might be apposite at this point. Over half the American states have enacted a constituency statute.[48] These statutes provide that directors may consider the interests of constituencies (and specifically including creditors), as well as shareholders,[49] when they make corporate decisions. In fact, consideration of these statutes has been primarily in the area of takeovers[50] and an examination of what interests directors have taken into account in considering whether to recommend the acceptance of takeover proposals. It has been argued that the existence of constituency statutes 'provides an obfuscation opportunity that facilitates [managerial opportunism]'.[51] That is, directors can assert that they adopted a particular course of conduct to benefit a particular constituency and this statement cannot be contradicted. The end result, so the argument goes, is that board accountability is attenuated and directors have the chance to foster self-interest by hiding behind the statutes. The same might be said about requiring a balancing of shareholder and creditor interests.

Fourth, and allied to the previous point, in any balancing exercise the danger is that the director whose actions are likely to be reviewed will simply pay lip-service to the need to consider the interests of both shareholders and creditors, and then make the decision that he or she wants, possibly based on self-interest. Of course, there is lip-service and there is lip-service, and while the activity of some directors might be sufficient to cause an adequate doubt in the mind of a judge that they had considered creditor interests, on other occasions it will be reasonably clear that directors have really only sought to appear to be taking the interests of creditors into account, and they have failed to do their duty.

Fifth, as Professor Victor Brudney has stated: 'The conflict between the interests of stockholders and bondholders does not permit management to be agent of both in a manner consistent with fiduciary principles.'[52] Consequently, it might be argued that requiring directors to effect a balance is unfair to directors[53] as it places them in invidious, no-win situations.

---

48 For example, Pennsylvania (the first to enact), New York, Wisconsin, Georgia, Illinois, Iowa, Massachusetts, Minnesota, Nebraska, New Jersey. A full list is set out by Miller, *op. cit.* fn 1 above at 1478, fn 49 and Mitchell, L, 'A theoretical and practical framework for enforcing corporate constituency statutes (1992) 70 Texas L Rev 579 at 579, fn 1.

49 This is except for Arizona where directors are required simply to consider long-term as well as short-term interests of the company (Arizona Revised Statute Ann, s 10–1202(A) (1987)).

50 A major reason for the introduction of the statutes was because of the takeover frenzy of the 1980s: Hanks, J, 'Playing with fire: non-shareholder constituency statutes in the 1990s' (1991) 21 *Stetson Law Review* 97 at 102.

51 *Op. cit.* fn 26 above at 622. See Macey, *op. cit.* fn 38 above at 36. Professor Jonathan Macey sees the statutes as providing directors with meaningful job security no matter at what level they perform (at 33).

52 'Corporate bondholders and debtor opportunism: in bad times and good' (1992) 105 Harv L R 1821 at 1837 fn 49.

53 *Op. cit.* fn 16 above at 1222.

Sixth, it might be argued that there is the danger that the natural tendency of directors is to favour shareholders, as they are the ones who can decline to re-elect them, or even dismiss them, pursuant to s 303 of the Companies Act 1985.[54] While directors might realise that whatever they do when their company is in financial distress could be the subject of close scrutiny at some later date by a court, the present reality of the possibility of dismissal could well lead to directors following a line that shareholders find palatable. The formulating of strategies to obtain a dismissal of directors does occur. For instance, in December 1994 Maurice Saatchi was removed as chairman of Saatchi and Saatchi plc at a general meeting after a consortium of US institutions moved against him.[55] In more recent times the mere threat of the calling of a meeting at which a removal motion would be put was successful in obtaining the dismissal of Patientline's chairman, Derek Lewis.[56] Lo Pucki and Whitford have maintained that if the elections of directors are permitted in relation to companies that are subject to Chapter 11 bankruptcy in the United States, then shareholders will use the threat of elections to induce the directors to follow policies that favour shareholder interests.[57]

Besides the issue of control and election, it needs to be noted that only shareholders are able to bring actions to challenge breaches of directors' duties[58] or even actions that are short of breaches of duty, provided that they can use s 459 of the Companies Act 1985 or bring a derivative action by successfully making out an exception to the rule in *Foss v Harbottle*. Apart from those creditors who have extended credit pursuant to an agreement that included covenants allowing some form of control, creditors, prima facie, cannot, unlike the shareholders who can vote at meetings, have any real input into management. There is evidence from the United States that bank creditors have been successful in having some effect on how companies are controlled by orchestrating the dismissal of directors,[59] but often banks have the standing of secured creditors and they do not have the same interest in monitoring and taking action if they are well secured, only being concerned that their security is safe,[60] so this will rarely provide any benefits for creditors

---

54 *Op. cit.* Mitchell, fn 48 above at 594.
55 Short, H, and Keasey, K, 'Institutional shareholders and corporate governance in the United Kingdom' in Keasey, K, *et al* (eds), *Corporate Governance: Economic, Management and Financial Issues*, 1997, Oxford: OUP, p 40.
56 Butler, S, 'Patientline hangs up on chief executive amid rebel attack' *The Times*, February 14 2006.
57 *Op. cit.* fn 11 above at 770.
58 Compare the position in Canada, where creditors may instigate derivative actions. See Chapter 16.
59 Gilson, S, and Vetsuypens, M, 'Credit control in financially distressed firms: empirical evidence' (1994) *Washington University Law Quarterly* 1005 at 1011–1015.
60 Jackson, T, and Kronman, A, 'Secured financing and priorities among creditors' (1979) 88 Yale LJ 1143 at 1154.

in general. The upshot is that, effectively, the shareholders are the only ones whom directors must fear.

Seventh, as was mentioned earlier, there are often different kinds of shareholders in companies, and while directors might be accustomed to having to balance the interests of such persons, the fact that there are multiple types of shares is likely to make the balancing exercise more complicated as the directors' task is not merely to consider shareholders' interests on one side, and creditors' on the other.

Creditors v creditors

Introduction

So much for the balancing of shareholder and creditor interests; but that is not the whole story. In the previous section of the chapter, it was noted that there are different kinds of shareholders. The fact of the matter is that there will be in most companies different kinds of creditor who do not have identical interests. Any company is likely to owe money to several groups of creditor who have different agenda, and who are dealt with in different ways by the law. Companies might have all or any of the following creditors: secured creditors; suppliers with a retention of title clause in supply contracts; trade creditors; suppliers under long-term contracts; lessors; holders of unexpired intellectual property licences; employees; Inland Revenue Commissioners; HM Customs; tort victims with claims; and customers who have paid deposits or the full price for goods or services to be supplied by the company. There is, for instance, likely to be a significant difference between the interests of a bank creditor with a charge over company assets compared with an unsecured trade creditor. In considering creditor interests, what does a director do if the interests of different groups do not accord?[61] There is going to be conflict, and this internecine conflict can be as difficult to resolve as the shareholder–creditor conflict. How does a director decide between different competing interests? On moral grounds? If so, then people like customers and tort victims might be favoured. The problem is that no formula can be established that provides directors with consistent guidance.[62]

As one might expect, there will be different risks assumed by different creditors. For instance, short-term creditors, such as suppliers,[63] often do not assume as high a risk as long-term creditors. The former will often enter into repeat transactions with companies and they can more easily respond to

---

61 This is assuming that all creditors are owed a duty. This is something which Professor Jonathan Lipson has questioned (*op. cit.* fn 16 above).

62 *Op. cit.* fn 2 above at 178.

63 Some suppliers might be more easily placed in the category of long-term creditors, when they invest in specific equipment or other capital items in order to service the company's business.

indications that companies are in a financial malaise. Long-term creditors bear a greater risk that the company with which they are dealing engages in some activity post-contract that heightens the chance of non-payment. For example, a creditor who is tied to the company in some way, such as installing in its factory special machinery that is only installed so that the creditor is able to supply the company, is particularly vulnerable as the supplier is at the mercy of the company, which might decide not to take the supplier's products any longer. Given all of this, it is more likely that long-term creditors will require restrictive covenants in the credit contract, and such creditors are more exposed to improper directorial behaviour that will cause them prejudice.

Before considering the various groups of creditor, it is worth noting that even creditors in the same group might not have the same interests. For instance, let us take the broad grouping of trade creditors. These creditors are generally treated in the same way by the law, and certainly they are when it comes to a liquidation of an insolvent company. This group might include, at one extreme, large companies that supply substantial quantities of goods to the company, and, at the other end of the spectrum, self-employed tradespersons, like plumbers. The former type of creditors might have a turnover of many millions of pounds per annum and are likely to be more willing to accept the directors embracing ventures and actions that involve a greater amount of risk, as large company suppliers are probably not so reliant as the tradespersons, whose turnover is likely to be only in the region of thousands of pounds, on being paid the debt owed. While the large company can gamble with its debt, tradespersons probably cannot. The latter would prefer to be assured of receiving, say half of what is owed, rather than seeing company funds used in such a way that *might* lead to full payment of the debt, but could just as likely lead to there being nothing left to pay creditors. In contrast, the large company might be ready to approve of a gamble because if it does not get paid, it can still survive.

Secured creditors

The main groups of creditor that are recognised by the law, as far as the rights to which they are entitled, particularly if the company enters some form of insolvency administration, are secured creditors, preferential creditors and unsecured creditors. In Anglo-American law, secured creditors retain their pre-insolvency right to recover what they are owed from the assets of the company over which they have security, in priority to any other creditors.[64] Absent significant devaluation of the secured assets or the fraudulent disposal

---

64 However, where a creditor holds a floating charge created on or after 15 September 2003, a certain part of the net proceeds (net property) from the realisation of the property covered by the floating charge must be set aside for the unsecured creditors: Insolvency Act 1986, s 176A. This does not apply where, *inter alia*, the company's net property is less than the sum, at

of such assets, secured creditors are generally in a strong position to recover their debt, and the actions of the directors might have little effect on them.[65] Provided that company action does not, or is not likely to, place a secured creditor's security in some jeopardy, secured creditors will not be too concerned about what the directors decide to do. In any event, those with fixed charges overwhelmingly include covenants in their loan agreement that provide that the value of the security is not to fall below a set multiple of the amount of the debt secured.[66]

Unsecured creditors: preferential and ordinary

Preferential creditors are those unsecured creditors who are entitled, if the company enters some form of insolvency regime, such as administration or liquidation, to be paid before other creditors. Most jurisdictions provide for a preferential creditor grouping, although there are jurisdictional differences as to the kinds of creditor that fall into the category. The most prevalent kind of preferential creditors are employees of the company. In the UK employees are effectively the only major type of preferential creditor since the corporate insolvency provisions of the Enterprise Act 2002 came into operation on 15 September 2003. Before then, and in common with many jurisdictions around the world, such as France, Spain, Ireland, South Africa and Italy, tax authorities also were accorded preferential status.

The group that is at the bottom of the priority ladder are the ordinary unsecured creditors, who are merely given the right to an equal and proportional claim to any company funds that remain after the secured and preferential creditors have been satisfied. They are the ones who usually lose out when companies become insolvent.

The preferential creditors would undoubtedly see it as being in their best interests for a company's business to be terminated where there were just sufficient company funds to satisfy what they are owed. While, in such a situation, the unsecured creditors would be in a similar position to the shareholders of an insolvent company, in that they would be content to see the company business continue, and maybe new ventures taken on, in the hope that there will be more funds produced over and above that owed to the

---

present, of £10,000 (Insolvency Act 1986 (Prescribed Part) Order 2003 (SI 2003/2097), reg 2) and the relevant office-holder thinks that the cost of making a distribution to the unsecured creditors would be disproportionate to the benefits received by the unsecured creditors (s 176A(3)(a)(b)).

65 Citron, D, 'The incidence of accounting-based covenants in UK public debt contracts: an empirical analysis' (1995) 25 *Accounting and Business Research* 139 and referred to in Mokal, R, 'The floating charge – an elegy' in Worthington, S (ed), *Commercial Law and Commercial Practice*, 2003, Oxford: Hart Publishing, p 487.

66 The debenture deed will permit the secured creditor to invoke a process to safeguard their position, such as the appointment of a receiver, if their security was in danger.

preferential creditors, with the consequence that there is something for them. Of course, the preferential creditors would be opposed to this as further activity might mean that the company's funds are diminished and that would imperil their return.

Future creditors

Is it also necessary for directors to have to balance the rights and interests of existing creditors as against those of future creditors? The main debate in this regard has been over whether a duty is actually owed to future creditors. While there are cases that have suggested in dicta that directors do owe a duty to future creditors, such as *Winkworth v Edward Baron Development Ltd* [1986] 1 WLR 1512 at 1516; [1987] 1 All ER 114 at 118, the suggestion has been the subject of a significant amount of robust criticism.[67] It seems to be the law that the interests of future creditors do not have to feature in the concerns of directors.

Assessment

In discharging their duties, should directors take into account the position that various creditors occupy as far as priority to payment is concerned? Against requiring this are three factors. First, directors would have to take legal advice as to what the priority order would be and that would hinder them in some cases in fulfilling their duties in a timely way. Second, directors might be somewhat hamstrung in trying to maximise benefits for the company if they were to consider creditor priority. Third, priority issues are only relevant if and when the company enters administration or liquidation as a result of being insolvent. Priorities established by the Insolvency Act 1986 have no application outside of these regimes, although secured creditors will enjoy the same rights whether or not a company enters a formal insolvency regime.

Although it does not resolve the problem that we are investigating, the decision in *Re Pantone 485 Ltd* [2002] 1 BCLC 266 is noteworthy, for it implicitly indicates that directors must effect a balance between the interests of all creditors. In this case the liquidator of a company failed in a claim that the directors of the company in liquidation had disposed of company property without taking into account the interests of one of the creditors, an unsecured creditor entitled to priority in a distribution of the company's assets. The court acknowledged that when a company was insolvent the

---

67 For example, see Sealy, L, 'Directors' duties – an unnecessary gloss' [1988] CLJ 175; Farrar, J, 'The responsibility of directors and shareholders for a company's debts' (1989) 4 Canta LR 12; Cheffins, B, *Company Law: Theory, Structure and Operation*, 1997, Oxford: Clarendon Press, p 338.

directors had to have regard for the creditors' interests (at 286–287). The claim failed because, according to the court, the directors had a duty to make decisions, when their company was insolvent, while having regard for all of the general creditors, and not one, or a section, of the creditors. Thus, if directors are found, in balancing the interests of creditors, that they have favoured one or more groups, they will have failed to discharge their responsibility.

Of course, the more creditor groups to whom money is owed by a company, the more difficult it is, potentially, for directors to take all creditors' interests into account in what they propose to do. The danger is that in some circumstances the directors are in a 'no-win situation' and might feel that the preferable thing to do, is nothing. Ultimately this could prejudice all creditors.

Summary

The idea of balancing the interests of the shareholder and creditor constituencies seems meritorious, but in practice it would be very difficult for a director, in many situations, to know what to do. The same could be said in relation to deciding what to do when an action discriminates between individual creditors. The main problem is that balancing is a fairly nebulous idea unless there is a goal that has been set for the balancing exercise. To what end is the balancing to be directed? To be effective any balancing must be done in the context of achieving an aim. Consequently, shortly under the heading of 'A Framework', I propose a framework that provides an objective to which directors should be working in making their decisions.

Governance in Chapter 11 bankruptcy

Deciding how directors should act necessitates consideration of how directors might be required to act in other circumstances to see if that provides us with any helpful pointers. One area that might be profitable is that of Chapter 11 bankruptcy in the United States. Companies are entitled in the United States to file proceedings in a bankruptcy court that enables them to the protection afforded by Chapter 11 of the Bankruptcy Code, such that the company is said to be subject to administration under Chapter 11. The main purpose that is fulfilled by Chapter 11 is to allow a company to 'catch its financial breath, propose a plan to reorganize and to thereby allow it an opportunity to cure its financial ills and continue in business' (*Re Continental Airlines Corp* (1984) 38 BR 67, 71 (SD, TX)).

When there is an administration like Chapter 11, the corporate governance of such companies can be highly instructive. A study of Chapter 11 does not tell us how directors should act, but it does provide us with an indication of how directors act in relation to companies that are subject to this form of administration and provides some guidance as to how directors should function. It has been accepted that the issue of on whose behalf the managers of the company are to act is one of the most critical.[68] There will be conflicting interests, just as with a company that is operating normally. Usually the company's management will remain in place;[69] this is known as the debtor-in-possession (DIP). It is usually asserted that this is the best way forward as the management knows the debtor's business and has the business skill and judgment to operate the business.[70] Of course, one might argue by way of riposte that the fact that the management got the company into the position in which it finds itself might indicate that management should not continue to operate the business, but that issue must be left for another day. The DIP is obliged by s 1107(a) of the Bankruptcy Reform Act 1978 to perform all of the duties of a trustee. The directors of the company owe fiduciary duties to both the shareholders and creditors.[71] But, it has been observed that managers of a company in Chapter 11 make 'decisions . . . often between courses of action that would serve either the interests of their shareholders or the interests of their creditors, one at the expense of the other'.[72]

When a company is in Chapter 11 bankruptcy the DIP's responsibility is to the estate.[73] What does this actually mean in practice? It is not clear. It has been said, in advocating the need to consider the rights of all claimants, that one has to rely on the discretion of the DIP, which must be exercised honestly and indicate a deference to the interests of all involved.[74] It is accepted that in fulfilling its role, some claimants might be harmed and some benefited by the DIP, and that the DIP is in a dilemma in some cases in knowing what to do.[75] It has been stated that 'often, it is best to simply acknowledge the dilemma and rely on the good faith of the DIP to resolve it in a reasonable manner'.[76] The DIP has the obligation of balancing the interests of all groups.[77] Some have said that it is necessary for the DIP to consider benefiting the whole estate even at the cost of sacrificing some creditors' interests, and creditors and shareholders alike are entitled to expect protection and fairness from the DIP.[78] While it is sometimes said that creditors are owed a duty, it is more accurate to say that directors owe a duty to the company and that will involve considering creditor interests,[79] a situation that is akin to that in the UK, where company directors are under an obligation to take into account the

---

68 Nimmer, R, and Feinberg, R, 'Chapter 11 business governance: fiduciary duties, business judgment, trustees and exclusivity' (1989) 6 *Bankruptcy Developments Journal* 1 at 25.
69 Bankruptcy Reform Act 1978, s 1108.
70 *Op. cit.* fn 68 above at 9.   71 *Op. cit.* fn 1 above at 1468.
72 *Op. cit.* fn 11 above at 672.   73 Section 1106(a).   74 *Op. cit.* fn 68 above at 29.
75 *Ibid* at 27.   76 *Ibid.*   77 *Ibid* at 33.
78 *Ibid* at 28; Davis, L, McCullough, M, McNulty, E, and Schuler, R, 'Corporate reorganizations in the 1990s: guiding directors of troubled corporations through uncertain territory' (1991) 47 Bus Law 1 at 15.
79 Minkel, H, and Baker, C, 'Claims and control in Chapter 11 cases: a call for neutrality' (1991) 13 *Cardozo Law Review* 35 at 60.

interests of creditors. There is a strong case for the creditors to be owed fiduciary duties, in addition to shareholders, because their right to take action against the company is subject to an automatic stay. In fact, while there are cases that hold that directors owe duties to both shareholders and creditors,[80] there are a growing number of statements in the US case law to the effect that duties are only owed to creditors, so any conflict between shareholders and creditors should be resolved in favour of the creditors.[81] Notwithstanding this, Lo Pucki and Whitford found that the interests that managers of companies in Chapter 11 served were diverse.[82] They also found that there is uncertainty about whose interests managers should be concerned for at a given time, and that lawyers found it difficult to provide well-grounded advice.[83]

Courts have given managers in companies broad discretion to exercise reasonable judgment, finding fault with them only where there is an indication of 'fraud, bad faith, gross overreaching or abuse of discretion'.[84] Directors must ensure that their actions and choices:

> ... reflect an honoured and reasoned effort to balance the competing interests ... These obligations do not require that the DIP elevate one interest to the exclusion of the other, nor do they require that each be evenly balanced against the other. The choices the DIP makes reflect the character of the insolvency proceeding, the causes of the bankruptcy, and the probable future of the business.[85]

The problem is, as with companies not in administration and yet where directors have to consider creditor interests, that the nature of duties owed to creditors remains obscure[86] and the courts have failed to articulate the duties owed to shareholders.[87] The result is that the task of the DIP is both 'open-ended and extremely difficult'.[88]

The conclusion to be reached from a consideration of Chapter 11 is that

---

80 For example, *Wolf v Weinstein* 372 US 633, 649–650 (1963) (US Sup Ct); *US v Byrum* (1972) 408 US 125 (US Sup Ct); *Re FSC Corp* 38 Bankr 346, 349 (Pennsylvania, 1983).

81 For example, *Federal Deposit Ins Corp v Sea Pines Co* 692 F 2d 973, 976–77; *Commodity Futures Trading Commission v Weintraub* 471 US 343, 355 (1985). See above *op. cit.* fn 11 at 708; Baird, D, and Jackson, T, 'Corporate reorganization and the treatment of diverse ownership interests: a comment on adequate protection of secured creditors in bankruptcy' (1984) 51 U Chi L Rev 97 at 103. Miller asserts that this is contrary to the scheme and purpose of Chapter 11: *op. cit.* fn 1 above at 1490. Nimmer and Feinberg take essentially the same view: *op. cit.* fn 68 above at 32.

82 *Op. cit.* fn 11 above at 751.   83 *Ibid* at 751–752.

84 *Treadway Co v Care Corp* 638 F 2d 357, 382 and quoted in Adams, E, 'Governance in Chapter 11 reorganizations: reducing costs, improving results' (1993) 73 *Boston University Law Review* 581 at 612.

85 *Op. cit.* fn 68 above at 34.   86 *Op. cit.* Davis fn 78 above at 15–16.

87 *Op. cit.* fn 5 above at 411.   88 Adams, *op. cit.* fn 84 above at 604.

there is a lack of certainty and a heavy reliance on the discretion of the management, which are similar concerns to those raised in the previous section of this chapter when dealing with balancing of interests.

A framework

It is simply not possible to formulate a single overarching principle or test to guide directors for the times when they are subject to a responsibility to consider creditor interests, as circumstances will be so varied and the issues that directors encounter are often complex and multifaceted. It is necessary to have flexibility. We have, therefore, to formulate a framework that embraces broad principles rather than specific rules, but something that has a pro-phylactic effect. The aim of arriving at a framework is to provide greater certainty for directors and to act in such a way so as to discourage directors from damaging creditors' interests.[89] Below I seek to develop a framework that has built into it flexibility and accountability.

Entity maximisation

When directors are not subject to an obligation to consider creditor interests we can assume, certainly for the purposes of this chapter, that directors will seek to maximise shareholder wealth,[90] a principle generally accepted as operating in Anglo-American corporate law.[91] But when directors have to take into account creditors' interests, it is submitted that directors should be seeking to implement a broader approach and the one that is advocated here is an entity maximisation approach.[92] This involves, in a nutshell, the directors making decisions that will maximise the general wealth of the company and enhance its sustainability. In other words, directors should do that which maximises the value of the corporate entity so that the net present

89 Mitchell, L, 'The fairness rights of bondholders' (1990) 65 NYULR 1165 at 1226.

90 It is submitted that there is significant authority in both the UK and the US that suggests that this approach is not completely established in law. The issue, though, is outside the ambit of this book. Under the Company Law Reform Bill, the government is proposing an enlightened shareholder value approach, but this still focuses on shareholder interests.

91 Lord Wedderburn, 'The legal development of corporate responsibility' in Hopt, K, and Teubner, G (eds), *Corporate Governance and Directors' Liabilities*, 1985, Berlin: Walter de Gruyter, p 5; Hirt, H, 'The company's decision to litigate against its directors: legal strategies to deal with the board of directors' conflict of interest' [2005] JBL 159 at 164–165. The view was made (in)famous by the comments of the Noble laureate economist, Milton Friedman, in 'The social responsibility of business is to increase its profits' *New York Times*, September 13, 1970, Section 6 (Magazine).

92 Referred to as the 'financial value maximization' in Chaver, A, and Fried, J, 'Managers' fiduciary duty upon the firm's insolvency: accounting for performance creditors' (2002) 55 Vanderbilt L Rev 1813 at 1815, the 'corporate value maximization' approach in Campbell at 580 and 'the maximization of firm value' approach in McDaniel, *op. cit.* fn 32 above at 309.

value to the company as a whole is enhanced (maximising the total financial value of the firm and taking into account the sum of the various financial claims that are made on the company[93]) and not just its equity.[94] Directors will endeavour to increase the 'total long-run market value of the firm',[95] by making the pie larger.[96] In doing this directors should have concern for 'the community of interest',[97] which would include the creditors.[98] This means that the common interest of all who have a stake in the company is to be fostered, but it does not mean that at some point one group will not benefit at the expense of another.[99] It might be argued, on the basis of hypothetical bargain theory,[100] that as entity maximisation endeavours to increase the value of all parties' interests *ex post*, creditors and shareholders would bargain for it *ex ante* if they could have done so.[101]

The approach discussed here is similar to saying that politicians are under a duty to do that which will make society better off, with 'society' meaning the sum of the interests of the people who constitute society.[102] It is to be remembered that the duty of directors is to the company, and, therefore, being concerned about entity maximisation is consistent with fulfilling that overall duty, more so, arguably, than shareholder primacy.

The entity maximisation approach takes into account the interests of those who have claims on the company, including the creditors, so that the most

---

93 Smith, T, 'The efficient norm for corporate law: a neotraditional interpretation of fiduciary duty' (1999) 98 *Michigan Law Review* 214 at 246.

94 Some scholars have taken this view even where companies are not in financial difficulties. See, for example, *ibid* at 223; Crespi, G, 'Rethinking corporate fiduciary duties: the inefficiency of the shareholder primacy norm' (2002) 55 *SMU Law Rev* 141 at 143, 152–153. This approach is criticised in Chaver and Fried, *op. cit.* fn 92 above on the basis that it might lead to inefficiency.

95 Jensen, M, 'Value maximisation, stakeholder theory, and the corporate objective function' (2001) 7 *European Financial Management* 297 at 299. Professor Jensen refers to this as 'value maximisation'.

96 McDaniel, M, 'Bondholders and corporate governance' (1986) 41 *Bus Law* 413 at 448.

97 *Credit Lyonnais Bank Nederland NV v Pathe Communications Corp* (1991 WL 277613; 1991 Del Ch LEXIS 215; (1992) 17 *Delaware Journal of Corporate Law* 1099 (Delaware Chancery Court) at [34] per Chancellor Allen. This might be said to overlap with the argument posited by some, namely that directors act as stewards who identify with their company and its corporate aspirations: Davis, J, Schoorman, F D, and Donaldson, L, 'Toward a stewardship theory of management' (1997) 22 *The Academy of Management Review* 20.

98 This was accepted in *Credit Lyonnais*.

99 This is accepted even by some advocates of stakeholder theory in relation to companies: Evan, W, and Freeman, R, 'A stakeholder theory for modern corporation: Kantian capitalism' in Beauchamp, T, and Bowie, N, (eds), *Ethical Theory and Business*, 1988, Englewood Cliffs: Prentice-Hall, p 103.

100 Sometimes referred to as 'hypothetical perfect contract'. See Rose, C, 'Stakeholder orientation vs shareholder value – a matter of contractual failures' (2004) 18 *European Journal of Law and Economics* 77 at 79.

101 *Op. cit.* fn 92 above at 244; Chaver, *op. cit.* fn 92 above at 1825.

102 *Op. cit.* fn 93 above at 244.

efficient outcome can be achieved for the benefit of the entity.[103] The decision in the American case of *Credit Lyonnais Bank Nederland NV v Pathe Communications Corp* 1991 WL 277613; 1991 Del Ch LEXIS 215; LEXIS 215; (1992) 17 *Delaware Journal of Corporate Law* 1099 (Delaware Chancery Court) at n 55 endorsed the approach formulated here. In this case the court said that when a company is in the vicinity of insolvency, the directors owed their duty to the corporate enterprise, which is 'an obligation to the community of interest that sustained the corporation . . . to exercise judgment in an informed, good faith effort to maximize the corporation's long-term wealth-creating capacity'.[104] Implicitly, this means that creditor interests are taken into account. In the American case of *Re Franklin Retail Stores Inc* (1998) 225 BR 646 (Bankr ND Ill) the court said (at 655) that the directors' duty was 'to serve the interests of the corporate enterprise, encompassing all its constituent groups, without preference to any. That duty, therefore, requires directors to take creditor interests into account, but not necessarily to give those interests priority'. Very recently, the Supreme Court of Canada in *Peoples Department Stores v Wise* [2004] SCC 68; (2004) 244 DLR (4th) 564 seemed to accept this approach. The court said (at [47]) that when a company's financial position has deteriorated significantly, directors should seek to act in such a way as to create a 'better corporation', which involves not favouring any one group of stakeholders. Arguably the notion of a 'better company' is encompassed by the concept of maximisation of entity wealth.

One of the concerns that we identified with the approach whereby directors simply seek to balance the interests of shareholders and creditors, was that it was difficult to implement. Is the entity maximisation approach any different? First, directors do not have to engage in active balancing between interests as their aim is to maximise entity wealth. Therefore, they do not have to feel that they must explain how they engaged in balancing the relevant interests. To be sure, the directors will inevitably have to undertake some balancing, as they do if applying the principle of shareholder primacy. For example, they have to decide what portion of profits to use to pay dividends and what portion should be used to purchase new equipment or stock etc. Second, according to empirical evidence derived in relation to a study of negotiated mergers, directors, when left alone, tend to maximise firm value rather than shareholder wealth,[105] which suggests that it can be, and is being, done.

So, how will directors have to act in order to achieve maximisation of entity wealth? They will have to evaluate the fairness of all investment opportunities when they are subject to the responsibility to consider creditor interests. Wild

---

103 *Op. cit.* Leung, fn 20 above at 605; Mitchell, *op. cit.* fn 48 above at 633.

104 At 109 (LEXIS) and quoted in Cieri, *op. cit.* fn 5 above at 418.

105 Dennis and McConnell, 'Corporate mergers and security returns' (1986) 16 *Journal of Financial Economics* 143. While this study is not recent, it accords with empirical evidence discussed in Stout, L, 'Bad and not-so-bad arguments for shareholder primacy' (2002) 75 *Southern California Law Review* 1189 at 1201–1207.

risk-taking must be eliminated, so that, for instance, directors will not be able to engage in 'bet the firm' enterprises, or go 'for double or nothing'. As Morey McDaniel has stated:

> A project is risky if it has a low probability of success but a big payoff if it succeeds, that is, a long shot. If such a project succeeds, stockholders reap most of the gain. The market value of the firm will increase, but most of the increases will accrue to stockholders.[106]

McDaniel's statement is apposite when one takes into account the fact that, according to empirical evidence,[107] when a company is near to insolvency the managers take greater risks,[108] and it has become axiomatic that this risk-taking will take place,[109] particularly where the directors are also the owners[110] in the context of closed corporations. If, because the directors have little to lose where their company is in financial distress, they engage in excessive risk-taking,[111] then the creditors will be the ones to lose out if the risk does not bear fruit.

A hypothetical case study may be helpful in order to illustrate what entity maximisation involves.[112] A company has a £22m judgment and this is its only asset. The company's only liability is a sum of £5m owed to unsecured creditors. The judgment is to be appealed. On appeal, there are three possible outcomes. First, the judgment has a 25 per cent chance of being upheld, giving an expected value of the judgment of £5.5m (25 per cent of £22m). Second, there is a 70 per cent chance that the judgment will be reduced to £2m, thus giving an expected value of £1.4m (70 per cent of £2m). Finally, there is a five per cent chance that the judgment will be overturned, giving an expected value of £0. Say that there are offers of settlement of £5m and £7m. The expected value of the judgment on appeal is £6.9m (the total of the values of the possible outcomes is £5.5m + £1.4m). The creditors would be happy with either offer, as that would satisfy all of them fully, whereas in

---

106 *Op. cit.* fn 96 above at 419.

107 Daniels, R, 'Must boards go overboard? An economic analysis of the effects of burgeoning statutory liability on the role of directors in corporate governance' in Ziegel, J (ed), *Current Developments in International and Comparative Corporate Insolvency Law*, 1994, Oxford: Clarendon Press, p 549. However, de R Barondes, *op. cit.* fn 23 above at 62 challenges this view.

108 This is known as the 'over-investment theory' in finance theory: de R Barondes, *ibid* at 46.

109 *Op. cit.* Adler, fn 23 above at 590–598; de R Barondes, *ibid* at 46 and 49.

110 Mokal, R, 'An agency cost analysis of the wrongful trading provisions: redistribution, perverse incentives and the creditors' bargain' (2000) 59 CLJ 335 at 353–354.

111 See Easterbrook, and Fischel, *op. cit.* fn 44 above at 60; Jelisavcic, *op. cit.* fn 38 above at 148; Adler, *op. cit.* fn 23 above at 590–598.

112 This example is based substantially on that given by Chancellor Allen in *Credit Lyonnais Bank Nederland NV v Pathe Communications Corp* 1991 WL 277613; 1991 Del Ch LEXIS 215; LEXIS 215; (1992) 17 *Delaware Journal of Corporate Law* 1099 (Delaware Chancery Court), at n 55.

the appeal court there is a 75 per cent chance of them receiving nothing or a much-reduced return on their debt. Neither of the offers is all that attractive to the shareholders, for pursuant to the former offer their wealth is not increased, and with the latter it is not anything like the original judgment of £22m. The shareholders would probably prefer to reject the offers and take their chances in the appeal court, on the basis that they have the least to lose and the most to gain from such a course of action. But, the directors, if applying entity maximisation would, in seeking the best for the corporate entity, accept any offer over £6.9m (the total of the values of the possible outcomes) and reject anything below that amount.

Let us take another example.[113] Say X Ltd has assets of £10m and debts of £8m, but has some financial concerns over projects that are ongoing. The directors are presented with two ventures. The first is quite conservative, involving a £5m outlay of funds with a 90 per cent chance of reaping £6m and a 10 per cent chance of being worth £4m. This effectively means that the company has a 90 per cent chance of making a gain of £1m and a 10 per cent chance of losing £1m. The full amount of any gain would go to the share-holders, so the creditors would not be particularly supportive of the venture, especially as there is a 10 per cent chance that some or all of them will not receive full payment of their debts. The second venture is more risky. It requires an outlay of £10m. There is a 10 per cent chance of a £100m return (making a gain of £90m), but it has a 90 per cent chance of producing a £10m loss. The shareholders are likely to support this as they will get *all* of it and the benefits are substantial, and even if the venture fails they will only lose their equity in X, something which is, in total, likely to be in the region of £2m before the venture is taken on. The creditors would be the ones who would bear most of the risk with the second venture. If the venture succeeds the creditors will be no better off and if it fails then they will get nothing. Directors following an entity maximisation model would dismiss the second venture, but might reason that the former is worthwhile, given the high probability of a gain.

An entity maximisation approach is attractive as it provides a happy medium between excessive risk and excessive caution.[114] If the directors were only concerned for shareholder wealth maximisation they would, potentially, be inclined to indulge in excessive risk, while if they were focusing on creditor wealth maximisation, then directors would engage in excessively cautious activity, thereby perhaps leaving potential value unrealised. This should mean that when directors are under an obligation to consider creditor interests, they are not to react by acting too cautiously, causing the company to miss out on good deals, and, conversely, they must ensure that they reconsider such things as their operating strategy in light of creditor interests. In other

---

113 Loosely based on that provided in Smith, *op. cit.* fn 93 above at 221–222.
114 *Op. cit.* fn 16 above at 1221.

words, the directors must undertake a balance so that creditors are protected and at the same time the company's ability to innovate and take some appropriate risks is not totally or unreasonably proscribed.[115]

An entity maximisation approach is not new. As indicated above, Chancellor Allen in *Credit Lyonnais* advocated it and empirical evidence seems to suggest that many directors choose that approach even when companies are not in financial difficulty.[116] Interestingly, Chancellor Allen is not alone in Delaware, reputed to be the most hard-line jurisdiction, when it comes to supporting the ruling out of any interests other than shareholders, for there are many cases where entity maximisation has been followed.[117]

In the framework suggested, it is critical that directors remember that they are not to act as advocates of any constituency or part of one, but rather 'as a neutral mediator and, when necessary, as a referee between divergent interests',[118] so that the most efficient outcome can be achieved for the benefit of the entity,[119] the directors take on the role of a mediating body,[120] in that they mediate between the sometimes-competing interests of the shareholders and the creditors, and the creditors *inter se*. But the mediating is done indirectly in that this occurs as they seek to maximise the entity's wealth. There is provision for director discretion, but they must always have in their mind that they might be accountable for their actions and that this will be tested pursuant to the entity maximisation principle.

The mechanics of the framework

This section of the chapter seeks to articulate the mechanics of the entity maximisation approach in the context of a responsibility to consider creditor interests. We specifically examine here, how directors are actually to operate properly in undertaking entity maximisation. Initially, we must acknowledge that there has to be an element of discretion allowed to directors because no two cases are going to be the same. Directors will be confronted with different situations and with different shareholder and creditor constituencies. Having said that, it is proposed that there are four broad elements that directors must address in implementing entity maximisation. These are prescribed in order to foster accountability of directors as well as providing them with

---

115 Schwarcz, S, 'Rethinking a corporation's obligations to creditors' (1996) 17 *Cardozo Law Review* 647 at 673.

116 *Op. cit.* Stout, fn 105 above at 1201–1207.

117 Strine, L, 'The social responsibility of boards of directors and stockholders in change of control transactions: is there any "there" there?' (2002) 75 *Southern California Law Review* 1169 at 1176.

118 *Op. cit.* Leung, fn 20 above at 590.

119 *Ibid* at 605; Mitchell, *op. cit.* fn 48 above at 633.

120 See Blair, M, and Stout, L, 'A team production theory of corporate law' (1999) 85 Va L Rev 247.

some guidance, without being overly prescriptive, thus leaving room for some flexibility.

First, directors, when taking the company's position into account, would have to have a real legitimate purpose of business in mind in taking any action. This excludes doing something for an improper objective, such as transferring property for less than market value. In the United States it was stated in the Massachusetts case of *Re Healthco Int'l Inc* (1997) 208 BR 288 by Judge Queenan that:

> A distribution to stockholders which renders the corporation insolvent, or leaves it with unreasonably small capital, threatens the very existence of the corporation. This is prejudicial to all its constituencies, including creditors, employees, and stockholders retaining an ownership interest. Surely it is not asking too much of directors that they honor their obligations of loyalty and care to avoid the corporation's destruction.

Likewise, some actions that are very risky would not be legitimate, but this would not exclude the taking of all risks, save perhaps where a company is teetering on the edge of insolvency.

Second, directors must ensure that they are adequately informed when deciding on a particular action, and they are to take the company's financial position into account before embarking on it. This is likely to include being completely aware of the financial position of the company, and, in accordance with what the law now requires of directors, they must be able to understand company accounts.[121] If they are not able to do so, then they must employ someone who can advise them appropriately (*Re Hitco 2000 Ltd* [1995] 2 BCLC 63). Actions of directors should include calling for cash flow projections and reassessing financial exposure at regular intervals, with the intervals between assessments becoming shorter the greater the severity of the company's financial woes. One thing that directors must be careful about doing is taking on additional debt, thereby worsening the prospects for the existing creditors. They must consider the impact of their decision on the creditors' ability to recover what they are owed (*Gwyer v London Wharf (Limehouse) Ltd* at [81]). Directors should take into account the position of the company, the reasons for its financial difficulty and the future of the business.

Third, directors must take the action being proposed in the good faith belief that it is reasonably likely to foster the long-term wealth of the company.[122] Fourth, a director must be persuaded in his or her mind that a reasonable

---

121 See the comments in *Re DKG Contractors Ltd* [1990] BCC 903 and referred to in Milman, D, 'Strategies for regulating managerial performance in the "twilight zone" – familiar dilemmas: new considerations' [2004] JBL 493 at 497.

122 This element is consistent with what the Supreme Court of Canada in *Peoples Department Stores v Wise* (2004) SCC 68; (2004) 244 DLR (4th) 564. The court said that this was the proper action of directors when their company is in financial difficulty (at [46]).

director in the position of the director armed with the relevant information, and with entity maximisation in mind, would agree to the proposal.

The second and third elements are derived from the American business judgment rule,[123] which pervades every aspect of corporate law in the United States.[124] This rule is designed to preserve directors' discretion and to protect the directors from courts using hindsight to find them liable. The rule provides, in a nutshell, that courts will not substitute their business judgment for that of the informed, reasonable director who acts bona fide in the best interests of the company.[125] Directors cannot be second-guessed by a court concerning their actions, provided that the directors made informed, reasonable decisions in good faith, and which were based on the details that were available to them when making the decisions. Incorporating elements that are derived from the business judgment rule serves to provide some protection for directors in an area where concern has been voiced that directors have to endure uncertainty.[126] It is worth noting that UK courts have tended not to second-guess the decisions that directors have made. They have tended to place a generous interpretation on what directors have done at times when they are alleged to have breached their duties to creditors. More will be said in this respect shortly under the heading 'Review by the courts'.

The approach advocated in the above elements is similar to that implemented by the constituency statute of the State of Indiana, which states that 'if a determination is made with respect to the interests of constituencies by a majority of disinterested directors in good faith after reasonable investigation, then that determination shall be presumed to be valid'.[127]

The last of the four elements introduces an objective aspect, necessary to achieve a fair result, and something that the courts have included when evaluating whether a director has acted bona fide in the best interests of his or her company (*Charterbridge Corp Ltd v Lloyds Bank Ltd* [1970] Ch 62; [1969] 2 All ER 1185). The traditional approach to assessment of directors in this area has been to use a subjective test (*Re Smith & Fawcett* [1942] Ch 304), but there are instances where courts have preferred an objective

---

123 For example, see *In re Healthco International Inc* 208 BR 288 at 306 (1997) (Ma).
124 Bainbridge, S, 'Director primacy: the means and ends of corporate governance' (2003) 97 *Northwestern University Law Review* 547 at 601.
125 For instance, see *Moran v Household International Inc* 500 A 2d 1346 at 1356 (1983) (De); *Spiegel v Buntrock* 571 A 2d 767 at 774 (1990) (De); *op. cit.* fn 5 above, at 408. The review of a director's action by a court, applying the business judgment rule, will involve a review of the objective financial interests of the directors, a review of the director's motivation and an objective review of the process by which a decision was reached by the director: *Re RJR Nabisco Inc. Shareholders' Litigation* (unreported, Delaware Chancery Court, 31 January 1989), referred to by Tompkins, A, 'Directors' duties to creditors: Delaware and the insolvency exception' (1993) 47 SMU L Rev 165 at 188.
126 *Op. cit.* Cieri, fn 5 at 422.
127 *Op. cit.* Committee on Corporate Laws of the Section of Business Law of the American Bar Association, fn 27 above at 2262.

approach.[128] The objective aspect of the test applied in relation to evaluating whether directors have breached their fiduciary duties was set out in *Charterbridge Corp Ltd v Lloyds Bank Ltd* and asks (at 74; 1194): whether an intelligent and honest man in the position of a director of the company involved, could, in the whole of the circumstances, have reasonably believed that the transaction was for the benefit of the company. Certainly the legislature has thought it appropriate to introduce an objective element into wrongful trading.

Professor Jonathan Lipson has said that the entity maximisation approach 'has a certain appeal, on both efficiency and fairness grounds. If one distils business reality down to certain understandings of rational economic behaviour, the entity maximisation approach is the most efficient as it brings risk and reward together'.[129] However, Lipson went on to criticise the entity maximisation approach on the basis, *inter alia*, that decisions that directors make will often benefit one constituency at the expense of another.[130] In response one might say that the framework articulated here attempts to provide a defence for directors in relation to any complaint brought against them, assuming that the directors have sought to entity maximise and followed the steps referred to above. It is submitted that the problem of balancing is in fact solved by employing the entity maximisation principle, as directors are not forced to weigh up the benefits and harm accruing to different shareholders or creditors as a result of a particular action. Their remit is to act to enhance the wealth of the entity.

Review by the courts

What is clear, and by way of safeguard for directors, is that courts, in reviewing the actions of directors, would, in applying the framework discussed above, have to dump the traditional approach used. Rather they would have 'to articulate more clearly the true reasons for their rulings',[131] instead of 'trotting out' without careful scrutiny the usual dicta from earlier cases.[132] But, given the framework articulated above, can the courts assess what directors have done? Sealy, who, in a significant contribution to the literature on this topic, asserts that in a commercial context this is not a justiciable issue. But, the courts have been judging the actions of fiduciaries for many years and, it is submitted, they are now more adept as doing so than ever before. It is contended that UK courts (and courts in other jurisdictions where the duty has been applied, such as in Australia), have increasingly become more competent at assessing the actions of directors. Moreover, the courts have not second-guessed the decisions that directors have made. They have generally

---

128 For instance, *Re Horsley & Weight Ltd* [1982] 3 All ER 1045 at 1056.
129 *Op. cit.* fn 16 above at 1221.   130 *Ibid* at 1223.   131 *Op. cit.* fn 2 above at 180.
132 *Ibid.*

been careful not to employ hindsight to find directors liable and have extended to directors reasonably wide latitude in interpreting how they have acted. Perhaps one example might suffice. In *Re Welfab Engineers Ltd* [1990] BCC 600 the action involved a claim that directors had breached their duty to the company, in that they failed to take into account the interests of creditors, because they accepted one bid for the company's property, while rejecting what appeared to be more substantial bids at a time when the company was in desperate financial straits. The court, in coming to a decision that the directors were not liable for breach of their duties, took into account the commercial environment at the time of the making of the transaction alleged to constitute the breach, even though it occurred some seven years before the hearing. At the time of the alleged breach the geographical region in which the company's business operated was suffering a harsh recession and this impacted markedly on the decision made.

Cases where directors have been found liable involve situations where the directors have clearly acted against creditor interests. An example is to be found in *West Mercia Safetywear Ltd*, the facts of which were discussed earlier.[133]

Dissension at board level

One practical issue warrants a brief discussion before this chapter draws to an end. It is quite possible that one can have the situation where there is dissent amongst the directors as to what action should be taken. What are those who want to take a cautious avenue, which they felt would enhance entity value or, if the company is insolvent, the best interests of the creditors (creditor maximisation), to do? What is to be the fate of these directors? This is a similar problem to the one facing a director who believes that his or her company has no reasonable prospect of avoiding insolvent liquidation. In such a case, unless something is done the director could be found liable under s 214 of the Insolvency Act for wrongful trading. A director has a defence to wrongful trading if he or she can establish that after the point when he or she first knew or ought to have concluded that there was no reasonable prospect that the company would avoid going into insolvent liquidation, the director took *every step* with a view to minimising the potential loss to the company's creditors as ought to have been taken (s 214(3)). Maybe some of the actions that have been suggested as constituting 'every step' in the context of s 214, some of which were mentioned earlier,[134] are relevant in determining what a director should do where there is dissension.

To what lengths must directors go to protect themselves? One possible action to take is to insist that the minutes of the relevant board meeting indicated that they dissented from the proposed course of action that is

133 Above at p 156.   134 Above at pp 111–116.

believed to be in breach of the obligation to consider creditor interests. Would resignation protect directors? If a majority decision is take a particular course of action and resignation by a dissenter occurred prior to the actual taking of the action that turns out to prejudice creditors' interests, it might be argued that the directors who resigned was not a party to the actions that caused loss to creditors. However, that might be too glib an approach. It might be contended that because the director was under a duty at the time that the proposed action(s) was discussed, he or she should do more than merely resign.

Conclusion

This chapter has examined what directors are to do when obliged to consider the interests of creditors. Undoubtedly, the first thing that has to be said is that there are difficulties in defining under what governance norms directors are to operate when they are subject to a responsibility to take creditor interests into account. While the exact circumstances that will precipitate the advent of the duty are not precise, how directors are to fulfil their responsibilities to creditors is even less clear. Much has been made of the fact that determining what is meant by taking into account the interests of creditors is difficult, and close to meaningless. Unfortunately the problem is that legal doctrine has not caught up with the economic reality where financially distressed companies are involved.[135] Without doubt, 'it is unsatisfactory that there should be no precise indication of the nature of the duty and the conduct that it demands from directors'[136] when they are subject to a duty to consider creditor interests.

It has been submitted that if a company is insolvent, because the interests of creditors are paramount, the task of directors is not so difficult. In all that they do, directors should have in mind the payment of creditors, and be implementing policies that maximise creditor wealth. The problem occurs where the company is in a position that is short of insolvency. In such a situation, the chapter considered the problems that exist if we simply require directors, when under an obligation to consider creditor interests, to balance the interests of creditors as against shareholders, as well as balancing the interests of creditors *inter se*. It was demonstrated that the task confronting directors in doing this is sometimes complex, primarily because of the existence of conflicting interests, and it is an invidious assignment for directors, with little in the way of a guide being given to directors as to how they should carry out the company's business.

The prime difficulty in devising resolutions to the problem is that there are no hard and fast rules concerning how directors are to act when creditor interests are to be taken into account. What is clear is that one cannot resort

---

135 *Op. cit.* fn 5 above at 415.   136 *Op. cit.* fn 4 above at 90.

to something akin to mathematical formulae. The issues that face directors are often complex and difficult to predict so it would not be feasible to lay down in advance how directors are to act in the light of future contingencies. The circumstances and conflicts of each case must be considered separately. We cannot get away from having to rely on directors' discretion. But this does not exactly help directors to know what they are to do. While accepting all of this, it has been submitted in the chapter that we can provide, at least, a framework within which directors should operate when subject to a responsibility to creditors. The framework advocated here is the entity maximisation approach which makes it incumbent on directors to make decisions that will maximise the general wealth of the company so that the net present value to the company as a whole is enhanced. The chapter has also sought to explain how directors should act in endeavouring to maximise entity wealth.

One critical advantage of adopting the entity maximisation model is that it avoids a total dependence on directors having to engage in a balancing exercise, weighing up the interests of the shareholder and creditor constituencies, which is extremely difficult to do. Some balancing will have to be undertaken, but the directors have an aim in what they doing, when they engage in the balancing, namely to ensure that entity value is maximised.

The framework proposed is an attempt to provide some guidance and a degree of certainty for directors, as well as providing some principles upon which courts could evaluate the actions of directors. Rather than having little on which to judge directors, courts would be able to assess whether directors sought to maximise entity wealth, and they would need to point to some aspect of the directors' mode of operation that meant that they had neglected the creditors.

15 A direct duty to creditors?

Introduction

An issue which has been the subject of some significant debate, and which warrants discussion in this book, is whether directors owe an independent or direct duty to creditors when the obligation to creditors is said to arise (an issue considered in passing in earlier chapters), or the duty is owed to the company and that duty requires directors to consider the interests of creditors. In other words, is the duty owed directly to creditors, or is it an indirect duty in that the duty is owed not to creditors, but to the company (whose interests do not include those of the creditors) to consider creditor interests, and the duty is mediated through the company? The concept of imperfect obligation may be used to describe this latter concept (*Re New World Alliance Pty Ltd; Sycotex Pty Ltd v Baseler* (1994) 51 FCR 425 at 444–445; (1994) 122 ALR 531 at 550 (Aust Fed Ct)). The issue as to whether directors owe a direct or an indirect duty is not merely an academic one, but can have several practical consequences. One important one is the identity of the person who has standing to take legal proceedings for a breach of the duty. It follows that while a direct duty would enable directors to enforce any breach, if the indirect duty approach is adopted, the creditors cannot enforce a breach of the duty; that can only be done by the company itself, to whom the duty is owed, or an office-holder such as a liquidator, an administrator or an administrative receiver acting for the company. In fact, it would seem that all of the UK, Irish and Commonwealth cases that have involved claims against directors for failing to consider creditor interests have been initiated by a liquidator. The situation has been a little different in the United States. In parts of the Commonwealth, most notably in the UK and Australia, administrators appointed to insolvent companies are entitled to bring proceedings in the name of companies in order to enforce a breach of duty.[1]

This chapter discusses the problems that have been identified if a direct duty were to be implemented. It then goes on to examine whether it is

---

1   See Insolvency Act 1986, Sched B1; Corporations Act 2001 (Aust), Part 5.3A.

possible to argue successfully, given the present state of the law, that creditors are owed a direct duty. It comes to the conclusion that it is not possible to do so, as the case law predominantly favours an indirect duty. Then, the Chapter investigates whether, from a normative perspective, the duty should be regarded as a direct duty.

The problems with a direct duty

There are several apparent problems with creditors being owed a direct duty.

Creditors taking proceedings

One of the primary advantages for creditors of a direct duty is that if the directors breached their duty, the creditors would be able to bring legal proceedings against the directors. But if that were the case it would lead, it has been argued, to problems.

First, because creditors could enforce breaches against directors, this might precipitate a greater amount of litigation (something which the rule in *Foss v Harbottle* (1843) 2 Hare 461; 67 ER 189 was designed to stop) which might lead to a waste of time and money. A way of restricting this is to require creditors to apply for leave to initiate substantial proceedings, and this enables the courts to filter out those claims that are without merit or are designed to achieve some ulterior purpose.[2] Such a mechanism is in place in some jurisdictions, such as Australia and Canada before derivative proceedings can be initiated. While this would be an acceptable process to apply here (and is proposed by the Company Law Reform Bill 2005), it would be necessary, in order to prevent directors from embarking on a course of action that could place the company in further financial danger, to permit creditors as a class to be able to seek injunctions prior to a liquidation.[3] These issues are broached again in the next chapter.

Second, a duty to creditors could lead to double recovery in that the creditors could sue individually and a liquidator could sue on behalf of the company if it is taken into liquidation, and, as Professor Dan Prentice has stated: 'This would obviously present the court with the difficulty of sorting out the respective rights of the company and the creditors so as to avoid the directors having to pay damages twice over with respect to a single wrong.'[4]

Third, providing for an indirect duty means that the collective procedure of

---

2   The Australian Company and Securities Law Review Committee took this view in relation to derivative proceedings (*Enforcement of the Duties of Directors and Officers of a Company by Means of a Statutory Derivative Action*, Report No 12, 1990, p 65).

3   Finch, V, 'Directors' duties: insolvency and the unsecured creditor' in Clarke, A (ed), *Current Issues in Insolvency Law*, 1991, London: Stevens, p 109. Also, see McDonnell, S, '*Geyer v Ingersoll Publications Co*: insolvency shifts directors' burden from shareholders to creditors' (1994) 19 *Delaware Journal of Corporate Law* 177 at 208.

4   Prentice, D, 'Creditors' interests and directors' duties' (1990) 10 OJLS 265 at 276.

liquidation (that is, creditors forfeit their respective individual rights to take action to enforce their claims and are given in exchange a right to prove in the liquidation) is preserved. Fourth, and allied to the two previous points, is the fact that if one or more creditors were able to bring successful proceedings against directors, for breach of duty, this might render the directors without funds to pay out other creditors who make claims later. It is likely that the powerful creditors will have the necessary knowledge and funds to be able to instigate proceedings before other creditors and this might be regarded as unfair. In *Mogal Corporation Ltd v Australasia Investment Ltd (in liq)* (1990) 3 NZBLC 101783, 101, 808–11 Smellie J of the New Zealand High Court warned about the use of the duty to benefit a particular creditor. In *Re Pantone 485 Ltd* [2002] 1 BCLC 266 the court said that directors had a duty to make decisions, when their company was insolvent, while having regard for all of the general creditors, and not one, or a section, of the creditors, so it might be concluded that a court would not want to see one or a section of creditors benefiting at the expense of the rest.

A fifth problem that presents itself is what award would the courts give if a creditor could sue? If there has been a diversion of assets to associates of the directors, the award could be fairly simple – an order taking into account the loss of value to the company (and ultimately to the creditors); although in such circumstances, a better course might be to take action under s 423 of the Insolvency Act 1986 (transactions defrauding creditors). But what happens if the action complained of is not so easily defined as a diversion of assets? In the American case of *Re Healthco International Co* 208 BR 288 (1997) (Bankruptcy District of Massachusetts) the court assessed the claim of a creditor by considering the decrease in the fair market value of the company that resulted from the actions of the directors (at 310).

While there are undoubtedly problems with permitting a direct duty, one important benefit to creditors is that if they could bring proceedings themselves for breach of duty, rather than having to wait for a liquidator to do so, a 'vast potential liability for company directors'[5] would exist. Proceedings could be taken before liquidation or administration, which might mean that creditors would receive payouts before the directors became liable pursuant to guarantees, given to cover company debts. Discharging such guarantees might well render directors impecunious by the time that proceedings are taken when the company is liquidated.

Interference with the pari passu *principle*

A further reason for not permitting creditors to recover under a direct duty is that it could damage the operation of the *pari passu* principle, which is often

---

5 Worthington, S, 'Directors' duties, creditors' rights and shareholder intervention' (1991) 18 MULR 121 at 140.

regarded as the foremost principle of insolvency law, and was mentioned as a reason as late as 2000 in the Australian High Court decision of *Spies v The Queen* (2000) 201 CLR 603; (2000) 173 ALR 529; [2000] HCA 43 at [93] for not having a direct duty. The principle is explained by Professor Charles Seligson as follows:

> Equality is equity. That maxim is a theme of bankruptcy administration – one of the cornerstones of the bankruptcy structure. All persons similarly situated are entitled to equality in treatment in the distribution of the assets of the bankrupt estate.[6]

With respect, this reason lacks weight now, for two reasons. First, there are so many exceptions to the *pari passu* principle that the principle is rarely determinative of who gets what in many insolvent regimes. For example, permitting set-off and debt subordination means that the principle is undermined. Furthermore, there will be payments that are made in priority to the general body of creditors, who receive payment on a *pari passu* basis. In a liquidation, before the general body are paid, the liquidator must discharge all costs and expenses of the winding up and pay, in full, all preferential creditors, such as employees and, in many jurisdictions, the tax authorities. Hence, as Dr Rizwaan Mokal has argued,[7] the *pari passu* principle does not mean much now. Therefore, if we interfered with it by granting creditors a right to enforce duties owed to them, then we would not exactly be overturning a principle that functions consistently.

Second, any action initiated by a creditor would be against the directors, and one is moved to ask how that interferes with the application of the *pari passu* principle to the company? It surely does not! Where the principle could apply, theoretically, is if the directors cannot pay all claims, and enter bankruptcy, then some creditors will have been paid in priority to others, and this would be, arguably, against the *pari passu* principle. But surely in such a situation the trustee in bankruptcy of the estates of the directors could recover payments made to creditors before bankruptcy eventuated, on the basis that such payments would constitute preferences under s 340 of the Insolvency Act 1986, provided that they were made within six months of the commencement of bankruptcy? Once recovered, these payments would swell the funds that are to be distributed to the general body of creditors who have claims against the directors.

---

6 Seligson, C, 'Preferences under the Bankruptcy Act' (1961) 15 Vanderbilt L Rev 115. For further discussion, see Jackson, J, *Logic and Limits of Bankruptcy Law*, 1986, p123, Cambridge, Mass: Harvard University Press; Eisenberg, T, 'Bankruptcy law in perspective' (1982) UCLA L Rev 953 at 963; Countryman, V, 'The concept of a voidable preference in bankruptcy' (1985) 38 Vanderbilt LR 713 at 738; Morris, C R, 'Bankruptcy law reform: preferences, secret liens and floating liens' (1974) 54 *Minnesota Law Review* 737 at 738.

7 For example in 'Priority as pathology: the *pari passu* myth' [2001] CLJ 581.

The situation where *pari passu* could be affected is where there was a direct duty owed to creditors, and individual creditors could threaten to sue directors if they did not get paid. Directors, fearful of action, might pay off from company funds these creditors, and not others, and given the weakness of the preference laws in England and Wales,[8] such payments might not be recovered if the company entered liquidation, thus leaving those creditors who did not threaten the directors with action losing out.

Interestingly, Canadian law subscribes to the *pari passu* principle and yet allows creditors the right to apply to courts under s 241(2)(c) of the Canadian Business Corporations Act 1985 (with *Re Sidaplex-Plastic Suppliers Inc* (1998) 40 OR (3d) 563 (Ontario Court of Appeal) constituting a recent example), which states that the court is able to give a remedy if the directors' powers have been exercised 'in a manner that is oppressive or unfairly prejudicial to or unfairly disregards the interests of any security-holder, *creditor*, director or officer'[9] (my emphasis). This is discussed further in the next chapter.

It is open to query whether one could tackle the interference with the *pari passu* principle by providing that a court is able to order a director against whom an action has been brought successfully by a creditor, to pay a sum to a trust fund for creditors so that all creditors might benefit. The problem with this strategy is that any incentive for many creditors to bring proceedings might be lost. The main issues are: how would the fund be administered; when would there be distributions; and which creditors would qualify for a distribution? These are difficult issues to resolve and this might militate against allowing creditor action.

Restricting the maximisation of profits

Professor Ross Grantham has argued that if one permitted a direct duty then this would clearly cut across the concept of a company being dedicated to the pursuit of maximising profits.[10] This is correct to a point. If the duty applies only during times of financial difficulty or where a venture is undertaken that could cause the company's insolvency, there is going to be a limit to the period when directors have a duty to creditors. Even then, I would submit, along the lines set out in Chapter 14, that the directors would, except where a company is insolvent, practice entity maximisation, and this does not mean that there can be no eye on profit-making. In fact the entity maximisation framework presented in Chapter 14 presupposes that there will be profit-making, but consistent with enhancing the value of the entity and not just benefiting of the shareholders.

---

8 See Keay, A, 'Preferences in liquidation law: a time for a change' (1998) 2 CfiLR 198.
9 See Thomson, D, 'Directors, creditors and insolvency: a fiduciary duty or a duty not to oppress' (2000) 58 *University of Toronto Faculty of Law Review* 31.
10 'The judicial extension of directors' duties to creditors' [1991] JBL 1 at 12.

The legal position

In introducing this part of the chapter, it should be noted that the relevant cases will not be considered in depth. Readers might care to refer back to Chapter 11 where cases were considered in their appropriate place as far as their contribution to the evolution of the responsibility to creditors, and several of them were examined in some depth.

Traditionally, directors clearly did not owe fiduciary duties to the creditors of their companies (*Re Wincham Shipbuilding Boiler & Salt Co* (1878) 9 Ch D 322 at 328; *Bath v Standard Land Co Ltd* [1911] 1 Ch 618 at 627). But is that still the case today? The case that can be regarded as really initiating the development of the responsibility of directors to creditors, *Walker v Wimborne* (1976) 137 CLR 1; (1976) 3 ACLR 529, has been relied on as supporting both a direct duty and an indirect duty. Mason J of the Australian High Court gave a dictum in *Walker* that has been relied on by many courts for the principle that directors have, in certain cases, an obligation to creditors of their company. His Honour said (at 6–7; 531):

> In this respect it should be emphasised that the directors of a company in discharging their duty to the company must take into account the interests of its shareholders and its creditors. Any failure by the directors to take into account the interests of creditors will have adverse consequences for the company as well as for them.

Mason J did not state whether directors had a duty to their companies to consider creditor interests or that directors had a distinct duty to creditors. But the dictum has been interpreted by some as a basis for establishing that directors owe a direct duty to creditors.[11] Others have said that all that his Honour was saying was that directors must consider, as part of their duty to their company, creditor interests. Clearly, the latter approach has attracted the most judicial and academic support. A few brief references to some of the relevant decisions may be helpful.

In *Re Horsley & Weight Ltd* (1982) Ch 442, one of the first UK cases to comment on the general area, the Court of Appeal made no reference to *Walker*. Buckley LJ, in whose judgment Cumming-Bruce LJ concurred, said expressly that the directors owe an indirect duty to creditors not to permit any unlawful reduction of capital, because the duty of the directors is to the company (at 454).

Nicholson v Permakraft (NZ) Ltd (1985) 3 ACLC 453 was one the first appellate court decisions after *Walker* where the latter case was expressly approved of. In *Permakraft*, Cooke J of the New Zealand Court of Appeal

---

11 For example, see Sappideen, R, 'Fiduciary obligations to corporate creditors' [1991] JBL 365 at 366.

seemed to indicate that there was no direct duty when he said (at 459) that: 'The duties of creditors are owed to the company. On the facts of particular cases this may require the directors to consider *inter alia* the interests of creditors.' However, later in his judgment his Lordship did talk about 'duties to creditors' (at 459), but it is likely that he was only using the reference to duties here loosely, in the manner that this book has done. Soon after *Permakraft* the New South Wales Court of Appeal in *Kinsela v Russell Kinsela Pty Ltd* (1986) 4 ACLC 215; (1986) 10 ACLR 395, was called upon to consider the issue. In delivering the leading judgment, Street CJ did not refer once to 'a duty to creditors'. Rather, his comments appear to affirm the indirect duty concept. His Honour said that when a company is insolvent, the creditors' interests intrude (221; 401), but he did not suggest that directors had a duty to the creditors. The approach of Street CJ was approved of by the Court of Appeal in *Liquidator of West Mercia Safetywear Ltd v Dodd* (1988) 4 BCC 30, but the court did not in its comments indicate a preference for the view that the directors owed a direct or indirect duty to creditors.

In the first Australian case that specifically considered the nature of the obligation of directors to creditors, *Re New World Alliance Pty Ltd* (1994) 122 ALR 531, Gummow J of the Federal Court took the view that the directors did not owe a direct duty. His Honour stated (at 550) that the duty is a duty of imperfect obligation owed to creditors and this cannot be enforced by creditors themselves to recover losses; reliance has to be placed upon a liquidator taking action.

The last UK case to mention specifically the issue of direct duty was *Yukong Lines Ltd of Korea v Rendsburg Investments Corp* [1998] BCC 870. Toulson J said (at 884) that a director 'does not owe a direct fiduciary duty towards an individual creditor, nor is an individual creditor entitled to sue for breach of the fiduciary duty owed by the director to the company'. Interestingly, his Lordship talked about no duty being owed to an individual creditor, but he does not expressly reject a duty owed to all creditors. The approach adopted may have some overlap with the decision in *Re Pantone 485 Ltd* [2002] 1 BCLC 266, where Richard Field QC (sitting as a deputy High Court judge) rejected a claim by one creditor that the company's directors had breached their duty to take into account creditor interests because the duty was owed to all general creditors, and not one, or a section, of the creditors.

While accepting, in *Millgate Financial Corporation Ltd v BCED Holdings Ltd* 2003 CanLII 39497 (Ont SC), that directors had to consider creditors' interests when the company 'is insolvent, or near insolvent, or where the impugned transactions place the corporation's solvency in jeopardy' (at [89]), Cullity J of the Ontario Superior Court of Justice rejected the idea of a direct duty to creditors.

Perhaps the most severe attacks that have been mounted against the concept of a direct duty have been in Australia and Canada, where the highest courts in both jurisdictions have rejected a direct duty. For the first time since

Walker, the Australian High Court had an opportunity to consider the issue under review in *Spies v The Queen*, although the case did not turn on whether directors owed a responsibility to creditors, and what the court had to say on the topic only constituted dicta at best. The court denied, clearly, it is respectfully submitted, that directors owe an independent duty to creditors (at [93–95]). The same result occurred in *Peoples Department Stores v Wise* [2004] SCC 68; (2004) 244 DLR (4th) 564. In this case, when it came before the Canadian Supreme Court, it was said, *inter alia*, that directors had a duty to act for the interests of their company and the interests of the company are not to be confused with the interests of the creditors or those of any other stakeholders (at [43]). While the Court stated that in determining whether directors have acted in the best interests of the company, it might be appropriate for the directors to take into account the interests of creditors, there is no duty owed to creditors, and this is even the case when a company is in the vicinity of insolvency (at [46]). The Court's decision followed a line provided in earlier cases (such as *Royal Bank of Canada v First Pioneer Investments Ltd* (1980) 27 OR (2d) 352) and it effectively reversed the judgment of Greenberg J, at first instance in the Quebec Superior Court (Bankruptcy and Insolvency Division) ([1998] QJ No 3571), where his Honour appeared to accept the notion that directors had a direct duty to creditors.

While the view that directors only have to consider creditor interests as part of their duty to their companies has predominated, those who argue for a direct duty are not without some support. The primary support lies in a judgment of Lord Templeman in *Winkworth v Edward Baron Development Co Ltd* [1986] 1 WLR 1512; [1987] 1 All ER 114, which was approved of by the other Law Lords sitting on the case. Lord Templeman said (at 1516; 118):

> [A] company owes a duty to its creditors, present and future. The company is not bound to pay off every debt as soon as it is incurred and the company is not obliged to avoid all ventures which involve an element of risk, but the company owes a duty to its creditors to keep its property inviolate and available for the repayment of its debts . . . A duty is owed by the directors to the company and to the creditors of the company to ensure that the affairs of the company are properly administered and that its property is not dissipated or exploited for the benefit of the directors themselves to the prejudice of the creditors.

Here his Lordship appears to countenance the idea that directors can owe a duty to the company and to the creditors. Certainly it has been stated in some UK decisions, from time to time, that directors owe duties to their company and the shareholders. The majority of commentators have taken the above comment of his Lordship as advocating a direct duty to creditors. The general approach adopted by his Lordship has found some judicial approval. In fact the Full Court of the Western Australian Supreme Court in *Jeffree v NCSC* (1989) 7 ACLC 556 expressly approved of his Lordship's words quoted above. Furthermore, while rarely referred to, Richardson J in the important New Zealand decision of *Permakraft*, said that when a company was insolvent the directors 'might be said to have a duty to them [the creditors]' (at 463). It must be added that his Lordship did say that when a company was not insolvent, but in a financial mire, the state of affairs was more difficult to determine.

In Ireland, McGuiness J in *Jones v Gunn* [1997] 3 IR 1; [1997] 2 ILRM 245, while not entering into a substantial consideration of whether a direct duty was owed, said that where a company is insolvent, at least, the directors owe a fiduciary duty to the creditors (at [48]). Interestingly, the approach taken by Richardson J and McGuiness J can be regarded as consistent with some decisions of American courts, a matter discussed shortly.

The dictum of Lord Templeman has certainly been the subject of substantial academic criticism. Points that can be made against the dictum representing the law are: no authority was cited by his Lordship in support; no case law was even discussed in the judgment; and given that the comments were, in many ways, groundbreaking, they were surprisingly brief. Chris Riley has noted that what his Lordship said could be seen as 'a novel suggestion in that it implies some sort of obligation owed by a company to its creditors over and above any contractual obligations incurred by the company in its dealings with each creditor'.[12] It is of interest that some three years after his comments in *Winkworth*, Lord Templeman, while a member of the Privy Council in *Kuwait Asia Bank EC v National Mutual Life Nominees Ltd* [1990] 3 All ER 404, concurred with the judgment of Lord Lowry, and the latter said: 'But although directors are not liable *as such* to creditors of the company, a director may by agreement or representation assume a special duty to a creditor of the company (at 421) (emphasis in the judgment).' This statement appears to suggest that no fiduciary duty could be owed directly to creditors.

There has been some suggestion that Jacobs J in *Grove v Flavel* (1986) 11 ACLR 161 was advocating that directors owed a direct duty to creditors, for in *Spies v The Queen* the Australian High Court said that *if* Jacobs J was suggesting that directors owed an independent duty, it was contrary to principle (at [95]). With respect, it is submitted that it is not possible to read what Jacobs J said as endorsing the concept of an independent duty, so I think that we can put *Grove v Flavel* to one side when considering the issue at hand. Of course, given what the High Court said in *Spies*, if Jacobs J was endorsing a direct duty, that view would not be very persuasive now.

One commentator[13] has sought to rely on a comment in an English judgment that pre-dates Lord Templeman's in order to bolster the argument for a direct duty. Lord Diplock in *Lonrho Ltd v Shell Petroleum Co Ltd* [1980] 1 WLR 627 stated that: 'It is the duty of the board to consider whether to

12 'Directors' duties and the interests of creditors' (1989) 10 Co Law 87 at 91.
13 *Op. cit.* fn 11 above at 387.

accede to the request [for inspection of documents] would be in the best interests of the company. These are not exclusively those of its shareholders but may include those of its creditors (at 634).' But it is to be noted that the upshot of what his Lordship said is that the directors *may* have to consider the creditors. He does not appear to be suggesting a continuing duty. In fact his Lordship seems to be stating that the duty is to the company and this might involve taking into account creditor interests. If this is correct then it is consistent with the argument that directors do not owe a direct duty, but as part of their duty to their company they have to consider the interests of creditors when some form of financial strife afflicts the company. In any event his Lordship's statement appears to be an aside that does not provide the necessary ammunition to argue for a full-blown doctrine of an independent duty.

There has been some lively debate on the issue in Australia. One commentator, Anil Hargovan, has trenchantly argued[14] that the Australian High Court in *Spies* has finished off the notion that directors could be held to owe an independent duty to creditors, while James McConvill asserts,[15] *inter alia*, that while the High Court did not approve of such a duty, the judgment in *Spies* does not bar a court from finding directors liable for breach of duty on a creditor's claim. His argument is that 'the decision in *Spies* did not make any authoritative determination as to the nature and scope of a director's obligation to the company's creditors'.[16] Much turns on the interpretation of the judgments in *Spies*, but it is submitted that it appears unlikely that an Australian court is going to permit the idea of an independent duty in light of *Spies*. Certainly, in two Western Australian cases heard subsequent to *Spies, The Bell Group Ltd (in liq) v Westpac Banking Corporation* [2001] WASC 315 and *Geneva Finance Ltd v Resource & Industry Ltd* (2002) 20 ACLC 1427, the Supreme Court of Western Australia found that the High Court in *Spies* was against the notion of an independent duty owed to creditors (at [103]). In the latter case, EM Heenan J said (at 1438):

> [T]he orthodox articulation of the duty is that a director of a company, especially if the company is approaching insolvency, is obliged to consider the interests of creditors as part of the discharge of his duty to the company itself, but that he does not have any direct duty to the creditors and certainly not one enforceable by the creditors themselves.

---

14 See Hargovan, A, 'Directors' duties to creditors in Australia after *Spies v The Queen* – is the development of an independent duty dead or alive?' (2003) *Company and Securities Law Journal* 390; '*Geneva Finance* and the "duty" of directors to creditors: imperfect obligation and critique' (2004) *Insolvency Law Journal* 134.
15 McConvill, J, 'Directors' duties to creditors in Australia after *Spies v The Queen*' (2002) 20 *Company and Securities Law Journal* 4; '*Geneva Finance* and the "duty" of directors to creditors: imperfect obligation and other imperfections' (2003) 11 *Insolvency Law Journal* 7.
16 See '*Geneva Finance*' ibid at 9.

Given the opinions of the High Court in *Spies*, and the Supreme Court of Canada in *Peoples Department Stores*, the most authoritative courts in their respective jurisdictions, the direct duty argument is likely to falter in most, if not all, Commonwealth jurisdictions, including the UK. While it might be argued that the concept of fiduciary relationship is developing on a case-by-case basis (*Hospital Products Ltd v United States Surgical Corporation* (1984) 156 CLR 41), and that would leave room for asserting the existence of an independent duty to creditors, the fact of the matter is that the predominance of the case law is against an extension of the duty to creditors. Furthermore, notwithstanding the gallant arguments of McConvill, academic opinion is firmly set against a direct duty.[17] The view that is often posited is that the idea 'that directors owe a fiduciary duty to creditors . . . [is] contrary to principle and to long-established authority'.[18]

As indicated in Chapter 11, the developments in the US have led to different approaches. Leaving aside the cases where the trust fund doctrine has been successfully pleaded, holding that a fiduciary duty is owed to creditors where the company is insolvent, there is not a large corpus of cases which have permitted creditors to proceed against directors on the basis of a direct duty. But it must be noted that there are some quite high-profile cases where creditors have been able to take proceedings against directors successfully claiming that the directors have breached their duty to the creditors, such as the Delaware Court of Chancery case, *Geyer v Ingersoll Publications Co* 621 A 2d 784 (1992) and the United States District Court case of *Re Buckhead America Corp* 178 BR 956 at 968 (1994). In the former case, Vice-Chancellor Chandler was of the view that on the occurrence of insolvency the directors owed fiduciary duties to the creditors (at 787). In the latter case it was held that a creditor can derivatively proceed against directors where the directors have failed to foster the interests of creditors. Chancellor Allen, in the most celebrated American case in this area, *Credit Lyonnais Bank Nederland, NV v Pathe Communications Corp* 1991 Del Ch WL 277613; LEXIS 215; (1992) 17 *Delaware Journal of Corporate Law* 1099, held that a fiduciary duty is owed to creditors (and the entire community of interest that makes up the company entity) when the company is in the vicinity of insolvency. There does seem more room in the US to argue for a direct duty, although some might well deny this.[19]

---

17   For example, see Prentice *op. cit.* fn 4 above at 275; Worthington, *op. cit.* fn 5 above at 151; Sealy, L, 'Personal liability of directors and officers for debts of insolvent corporations: a jurisdictional perspective (England)' in Ziegel, J (ed), *Current Developments in International and Comparative Corporate Insolvency Law*, 1994, Oxford: Clarendon Press, p 486.

18   Renard, I, Commentary to Heydon, J, 'Directors' duties and the company's interests' in Finn, P D (ed), *Equity and Commercial Relations*, 1987, Sydney: Law Book Co, pp 120, 140.

19   Ribstein, L, and Alces, K, 'Directors' duties in failing firms', University of Illinois College of Law, Law and Economics Working Papers, Paper 50, 2006, accessible at www.law.bepress.com/uiuclwps/papers/art50; Bainbridge, S, 'Much ado about little? Directors' fiduciary duties in

Finally, one other approach should be adverted to. Although it has never been taken up by any court, Cooke J in *Permakraft* appeared to propose the possibility of a direct duty, based on a breach of a duty of care that derives from negligence principles. The example given by his Lordship was where directors obtain credit when they ought to know (as against, one assumes, when they actually know) that the creditor incorrectly understood a particular asset was owned by the company. The judge did not pursue this line of thinking in the case as the facts did not warrant it. But it is worth addressing. The problem with what his Lordship was positing is determining whether directors should have known that the creditor had a view about a particular asset of the company. Obviously if a creditor were to mention it directly then the directors would have no answer, but this is unlikely to be the case. It would be hard to impute directors with knowledge of something to which creditors might not have even given any thought. The approach mentioned by Cooke J has not met with any support and has been criticised,[20] *inter alia*, on the basis that such a duty would be at odds with the director's function as a risk-taker.[21] Certainly Professor Len Sealy did not think that this was maintainable and has said that 'the duty of care and the liberty to embrace risk are incompatible bedfellows'.[22]

Should there be an independent duty?

If the conclusion to the last section of the chapter is correct, and the courts are set against a direct duty, we must then ask: should there be an independent duty?[23] Have the majority of courts got it wrong from a normative perspective?

Some of the arguments that are considered in Chapter 19 in favour of there being some directorial responsibility to creditors are able to be applied in arguing for an independent duty. A prime example is that creditors are unable to protect themselves adequately through contractual means, as they are not in an equal bargaining position, so they warrant some kind of protection outside of contract. Having noted that, it could be said that while there are certainly problems for creditors in protecting themselves against loss of the credit that they have extended, it is sufficient if directors are required to

the vicinity of insolvency' *Journal of Business and Technology Law*, forthcoming, available at SSRN: www.ssrn.com/abstract=832504 (University of California at Los Angeles Law and Economics Research Paper Series, Paper No 05-26, 2005).

20 Sealy, L, 'Director's wider responsibilities – problems conceptual practical and procedural' (1987) 13 *Monash University Law Review* 164 at 176 and 186.
21 Finch, V, 'Creditor interests and directors' obligations' in Sheikh, S, and Rees, W (eds), *Corporate Governance and Control*, 1995, London: Cavendish, p 113.
22 *Op. cit.* fn 20 above at 176.
23 Arguments that might support the existence of some form of duty, whether it be direct or indirect are considered in Chapter 19.

consider their interests, and if they fail to do so, an administrator or liquidator can seek compensation where the company falls into insolvency and cannot pay the creditors. The riposte that might be put by those advocating a direct duty is probably that directorial decision-making has the potential in some cases to damage creditors before the debtor company falls into financial difficulty.[24] The test for determining when the directors' obligation to consider the interests of creditors is triggered, as posited in Chapter 13, does address this issue to a point. In Chapter 13 it was argued that the most appropriate trigger for the advent of the obligation would be where a company's situation is such that a director can reasonably expect that the action upon which he or she is going to embark could lead to the insolvency of the company. But, of course, that still does not mean that a creditor can do anything about the actions of the director.

Those in favour of a direct duty might contend that it is more likely that creditors will be compensated where the directors have acted wrongly, if there is direct duty. The reason is that the ultimate benefit of a direct duty over an indirect one is that actions against directors for breach might be more advantageous for creditors than where the creditors have to wait for an administrator or a liquidator to bring proceedings. As mentioned earlier, directors may well be impecunious by the time that liquidators get around to suing them, because, in many cases, they have had to discharge the company's liability to banks that hold guarantees signed by the directors. While payments under guarantees might be regarded as preferences, if the directors were to be made bankrupt, at the behest of a liquidator, it is probable that they could not be attacked by trustees in bankruptcy as the directors would not have been influenced in deciding to give the payments by a desire to see the banks receive preferences, an element that has to be proved by bankruptcy trustees according to s 340(4) of the Insolvency Act 1986, and explained by Millett J in *Re M C Bacon Ltd* [1990] BCC 98.

It is likely that an independent duty would mean that the responsibility placed on directors would be more effective as the creditors, the ones with the greatest interest in the institution of proceedings, would, themselves, be able to enforce any breach.[25] Allied to this is the fact that a direct duty would provide a broader range of remedies for creditors based on the fact that creditors could bring proceedings themselves.[26] It might also be argued, that an independent duty should exist on the basis that it serves to protect creditors from the effects of limited liability. Limited liability places creditors in an unenviable position and fairness dictates that the creditors receive some advantage to offset the benefits of limited liability to

24 *Op. cit.* fn 11 above at 365.
25 Riley, C, 'Directors' duties and the interests of creditors' (1989) 10 Co Law 87 at 91.
26 McConvill (2002), *op. cit.* fn 15 above at 14.

companies.[27] For limited liability 'confers very significant benefits on owners of closely held corporations and provides numerous opportunities for deviant conduct by management'.[28]

Another reason why a duty should be owed to creditors is that when a company is in serious financial difficulty, the creditors are the residual claimants as far as company assets go, and they should be entitled to be owed a duty, just as a duty is often said to be owed to the shareholders when the company is solvent (*Hutton v West Cork Railway Co* (1883) 23 LR Ch D 654), the shareholders being the residual claimants at that point (discussed in Chapter 12). The response to that, particularly from contractarian scholars (see Chapter 19), is that creditors should not be owed fiduciary duties as they have the medium of the contract to protect them.[29]

A significant argument that is against a direct duty is that a direct duty might enable creditors to interfere in the management of the company when it is not appropriate to do so.[30] This would take the form of either threatening, or actually taking, legal proceedings against the directors, perhaps in an attempt to influence what the directors do. It is possible that directors could be threatened with proceedings by several creditors and this might place directors in a difficult position so far as deciding what decisions should be taken for the company. In Chapter 14 we considered the problems that confront a director who has to balance the interests of various kinds of creditors.

A second argument is that, as mentioned earlier, a direct duty could precipitate a multiplicity of proceedings, and this would 'eat up' significant time and expense.

Another conceivable argument against a direct duty is the fact that it would enable creditors to be able to bring proceedings and one would have to determine which creditors are owed the duty and are, therefore, entitled to institute proceedings. This issue is considered further in Chapter 17.

Conclusion

There is no doubt that there are difficulties and complexities, of both a practical and a theoretical nature, in arguing for an independent duty.[31]

---

27 Dabner, J, 'Directors' duties – the schizoid company' (1988) 6 *Company and Securities Law Journal* 105 at 114.
28 Ziegel, J, 'Creditors as corporate stakeholders: the quiet revolution – an Anglo-Canadian perspective' (1993) 43 *University of Toronto Law Journal* 511 at 530. Also, see McConvill (2002), *op. cit.* fn 15 above at 13–14.
29 For instance, see Macey, J, 'An economic analysis of the various rationales for making shareholders the exclusive beneficiaries of corporate fiduciary duties' (1991) 21 *Stetson Law Review* 23 at 38.
30 Beveridge, N, 'Does a corporation's board of directors owe a fiduciary duty to its creditors?' (1994) 25 *St Mary's Law Journal* 589 at 621.
31 McConvill (2002), *op. cit.* fn 15 above at 24.

Furthermore, as demonstrated in this chapter, the law is against it, and given what the government has said in recent White Papers on company law reform and in the Company Law Reform Bill (discussed in Chapter 11), the law is unlikely to be changed, certainly in the short term. Even leaving this aside, while there are some strong normative arguments in favour of a duty, there are also some substantial points that militate against it, particularly the fact that many of the reasons that can be raised in favour of some protection of creditors can be satisfied by an indirect duty, which presents fewer practical problems and is less intrusive as far as company management is concerned.

16 Commencement of proceedings

Introduction

If directors have breached their obligation to the company's creditors, then, absent a settlement out of court, proceedings will have to be taken to obtain recompense. Who has standing to commence those proceedings depends on the nature of the duty. If it can be established that creditors are owed a direct duty by directors, then creditors will be entitled, short of some restriction being placed on this right, to initiate proceedings against the company's directors if there is a breach of duty, and a creditor can establish that fact. As mentioned in the previous chapter, this is one of the main attractions of having a direct duty. But, if the duty is owed to the company to take into account creditor interests, then, pursuant to the thrust of the rule in *Foss v Harbottle* (1843) 2 Hare 461, only the company is entitled to bring proceedings if there is a breach. As directors are highly unlikely to sanction the initiation of proceedings against themselves, or one of their number, creditors will usually have to wait until a liquidator or administrator is appointed in relation to the affairs of the company, and hope that he or she will bring proceedings, technically on behalf of the company, but, in reality, on behalf of the creditors. Proceedings would usually be commenced pursuant to s 212 of the Insolvency Act 1986 (commonly known as 'misfeasance proceedings') where a company is in liquidation. It is a major point made by those who have argued against the existence of any obligation of directors to creditors that, because the obligation to creditors in fact involves an indirect duty, and not a direct duty to creditors, creditors have no right to bring proceedings against directors.[1] In the words of Morey McDaniel, 'a right without a remedy is worthless'.[2]

---

1   Sealy, L, 'Directors' duties – an unnecessary gloss' [1988] CLJ 175 at 177. Sealy points to s 309 of the Companies Act 1985. Also, see Hartman, R F, 'Situation-specific fiduciary duties for corporate directors: enforceable obligations or toothless ideals' (1993) 50 *Washington and Lee Law Review* 1761 at 1767 commenting in the wake of *Credit Lyonnaise Bank Nederlander NV v Pathe Communications Corp* 1991 Del Ch LEXIS 215; (1992) 17 *Delaware Journal of Corporate Law* 1099.
2   McDaniel, M, 'Bondholders and stockholders' (1988) 13 *Journal of Corporation Law* 205 at 309.

However, as case law in the UK and the Commonwealth patently demonstrates, actions for breach of the duty can be commenced and prosecuted by a liquidator (or an administrator of the company) acting on behalf of the collective that is constituted by the unsecured creditors in a liquidation, and so the fact that there is no independent cause of action 'presents no conceptual difficulties'.[3] That said, there are clear practical problems that can occur for creditors.

In all of the cases that have been decided in the UK, Ireland and the Commonwealth, where directors have been found to be liable for breaching their obligation to the creditors, proceedings were commenced by a liquidator. The problem with the duty being indirect is that, short of instituting winding-up or administration proceedings, creditors can do nothing to arrest any action taken by directors that prejudices the repayment of the debts that they are owed, unless they have some rights pursuant to covenants in the contract under which they extended credit. It might be added that creditors themselves would also have a right to bring misfeasance proceedings against the directors, pursuant to s 212(3) of the Insolvency Act 1986, where the company is in liquidation. Creditors might be reluctant to do so, given the costs involved and the fact that all creditors would benefit from any award. Creditors might prefer to wait for the liquidator to commence proceedings. Of course, if proceedings are brought by a liquidator and they are successful, the unsecured creditors might not benefit at all, as a secured creditor with a floating charge over company assets might be entitled to the total sum recovered (*Re Anglo-Austrian Printing & Publishing Union* [1895] 2 Ch 891). If the liquidator declines to initiate proceedings against directors a creditor has the option of taking action himself or herself, as mentioned above, or of challenging the decision of the liquidator not to take action, under s 168(5) of the Insolvency Act 1986.[4] The other possibility is for a creditor to seek the assignment of the liquidator's cause of action against the directors. Before making an assignment, a liquidator will probably want some consideration being paid.

This chapter examines the issues and problems surrounding the commencement of proceedings against directors, and considers possible reform measures, with some consideration given to a couple of possible solutions to the argument that the obligation could not be enforced by creditors.

Shareholders and creditors

While shareholders can find themselves in a similar position to creditors in that no duty is owed by directors to them individually (*Percival v Wright* [1902] 2 Ch 421; *Multinational Gas and Petrochemical Co v Multinational Gas*

---

3   Dabner, J, 'Directors' duties – the schizoid company' (1988) 6 *Company and Securities Law Journal* 105 at 114.
4   See Keay, A, 'The supervision and control of liquidators' [2000] Conv 295.

and Petrochemical Services Ltd [1983] Ch 258, CA; *Peskin v Anderson* [2000] BCC 1110; [2000] 2 BCLC 1 (affirmed on appeal by the Court of Appeal [2001] BCC 874)), the difference is shareholders are able to rely at common law on derivative actions (where the company's rights have been injured)[5] or proceedings under s 459 of the Companies Act 1985 (where the shareholders' interests have been unfairly prejudiced) to right obvious wrongs.[6] A shareholder probably cannot bring an action under s 459 where directors have breached their duties to creditors, unless it affects the rights of members, as the provision requires the action complained of to be unfairly prejudicial to the interests of the members including at least the petitioner's interests. Could an action be brought where a member was also a creditor? It is permissible in Australia, for under s 234 of that country's Corporations Act 2001, a member is able to bring proceedings in a capacity other than as a member. But in the UK a member who launches a s 459 petition must establish conduct that is unfairly prejudicial to the member's interests as a member, and not in relation to non-member interests (*Re A Company (No 00314 of 1989)* [1991] BCLC 154 at 160).

Misfeasance proceedings

Before dealing with more controversial issues, we should discuss briefly the fact that a liquidator who wishes to bring breach of duty proceedings against a director might well find help in the shape of s 212 of the Insolvency Act. It provides a liquidator[7] with the right to initiate what are usually known as 'misfeasance proceedings' against certain persons, including officers of the company. Over the years, proceedings have frequently been brought by liquidators against directors pursuant to s 212 and its precursors. But, s 212 does not take one too far as the section does not create any new rights. For a misfeasance action to succeed under s 212, it must be founded on some action in relation to which the company could have initiated proceedings prior to winding up, namely a breach of any fiduciary or other duty in relation to the company;[8] so under s 212 an applicant must 'establish actionable wrongdoing by the respondent independently of s 212'.[9] The role of s 212, in accordance

---

5   The Company Law Reform Bill provides in Chapter 11 for a statutory derivative action for shareholders.

6   The distinction between corporate and shareholders' personal rights is a vexed issue. See, for example, Sugarman, D, 'Reconceptualising company law – reflections on the Law Commission's Consultation Paper on Shareholder Remedies' in Rider, B A K (ed), *The Corporate Dimension*, 1998, Bristol: Jordans, p 206; Hirt, H, 'In what circumstances should breaches of directors' duties give rise to a remedy under ss 459–461 of the Companies Act 1985?' (2003) 24 Co Law 100.

7   As well as other possible applicants, namely, the official receiver, a creditor and a contributory.

8   For a recent instance of a misfeasance action, see *Re Simmons Box (Diamonds) Ltd* [2000] BCC 275, which involved directors failing to act carefully.

9   Oditah, F, 'Misfeasance proceedings against company directors' [1992] LMCLQ 207 at 208.

with its legislative precursors, is essentially procedural as it provides an alternative summary procedure which is designed to facilitate recovery of assets improperly dealt with, and to enable the liquidator to obtain compensation for misconduct which had caused loss to the company (*Re B Johnson & Co (Builders) Ltd* [1955] Ch 634). As misfeasance covers the whole spectrum of directors' duties (*Re D'Jan of London Ltd* [1993] BCC 646; *Re Westlowe Storage and Distribution Ltd* [2000] BCC 851), a liquidator could rely on a breach of duty to take into account the interests of creditors, and s 212 could be used as the means by which the claim could be initiated and prosecuted, as was the case in *Liquidator of West Mercia Safetywear Ltd v Dodd* (1988) 4 BCC 30. This strategy would appear to be in accord with the views expressed by Toulson J in *Yukong Lines Ltd v Rendsburg Investments Corporation* [1998] BCC 870 at 884.

Class actions

An argument advocated by Vanessa Finch is that, while directors might not be said to owe a duty to individual creditors, consideration should be given to directors owing a duty to unsecured creditors as a class.[10] Finch points out that: 'This is consistent with the principle that insolvency law confers a class action for the benefit of creditors generally because it is in practice only the unsecured creditors who are bound by the collectivist principle.'[11] The learned commentator accepts that final enforcement would have to wait until liquidation (or perhaps administration) or else the wrongful trading provisions might be undermined, but a class action would still provide advantages. As the action would be granted to creditors as a class, the holders of charges would not be able to claim priority to any sums recovered,[12] which they can claim at present if a liquidator succeeds in recovering sums from directors. Hitherto, concern has been voiced[13] about allowing creditors to proceed against directors as it could undermine the operation of the *pari passu* principle.[14] But giving creditors a right of action as a class would not affect the principle, as the principle is designed to safeguard creditors generally and this is precisely what a class action would do,[15] and as stated in Chapter 15, the *pari passu* principle has little effect in today's world anyway.

---

10 'Directors' duties: insolvency and the unsecured creditor' in Clarke, A (ed), *Current Issues in Insolvency Law*, 1991, London: Stevens, pp 104 *et seq*; 'Creditor interests and directors' obligations' in Sheikh, S, and Rees, W (eds), *Corporate Governance and Control*, 1995, London: Cavendish, pp 129 *et seq*.
11 *Ibid* at 105 (1991).   12 *Ibid*.
13 For example, see Prentice, D, 'Creditors' interests and directors' duties' (1990) 10 OJLS 265 at 275–276.
14 See the comments of the High Court of Australia in *Spies v The Queen* (2000) 201 CLR 603 at 636.
15 *Op. cit.* Finch, fn 10 above (1991) at 110.

Finch submits that creditors as a class should be able to seek injunctions prior to a liquidation so as to prevent directors from embarking on a course of action that could place the company in further financial danger.[16] If injunctive relief were available then it would be necessary for the creditors to establish a prima facie case that the company would become insolvent if the action that is impugned, was actually taken, and this could, as Finch notes, be onerous.[17] The need for establishing a prima facie case is important for two reasons. First, this would eliminate the more trivial claims and ensure that there is not a multiplicity of proceedings. Second, if one is going to allow interference in the management of companies, then there has to be a good basis for doing so. But on what basis could an injunction be granted? Could it be said that the creditor who takes action can argue that he or she has an interest in the company that needs protecting? The creditor could get no relief at common law, but equity might be willing to provide some. A significant benefit of the use of class actions is that it would reduce the volume of proceedings, a concern that was discussed in Chapter 15 in relation to accepting the notion of a direct duty to creditors.

There are undoubtedly practical issues that would have to be resolved if a class action is to be permitted. As Finch asks, what does one do with creditors who want to freeride, namely those who decline to contribute to the initiation of the class action, but want to share in any proceeds of an action? One answer would be to deduct from the creditor's share of any fund recovered, a sum to reflect the costs that are not able to be recovered under the court order. Of course, this still might be seen as unfairly benefiting the non-contributing creditor who bears no risk in the commencement of the action. If there is a disagreement amongst creditors as to whether an action should be commenced or not, then, as Finch states, the court could convene a meeting of creditors, as it is empowered to do under s 195 of the Insolvency Act 1986.[18]

Derivative actions

A second response to the enforceability issue is that given by Professor Rutheford Campbell, who argues for the introduction of a derivative action for creditors so as to bring creditors into line with shareholders in the United States.[19] Presently, in the United States derivative actions can only be initiated

---

16 *Ibid* at 109. Also, see McDonnell, S, '*Geyer v Ingersoll Publications Co*: insolvency shifts directors' burden from shareholders to creditors' (1994) 19 *Delaware Journal of Corporate Law* 177 at 208.

17 *Op. cit.* Finch, fn 10 above at 110 (1991); 130 (1995).

18 *Op. cit.* Finch fn 10 above at 111 (1991).

19 'Corporate fiduciary principles for the post-contractarian era' (1996) *Florida State University Law Review* 561 at 606. This is also a position advocated by Professor Lawrence Mitchell in 'A theoretical and practical framework for enforcing corporate constituency statutes' (1992) 70 Texas L Rev 579 at 630–643.

by creditors when the company which owes them money is insolvent (*Re Buckhead America Corp* 178 BR 956 (1994)),[20] which is, as we shall see, more than is available to creditors in UK law.

With a derivative action in company law the applicant is bringing proceedings to enforce rights of the company. So, if derivative proceedings were permitted and we take the view that directors owe an indirect duty to creditors, that is that they owe a duty to their company to take into account the interests of the creditors, and the directors fail to do so, creditors could initiate proceedings to enforce the breach committed against the company, although obviously we are really talking about creditors enforcing rights indirectly due to them.

The Law Commission[21] recommended the introduction of a statutory derivative action for shareholders and the Company Law Review Steering Group supported this proposal. The Company Law Reform Bill that was introduced in November 2005 included provision for a statutory derivative action in Chapter 1 of Part 11 for England and Wales and Northern Ireland, and provision in Chapter 2 for Scotland. A statutory derivative action has been introduced in Australia as far as shareholders are concerned (Corporations Act 2001, s 236), but while the Company and Securities Law Review Committee, a body that reviews company law and considers changes to corporate legislation in Australia, favoured giving a derivative action to creditors as well as shareholders,[22] this view did not gain the imprimatur of Parliament and, hence, did not find its way into legislation. Section 236 of the Corporations Act 2001 allows only members, former members and officers of the company to bring derivative proceedings. Importantly though, in the general scheme of things, Australian creditors arguably could secure relief under s 1324 of the Corporations Act, which enables anyone affected, or who could be affected, by a contravention, or proposed contravention, of the Act to seek injunctive relief. Such relief is not available in the UK.

It could be argued that the use of the derivative action in the circumstances envisaged here seems to fit in with the rationale for such an action. Professor Bert Prunty stated that this kind of action 'was born and nurtured as a corrective for managerial abuse in economic units which by their nature deprived some participants of an effective voice in their administration'.[23]

The derivative action has been permitted in some cases in the United States. For instance, in *Re Buckhead America Corp* the United States District Court in Delaware effectively held that a creditor can proceed by way of

---

20 Millon, D, 'New game plan or business as usual? A critique of the team production model of corporate law' (2000) 86 Va L Rev 1001 at 1013.
21 *Shareholders Remedies*, Report No 246, 1997, at para 6.1
22 *Enforcement of the Duties of Directors and Officers of a Company by Means of a Statutory Derivative Action*, Report No 12, 1990.
23 'The shareholders' derivative suit: notes on its derivation' (1957) 32 NYULR 980 at 982.

derivative action against the directors where they have failed to foster the interests of creditors.

The concern about allowing derivative actions is that it might well precipitate a multiplicity of proceedings or be abused by creditors. One way to prevent this, at least to some degree, would be to require creditors to obtain leave before being able to initiate the substantive proceedings. The Law Commission for England and Wales recommended this in relation to a proposed derivative action for shareholders.[24] While the requirement to obtain leave might deter some who might 'float' proceedings with the idea of forcing companies to talk to them about some form of settlement, the shortcoming with this is that there would be an added cost element (even though it might reduce costs in that only bona fide proceedings would find their way to court) as all proceedings would have to be preceded by a pre-hearing. It would appear that leave has been used in Canada (Canada Business Corporations Act 1985, s 239(1)) successfully, in that it has prevented an avalanche of litigation. Under the Canadian Business Corporations Act 1985, creditors might be able to proceed by way of a derivative action if they can convince a court that they are a proper person to make an application (s 238). Further, creditors have to establish that they are acting in good faith and it appears that the action is in the interests of the company (s 239(2)(b)(c)). In addition, creditors would have to give 14 days' notice to the directors of the company that they are going to initiate derivative proceedings (s 239(2)(a)). The Canadian courts have further limited the right of creditors to proceed by requiring them to establish that they have either a direct financial interest in the affairs of the company or a particular legitimate interest in the way that the company is being managed (*Re Daon Development Corp* (1984) 54 BCLR 235 at 243; *Jacobs Farms Ltd v Jacobs* [1992] OJ No 813 at 6–7).[25] Also, the courts have required creditors to demonstrate that they are in a position that is analogous to minority shareholders who have no legal right to influence the things that they regard as abuses of management (*Daon Development* at 243).

Another measure that could be introduced to thwart the abuse of derivative proceedings by creditors is, as Finch notes, use of a provision that provides that if a court is satisfied that creditors have abused the process, it may order that creditors pay not only their own costs, but those of the directors, the company and any other interested parties.[26]

If an award of damages was ordered pursuant to a successful derivative action, the award would be made in favour of the company. The danger with this is that the directors would be in control of the award, and the money

---

24 *Shareholders Remedies*, Report No 246, 1997, at para 6.69.
25 Referred to by Sarra, J, 'Taking the corporation past the "Plimsoll line" – director and officer liability when the corporations founders' (2001) 10 *International Insolvency Review* 229 at 244.
26 *Op. cit.* Finch, fn 10 at 131 (1995).

could be frittered away and the creditors would be no better off. It would seem that the appropriate measure would be for a court to order that the award be held in trust for payment of creditors.

Opponents of the use of derivative proceedings by creditors might argue that creditors have the right to commence winding-up or administration proceedings, and if they feel that a company's affairs are being administered in a way that is prejudicial to their interests, they should seek a winding-up or administration order, provided that the company is insolvent or, in the case of administration, likely to become so. However, there might well be occasions where the directors' obligation to creditors has arisen and creditors can see that the directors are taking the company down a path that might lead to further financial stress, but a winding-up or administration order might not be able to be secured because the company is not technically insolvent.

Oppression and/or unfair prejudice remedy

Another possible way of providing creditors with a right to take action, but in quite a different way, as it does not involve arguing that directors have a duty to creditors, has been pioneered in Canada. Section 241(2)(c) of the Canadian Business Corporations Act 1985 (and provincial statutes based on this provision) states that the court is able to give a remedy if the directors' powers have been exercised 'in a manner that is oppressive or unfairly prejudicial to or unfairly disregards the interests of any security holder, *creditor*, director or officer'[27] (my emphasis). It must be noted that to be able to bring an application under the federal Canadian provision, a creditor must either be a registered holder of a security or must be deemed to be 'a proper person to make an application' (s 238). Who is a proper person is squarely within the discretion of the court. Section 241(3) gives courts an unfettered discretion as to what order they think appropriate, although some examples of orders are set out, in a similar manner to s 461 of the UK's Companies Act 1985.

It has been made patent by the Canadian courts that creditors are not going to be able to use the oppression action to recover run-of-the-mill debts (*Royal Corporation Trust of Canada v Hordo* (1993) 10 BLR (2d) 86 at [12]). In Ontario, for instance, it has been said that for a creditor to be able to proceed, it must be demonstrated that the creditor has a legitimate interest in the manner in which the company is being run or has a direct financial interest in how directors are managing the company's affairs (*Hordo; Jacobs Farms Ltd v Jacobs* [1992] OJ No 813 at 12–14).[28] Professor Janis Sarra has asserted that the courts will not grant the right to creditors where their claims

---

27 See Thomson, D, 'Directors, creditors and insolvency: a fiduciary duty or a duty not to oppress' (2000) 58 *University of Toronto Faculty of Law Review* 31.
28 Referred to by Sarra, *op. cit.* fn 25 above at 240.

are too remote, there is lack of good faith, the creditors were not creditors at the time when the actions that are challenged occurred, or where actions that are the subject of applications are not related to the debts claimed by creditors.[29] It has been held, in relation to the derivative action which lays down similar requirements for applicants in Canada, that it is not sufficient if the only interest a creditor can point to as far as the management of the company is concerned is a 'general and indirect one of wishing to see the company prosper' (*Re Daon Development Corp* at 243). Creditors have succeeded most often where the company is closely held and the actions that are challenged benefited the director(s) personally.[30] One example of the use of the provision is *Prime Computer of Canada Ltd v Jeffrey* (1991) 6 OR (3d) 733 where a director had increased his salary substantially at a time when he was aware that his company was in financial straits. On the application of a creditor the court ordered the director to repay the increase in salary on the basis that the director's action was unfairly prejudicial to the creditor, as the funds used to increase the director's salary were largely, in effect, those of the creditor. A further example of the use by a creditor of the oppression provision occurred in *R v The Sands Motor Hotel Ltd* [1985] 1 WWR 59 where the application of the Department of National Revenue was successful. The claim was for the setting aside of a dividend declared in breach of the relevant companies legislation. The court ordered that the dividend was not to be distributed until back taxes were fully paid.

Provincial legislation employs the same type of provision, and reproduces the wording of s 241 of the federal statute. For instance, see s 166(2) of New Brunswick's Business Corporations Act 1981 and s 242(2) of the Alberta Business Corporations Act 2000. But in some provinces, such as New Brunswick (s 163(c)) and Alberta (s 239(b)(iii)), the provisions which state who can bring oppression actions expressly include creditors, so creditors in these provinces do not have to rely on the courts regarding them as proper persons to bring actions; they can bring proceedings as a matter of right. This has the attraction of providing a little more certainty in specifying that creditors have standing to bring proceedings.

Unlike with directors' duties to creditors, which seem to depend on the establishing of the company's financial distress, for a claim under the Canadian provisions there is no need to prove that the company is suffering from financial strife. The critical issue is whether the action complained of is oppressive or unfairly prejudicial. While creditors do not have an automatic right to make an application under provisions in some Canadian jurisdictions, the criteria for a claim give plenty of scope for creditors – far wider than where a claim for a breach of duty is involved. This is because the Canadian courts have interpreted the concepts 'oppression, unfair prejudice and unfair disregard' widely. Section 459 of the UK Companies Act 1985

---

29 *Ibid.*   30 *Ibid* at 240–241.

uses the concept of unfair prejudice and the courts have also given it a broad meaning. The Australian equivalent of s 459 (Corporations Act 2001, s 232) uses 'oppression' as well as 'unfair prejudice' and both expressions are applied widely. The Ontario Court of Appeal in *Brant Investments Ltd v Keep-Rite Inc* (1991) 3 OR (3d) 289 at 303 said that as 'the statutory scheme of [s 241] is so broadly formulated, the evidence necessary to establish a breach of fiduciary duty would be subsumed in the broader range of evidence which would be appropriately adduced on an application under the [oppression] section'.[31] As one would expect, the courts have developed some guidelines. For instance, the courts will have reference to the history and nature of the company, the relationship between the company and the applicant creditor as well as general commercial practice (*First Edmonton Place Ltd v 315888 Alberta Ltd* (1988) 60 Alta LR (2d) 122 at 146).[32]

If it is correct to say that no independent duty is owed by directors to creditors, something that the predominance of the case law seems to hold, one way to provide added protection for creditors would be to include in s 459 of the Companies Act 1985 provision for creditors to take proceedings when their interests are unfairly prejudiced. This would allow for a similar provision to the Canadian, although the grounds on which one can base proceedings in Canada includes, as well as unfair prejudice, oppression, which was the ground for proceeding under the precursor section to s 459 in the UK (s 210 of the Companies Act 1948). If s 459 were enlarged as proposed, it is submitted that it would be appropriate to require creditors to obtain leave before being able to commence proceedings. As with derivative proceedings, this would prevent vexatious and trivial litigation. The Law Commission in its report in 1997 on shareholder remedies (*Shareholders Remedies*, Report No 246) was concerned to streamline proceedings under s 459 as much as possible and obliging a creditor to obtain leave would satisfy this concern.

A possible objection to this approach might be that it will precipitate, as with permitting derivative actions brought by creditors, a proliferation of litigation, as well as the abuse of proceedings in order to disrupt the management of a company. Yet, this is not the Canadian experience. Its legislation has not, interestingly, precipitated a large number of claims by creditors,[33] so perhaps providing some process allowing creditors to bring proceedings might not lead to the floodgates being opened, nor would it be subject to abuse.

---

31 Quoted by Thomson, *op. cit.* fn 27 above at 48.
32 Nevertheless, one learned commentator has criticised the vagueness of the legislation (Ziegel, J, 'Creditors as corporate stakeholders: the quiet revolution – an Anglo-Canadian perspective' (1993) 43 *University of Toronto Law Journal* 511 at 531).
33 *Ibid* at 527; *op. cit.* Thomson, fn 27 at 47.

Why might some creditors not want to pursue proceedings?

It is questionable whether some creditors would want to initiate proceedings against directors, even if they were entitled to do so. Secured creditors, in most cases, would probably be happy to rely on their security. Those creditors who would enjoy preferential rights in an administration or liquidation may be reluctant to take proceedings except where it is clear that in an administration or liquidation of the company no dividend would be paid to them. Unsecured creditors might, for a number of reasons, be hesitant to take proceedings unless they are owed a substantial amount, and the company is clearly insolvent or close to being so. First, there are the obvious ones that apply to any litigation, namely the risk of losing and the amount of the costs of litigating. Second, establishing that there has been a breach might not be easily achieved, especially in light of the fact that the courts have not either laid down, certainly consistently, the trigger(s) for the duty or actually provided any guidelines as to what director are to do when subject to a duty to creditors. Third, any creditor considering initiating proceedings takes the risk that the directors against whom proceedings have been commenced are impecunious. It is bad enough when a liquidator secures a judgment and cannot enforce it, but it would be even worse for a creditor when he or she has initiated and pursued the proceedings to judgment.

Conclusion

Where there has been a breach of the obligation of directors to creditors, actions for compensation have thus far only been initiated by liquidators. This is understandable if the obligation constitutes an indirect, and not a direct, duty to creditors, for creditors would not be entitled to commence actions. Undoubtedly, there are significant drawbacks for creditors if they are not able to commence proceedings. This chapter has examined the possibility of options that might be considered and made available to creditors in the future. These are a class action in relation to a duty owed to the class of creditors or a derivative action. While these might remedy the difficulties facing creditors, it is unlikely that the government is going to consider providing for such actions, especially, in relation to derivative actions, as it has not, in the provisions in the Company Law Reform Bill, included creditors in the class of persons who can apply for the right to commence derivative proceedings. The chapter has also considered that it might be appropriate to enlarge the scope of s 459 of the Companies Act 1985 by allowing creditors to commence proceedings where their interests are unfairly prejudiced. A similar right has apparently met with some success in Canada, and there is evidence to suggest that it has not been abused.

17 Are all creditors to be favoured?

Introduction

We have considered thus far that directors have some obligation to creditors where their company is in some form of financial difficulty. What we have not examined is whether this obligation is owed to all creditors. This chapter asks whether we should seek to distinguish between creditors who are owed the obligation. In other words, if the obligation to creditors arises at a particular point, do directors have to consider the interests of all creditors who existed at the time of the obligation being triggered? Also, this issue requires us to consider the position of future creditors. Is there an obligation to these creditors? If not, should there be an obligation? This chapter focuses particularly on the position of these creditors, and examines the case law and the arguments that might be put for and against the inclusion of such creditors.

The issues

If the conclusion reached in Chapter 15 is that directors only owe an indirect duty to creditors, then, as we have seen, no proceedings will be able to be brought until an administrator or liquidator is appointed, and the relevant office-holder initiates proceedings on behalf of the company, but, in effect, on behalf of all creditors. This is because these regimes involve collective proceedings. Let us concentrate on liquidation as all actions that have been brought thus far have been instigated by liquidators, and it is likely that that will be, for the most part, the case in the future. Liquidation is a procedure of an inherently collective nature,[1] in that as a result of its commencement each creditor forfeits the individual right to take action to enforce the debt owed, and in lieu thereof the creditor must depend on the result of the collective

---

1   See *Re Western Welsh International System Buildings Ltd* [1985] 1 BCC 99, 296 at 99, 297 per Harman J; *Re Lines Bros Ltd* [1983] Ch 1 at 20 per Brightman LJ; Fletcher, I F, *The Law of Insolvency*, 2nd edn, 1996, London: Sweet and Maxwell, p 2; Report of the Insolvency Law Review Committee, *Insolvency Law and Practice*, Cmnd 8558 (1982) at paras 224–227, 232 (the 'Cork Report').

proceedings.[2] This means that the primary beneficiary of the proceedings is the general group of unsecured creditors, each of whom is affected by the winding up, albeit to different degrees.[3] So, any action that is taken and produces funds will be distributed according to the liquidation scheme, as with actions, for example, under the adjustment provisions in the Insolvency Act 1986 (ss 238–246), and so it is likely that we cannot distinguish between creditors. Arguably, provided that a person is owed a debt when liquidation commences (Insolvency Rules 1986, r 12.3), he or she is entitled to share in any assets or money obtained by the liquidator, as the assets or money is obtained for the company and the creditors are owed money by the company (provided that the liquidator accepts his or her proof of debt).

If it can be submitted that creditors are entitled to a direct duty, and they can, therefore, proceed to seek compensation if directors breach the duty, the question of which creditors are owed the obligation is similar to that considered above, although it is more of a pressing problem. The reason for saying this is that if only an indirect duty is owed the liquidator, once he or she has recovered funds from errant directors, has the chance to assess whether all creditors could share in the funds, and even to seek directions from the courts. However, if a direct duty is owed, creditors needs to know whether they are entitled to commence proceedings, or else if they did commence proceedings they could be subjected to a strike-out application if the view is taken that they have no standing to bring the proceedings.

Future creditors

It must not be forgotten that the obligation to creditors might have been triggered some time before the advent of liquidation, and several of those claiming in the liquidation could have become creditors after the directors' obligation arose. Should this make any difference? The argument might be put that directors should only be responsible in relation to the interests of those who were creditors when the necessary conditions for the obligation actually occurred. Furthermore, it might be argued that those creditors who became creditors after the triggering of the directors' obligation, had a chance to ascertain the fact that the company was in some financial difficulty and if they still extended credit, then they have to accept that they might not get paid. However, the response to that is, and this is considered in detail in Chapter 19, that many creditors do not have the knowledge or opportunity to find out about the company's position. Certainly, if future creditors were to be excluded then the liquidator would have to be more precise as to when the

---

2   Jackson, T, 'The avoiding powers in bankruptcy' (1984) 36 *Stanford Law Review* 725 at 758; Friedman, J, 'Lender exposure under sections 547 and 550: are outsiders really insiders?' (1990) 44 *Southwestern Law Journal* 985 at 993.
3   Cork Report at para 232.

directors' obligation to creditors was triggered. While I have sought to do that in Chapter 13, thus far the courts have not embraced a test similar to that described in Chapter 13, and the case law does no exhibit any great consistency.

One kind of creditor that has excited some debate is the future tort claimant. Directors may not be able to foresee whether their company will be liable in tort in the future, but it seems unfair to say that these creditors are not owed a duty merely because the company has not yet caused them injury when the obligation to creditors arises. We are dealing here with creditors who have no say whatsoever in becoming creditors of the company. They become creditors through misfortune, and warrant being able to take action if the directors have breached their duty at some stage. Professor Jonathan Lipson has contended that an appropriate way of dealing with this is to say that if the liability 'was not, with reasonable prudence, discoverable by the directors, then no duties should have been owed by the directors'.[4] However, this might be perceived as too restrictive an approach. Lipson's exception is likely to cover a long-standing deficiency in goods that have been supplied to the public and that are capable of causing injuries to consumers (Lipson suggests the Dalkon Shield birth control device), but what about deficiencies in goods that are built into the manufacturing process after the obligation to creditors arises? Should consumers injured by them be in a worse position than those consumers who purchased goods before the triggering of the obligation? Consumers are not, generally speaking, in a position to know the financial state of a company whose goods they are acquiring, and, hence, they do not know whether the company owes a duty to creditors.

Distinguishing between creditors

The primary issue is that, if one is going to make distinctions between those creditors who can claim and those that cannot, one must be able to identify criteria on which to base one's decision. But, it is very difficult to arrive at such criteria.

Lipson has argued[5] that only certain kinds of creditor should benefit from a duty owed to them. Essentially these are creditors who possess low levels of volition (voluntariness), cognition (information) and exit (ability to extract oneself from an investment). While he does not purport to provide a complete list of the creditors that are in view, Lipson mentions: tort creditors; employees whose employment has been terminated; revenue authorities; and certain trade creditors.[6] Lipson contrasts these creditors with those whom he says have high levels of volition, cognition and exit, such as banks and

4   Lipson, J, 'Directors' duties to creditors: volition, cognition, exit and the financially distressed corporation' (2003) 50 UCLA LR 1189 at 1255.
5   *Ibid.*   6   *Ibid* at 1245.

bondholders.[7] The learned commentator argues that it is not the actual creditor that is critical, but the circumstances and relationships that give rise to the claim that a creditor possesses.[8]

The approach taken by Lipson has a lot to commend it. With respect, he has sought to address many of the problems that confront creditors and which are discussed in depth in Chapters 19 and 20, such as the fact that not all creditors are equal. The views which the learned writer conveys only seek to benefit those creditors who are not able to protect themselves, and he favours not holding directors responsible to those that could be called 'powerful creditors'. The primary problem with Lipson's approach is that it produces a lack of certainty for all parties. Whether a creditor falls within the general categories of creditors who are to be favoured with a fiduciary duty or not is unclear, and can probably be only ascertained after a court hearing that will involve the giving of evidence. As Lipson himself acknowledges: 'It may be difficult – *ex ante* or *ex post* – to determine whether these power imbalances exist, and, if so, whether they are sufficient to justify the imposition of a fiduciary duty.'[9] This leads me to question whether it is possible as a matter of fairness and practicality to distinguish between creditors.

The case law

It is fair to say that the courts have not spent any significant time considering the issue on which this chapter is focused. Most decisions contain no reference to it and those that do dispose of it in a few words, and without discussion of the issues. The main question that has been considered is whether a duty is owed to future creditors.

The view that is the most unequivocal on the subject of future creditors is that of Lord Templeman in *Winkworth v Edward Baron Development Co Ltd* [1986] 1 WLR 1512; [1987] 1 All ER 114. His Lordship plainly said: '[A] company owes a duty to its creditors, present and future (at 1516; 118).' Lord Templeman's approach was approved of in *Jeffree v NCSC* (1989) 7 ACLC 556, and Wallace J specifically recognised (at 560) the fact that a duty was owed to present and future creditors. In the same case, Brinsden J said that the duty owed was also owed to prospective creditors (at 565). It was necessary in this case (the facts of which were explained earlier[10]) to accept the extension of the duty to future creditors, if the director/defendant was to be liable, for in that case at the time when the director committed the alleged breach of duty, namely transferring the business of his company (W) to another company, the party (L) who allegedly suffered from the breach was not a creditor. L had had a dispute with W and arbitration proceedings were instituted. Evidence was led that the director feared an adverse award against W, and this precipitated the transfer of W's business. Obviously, if L succeeded

---

7   *Ibid* at 1249.   8   *Ibid* at 1251.   9   *Ibid* at 1253.
10   See above at pp 155–156.

in obtaining an award, and this would be after the transfer of the business, there would be no assets on which he could execute the award. In fact, after the transfer of W's business, the 'cupboard was virtually bare' (at 559).

The Court of Appeal said, in its judgment in *Fulham Football Club Ltd v Cabra Estates plc* [1994] BCLC 363 at 379, that: 'The duties owed by the directors are to the company and the company is more than just the sum total of its members. Creditors, both present and *potential*, are interested (my emphasis).' The use of the word 'potential' with creditors suggests that an obligation was owed to future creditors of the company, although it must be pointed out that the court was not addressing the typical situation considered in this book, where creditors lose out because of the actions of the directors, and the remark might be regarded very much as an aside. But more recently the majority of a bench of the Australian High Court in *Spies v The Queen* (2000) 201 CLR 603; (2000) 173 ALR 529; [2000] HCA 43, said that:

> It is true that there are statements in the authorities, beginning with that of Mason J in *Walker v Wimborne* which would suggest that because of the insolvency of Sterling Nicholas [the company], the appellant, as one of its directors, owed a duty to that company to consider the interests of creditors and *potential creditors* of the company ... (at [93], my emphasis).

As with *Fulham Football Club v Cabra Estates*, the judges seem to be ready to accept that future creditors have a right to be considered, and in this case, in the passage quoted, as well as in surrounding passages, the court was dealing with the issue of whether directors owed any obligation to creditors.

The view that the interests of future creditors are to be considered is in line with the general position as far as shareholders are concerned, namely directors are said to owe a duty to shareholders, present and future (*Brady v Brady* (1987) 3 BCC 535 at 552, CA).

In one of the first cases to consider the matter, post-*Walker v Wimborne*, *Nicholson v Permakraft (NZ) Ltd* (1985) 3 ACLC 453, Cooke J said that it was appropriate for directors to consider the payment of debts owed to current and continuing trade creditors, but it would be much more difficult to 'make out a duty to future new creditors' (at 459). The reasoning behind this was that such creditors have to take a company as they find it when they decide to do business with it (at 459). However, the response to that is, and this is considered below and, in detail, in Chapter 19, that many creditors do not have the knowledge or opportunity to find out about the company's position. Also, of importance is the fact that his Lordship was not ruling out the fact that the duty was owed to future creditors; he merely felt that it was more difficult to make out a case for them.

While not addressing the issue head on, in *Brady v Brady* (at 552), Nourse LJ did state, after commenting that the interests of the shareholders were foremost in solvent companies, that if a company is insolvent or doubtfully solvent the interests of existing creditors were critical. No reference was made to future creditors.

Recently, in the New South Wales Court of Appeal, Young CJ in Eq, in *Edwards & Ors v Attorney General & Anor* [2004] NSWCA 272 at [153], seemed to imply that at the moment future creditors are not covered by the principle that has developed from *Walker v Wimborne*. But his Honour said that a court might extend the principles devised thus far in relation to directors' duties to creditors, and hold that a company in a precarious financial position might not only owe duties to the shareholders and creditors but also to likely future creditors. His Honour did not elaborate any further as the case before him did not involve consideration of whether the directors were liable for breach of their duties to creditors.

Most of the cases that have been central to the development of the juris-prudence dealing with the obligation of directors to creditors have not addressed the issue of future creditors. This could, of course, mean that the courts did not think that it was an issue that required consideration in the matters before them, the express omission of a reference to future creditors was intended to indicate that only existing creditors were in view, or a refer-ence to creditors was intended to cover all kinds of creditors, including future ones.

There has been a significant amount of academic commentary, particularly in the UK, that has robustly criticised any approach that has called for con-sideration of the interests of future creditors.[11] However, as demonstrated by a survey of the cases, it is not possible to say that the courts are set firmly against future creditors. But it is very difficult to say without equivocation that future creditors are included. The comments of Young CJ in Eq, referred to above in *Edwards*, indicate that the jurisprudence has not developed to a point of complete certainty and probably the issue is not closed.

Conclusion

Whether all creditors of the company are able to share in any compensation paid by the directors for breach of their obligation to creditors is not clear, but it is reasoned in this chapter that they should be able to, and also it would be very difficult to make distinctions between creditors. The main issue that has been raised is whether those who were not creditors at the time when the obligation of the directors to creditors arose are able to share in the fruits of any claim. This chapter has shown that while the predominant academic view is that they should not, and there are no strong statements in the authorities supporting future creditors, there are more *obiter* comments from the courts that favour future creditors sharing in the benefits, than are against.

---

11 For example, see Sealy, L, 'Directors' duties – an unnecessary gloss' [1988] CLJ 175; Farrar, J, 'The responsibility of directors and shareholders for a company's debts' (1989) 4 Canta LR 12.

Part E
Theoretical analysis

18 An introduction to theoretical analysis

Thus far the book has been focusing, primarily, although far from exclusively, on what is the doctrinal position concerning the responsibilities that are owed by directors to creditors, and providing some commentary of the positions in jurisdictions other than the UK. Chapter 14 is, perhaps, the main exception to the general focus on doctrinal issues as it endeavoured to develop a theoretical framework which could be implemented to deal with determining how directors should act when subject to a responsibility to creditors at common law. In this part of the book, we now change emphasis and examine, in Chapters 19 and 20, whether directors should, from a theoretical perspective, owe the responsibilities to creditors that we have considered. In other words, are the wrongful trading provision and the obligation of directors to consider creditor interests as part of the directors' duty to their company (or, possibly, the directors' duty to creditors) normative? These issues warrant significant consideration because there have been some divergent views expressed in the literature on the topic. It should be said that there is no substantial examination of fraudulent trading, and the reason for this is given later in this chapter. After a consideration of the theoretical issues affecting directors' duties to creditors and wrongful trading, the part examines, in Chapter 21, whether it is possible for the parties to opt out of the application of the duties to creditors, and the fraudulent trading and wrongful trading provisions, and whether the parties should be able to do so.

A theoretical perspective involves 'academic analysis of the law which requires a degree of abstraction from the principles stated in case law and statute-based law'.[1] Principally, the discussion focuses on those factors that are most pertinent to any investigation of whether there is a theoretical justification for law regulating so-called wrongful trading and imposing a responsibility on directors to consider creditor interests. In the course of this investigation, arguments that are able to be derived from what are, arguably,

---

1 Nygh, P, and Butt, P (eds), *Butterworths Australian Legal Dictionary*, 1997, Sydney: Butterworths, p 681 and quoted in Cheffins, B, 'Using legal theory to study law : a company law perspective' (1999) 58 CLJ 197 at 198.

the two main approaches to corporate law, namely those taken by the contractarian and the progressive (or communitarian) schools of thought, are articulated and discussed. Chapter 19 begins with an explanation of these two schools of thought, and their general position on whether the responsibilities discussed here are normative, before going on to assess the theoretical arguments for some regulation by the legislature or by the courts. Chapter 20 initially examines the case that is made against the existence of a wrongful trading-type provision by focusing on the work of three scholars approaching the area from a contractarian perspective, and then it considers the arguments for a section that deals with wrongful trading.

I should mention that there is an overlap of issues that are broached in Chapters 19 and 20, because both wrongful trading and a duty to consider creditor interests involve extraordinary protection of creditors. Where possible I have sought to avoid repetition, but on some occasions it is worthwhile repeating a discussion in some depth, or in a different way, in an appropriate context, as it saves the reader having constantly to refer to another chapter, and it facilitates exposition of the issues.

The overall objective of the part is to assess the arguments that are given for and against the existence of the responsibilities to creditors that are the subject of the book and to conclude whether the responsibilities should be regarded as normative.

Before closing this brief chapter, a few words need to be written in relation to fraudulent trading. As mentioned above, this part does not consider whether fraudulent trading is normative. It is submitted that commercial morality demands that there is a proscription of such activity. Creditors are clearly entitled to expect, when extending credit, that the company's directors will not engage in fraudulent activity. The only argument that might be put is that the social cost of enforcing a breach of the obligation to avoid fraudulent trading would be greater than the distributive justice secured by enforcement,[2] so it would be better not to proscribe fraudulent trading expressly. It might be argued that there are other avenues available to find a director liable where he or she has engaged in fraudulent trading type activity, such as breach of the duty to creditors or a contravention of s 423 of the Insolvency Act 1986, namely entering into transactions with the purpose of either putting assets beyond the reach of a person who is making, or who may make at some time, a claim against the debtor, or otherwise prejudicing the interests of such a person (a creditor or potential creditor) in relation to the claim. The latter ground was discussed in Chapter 12. It was noted there that there are a number of significant obstacles that liquidators have to negotiate to be able to mount a successful claim under s 423. Another reason for including

---

2   A point made in relation to the disclosure requirement in s 317 of the Companies Act 1985: Lee, P-W, 'Reassessing the crime of non-disclosure under section 317 of the Companies Act 1985' (2005) 5 JCLS 139 at fn 82.

a provision like s 213 is to ensure that the process of private ordering is protected from abuse. Without such protection, confidence in the process will be undermined.[3] It is the kind of mandatory provision that even the most extreme contractarian would support. For instance, Judge Frank Easterbrook and Professor Daniel Fischel, ardent contractarians, take the view that fraud needs to be deterred.[4]

It is, of course, another matter whether the fraudulent trading provision that we have at present should be retained in the same form. That was an issue considered in Chapter 6. Also, it is another matter whether there should be criminal sanctions for the action, as contained in s 458 of the Companies Act 1985. The book does not seek to address this latter issue.

---

3 Goddard, R, 'Modernising company law: the government's White Paper' (2003) 66 MLR 402 at 407
4 'Optimal damages in securities cases' (1985) 52 U Chi L Rev 611 at 613, 621–622.

19 A theoretical analysis of the duty to consider creditors

Introduction

Part D focused primarily on a doctrinal examination of the law as far as it requires directors to consider interests of creditors. This chapter aims to provide a theoretical examination of the subject, with the objective of establishing whether the duty can be justified as normative. The examination discusses those issues that pertain to any assessment of whether a duty should be imposed or not and also contains a consideration of arguments that have been or might be put forward by scholars who align themselves with the two leading schools when it comes to corporate law theory, namely the contractarian school and the progressive (or communitarian) school.

The rationale for the chapter is the fact that commentators are sharply divided over whether or not directors should or should not be subjected to a responsibility to creditors. Some, such as most of those taking a contractarian approach, are of the opinion that the market and freedom of contract are adequate factors to protect creditors, while others, some of whom advocate what is referred to as the progressive or communitarian theory of the company, are of the view that creditors, amongst other stakeholders in the company, remain in a vulnerable position and should be protected more adequately by mandatory rules. The Chapter considers the approach taken by these two leadings schools of thought in the corporate field, and then examines pertinent issues that affect whether a duty is normatively acceptable.

The contractarian paradigm and the law and economics movement

The purpose of this part of the Chapter is to examine the primary arguments that have been articulated by those contractarians who have condemned the imposition of additional responsibilities on directors, such as requiring them to take into account creditor interests. Predominantly, although not exclusively, these scholars have embraced a law-and-economics approach to corporate law, and it is upon the law-and-economics brand of contractarianism that we will focus.[1]

The contractarian approach

In a nutshell, the contractarian approach emphasises the contractual relationships that exist between persons involved in the affairs of the company, and, accordingly, holds to the principle of the sanctity of contract. Many contractarians[2] regard the company as nothing more than a number of complex, private consensual contract-based relations,[3] either express or implied, and they consist of many different kinds of relation that are worked out by those voluntarily associating in a company.[4] The parties involved in these contracts are regarded as rational economic actors, and include shareholders, managers, creditors, suppliers and employees, and it is accepted that each of these constituencies endeavour in their contracting to maximise their own position, with the intention of producing concomitant benefits for themselves.[5] This scheme is usually known as 'a nexus of contracts'.[6] Where the contracts of the parties are not complete, the theory accepts that corporate law will fill the gaps; for instance, limited liability in corporate law provides an allocation of risk.[7] The structure of corporate law, according to contractarianism, should be that of a body of default rules, which the parties

1 Professor Paddy Ireland refers to law and economics that focuses on neo-classical microeconomics as the more extreme version of contractarianism ('Defending the rentier: corporate theory and the reprivatisation of the public company' in Parkinson, J, Gamble, A, and Kelly, G (eds), *The Political Economy of the Company*, 2000, Oxford: Hart Publishing, p 142 fn 4.

2 For example, Fama, E, 'Agency problems and the theory of the firm (1990) 99 *Journal of Political Economics* 288 at 290.

3 Referring to the relations as contracts is probably incorrect. Some authors refer to the relations as bargains as some of the relations do not constitute contracts in a technical sense. See Klausner, M, 'Corporations, corporate law and networks of contracts' (1995) 81 *Virginia Law Review* 757 at 759.

4 Easterbrook, F H, and Fischel, D R, 'The corporate contract' (1989) 89 Colum L Rev 1416, at 1426. At p 1428 the learned commentators give examples of some of the arrangements.

5 See, Butler, H N, 'The contractual theory of the corporation' (1989) 11 *George Mason University Law Review* 99; Riley, C A, 'Understanding and regulating the corporation' (1995) 58 MLR 595 at 598.

6 The literature considering the nexus of contracts is too voluminous to cite. But see, for example, *op. cit.* fn 2 above at 290; fn 4 above at 1426–1427. The nexus of contracts approach is critiqued by Bratton Jr, W, 'The "nexus of contracts corporation": a critical appraisal' (1989) 74 Cornell L Rev 407 at 412, 446–465. The scheme has been referred to as 'a nexus of incomplete contracts'. For recent comments, see, for example, Deakin, S, and Hughes, A, 'Economic efficiency and the proceduralisation of company law' (1999) 3 CfiLR 169 at 176–180; McNeil, I, 'Company law rules: an assessment from the perspective of incomplete contract theory' (2001) 1 JCLS 107.

7 Whincop, M J, 'Painting the corporate cathedral: the protection of entitlements in corporate law' (1999) 19 OJLS 19 at 28.

may chose to vary or omit.[8] So, the theory is anti-regulatory and, therefore, tends to eschew mandatory legal rules.[9] In general it favours the view that parties should be able to opt out of rules if they so wish, although it must be acknowledged that there are contractarians who recognise that some rules are necessary. Classic contractarianism focuses on voluntary contracting and individualism, so that contractarians do not see the company as a hierarchy, with senior management at the pinnacle controlling the company subject to company law. Rather, contractarians in general tend to regard the managers of the company as the agents of the shareholders (the so-called 'agency theory'), but this is only in economic terms as it is not asserted that this constitutes a legal relationship. Furthermore, contractarians see the company as a private initiative that does not have public functions,[10] and as a consequence 'the state has no greater standing to intervene in corporate affairs than it has in the individual affairs of the citizens who make up the company'.[11]

The law-and-economics movement

Introduction and relationship to contractarianism

Law and economics has played a large part in legal scholarship for at least 25 years. Corporate law in the United States has embraced the law-and-economics approach more than most areas of the law, and this has led Professor Brian Cheffins to proclaim that, in the United States, it has become the most influential school of thought in the academic study of corporate law,[12] and it has been embraced by the Law Commission in its Consultation Paper on *Corporate Directors*[13] in 1997, and later the Company Law Review Steering Group, when reporting on the need for company law reform.[14] Consequently, the view that is generally put by

---

8 Having fiduciary duties as default provisions can foster economic efficiency in that the parties are saved the expense of negotiating all of the terms governing relations. This is discussed later in the Chapter. Also, see Chapter 21.

9 Although some contractarians acknowledge that mandatory rules are needed where 'bargaining is likely to be extremely costly or where there is an imbalance of power or information between the parties': The Law Commission, 'Company Directors: Regulating Conflicts of Interests and Formulating a Statement of Duties', Consultation Paper No 153, 1998 at para 316.

10 This is to be contrasted with the approach of communitarians.

11 Parkinson, J E, *Corporate Power and Responsibility*, 1993, Oxford: OUP, p 27.

12 'Using theory to study law: a company law perspective' (1999) 58 CLJ 197 at 209. Also see his book, *Company Law: Theory, Structure and Operation*, 1997, Oxford: Clarendon Press, p 3.

13 LCCP No153.

14 See, for example, *Modern Company Law for a Competitive Economy: The Strategic Framework*, 1999, London: DTI at para 2.4.

commentators addressing the law from an economic perspective warrants careful consideration.

Frequently no distinction is made between contractarianism and law-and-economics theory in much of the corporate law literature,[15] and the majority of law-and-economics scholarship in corporate law is founded on the contractarian approach, sometimes referred to as the neo-classical model, but economic analysis of law can be distinguished from classic contractarianism. But first we should acknowledge the assumptions that both theories share. Like contractarianism, law-and-economics theory presumes that individuals should be at liberty to live how they choose and make whatever agreements they see fit,[16] and be permitted to opt out of the application of legal rules. In common with much contractarian thought, law-and-economics theorists are opposed to the strict imposition of fiduciary duties as they hold that such duties do not operate without cost and so the parties should be entitled to opt out of these duties.[17] This undoubtedly affects their views on the proposition that directors should take into account creditor interests in discharging duties to their company. Law and economics, following contractarianism, accepts that companies are private initiatives. Also presumed, in common with contractarianism, is that all actors in the nexus of contracts are rational and desire to maximise their benefits. But, unlike classic contractarianism, the economic-analysis approach focuses on market forces.[18] The starting point for law-and-economics scholars is the market (including capital, labour and product markets) which is 'the glue that holds together the nexus of contracts'.[19] And market forces, so the argument goes, provides a more effective incentive towards efficient managerial conduct. Law and economics adds to its contractarian base by emphasising financial economics and the need to reduce transaction costs so as to improve efficiency.[20] Emphasis on efficiency, which is the very heart of this theory, is the factor that further characterises law-and-economics scholarship. We will consider the meaning of efficiency shortly.

In sum, several of the foundations of law-and-economics theory as applied to corporate law are common to classic contractarianism, and as a result

---

15 For example, see Campbell Jr, R B, 'Corporate fiduciary principles for the post-contractarian era' (1996) 23 *Florida State University Law Review* 561 at 561.

16 Millon, D, 'New directions in corporate law: communitarians, contractarians and crisis in corporate law' (1993) 50 *Washington and Lee Law Review* 1373 at 1382.

17 See Butler, L E, and Ribstein, H, 'Opting out of fiduciary duties: a response to the anti-contractarians' (1990) 65 *Washington Law Review* 1. Also, see Chapter 21.

18 These include, amongst other factors, pressures from employees, managers, capital markets and corporate control markets: Millon, D, 'Theories of the corporation' [1990] Duke L J 201 at 231.

19 *Op. cit.* fn 17 above at 24.

20 In corporate law transaction costs are reduced by the organisational design of the company: Williamson, O E, 'Transactional-cost economics: the governance of contractual relations' (1994) 21 *Journal of Law and Society* 168.

it can be seen as a variant of contractarianism.[21] It is this variant of contractarianism that is the most popular form of contractarianism, and which is the focus of parts of this chapter.

Duties to creditors

Any theoretical consideration of any aspect of corporate law warrants some reference to the work done by those in the law-and-economics school. It is not intended to indulge in a prolix discussion of the contribution of law-and-economics scholarship to corporate law, as the literature is voluminous. What I wish to do is to focus on the approach taken by scholars who hold to this paradigm as far as duties of directors are concerned. The discussion has to be framed in general terms and it is accepted that not all scholars hold to all of the views articulated here.

Law-and-economics scholars differ concerning the appropriate level of legal regulation that should exist, with many opposed to the strict imposition of fiduciary duties on the basis that such duties do not operate without cost, and restrict free bargaining between parties.[22] The corollary is that the parties should be entitled to opt out of these duties,[23] and this means that law-and-economics scholars are generally against directors being required to take into account creditor interests in discharging duties to their company.

The emphasis on efficiency

The focus of law-and-economics scholars, when considering whether a legal rule is normative or not, is to consider the efficiency of the rule[24] (defined as the relationship between the aggregate benefit of a legal rule and the aggregate costs of that legal rule[25]), with the result that the common law is

---

21 The renowned American company law academic, Professor Robert Clark, has said the contractarianism has dominated the thinking of most 'economically oriented corporate law scholars who focus on the theory of the corporation' ('Contracts, elites and traditions in the making of corporate law' (1989) 89 Colum L Rev 1703 at 1705).

22 For perhaps an example of the extreme view, see Ribstein, L, 'The mandatory nature of the ALI code' (1993) 60 *George Washington Law Review* 984.

23 See *op. cit.* fn 17 above at 6, 13–15. Also, see Chapter 21.

24 Law and economics does rely, on occasions, on values other than efficiency when justifying their position. See Posner, R, 'The ethical and political basis of the efficiency norm in common law adjudication' (1980) 8 *Hofstra Law Review* 487 at 494. This is certainly the case in Britain. For example, see Deakin, S, and Hughes, A, 'Economics and company law reform: a fruitful partnership' (1999) 20 Co Law 212 at 218; Armour, J, 'Share capital and creditor protection: efficient rules for a modern company law' (2000) 63 MLR 355 at 358.

25 Polinsky, A M, *An Introduction to Law and Economics*, 1989, Boston: Little Brown & Co, p 7 and referred to in Yeo, V, and Lin, J, 'Insolvent trading – a comparative and economic approach' (1999) 10 *Australian Journal of Corporate Law* 216 at 234.

explained best as a system that fosters economic efficiency.[26] Many, but far from all, commentators take the view that the efficiency goal of maximising the company's value to investors is the principal function of corporate law.[27]

The kind of efficiency[28] that is commonly relied on in law-and-economics scholarship is Kaldor-Hicks efficiency,[29] a derivative of, but to be contrasted with, Pareto efficiency. These are the kinds of allocative efficiency recognised by economists. There are two principal forms of Pareto efficiency. There is a third one, namely, Pareto inferiority, but it is rarely relied on. Something is Pareto superior[30] (often regarded as being based in classical utilitarianism[31]) where, given two possible states of affairs, say X and Y, Y is Pareto superior to X if no one prefers X to Y and at least one person prefers Y to X, so the utility of at least one person is increased while not making anyone else worse off;[32] this obviates the need to compare the relative gains and losses of winners and losers so as to gauge whether a course of action increases total utility. So, if any person is prejudiced by an action, then we cannot have Pareto superiority. It is generally agreed that the conditions required for Pareto superiority are never found in the real world. The third form is Pareto

---

26 Achieving 'economic efficiency' demands that the parties be permitted to trade without governmental or other restraints: *op. cit.* fn 15 above at 565.

27 For example, see Black, B, and Kraackman, R, 'A self-enforcing model of corporate law' (1996) 109 Harv L Rev 1911 at 1921. Some law-and-economics scholars accept other virtues besides efficiency are relevant (for example, Bainbridge, S, 'Community and statism: a conservative contractarian critique of progressive corporate law scholarship' (1997) 82 *Cornell Law Review* 856 at 883). For examples of scholars in Britain who do not see efficiency as the only virtue, see Deakin and Hughes, *op. cit.* fn 24 above at 218; Armour, *op. cit.* fn 24 above at 358.

28 For comment on the different meanings of 'efficiency', see Deakin and Hughes, *op. cit.* fn 6 above at 173–175.

29 See Kaldor, N, 'Welfare propositions of economics and interpersonal comparisons of utility' [1939] *The Economic Journal* 549; Hicks, J R, 'The valuation of the social income' [1940] *Economica* 105. For a recent discussion of the concept, see Trebilcock, M, 'The value and limits of law and economics' in Richardson, M, and Hadfield, G (eds), *The Second Wave in Law and Economics*, 1999, Sydney: Federation Press, pp 20–22. The rule has been subject to criticism. For example, see Hardin, R, 'The morality of law and economics' (1992) 11 *Law and Philosophy* 330 at 346.

30 Many regard Pareto superior as unobtainable. For a discussion of Pareto, see the following works of Coleman, J L: 'Efficiency, utility and wealth maximization' (1980) 8 *Hofstra Law Review* 509 at 513; 'Efficiency, exchange and auction: philosophic aspects of the economic approach to law' (1980) 68 *California Law Review* 221 at 226–227. Also, see Trebilcock, *ibid* at 17–20; McDaniel, M, 'Bondholders and stockholders' (1988) 13 *Journal of Corporation Law* 205 at 222 and Wiegers, W, 'Economic analysis of law and "private ordering": a feminist critique' (1992) 42 *University of Toronto Law Journal* 170 at 187–198. For a critique of Pareto, see Calabresi, G, 'The pointlessness of Pareto: carrying Coase further' (1991) 100 Yale LJ 1211; Macintosh, J, 'Designing an efficient fiduciary law' (1993) 43 *University of Toronto Law Journal* 425 at 435–440.

31 Coleman, J L, 'Efficiency, utility and wealth maximization' *ibid* at 515.

32 *Ibid* at 515; Lawson, G, 'Efficiency and individualism' (1992) Duke LJ 53 at 85.

optimal and it occurs if one gets to the point where any further change to states of affairs would not enhance the welfare of one person and would make somebody else worse off. Consequently, Pareto-optimal distributions have no distributions Pareto-superior to them.[33] Under the Kaldor-Hicks test, efficiency exists, essentially, where the aggregate benefits of a system that is proposed exceeds the costs to such an extent that the winners could compensate the losers. Whether or not the winners do in fact compensate the losers is not critical,[34] and usually the losers are not compensated.[35] If the losers were paid compensation then we would have Pareto superiority.

While the renowned law-and-economics scholar, Judge Richard Posner, has said that efficient company law does not favour creditor protection or corporate freedom, but mediates between these two objectives so as to minimise the costs of investment,[36] the fact of the matter is that many scholars[37] have said that requiring directors to consider creditor interests is not appropriate for the most part because of the costs which it can precipitate. This view emanates from one of the foundations of law and economics, the Coase theorem (developed by Ronald Coase in one of his seminal pieces[38]). The Coasean theorem holds that transaction costs might prevent resources being put to the most allocatively efficient use (the maximum productive use of resources), and, hence, imposing additional duties on directors would increase transaction costs and prevent resources being utilised in the most efficient way. Put in other words, the concern is that any greater impositions on directors will make them less efficient in their role as agents of the shareholders of the company, because amongst other things, they will start to think of their own positions,[39] rather than maximising profits. So, as many argue, any expansion of the responsibility of directors will produce inefficiencies in corporate governance.[40] To be

33 Coleman, J L, 'Efficiency, utility and wealth maximization' *ibid* at 517.

34 *Ibid* at 513.

35 Whincop, M J, 'Painting the corporate cathedral: the protection of entitlements in corporate law' (1999) 19 OJLS 19 at 33.

36 Posner, R, 'The rights of affiliated corporations' (1976) 43 *University of Chicago Law Review* 499 at 509.

37 For example, Butler and Ribstein, *op. cit.* fn 17 above; Macey, J, 'An economic analysis of the various rationales for making shareholders the exclusive beneficiaries of corporate fiduciary duties' (1991) 21 *Stetson Law Review* 23; Lin, L, 'Shift of fiduciary duty upon corporate insolvency: proper scope of directors' duty to creditors' (1993) 46 *Vanderbilt Law Review* 1485; Macintosh, *op. cit.* fn 30 above; Byrne, M, 'An economic analysis of directors' duties in favour of creditors' (1994) 4 *Australian Journal of Corporate Law* 275; van der Weide, M, 'Against fiduciary duties to corporate stakeholders' (1996) 21 *Delaware Journal of Corporate Law* 27.

38 'The problem of social cost' (1960) 3 *Journal of Law and Economics* 1. For some discussion of Coase's work, see Jules L Coleman, 'Efficiency, exchange and auction', *op. cit.* fn 30 above at 223–226.

39 Glasbeek, H J, 'More direct director responsibility: much ado about … what?' [1985] *Canadian Business Law Journal* 416 at 421.

40 *Ibid*, 421; van der Weide, *op. cit.* fn 37 above at 84; Bainbridge *op. cit.* fn 27 above at 877.

comprehensive, I should say at that this point that because the law-and-economics framework is methodologically neutral, other law-and-economics scholars[41] have taken the view that the kind of duty considered here is to be supported on efficiency grounds because, on their assessment, the benefits produced outweigh the costs incurred if a duty applies. The resolution of the divergence of opinion in law-and-economics scholarship depends on empirical findings.

We now turn to another approach to corporate law to see what it offers in relation to consideration of a theoretical basis for imposing a duty on directors to consider creditor interests.

Progressive scholarship

In the past decade or so, a group of scholars, largely located in the United States,[42] who have sometimes referred to themselves as advocating a progressive view[43] on corporate law,[44] have, largely, sought to provide responses to the opinions propounded by some from the law-and-economics school.[45] It is not intended to provide a detailed discussion of the positions taken by progressives,[46] but merely to indicate the main ideas posited.

While law-and-economics scholars have turned to finance theory and

---

41 For example, Grantham, R, 'The judicial extension of directors' duties to creditors' [1991] JBL 1; Schwarcz, S, 'Rethinking a corporation's obligations to creditors' (1996) 17 *Cardozo Law Review* 647; Whincop, M J, 'Taking the corporate contract more seriously: the economic cases against, and a transaction cost rationale for, the insolvent trading provisions' (1996) 5 *Griffith Law Review* 1; Mokal, R J, 'An agency cost analysis of the wrongful trading provisions: redistribution, perverse incentives and the creditors' bargain' (2000) 59 CLJ 335.

42 Some of the foremost have been Professors Douglas Branson, William Bratton, Lyman Johnson, David Millon, and Lawrence Mitchell. A similar approach, called the pluralist approach, has been advocated in the UK by some, such as Professor John Parkinson (*op. cit.* fn 11 above) and (with Gavin Kelly), 'The conceptual foundations of the company: a pluralist approach' in Parkinson, J, Gamble, A and Kelly, G (eds), *The Political Economy of the Company*, 2000, Oxford: Hart Publishing.

43 The appellation is challenged by some, such as Professor Stephen Bainbridge *op. cit.* fn 27 above at 856. Certainly the progressives are numbered amongst the anti-contractarians in corporate law: see Butler and Ribstein, *op. cit.* fn 17 above. For a critique of the approach, see Bainbridge, *op. cit.* fn 27 above.

44 The literature is voluminous and too extensive to cite in full. Examples of the scholarship can be seen in the monograph, Mitchell, L E (ed), *Progressive Corporate Law*, 1995, Boulder, Colorado: Westview Press, and the following works: Bratton, *op. cit.* fn 6 above; Mitchell, L, 'The fairness rights of bondholders' (1990) 65 *New York University Law Review* 1165; Millon, *op. cit.* fn 18 above; Johnson, L, 'The Delaware judiciary and the meaning of corporate life and corporate law' (1990) 68 *Texas Law Review* 865. For critiques of progressive scholarship, see, for example, DeBow, M, and Lee, D, 'Shareholders, non-shareholders and corporate law: communitarianism and resource allocation' (1993) 18 *Delaware Journal of Corporate Law* 393; Bainbridge, *op. cit.* fn 27 above.

45 Some writers, such as, Mitchell, 1990, *ibid*, have also sought to construct positive agenda.

46 Possibly the best articulation of progressive views in the one location is to be found in Mitchell, 1995, *op. cit.* fn 44 above.

neoclassical economics, the progressive school has embraced views from the humanities and social sciences, and has sought to focus on the fact that those involved in, and dealing with, companies are humans and corporate law should not be depersonaliscd.[47] In the progressive assessment a greater array of social and political values are considered, and progressives opine that whether the company is useful is measured by seeing how it assists society gain a richer understanding of community by respecting human dignity and overall welfare.[48] Progressives, also known as communitarians,[49] embrace a different normative world view to law-and-economics scholars, for the former emphasise the fact that people are part of a shared community who inherit the benefits, values and goals of the community, thus the cultural milieu in which people find themselves cannot be ignored.[50] The law-and-economics approach is criticised for being too focused on self-interest,[51] while progressives are interested in community benefits. It has been argued in the progressive literature,[52] *inter alia*, that companies are public institutions with public obligations and it is necessary to have mandatory rules to control what they and their managers do.[53] The company is perceived not as a nexus of contracts but as 'a community of interdependence, mutual trust and reciprocal benefit'.[54] To progressives, contract is not able to explain the many relationships that are involved in the life of a company.[55] Rather than being concerned about the reduction of transaction costs, the progressives are concerned about the social effects of corporate activity.[56] Progressive scholars

---

47 For example, see Mitchell, L, 'Groundwork of the metaphysics of corporate law' (1993) 50 *Washington and Lee Law Review* 1477 at 1479–1481. In another work, the learned commentator states that 'The corporation is a human enterprise' ('The death of fiduciary duty in close corporations' (1990) 138 U Pa LR 1675 at 1675).

48 Sullivan, D, and Conlon, D, 'Crisis and transition in corporate governance paradigms: the role of the Chancery Court of Delaware' [1997] *Law and Society Review* 713 and referred to by Dine, J, 'Companies and regulations: theories, justifications and policing' in Milman, D (ed), *Regulating Enterprise: Law and Business Organisations in the UK*, 1999, Oxford: Hart Publishing, p 295.

49 For example, see, Millon, D, 'Communitarianism in corporate law: foundations and law reform strategies' in Mitchell, 1995, *op. cit.* fn 44 above at 1; DeBow and Lee, *op. cit.* fn 44 above at 394. But some who are labelled as 'communitarians', reject the label (for example, Mitchell, L, 'Trust. Contract. Process' in Mitchell, 1995, *op. cit.* fn 44 above at 185, 186–187).

50 *Op. cit.* fn 16 above at 1382.   51 Mitchell, 1993, *op. cit.* fn 47 above at 1485.

52 Of course, just as with the law and economics school, not all progressives adhere to the same view on all matters.

53 For example, see Branson, D, 'The death of contractarianism and the vindication of structure and authority in corporate governance and corporate law' in Mitchell 1995, *op. cit.* fn 44 above at 93.

54 Millon, *op. cit.* fn 49 above at 10.

55 For example, see Brudney, V, 'Corporate governance, agency costs, and the rhetoric of contract' (1985) 85 Colum L R 1403; Eisenberg, M, 'The structure of corporation law' (1989) 89 Colum L R 1461; Frankel, T, 'Fiduciary duties as default rules' (1995) 74 *Oregon Law Review* 1209.

56 Millon, *op. cit.* fn 16 above at 1379.

have posited the need for mandatory rules to provide adequate protection for some people.[57] In particular, the progressives have asserted that the interests of shareholders are not the only interests that should be considered by directors when carrying out their functions; they have argued that there are other important constituencies that warrant consideration from directors,[58] such as creditors, employees, suppliers and the general community.

Many progressives have argued for respect, trust and fairness and other virtues to be considered when determining what shape corporate law should take.[59] In several ways this school has echoed the views presented by Professor E Merrick Dodd in the 1930s and 40s, particularly in relation to his debates with Professor Adolf Berle, when the learned commentator argued that the company 'has a social service as well as a profit-making function'.[60]

Progressives reject the idea of the market being a satisfactory institutional means to achieve justice. Rather, they focus on a broad, admittedly imprecise, concern for justice that is based on stability and fair dealing.[61] Advocates of this approach are more ready to contend for the use of legal rules to structure relations among the various groups who can be regarded as having a stake in the company, on the basis that company law needs to confront the effects of managers pursuing shareholder wealth maximisation. Therefore, it would seem that progressives would be more ready to embrace a duty to creditors.

We now turn to considering the duty to creditors in the context of a number or factors and in light of the corporate law theories just discussed.

Distributional fairness

Any decision to hold directors in breach of a duty to creditors would, in effect, constitute a distribution of resources that was not contracted for. And this is a major concern for law-and-economics scholars as they focus on maximising aggregate social welfare and not distributional fairness.[62] In contrast, we have seen that progressive scholars advocate virtues such as trust, respect and interdependence in corporate law, and, consequently, they argue

---

57 Millon, *op. cit.* fn 49 above at 4.
58 For example, Professor Lawrence Mitchell criticises the whole notion of shareholder maximisation in corporate law ('A theoretical and practical framework for enforcing corporate constituency statutes' (1992) 70 *Texas Law Review* 579 at, 640). See Millon, *op. cit.* fn 49 above at 7–9. Progressives differ among themselves concerning the strength of the claims of various non-shareholder constituencies to warrant legal intervention.
59 For example, Mitchell, 'Trust', *op. cit.* fn 49 above at 185.
60 Merrick Dodd, E, 'For whom are corporate managers trustees?' (1932) 45 Harv LR 1145 at 1148.
61 For example, Millon, *op. cit.* fn 49 above at 9.
62 Easterbrook, F, and Fischel, D, *The Economic Structure of Company Law*, 1991, Cambridge, Mass: Harvard University Press, p 122.

for fairness in the distribution of wealth, because that promotes social welfare, stability and fair dealing, and that is more likely to ensure that there is reciprocal benefit. Resolving issues relating to distributional justice in corporate law is never easy, and the way that the theory of law and economics deals with the issues is to turn a blind eye to them. It is unconcerned with distribution; losses fall where they fall. Law and economics has no regard for effects that contracts have on third parties;[63] it is just not pertinent who gains and who loses. This approach is based on the argument that the parties are able, through contract, to decide what price they should demand for their agreement, and hence this process alone will determine where the benefits and burdens fall. The approach might seem to be an attractive approach in that people get what they bargain for, and of itself the theory does not exacerbate existing inequalities; it is neutral on that point as it respects inequalities. When contracting, law-and-economics scholars will argue that creditors are able to 'price up' a deal to compensate for the risk that they are taking on, and so the parties are distributing the benefits and burdens amongst themselves. The consequence, arguably, is that there is Pareto efficiency (each party is left in a better position). But that fails to account for things like information asymmetry and unforeseeable *ex post* conduct of directors. Furthermore, creditors will often not appreciate the state of the law and fail, consequently, to make provision for it and thus obtain a redistribution of benefits and burdens. Moreover, contracting in the context we are contemplating often involves inequality of bargaining power, that is, creditors are not able to make the bargain that they really want because of their circumstances.

Progressives might posit that in developing policy there cannot only be a focus on what is the most optimal allocation of resources, a major concern of law-and-economics scholars, but concern must be shown for the appropriate distribution of resources.[64] Some economic analysts regard efficiency as either the sole value to be taken into account, or at least to be weighted higher than other values.[65] But if there is exclusive focus on efficiency this may 'mask the consequences of risk shifting for certain groups who are the losers, at the expense of others'.[66] In our context the losers would be unsecured creditors. The upshot is that we cannot reduce company law to one normative value, such as efficiency, which is, after all is said and done, only an 'abstract concept which is the outcome of a theoretical model of how resources can be best

---

63 *Op. cit.* fn 4 above at 1429–1430.

64 Ogus, A, 'Economics, liberty and the common law' (1980) 5 *Journal of the Society of Teachers of Law* 42 and referred to in Freedman, J, 'Limited liability: large company theory and small firms' (2000) 63 MLR 317 at 320.

65 Maughen, C, and Copp, S, 'The Law Commission and economic methodology: values, efficiency and directors' duties' (1999) 20 Co Law 109 at 112.

66 Freedman, *op. cit.* fn 64 above at 320.

allocated in society'.[67] We might find it beneficial to society if we consider values that do not carry 'price tags'.[68]

While some commentators[69] in the law-and-economics movement, and particularly those in Britain,[70] do not advocate the view that efficiency is the sole factor to be considered in determining what the law should be, many do. Let us make no mistake, efficiency is certainly a factor in 'any system in which private ordering through the mechanism of contract has a prominent role',[71] and must not be ignored. Efficiency is a useful value and warrants being considered in deciding what the law should be, but it is only one of a number that deserve consideration,[72] and should not been seen as an end in itself.[73] It is unfortunate that efficiency all too often dominates in the analysis of the law by some contractarians to the exclusion of other values. Concentrating solely on efficiency as a value, or as an end, tends to produce overly harsh results. 'A world dominated by the pursuit of economic efficiency is often lacking in grace and kindness, those wonderful human qualities that society in its finer moments finds so attractive.'[74] It has been said that much of what is 'written in the name of law and economics is . . . insensitive to the limits within which economic analysis might prove fruitful'.[75] The position taken by the law-and-economics scholars as far as distributional justice is concerned, with its focus on the optimal allocation of resources, leads to economic analysis being criticised as cold and uncaring.

Having accepted the need to consider efficiency, we must be careful that other values are not overwhelmed by efficiency.[76] One value that deserves consideration is fairness, as acknowledged by some of the literature in this field. The problem is that there is a profound lack of any explanation as

---

67 *Op. cit.* fn 65 above at 112.
68 Hardin, R, 'The morality of law and economics' (1992) 11 *Law and Philosophy* 330 at 339.
69 For example, see *op. cit.* fn 7 above at 19–20.
70 For example, see Deakin and Hughes, *op. cit.* fn 24 above at 218; Armour, *op. cit.* fn 24 above at 358.
71 McNeil, *op. cit.* fn 6 above at 110.
72 Posner ultimately accepted that efficiency cannot be the sole principle to consider in dispensing justice: *The Problems of Jurisprudence* (1990) at 379 and referred to in Farber, D, 'Economic efficiency and the ex ante perspective' in Kraus, J, and Walt, S (eds), *The Jurisprudential Foundation of Corporate and Commercial Law*, 2000, Cambridge, Mass: Cambridge University Press, p 63.
73 Riley, C, 'The Law Commission's questionable approach to the duty of care and skill' (1999) 20 Co Law 196 at 198.
74 *Op. cit.* fn 15 above at 623.
75 Coleman, 'Efficiency, exchange and auction', *op. cit.* fn 30 above at 221.
76 It has been noted that '[a] society that thinks only of alleged Efficiency regardless [of] the consequences to human beings, works its own ruin' (Kirk, R, *The Politics of Prudence*, 1993 at 122 and quoted by Bainbridge, *op. cit.* fn 27 above at 883 fn 127). See the comments of Hardin, *op. cit.* fn 68 above at 339. A value can be viewed as an objective of the legal order and shape the decisions of courts (Dias, R, *Jurisprudence*, 1985, London: Butterworths, p 196).

to what is meant by the word, 'fairness'; writers gloss over what is meant by it, assuming that we know what the term entails.[77] This is probably because fairness is 'one of the great unexplained mysteries of corporate law'.[78] Undoubtedly, one reason for this is the fact that 'fairness' is intuitive. Nevertheless, we need to put some substance into the term for the purposes of this discussion.

First, we must accept that fairness is incapable of precise definition.[79] There are potentially many dimensions to the value of fairness (as in fact there are in relation to many values, including efficiency[80]) and it is not possible to provide an exposition of all of them here. But there are some aspects that are relevant, particularly in the context of the duty under discussion. Of relevance to our discussion is the fact that fairness is often used to refer to how wealth is distributed in society.[81] So, unlike efficiency, fairness is concerned with the end effect of wealth distribution. I will return to this point later. While fairness has no single accepted meaning, here it is used in the context of company–creditor transactions and produces the results one would obtain where there is a bargain between unrelated parties with approximately equal bargaining power,[82] namely where there is fair dealing and a fair price.[83] This accords with the general idea that fairness, throughout our legal system, involves balance and proportionality as far as the parties to transactions or proceedings are concerned.[84] This notion of fairness, consistent with our legal tradition, assumes support for those who are vulnerable and the meeting of people's reasonable and legitimate expectations. Some creditors are vulnerable *ex ante* because, as we have seen, they often do not have the necessary information, knowledge or bargaining position that enables them either to protect themselves adequately or to charge a price for the credit that is commensurate with the risk that is taken. Furthermore, many creditors are vulnerable after the extension of credit as they receive no information from the company, having few or no ways of securing such information (except, perhaps, by freeriding (that is relying on the monitoring of the company by other creditors)), having little or no influence on the company's management, and the directors might take action to change the gearing of the company so that existing arrangements do not reflect the risks to which creditors are

---

77 For instance, Mitchell, 1990, *op. cit.* fnn 7, 44 and 68 above; Farber, *op. cit.* fn 72 above at 54. The same situation exists in literature in other areas of the law. For example, see Oliver, D, 'Common values in public and private law and the public/private divided' [1997] PL 630.

78 Mitchell, L, 'Fairness and trust in corporate law' (1993) 43 *Duke Law Journal* 425 at 428.

79 *Ibid* at 451.

80 See, for example, Deakin and Hughes, *op. cit.* fn 24 above and *op. cit.* fn 6 above at 173–175; Orts, E, 'The complexity and legitimacy of corporate law' (1993) 50 *Washington and Lee Law Review* 1565 at 1566, 1587.

81 Anderson, A, 'Conflicts of interest: efficiency, fairness and corporate structure' (1978) 25 UCLA L Rev 738 at 745.

82 See, *ibid* at 746.   83 *Op. cit.* fn 78 above at 446.   84 See, *ibid* at 425.

exposed. The result of all this is that directors can act as they choose, even though they are doing it with the creditors' money! Where there is information asymmetry and uneven bargaining power, there is not fair dealing and not a fair price being given, so the law has to compensate the vulnerable in order to ensure that a fair outcome is produced; where directors have a responsibility to creditors, the latter are compensated for what they have been deprived of by the actions of the directors.

Fairness in progressive thought dictates that the actions of management should not directly or indirectly transfer wealth from creditors to shareholders, either by the shifting of funds or causing an increase in risk. In not having regard for creditor interests when resources are scarce, such as when the company is near to, or in, insolvency, it might be argued that the directors are cheating[85] as they are effecting a wrongful distribution of wealth away from those who are the residual claimants of company property. All that the law can do, apart from requiring that creditors are to be treated equally at the time of contracting, is to impose some form of *ex-post* judgment to redress unfairness.

The concept of reasonable and legitimate expectations was mentioned above. It is grounded in fairness,[86] and to have these sorts of expectations is to have moral claims on the grounds of fairness.[87] It has had a significant influence in the law of contract,[88] although arguably its effect is wider in scope.[89] In contract, the object of the employment of reasonable and legitimate expectations is to fill in the gaps in a contractual relationship. It has been taken to mean: what the parties would have wanted had they thought about the gap;[90] what reasonable parties would have wanted to have included in their contract had they thought about the gap;[91] or what the parties actually anticipated the contract would require in the situation that has in fact occurred.[92] It is submitted that the second of the meanings is preferable as it accepts the need for some form of objectivity, which is to be preferred over tests focused on the subjective hopes of a party for the future.[93] It permits

---

85 A word used by Professor Alison Anderson in *op. cit.* fn 81 above at 750.

86 Hsieh, N, 'Moral desert, fairness and legitimate expectations in the market' (2000) 8 *Journal of Political Philosophy* 91 at 103. In *R v IRC* [1990] 1 WLR 1545 at 1569 Bingham LJ said that '[t]he doctrine of legitimate expectations is rooted in fairness'.

87 Hsieh, *ibid* at 102.

88 See, Mitchell, C, 'Leading a life of its own? The roles of reasonable expectation in contract law' (2003) 23 OJLS 639.

89 Roscoe Pound suggested that the norm of reasonable expectations generates all legal rules: *Introduction to the Philosophy of Law*, 1922 at 189 and referred to in Kuklin, B, 'The plausibility of legally protected reasonable expectations' (1997) 32 *Valparaiso University Law Review* 19, fn 3.

90 Bratton, W, 'The interpretation of contracts governing corporate debt relationships' (1984) 5 *Cardozo Law Review* 371 at 381–382.

91 Mitchell, 1990, *op. cit.* fn 44 above at 1224.   92 *Ibid* at 1225.

93 *Op. cit.* fn 88 above at 642.

factors such as the nature of the company's business and its future, and the kind and position of the creditor providing credit to be considered. In assessing reasonable and legitimate expectations, progressives would argue that the assessment should involve a consideration of community values of fairness and decency.[94]

It is fair that a creditor's reasonable expectations at the time of extending credit are fulfilled. It would be reasonable and legitimate for creditors to hold an expectation that the company will behave in good faith,[95] and to expect certain things of directors, such as not transferring assets of the company to third parties at an undervalue, and taking creditor interests into account when the company is, or potentially is, in financial distress, as the creditors have the residual claim over the company. If these expectations are not met then creditors can reasonably expect that directors would be held responsible.

A fair distribution of resources would, if there were a duty to creditors, result in creditors being compensated in a liquidation or administration by the directors for any of their losses that were occasioned by the directors' failure to give proper consideration to the creditors' interests when the company was in financial difficulty, or even potential difficulty. The compensation would be justified on the basis that at a time when the company's residual claimants were the creditors, the directors ignored their interests and transferred resources to the shareholders.

Perhaps it is also possible to say that the imposition of a duty will promote fairness in that the duty could prevent wide-ranging effects on society. For example, if creditors, because their interests are ignored, lose out, it is highly likely that some creditors will not be able to pay their own creditors, and so on down the chain of debt, and this will not only affect individual creditors but also diminish the collective welfare of society. Also, the enforcement of reasonable and legitimate expectations can have an efficiency benefit as well as providing for fairness in that it enables parties to engage in negotiating complicated contracts without incurring high transaction costs.

Clearly, efficiency and fairness are both appropriate values to be taken into consideration. While many see tensions between fairness and efficiency,[96] in that, *inter alia*, the former demands regulation, and the latter the restriction of regulation, and some commentators have said that there is a need to strike a balance between the two values (necessarily involving a compromise between them, that is, a trade-off),[97] it has been argued by Dr Rizwaan

---

94 *Ibid.*

95 Carney, W, 'Does defining constituencies matter?' (1990) 59 *University of Cincinnati Law Review* 385 at 390.

96 For instance, see Anderson, *op. cit.* fn 81 above at 745, 748, 754, 756 and 761.

97 For an economic assessment of the trade-off between fairness and efficiency, see Tadenuma, K, 'Efficiency first or equity first? Two principles and rationality of social choice' (2002) 104 *Journal of Economic Theory* 462.

Mokal[98] that as fairness is a goal and efficiency is only a method in assessing goals, fairness and efficiency should not be compared. Accepting that latter argument in this context does not attenuate the progressive approach as the enforcement of reasonable and legitimate expectations can in fact be assessed positively as producing more benefits than costs, and therefore be regarded as efficient. This is discussed later under the heading of 'Efficiency'.

On the subject of efficiency, the argument might be put that while one is making some people better off, namely the creditors, by imposing liability, one is making others, namely the directors worse off, and that is unfair. This is true up to a point, but the response might be that, firstly, the unsecured creditors are not better off as they are only getting what they reasonably expected to get, and, secondly, the directors are only worse off because they failed to discharge their responsibilities properly and breached their duty of trust to the creditors.

If a duty to creditors is regarded as fair, it does not necessarily mean that in all cases where unsecured creditors lose out in a liquidation or administration that the directors will be liable to pay them compensation. Whether there has been a breach or not will be determined by the courts, which are an integral element of the fairness framework discussed above. It is the courts that will determine whether directors should have considered creditor interests at a particular point in time, and if they should have done so, whether they in fact did so. If the answer to the latter inquiry is negative then the court is entitled to provide compensation, as parties contract 'under the shadow of the law'.[99] The compensation would be justified on the basis that at a time when the company's residual claimants were the creditors, the directors effectively ignored their interests and transferred resources to the shareholders. In this way *ex post* judicial review effectively acts as the counterbalance to the contractual freedom that is at the heart of the law-and-economics theory.

In sum, it is submitted that a duty to take into account creditor interests is fair as it compensates for things like informational asymmetry, legitimate expectations and the vulnerable positions in which creditors often find themselves *ex ante*. This might well produce some negatives as far as efficiency goes (and discussed in the next section), but these are warranted given the circumstances in which a large portion of creditors find themselves.

---

98 Mokal, R, 'On fairness and efficiency' (2003) 66 MLR 452. Also, see in this regard, Deakin and Hughes, *op. cit.* fn 6 above at 171.

99 Coffee, J, 'The mandatory/enabling balance in corporate law: an essay on the judicial role' (1989) 89 Colum LR 1618 at 1622.

Efficiency

This is a value, the meaning of which was discussed earlier,[100] that is clearly at the centre of law-and-economics thinking. One law-and-economics scholar, Professor Gillian Hadfield, has described efficiency as '[t]he bedrock of gold that has carried economic analysis of law through three decades now'.[101] For many law-and-economics scholars, saying that a legal rule is 'efficient' is tantamount to saying that the benefits of its imposition outweigh the costs. Many commentators take the view that the efficiency goal of maximising the company's value to investors is the principal function of corporate law.[102] In the economic analysis of corporate law there is particular emphasis on the promotion of an efficient capital market;[103] some argue that any expansion of the responsibilities imposed on directors will produce inefficiencies in corporate governance,[104] because requiring directors to consider creditor interests is not appropriate for the most part because of the costs which it can precipitate.

While progressives have mounted critical attacks on what they see as the fixation of the law-and-economics school on efficiency, with some arguing that it promotes greed and self-interest and the acceptance of the idea of 'losers',[105] their principal concern is not that efficiency is a virtue totally without merit, but that efficiency should not be the subject of unrestrained pursuit and used as the appropriate criterion for determining whether a law should be implemented. The progressives do not appear to have any problem with consideration of the efficiency of a rule, provided that it is considered in conjunction with other virtues, such as fairness, morality and justice.[106] Generally this accords with the fact that many scholars would accept that efficiency is a factor in 'any system in which private ordering through the mechanism of contract has a prominent role',[107] but company law cannot be reduced to one normative value, such as efficiency.

Assuming that a duty to creditors fulfils the demands of fairness, what effect then would a duty to creditors have on transaction costs? Many have argued that the imposition of an obligation on directors reduces efficiency, and these are now discussed and evaluated. In particular it has been argued that the imposition of the duty will reduce efficiency in two principal ways.

---

100 See above, pp 290–292.
101 'The second wave of law and economics: learning to surf' in Richardson, M, and Hadfield, G (eds), *The Second Wave in Law and Economics*, 1999, Sydney: Federation Press, p 56.
102 For example, see Black, B, and Kraackman, R, 'A self-enforcing model of corporate law' (1996) 109 Harv L Rev 1911 at 1921.
103 Halpern, P, Trebilcock, M, and Turnbull, S, 'An economic analysis of limited liability in corporate law' (1980) 30 *University of Toronto Law Journal* 117 at 124, 125.
104 *Op. cit.* fn 39 above at 421; van der Weide, *op. cit.* fn 37 above at 84.
105 Campbell, *op. cit.* fn 15 above at 563, 575.   106 See, for example, *ibid* at 576.
107 McNeil, *op. cit.* fn 6 above at 110.

Restricting risk-taking

It is axiomatic that companies need to take risks[108] to prosper. Cheffins has said that 'those in charge will take risks in order to pursue and exploit potentially lucrative projects and ventures'.[109] It is acknowledged that without risks being taken, we would not enjoy some of the things that we enjoy in society today, such as the railways and other technology.[110] One of the principal arguments of those who question the existence of a duty to creditors is, *inter alia*, that directors are placed under greater pressure when making decisions and the company's development might be stifled as directors, rather than taking risks, will adopt a defensive posture, becoming extremely cautious[111] and risk-averse, with the consequence that they either minimise the taking of risks[112] or even refuse to take any at all. The result is that the company ultimately ends up with a lower positive net value, and so efficiency is not fostered.[113] It has been said that a duty to creditors 'results in the inability of directors to take risks with corporate assets for the purposes of extinguishing or minimising the firm's temporary financial distress'[114] and changes the role of directors from an 'active management mode to one of passive asset preservation'.[115] Of concern to the shareholders is that directors will focus on protecting their own positions rather than focusing on what the shareholders

---

108 Risk is defined by Peter A Diamond and Joseph Stiglitz in 'Increases in risk and in risk aversion' (1974) 8 *Journal of Economic Theory* 337 (referred to in Rose-Ackerman, S, 'Risk taking and ruin: bankruptcy and investment choice' (1991) 20 *Journal of Legal Studies* 277 at 283) as 'what increases when a frequency distribution is changed by a mean-preserving spread'.

109 Cheffins, B, *Company Law: Theory, Structure and Operation*, 1997, p 541, Oxford: Clarendon Press. See Flannigan, R, 'The economic structure of the firm' (1995) 33 *Osgoode Hall Law Journal* 105 at 108. Also, see Yeo, V, and Suet Lin, J, 'Insolvent trading – a comparative and economic approach' (1999) 10 *Australian Journal of Corporate Law* 216 at 234.

110 Sealy, L, 'Directors' wider responsibilities – problems conceptual practical and procedural' (1987) 13 Mon U LR 164 at 181. Also, see *op. cit.* fn 62 above at 41–44 and referred to by Telfer, T, 'Risk and insolvent trading' in Rickett, C, and Grantham, R (eds), *Corporate Personality in the 20th Century*, 1998, Oxford: Hart Publishing, pp 127–128. Mannolini, J J, in 'Creditors' interests in the corporate contract: a case for the reform of our insolvent trading provisions' (1996) 6 *Australian Journal of Corporate Law* 14 at 32 regards risk-taking as the 'motor for the entrepreneurial economy'.

111 This was recognised by the Company Law Steering Group in its Final Report for *Modern Company Law for a Competitive Economy*, vol 1, at para 3.19.

112 See Tauke, D, 'Should bondholders have more fun? A re-examination of the debate over corporate bondholders' rights' [1989] *Columbia Business Law Review* 1 at 134.

113 Daniels, R, 'Must boards go overboard? An economic analysis of the effects of burgeoning statutory liability on the role of directors in corporate governance' in Ziegel, J (ed), *Current Developments in International and Comparative Corporate Insolvency Law*, 1994, Oxford: Clarendon Press, p 564.

114 Stilson, A, 'Re-examining the fiduciary paradigm at corporate insolvency and dissolution: defining directors' duties to creditors' (1995) 20 *Delaware Journal of Corporate Law* 1 at, 91. Also, see Yeo and Lin, *op. cit.* fn 109 above.

115 Stilson, *ibid*.

want, namely profit maximisation.[116] This concern might be exaggerated for, as discussed in Chapter 14, it is possible for directors to seek to increase the net value of the company if an entity maximisation approach is implemented when directors are subject to a responsibility to take into account the interests of creditors.

Director caution, so it is argued, might cause directors, out of concern for their personal liability, to place the company into liquidation prematurely,[117] an issue that is discussed in relation to wrongful trading in Chapter 20. Undoubtedly companies might be prematurely placed in liquidation on occasions, but it must not be forgotten that directors could decide to take the company into administration,[118] thereby protecting themselves and ensuring that their company's position will be carefully evaluated by a licensed insolvency practitioner. That evaluation might conclude that the company can be rescued from its problems, and a viable strategy for the carrying on of the business of the company, producing an optimal outcome for all stakeholders, might be implemented.

Too much is often made of the argument that a duty to creditors will stifle the development of a company's business. Admittedly there is empirical evidence, at least from the United States, although only relating to large listed companies,[119] to suggest that directors might be more risk-averse when their companies are struggling financially. It might be said that this evidence is of little relevance to companies that are closely held. The directors of closely held companies are usually also the major shareholders and they are frequently so caught up in the enterprise that they will seek to take every risk possible to extricate their company from its financial malaise. With some closely held firms, shareholder-managers are sentimentally attached to their firms and have often sunk their life savings into them as well as a lot of effort, and they are ready to try anything to keep their enterprise going.[120]

If one accepts, for argument's sake, that there might be some director caution when a company is in difficulty, placing an obligation on directors to take into account the interests of creditors does not automatically mean that directors are hamstrung, unable to take some risks and liable if things do not work out. It is submitted that while the imposition of a duty will necessarily limit risk-taking to some degree, it will not eliminate it. This was

---

116 Glasbeek, *op. cit.* fn 39 above at 432.
117 Yeo and Suet Lin, *op. cit.* fn 109 above at 231; McDonnell, S, '*Geyer v Ingersoll Publications Co*: insolvency shifts directors' burden from shareholders to creditors' (1994) 19 *Delaware Journal of Corporate Law* 177 at 207.
118 Insolvency Act 1986, Sched B1.
119 Lo Pucki, L, and Whitford, W, 'Corporate governance in the bankruptcy reorganisation of large, publicly held companies' (1993) 141 *University of Pennsylvania Law Review* 669.
120 Mokal, *op. cit.* fn 41 above at 353–354.

demonstrated in Chapter 14. The policy of the present UK government[121] is clearly to foster an entrepreneurial culture which involves risk-taking, but the risk-taking is to be responsible risk-taking.[122] There clearly is a line, beyond which one is moving from acceptable and responsible risk-taking into the region of irresponsible risk-taking, perhaps better designated as foolhardiness. Unless personal liability is imposed there might be no barrier to directors engaging in excessive risk-taking.[123] If directors do overstep the mark and indulge in excessive risk-taking, shareholders *might* eventually rein them in, but this is likely to be too late, as the damage to creditors might well be irreparable by that stage. The degree of risk permitted should depend on the actual level of financial difficulty. If the company is financially embarrassed the shareholders and directors might have nothing to lose by embracing a high-risk strategy;[124] the taking of substantial risks could be highly profitable and might 'make the company'. But if the gamble does fail then the ones 'picking up the tab' are the creditors. The directors do not have the right to gamble with what might be seen as the creditors' money. This does not mean that directors must sit on their hands or refrain from seeking to take the company forward; their only obligation is to refrain from taking action that cannot be calculated overall to be in the interests of the creditors. The degree of financial instability and the degree of risk are interrelated[125] and the latter must be determined by the former. Hence, the more obvious it is that the creditors' interests are at risk, the less risk to which the directors should expose the company.[126] So, providing that a director must, in certain cases, have concern for the interests of creditors does not mean that risk-taking is to be totally proscribed. Even in *Winkworth v Edward Baron Development Ltd* [1986] 1 WLR 1512, perhaps the high-water mark as far as decisions go in relation to a duty to creditors, Lord Templeman did not suggest that the

---

121 *Our Competitive Future: Building the Knowledge-Driven Economy* Cm 4176 (1998), at para 2.7; Budget Statement 9 March 1999, [1999] STI 381 in Freedman, *op. cit.* fn 64 above at 320. Also, see the White Paper, *Opportunity for All in a World of Change*, Cm 5052 (2001).

122 Speech of the Rt Hon Stephen Byers MP, then Secretary of State for Trade and Industry, to the British Chamber of Commerce Conference (4 April 2000).

123 Sarra, J, 'Taking the corporation past the "Plimsoll line" – director and officer liability when the corporation founders' (2001) 10 *International Insolvency Review* 229 at 239.

124 Bainbridge, S, 'Much ado about little? Directors' fiduciary duties in the vicinity of insolvency' *Journal of Business and Technology Law*, forthcoming, available at SSRN: www.ssrn.com/abstract=832504 (University of California at Los Angeles Law and Economics Research Paper Series, Paper No 05-26, 2005). Ironically, in such circumstances, absent any duty to take creditors' interests into account, directors might not be liable in taking such action, even though the action is close to reckless, because the shareholders would not complain.

125 See *Kinsela v Russell Kinsela Pty Ltd* (1986) 4 ACLC 215 at 223; *Equiticorp Finance Ltd (in liq) v BNZ* (1993) 11 ACLC 952 at 1017.

126 *Ibid.* Also, see the view of Rao, R, Sokolow, D, and White, D, 'Fiduciary duty á la Lyonnais: an economic perspective on corporate governance in a financially distressed firm' (1996) 22 *The Journal of Corporation Law* 53 at 65.

taking of a risk should be prohibited. Risk-taking should be permitted where the decision to undertake particular activities is made in the informed, good-faith belief that the action taken is likely to enhance the company's long-term wealth, which, as a concomitant, should benefit creditors.[127] We have already seen, in Chapter 14, that if an entity maximisation approach is employed by directors when they are required to consider creditor interests, all risk-taking is not forbidden. It must, however, be consistent with seeking to enhance the net present value of the company.

The view of contractarians might well be that even if one accepts the fact that all risk-taking is not eliminated, a director will have in the back of his or her mind that the decisions which are taken might come under the scrutiny of a court at some point in the future and it is not possible to know what attitude will be adopted by the court. While it is questionable whether substantial numbers of directors are so concerned, let us accept that this might be a legitimate concern that needs to be addressed. The issue of whether or not a duty to creditors has been breached will fall to the courts. Some law-and-economics scholars, such as Cheffins, have serious doubts about whether the courts are suitably qualified to determine what constitutes responsible risk-taking.[128] The learned commentator states:

> Judges throughout their legal career, deal with commercial arrangements which have yielded disappointing outcomes. They correspondingly may develop a bias against risky business strategies which lead them to rely on hindsight to evaluate too critically rapid decisions taken in the light of uncertain events. Moreover, judges have little contact with the business world. As a result, they may well not have the expertise required to ascertain whether managerial conduct is within the bounds of suitable business practice (footnote omitted).[129]

Nevertheless, hitherto, courts, when reviewing what occurred to a company, often some years before the hearing of the breach of duty action, have demonstrated a good deal of understanding of the positions in which directors found themselves at the relevant time. They have not engaged in second-guessing the judgments of directors and, in some ways, they have applied a quasi-business judgment rule,[130] which tends to protect directors. Decisions like *Nicholson v Permakraft (NZ) Ltd* (1985) 3 ACLC 453, *Re Welfab Engineers Ltd* [1990] BCC 600,[131] *Linton v Telnet Pty Ltd* (1999) 30 ACSR 465[132] and *Brady v Brady* (1988) 3 BCC 535 manifest the fact that courts have taken

---

127 Varallo, G, and Finkelstein, J, 'Fiduciary obligations of directors of the financially troubled company' (1992) 48 *The Business Lawyer* 239 at 243.

128 Cheffins, *op. cit.* fn 109 above at 543.   129 *Ibid.*

130 A rule that is employed frequently in the United States and which 'insulates managerial decision-making from shareholder (and judicial) scrutiny': Millon, *op. cit.* fn 18 above at 249.

131 See above p 213.   132 See above pp 160–161.

into account all relevant factors and erred, if anything, in favour of directors. Some of these cases have been discussed already and will not be discussed again. In *Permakraft* the New Zealand Court of Appeal did not hold directors liable for taking action to implement a scheme of reconstruction, as the action was commercially justifiable.[133] The court may, as it did in this case, look at the company's position at the time when directors took the action that is argued to have caused a breach of duty to creditors. Further, in *Facia Footwear Ltd (in administration) v Hinchliffe* [1998] 1 BCLC 218, Sir Richard Scott V-C acknowledged that in continuing trading, the directors were taking a risk, but his Lordship went on to say (at 228), with, it is respectfully suggested, an understanding of business, that 'the boundary between an acceptable risk that an entrepreneur may properly take and an unacceptable risk . . . is not always, perhaps not usually, clear cut'.

It seems that courts take great care to ensure that their assessment of the conduct of the directors is not coloured by hindsight. This is demonstrated clearly by the comments in *Re Sherborne Associates Ltd* ([1995] BCC 40), a wrongful trading case, where the judge warned that it is dangerous to assume that 'what has in fact happened was always bound to happen and was apparent' (at 54). Likewise in *Facia Footwear Ltd*, Sir Richard Scott V-C said that 'the benefit of hindsight was not available to the directors at the time', implying that he was not going to rely on it. The same approach is evident in the director disqualification case, *Secretary of State for Trade and Industry v Gill* [2004] EWHC 933, a case that was concerned with the past activities of a director. Blackburn J made it clear that hindsight should not be employed when dealing with a consideration of the finely balanced judgments of directors. In sum, while judges will, it is acknowledged, often have to wrestle with difficult questions flowing from differing views of what constitutes right action in the circumstances in which companies operated,[134] they are able to make a fair and competent assessment of the actions of creditors.

Imposing a duty to creditors may be no more stringent and stifling of risk-taking than when the wrongful trading provision, s 214 of the Insolvency Act 1986, was introduced. While it might be argued that from a normative perspective s 214 itself is not defensible for the same reasons that contractarians challenge the existence of a duty to creditors (an issue considered in Chapter 20), it is interesting to note that there is no evidence that the advent of s 214 has caused a reduction in the amount of risk-taking that occurs in UK markets.

If one accepts that directors will become more risk-averse if there is a duty

---

133 Directors might be concerned that a court might not see the commercial justification for the action that the directors took, but such a concern applies across the board when considering directors' duties.

134 Allen, W, 'Ambiguity in corporation law' (1997) 22 *Delaware Journal of Corporate Law* 894 at 899.

to creditors, they might be able to safeguard their position at the same time as embracing risky policies, by obtaining insurance. Section 309A of the Companies Act 1985 (clauses 216 and 217 of the Company Law Reform Bill 2005 as introduced to the Commons provide similarly) permits companies to purchase insurance for their officers against liability, *inter alia*, for breach of duty. The marketplace seems to make such insurance available to companies, and, compared with the situation in the United States, it has been available at a reasonable cost, especially if purchased by the company itself.[135] The taking out of such insurance increased during the 1990s,[136] but query whether this will be sustained given the fact that in the past couple of years or so there have been significant price rises in premiums in the UK,[137] in the United States (30 per cent),[138] and Canada,[139] although it has been argued that policies in the UK were under-priced for many years and the increases in the UK have been by way of market correction.[140] The possible drawback for shareholders, if insurance is taken out, is that directors, knowing that they are insured, might adopt unreasonably high-risk policies that are unwise and prejudicial for shareholders as well as possibly causing adverse social costs,[141] such as the loss of jobs if the company fails, and losses to the community in which the company and its workforce are located.

Monitoring and the increase in costs

A second concern, as far as efficiency is concerned, is that imposing a duty to creditors would require directors to have to engage in more monitoring so as to minimise risk, and that, as a necessary concomitant, would increase the company's costs, thereby producing less-efficient use of company resources.[142] Perhaps of greater concern to shareholders is that the monitoring is being done principally to protect the directors, and this increases agency costs without any corresponding increase in profits.[143]

The existence of a duty to creditors will, in many cases, produce an increase

---

135 Finch, V, 'Personal accountability and corporate control: the role of directors' and officers' liability insurance' (1994) 57 MLR 880, especially at 890 and 902. According to Finch, insurance for directors has not been placed under the same stress as insurance for auditors (at 905).

136 *Ibid* at 900.

137 'Directors face liability dilemma', *Corporate Finance*, May 2003, 1 at 1.

138 O'Rourke, M, 'D & O premiums continue to rise' (2003) 50 *Risk Management* 9.

139 Wojcik, J, 'Frequency, severity of claims hike D & O pricing' (2003) 37 *Business Insurance* 35.

140 'Directors face liability dilemma', *Corporate Finance*, May 2003, 1 at 1; Hodge, N, 'UK companies say D & O rate increases don't reflect risks' (2003) 37 *Business Insurance* 4.

141 See the view of Professor Freedman, *op. cit.* fn 64 above at 340–341.

142 For example, *op. cit.* fn 103 above at 125; *op. cit.* fn 113 above at 564; Triantis, G, and Daniels, R, 'The role of debt in interactive corporate governance' [1995] 83 *California Law Review* 1073 at 1079.

143 For some examples of agency costs, see Fama, E, and Jensen, M, 'Agency problems and residual claims' (1983) 26 *Journal of Law and Economics* 327 at 327.

in a company's costs as directors might well have to undertake investigations to ascertain whether their contemplated actions could precipitate insolvency or worsen an already-insolvent position, and these investigations, it may be argued, could occupy inordinate periods of time and perhaps even reduce the company's profitability. This might entail, by way of protection for the directors, the securing of more expert opinions than is normal, undertaking copious checks and even obtaining some valuations of the company's assets, all of which would add to the company's operating costs. These arguments certainly have substance. However, it is suggested that courts will take into account, when assessing the actions of directors, the costs that are associated with undertaking inquiries and realise that companies' finances cannot be used for every check possible and that directors must act quickly in some situations. As demonstrated earlier, British and Commonwealth courts have tended to view the position that confronts directors pragmatically in coming to decisions concerning the conduct of directors.

The argument that monitoring activity is costly and reduces efficiency masks the fact that monitoring is a necessary element of responsible corporate governance and a natural part of directors' functions, whether or not a duty to creditors exists.[144] When considered in the context of protecting shareholders and good corporate governance, monitoring is regarded positively, but it is often regarded negatively if it is considered in the context of protecting creditors. The fact of the matter is that monitoring can provide advantages for all constituencies: for shareholders as well as creditors, employees and so forth. Generally, directors should be reviewing all available material information relating to the financial standing of the company before embarking on any actions that could impact negatively on shareholders. The monitoring process, consisting of acquiring, processing, interpreting and verifying information about the firm,[145] should not necessarily be seen in a negative light as far as shareholders are concerned. Rather than inhibiting efficiency, it might well lead to the identification of improvements that could be made in the company's procedures and profit-making processes which, in turn, could lower costs and increase profits, thereby promoting overall efficiency. Thus, it is possible that the imposition of a supplementary duty on directors might well 'exploit intra-firm economies of scope'.[146] Ultimately, monitoring might well improve the lot of shareholders. Further, there are several recent cases in England alone where courts have emphasised the need for directors to engage in the careful monitoring of their company's affairs (*Norman v Theodore Goddard* [1992] BCLC 1028; *Re D'Jan of London Ltd* [1994] 1 BCLC 561; *Re Barings plc (No 5)* [1999] 1 BCLC 433). Besides, directors should, in the normal course of things, engage in significant monitoring to ensure that their companies adhere to relevant

144 For instance, see the comments in *Re Barings plc (No 5)* [1999] 1 BCLC 433 at 489.
145 Triantis and Daniels, *op. cit.* fn 142 above.   146 Daniels, *op. cit.* fn 113 above at 560.

regulations.[147] Of importance in this context is the fact that directors must be informed so that they can ensure that their company is not engaging in wrongful trading under s 214 of the Insolvency Act.

Even if directors are required to take into account creditor interests, the problem is monitoring how the directors act. It is difficult for shareholders, but it can be even more difficult for creditors as they are not entitled to some of the information to which shareholders are entitled. But does this matter? The fact is that given the present law, the creditors are not able to enforce any breach of duty by creditors. They have to wait for an administrator or a liquidator to be appointed and that person can enforce breaches of duty.

Benefits: the responsibility producing efficient outcomes

If one were only to consider the value of efficiency in determining whether a duty ought to be imposed, there are arguments in favour of the duty's existence. This is notwithstanding the fact that there is going to be some increase in costs for there is an upside as far as efficiency is concerned as the duty is able to provide benefits through the employment of an *ex-post* adjustment. Some benefits were identified in the previous section of the chapter. Some further ones are now identified.

First, it might be argued that limited liability, without the counterbalance of a director's duty to creditors, is inefficient as shareholders are able to 'effect uncompensated transfers of business risks to creditors, thus creating incentives for excessive (inefficient) allocations of social resources to risky economic activities'.[148] Second, a duty imposed on directors can produce benefits in that it could reduce the need for creditors to insist on lengthy and complex contracts when entering into agreements with companies; it would reduce the onus on creditors to formulate protective covenants. Third, it is more efficient if directors have a duty to take into account creditor interests as the imposition of the duty envisages that there will be an *ex-post* adjustment. The existence of the duty has the benefit of reducing both the costs of inquiring about, and assessing, the company's position *ex ante*, and the monitoring costs incurred by creditors *ex post*.[149] So, in cases where creditors commonly build inquiry and monitoring costs into contracts with companies, there is a cost saving that could be passed on to the company, namely the reduction of the cost of the credit given as it would mean that creditors would not need to monitor the affairs of the company, both before and after the making of a contract, so strictly, or at all, and make an assessment about the company's position. So, in the second and third points the duty is a substitute

---

147 Particularly pertinent now is the need for many businesses to engage in monitoring to ensure that there is no breach of environmental legislation.

148 *Op. cit.* fn 103 above, at 126.   149 *Op. cit.* fn 112 above at 28.

for more expensive transaction costs. Costs, such as those associated with negotiating, drafting and executing complex contracts, and those related to the monitoring of a company's affairs, would be saved. This cost saving could be passed on to the company, namely reducing the cost of the credit given.

A fourth benefit of a duty is that it is possible that it might act as a deterrent as far as directors are concerned, and thereby reduce social costs. First, and most obviously, a responsibility on directors to consider creditor interests could have a calming effect on directors and might mean that they refrain from pursuing questionable courses of action, such as high-risk strategies, in an attempt to turn around their companies which could fail and leave the creditors, and others such as the employees, as the losers. Second, it might deter some non-executive directors from passively acquiescing to risky actions proposed by other directors; the former knowing that they might be liable if things go awry could well be encouraged to be more diligent in their monitoring of the activities of executive directors. Third, the concern over possible liability might be the necessary counterweight to the pressure of shareholders on directors to embrace risky actions.

The final benefit of the existence of a duty to creditors is that it might cause creditors, on some occasions, to refrain from initiating proceedings against the company, including those leading to liquidation, as they know that if the directors take improper action, failing to consider creditor interests, the directors are likely to be liable for breach of duty.[150] The fact that creditors refrain from instituting proceedings might give directors more time in which to turn around their companies without resorting to virtually gambling with the company's assets. This might have potential benefits not only for creditors, but for the shareholders and other constituencies, such as a company's workforce. But it must be acknowledged that this benefit must be qualified by the findings in the empirical work undertaken by Professors Julian Franks and Oren Sussman, suggesting that often the issue of whether a debtor company in difficulty will be permitted to continue to operate will be a decision for the main bank of the company.[151]

In sum, there are benefits to be had from a duty to creditors. Arguably, the social benefits are capable of outweighing the costs that will be incurred by the imposition of a duty, thereby producing an efficient result. Of course, whether this is strictly correct is an empirical question.

---

150 It is acknowledged that the creditors will have to factor into their decision that the directors might be impecunious by the time the company collapses.

151 Franks, J, and Sussman, O, 'The cycle of corporate distress, rescue and dissolution: a study of small and medium-size companies' (April 2000).

Commentary

Law-and-economics theorists warn that if directors are subjected to any more responsibilities, then inefficiencies will result. Yet there is no clear empirical evidence to support such a conclusion, certainly in relation to small to medium-sized enterprises. There are, undoubtedly, points of substance in the arguments proffered in the law-and-economics literature, but the force of the points are attenuated somewhat by the fact that the theory focuses on large listed public companies, almost to the exclusion of any consideration of the position of closely held companies.[152] Yet around 99 per cent of companies in the UK do not fit into the large listed company mould (Companies House Annual Report for 2004/2005), and this is certainly the case in many other countries. Also, a study of the reported cases indicates that it is in relation to closely held companies that creditors are at most risk.[153] Lastly, the economic arguments focus on creditors such as banks and other institutional lenders, and these are not representative of the vast bulk of creditors. We will return to this later when considering the issue of protection of creditors in the next section of the Chapter.

Creditor protection – is it warranted?

Undoubtedly, a duty owed to creditors by company directors enhances the protection of creditors over and above that which already exists under statute and common law. The critical issue that follows from this is whether creditors should be protected in this way? Many law-and-economics scholars argue that creditors are able to take care of their own interests and do not need any protection other than that which is granted either by existing legislation or by the terms of the contract under which credit is extended. Put another way, the argument is that if creditors are willing to extend credit, then they should ensure that they gain adequate protection through market forces, and insist on either sufficient compensation or some protection in the contract entered into with the company. True to their contractarian roots and their focus on voluntary contracting, law-and-economics scholars have submitted that a person or company is not forced to become a creditor – it is their choice – but if they do they then should seek to ensure that they gain adequate protection through market forces. Consequently, so the argument goes, there are opportunities for creditors to protect themselves adequately, and if a duty to creditors is imposed on directors then creditors are being overprotected. It has been argued that creditors can embrace a number of protective strategies and they are now discussed.

---

152 According to Professor Feldman, the closely held corporation is 'something of an irritant' to the law-and-economics school (*op. cit.* fn 64 above at 331).

153 Worthington, S, 'Directors' duties, creditors' rights and shareholder intervention' (1991) 18 MULR 121 at 139. Also see an American view in Lin, *op. cit.* fn 37 above at 1518.

Security

Security is the most favoured protection for banks and other institutional credit providers.[154] It clearly reduces their financial exposure as they are given a privileged position if the debtor company becomes insolvent. While favoured by banks and other institutional credit providers,[155] security is not a viable option for many creditors, especially smaller ones, as the costs and time involved in organising security could well mean that their profit margins are cut to the bone,[156] and it is likely that they will not be familiar with the necessary arrangements for the taking, and the benefits, of security. Furthermore, these creditors might not have the resources or know-how to undertake the necessary monitoring of a security arrangement, and, in any event, large companies with good credit ratings might well refuse to give security and threaten to go elsewhere for credit.[157] On the other side of the coin, it might well be difficult for companies to find security for creditors, given the fact that companies have usually borrowed substantial sums from banks and other lenders, and they have probably agreed that most, if not all, assets of the company are to be covered by fixed and floating charges granted to lenders. So, the transaction costs of and incidental to, and the time involved in, taking security is likely to count against many creditors availing themselves of this option, even if companies would be willing to grant security.

Guarantees

The point is often made that creditors can insist, before extending credit, that the directors of the debtor company provide personal guarantees in which they covenant to repay the debt of their company if it fails to do so.[158] Frequently, banks and other large credit providers, particularly when dealing with small to medium-sized and undercapitalised companies, will demand that the directors give personal guarantees. In taking this action the creditor is often protected completely, or at least its exposure is significantly reduced. Creditors, other than banks, rarely have the necessary financial muscle to demand guarantees. Most of the points made in the previous section under 'Security' are pertinent to guarantees.

However, it is true to say that where a bank has been given guarantees, smaller creditors are able to 'freeride' on the fact that the directors who have given the guarantees might be deterred from excessive gambling with

---

154 See Cheffins, *op. cit.* fn 109 above at 498.   155 See *ibid.*

156 See Finch, V, 'Directors' duties: insolvency and the unsecured creditor' in Clarke, A (ed), *Current Issues in Insolvency Law*, 1991, London: Stevens, p 90.

157 Finch, V, 'Security, insolvency and risk: who pays the price?' (1999) 62 MLR 633 at 638.

158 For example, see Posner, *op. cit.* fn 36 above at 505.

the creditors' money and this will benefit all creditors.[159] Nonetheless, creditors who cannot demand guarantees may be significantly affected as the directors who gave the guarantees are, in effect, encouraged to prefer those creditors holding guarantees, by paying them before they pay other creditors. If a company were to go into administration or liquidation within six months of the payment of creditors holding guarantees, realistically an administrator or liquidator might be hard-pressed to succeed because of the many problems facing office-holders who wish to challenge preferences under s 239 of the Insolvency Act 1986, if the company gave the preference to a party not connected with the company.[160] The upshot is that perversely the taking of guarantees and subsequent payments pursuant to them will usually be at the expense of the other creditors.

Higher interest rates

One of the fundamental arguments of many from the law-and-economics school is that creditors should undertake a risk assessment of a company before extending credit, and then they will be able to determine what interest rate they need to set so as to ensure that they receive adequate compensation for the risk that they are accepting.[161] In other words, the credit provider builds into the interest charge a percentage for the risk being undertaken, and, normally, the greater the risk, the higher the interest rate.[162] It is acknowledged by contractarians that to the extent that the company takes action that was not anticipated before the providing of credit, the company has been able to get credit at a rate that fails to compensate the creditor fully for the risk that has been assumed.[163] The problem is that even though a creditor has been diligent in assessing risk and setting a price which is thought to be adequate for the credit extended, events following the extension of credit will affect the probability of default and many of these cannot be foreseen.[164] A risk might escalate due to any number of events, such as a benevolent dividend policy, a risky investment policy, the disposal of assets, major changes in market or

---

159 I am indebted for this point to the anonymous referee of my article, 'A theoretical analysis of the director's duty to consider creditor interests: the progressive school's approach' (2004) 4 *Journal of Corporate Law Studies* 87.

160 See Keay, A, 'Preferences in liquidation law: a time for a change' (1998) 2 CfiLR 198. Compare the situation in both the United States and Australia where office-holders have an easier time of it due partially to the fact that these jurisdictions have an objective theory of preference avoidance, while in England a subjective theory applies.

161 For example, see *op. cit.* fn 36 above at 508; *op. cit.* fn 103 above at 128.

162 *Op. cit.* fn 36 above at 501; Cheffins *op. cit.* fn 109 above at 501; van der Weide, *op. cit.* fn 37 above at 47.

163 *Op. cit.* fn 103 above at 125.

164 Professor David Millon, *op. cit.* fn 49 above at 6, states that even if contingencies are foreseeable, the parties might choose not to negotiate about them because their occurrence is remote.

industry conditions,[165] or the subsequent borrowing of funds at high rates of interest. And as Posner notes, it is impossible to compensate creditors for risks that are unpredictable.[166] So, to the extent that a creditor does not foresee an event that impacts on its repayment prospects, such as the company entering a much more risky field of business (and this was not disclosed *ex ante*),[167] or the directors engaging in divergent behaviour post-contract,[168] the creditor is not being compensated fully for the risk that has been adopted.[169]

Notwithstanding the emphasis on the setting of an appropriate interest rate, given the risks involved in extending credit, it appears, and this is conceded by Cheffins,[170] that there is little evidence that creditors charge a higher interest rate when dealing with a limited liability company, compared with other creditors. But the learned commentator then states:

> In other contexts, however, the rate of return which creditors charge varies in accordance with the risk that there will not be full repayment. For instance, banks charge greater interest rates to high-risk corporate borrowers.[171]

It is probably not by accident that banks are referred to here because in the law-and-economics system when creditors are discussed, banks are the main focus. Posner sees the 'consortium of banks' as the paradigm group of creditors.[172] Undoubtedly, banks are creditors who do assess risk and factor the conclusions they reach into the rate charged, but they are hardly representative of all, or even many, creditors. Posner concedes that creditors, other than financiers, labour, generally, under the disadvantage of not being able to appraise credit risks.[173]

Setting an appropriate rate of interest for the supply of credit depends, as Posner acknowledges,[174] on obtaining an accurate view of the risk. Yet the cost of doing so is, for many creditors, often disproportionate to the value of the transaction.[175] Take for instance a trade creditor who agrees to supply timber worth £2,000 to a company. It is highly unlikely that the creditor will

---

165 Fischel, D, 'The economics of lender liability' (1989) 99 Yale LJ 131 at 134.

166 *Op. cit.* fn 36 above at 504–505.   167 A possibility conceded in *ibid* at 508.

168 It has been recognised that it is impracticable and irrational for a creditor to research thoroughly such a critical aspect of the risk: Mannolini, *op. cit.* fn 110 above at 25.

169 In any event, it might be argued that foreseeability is not a sufficiently certain factor to be considered in undertaking a risk assessment: Wishart, D, 'Models and theories of directors' duties to creditors' (1991) 14 NZULR 323 at 336.

170 Cheffins, *op. cit.* fn 109 above at 501.   171 *Ibid.*

172 Posner, *op. cit.* fn 36 above at 522. See Triantis and Daniels, *op. cit.* fn 142 above where the authors focus on banks.

173 Posner, *ibid* at 523.   174 Posner, *ibid* at 508.

175 Landers, J, 'Another word on parents, subsidiaries and affiliates in bankruptcy' (1976) 43 *University of Chicago Law Review* 527 at 529; Bebchuk, L, and Fried, J, 'The uneasy case for the priority of secured claims in bankruptcy' (1996) 105 Yale L J 857 at 885.

assess the risk of non-payment, for if it did then that would probably erode much of the profit that it earns from the transaction. Also, many creditors, such as trade creditors, do not have the expertise or the time to conduct such assessments,[176] which entail obtaining accurate information about the existing and expected assets and liabilities of the company and its debtors.[177] Many trade creditors, even if they could assess risk, do not do so as they have standardised prices and terms of credit.[178] Those creditors that do assess rely on the debtor's past payment history and its tangible assets, but that leaves many components of risk that cannot be estimated.[179] Furthermore, creditors are not always able to access full and up-to-date information and become conversant with all of the relevant facts that determine the price of credit.[180] Yet much of the law-and-economics literature assumes that transactors have full information concerning prices, notwithstanding the fact that those involved in transactions will rarely be in such a position.[181]

Even if current and accurate information that determines risk is available, two points are worth noting. First, different creditors will in fact possess or ascertain different amounts of information, so creditors will be assessing risk on divergent facts. Second, a company's financial position can change rapidly in today's economic climate,[182] with the result that the information on which risk was assessed is rendered meaningless.

Contracts

As the contractarian approach emphasises freedom of contract, it is not surprising to see its proponents arguing that, as creditors can agree to enter into whatever contract they see fit, they are adequately protected.[183] Certainly some creditors who are involved in extending credit will, in their contract with the company, insist upon the inclusion of covenants that circumscribe what the company may do,[184] in order to attempt risk minimisation and to reduce the possible effect of moral hazard, that is managers conducting a company's business in ways that are self-serving, adverse to creditor interests and outside of the expectations that creditors had concerning the behaviour

---

176 Hudson, J, 'The case against secured lending' (1995) 15 *International Review of Law and Economics* 47 at 56.

177 *Op. cit.* fn 36 above at 508.

178 Landers, *op. cit.* fn 175 above at 530; Petersen, M, and Rajan, R, 'The benefits of lending relationships: evidence from small business data' (1994) 49 *Journal of Finance* 3 at 23–25 and referred to in Bebchuk and Fried, *op. cit.* fn 175 above at 886.

179 Landers, *op. cit.* fn 175 above at 531.   180 Cheffins, *op. cit.* fn 109 above at 9.

181 *Ibid* at 9. This is also implied by Posner, *op. cit.* fn 36 above at 523.

182 Ziegel, J, 'Creditors as corporate stakeholders: the quiet revolution – an Anglo-Canadian perspective' (1993) 43 *University of Toronto Law Journal* 511 at 530

183 *Op. cit.* fn 15 above at 562. Also, see Macey, J, and Miller, G, 'Corporate stakeholders: a contractual perspective' (1993) 43 *University of Toronto Law Review* 401 at 406–407.

184 Often referred to as 'restrictive covenants'.

of the controllers.[185] For instance, it might be provided in the contract, in order to prevent claim dilution, that: the company is not to change the nature of its business; the company is to supply to the creditor certain financial information; the company is not to dispose of certain assets; there are constraints on dividend policy and/or on the creation of new debt imposed; there is an acceleration in the payment of the outstanding balance if it is determined that the directors have entered into transactions that would reduce the company's net worth; if funds are loaned, the creditor may place restrictions as to the uses which funds can be put; and the creditor, if a supplier, is to retain title in the goods supplied until payment is made.

But, as most recognise, *ex ante* contracts have their limitations as far as protecting a creditor.[186] As Halpern *et al* have said: 'The difficulty of specifying such constraints in sufficient detail to provide protection against all the possible means by which the corporation could increase the risk to creditors limits the usefulness of such a strategy.'[187] Including particular terms in a contract might safeguard the creditor to some degree, however, it is impossible to draft a contract that encapsulates all of the matters that the parties might want to address and which covers every possible contingency.[188] Contracts often are only as good as the foresight of the parties and their advisers. As Professor Dale Tauke has said:

> The ability of contracting parties to enter into complete contingent claims contracts in the face of complex and uncertain contingencies is limited by the bounded rationality of the parties – the limits of the human mind in comprehending and solving complex problems.[189]

Creditors are not able to anticipate some of the things that a company might do, for example creditors cannot be expected to foresee the fact that directors might invest in risky assets or lend to borrowers with poor credit ratings.[190]

Some creditors, particularly banks,[191] are able to rely on covenants that restrict the activities of companies,[192] in order to make some attempt at

---

185 See, for example, *op. cit.* fn 112 above at 2–3; *op. cit.* fn 17 above at 27–28. Also, see *op. cit.* fn 169 above at 335.

186 *Op. cit.* fn 7 above at 30–31.

187 *Op. cit.* fn 103 above at 125. Also, see McDaniel, M, 'Bondholders and corporate governance' (1986) 41 *Business Lawyer* 413 at 434; *op. cit.* fn 112 above at 16, 21; Flannigan, *op. cit.* fn 109 above at 115; Schwarcz, *op. cit.* fn 41 above at 647, 652.

188 See the comments of Riley, C, in 'Contracting out of company law: section 459 of the Companies Act 1985 and the role of the courts' (1992) 55 MLR 782 at 786 in this regard.

189 *Op. cit.* fn 112 above at 15, fn 28.

190 Ferran, E, 'Creditors' interests and "core" company law' (1999) 20 Co Law 314 at 316.

191 Fraser, J, 'The art of the covenant' (1997) 19 *Inc Boston* 99 at 99–100.

192 The most common financial covenants found in private loan documentation by a study in the mid-1990s were related to balance-sheet gearing, interest cover and minimum tangible net worth (Day, J, and Taylor, P, 'Bankers' perspectives on the role of covenants in debt

minimising risk, such as requiring the company to supply financial information, specifying that the company is not to dispose of certain assets, demanding minimum working capital requirements, or some other cap on the level of corporate activity. Yet an empirical study which examined the implications of accounting-based debt covenant restrictions in the United States found that 15.5 per cent of the companies studied did not have such covenants in their loan contracts,[193] thereby suggesting that a significant number of creditors were: not aware of the use of such covenants; aware of them, but decided not to utilise them; or unable to get the debtor to agree to their inclusion in the credit contract for one reason or another. The last reason could well be the one that is most common in the UK, given the fact that in 1996 the annual Banking Act Report stated that 'many borrowers continued to resist the inclusion of certain loan covenants in documentation'.[194] A study by Professors Gilson and Vetsuypens[195] discovered that, while banks were able to use covenants to influence corporate actions, this was not the case with trade creditors, suggesting one of the following: that trade creditors availed themselves of covenants rarely; that trade creditors had covenants included in contracts, but did not monitor companies sufficiently; or (the least likely) trade creditors did not feel that they could influence the companies to good effect by enforcing the covenants.

An empirical study investigating the use of loan covenants by banks found that banks limited their use of standard contracts, preferring to draft term-specific contracts,[196] but trade, and many other kinds of, creditors did not have the experience or the time to negotiate special terms, or the financial clout of banks to demand such terms.

Admittedly, if banks are able to demand covenants restricting companies, less powerful creditors might be able to 'freeride' on such covenants, that is relying on the efforts of the bank to monitor adherence to the covenants in its contract with the company.[197] Of course, smaller creditors would have to be convinced that the bank is conducting adequate monitoring of the affairs of the company. In any event, the results of a study by Professors Mitchell

---

contracts' (1996) 11 JIBL 201). In another study other common covenants that were found were negative pledges and covenants limiting disposal of assets (Day, J, and Taylor, P, 'Loan contracting by UK corporate borrowers' (1996) 11 JIBL 318 at 322).

193 Duke, J, and Hunt III, H, 'An empirical examination of debt covenant restrictions and accounting-related debt proxies' (1990) 12 *Journal of Accounting and Economics* 45 at 55.

194 See, Hart, J, 'Corporate lenders could do with a bit of discipline' *Evening Standard* (London), 24 May 1996, at 40.

195 'Credit control in financially distressed firms: empirical evidence' (1994) *Washington University Law Quarterly* 1005 at 1010, 1011.

196 *Op. cit.* fn 192 above, 'Loan contracting' at 319.

197 The danger is, as Professor Saul Levmore has noted ('Monitors and freeriders in commercial and corporate settings' (1982) 92 Yale LJ 49 at 49), if freeriding is widespread then this will lead to undermonitoring.

Petersen and Raghuram Rajan seemed to exclude the possibility that suppliers depend on banks to monitor for them.[198] This is probably a realistic position to adopt given the fact that while it has been found that banks do undertake significant monitoring, they use their power and information to transfer risk to trade creditors where debtor companies are in financial stress.[199]

Another critical factor, something that was acknowledged by Coase,[200] is the high cost of entering into formal and widely drawn contracts,[201] which, in turn, drives up the cost of extending credit. Even if a contract is entered into, it might still fail to do the job, probably because directors are likely to resist covenants in the contract that restrict 'their ability to take value-increasing actions'.[202]

Of more of a concern is the fact that the majority of trade creditors, as well as other kinds of creditors, find it difficult to document transactions; they frequently provide goods and services on 'open account' terms without entering into a formal written contract containing agreed terms.[203] Even if trade creditors turned their mind to the issue and were inclined to have a contract drafted, the circumstances surrounding the order and supply of goods or services is often such that it is impracticable to draw up a complete specification of the rights of the parties.[204] An allied point is that creditors often do not have the necessary strength to extract the promises that they would like to get from management.[205]

If a creditor has a restrictive covenant inserted in a contract then it is only any use, in most cases, if the creditor is willing to monitor the affairs of the company. The necessary monitoring can be time-consuming and costly, and even then it might not be sufficient to keep the creditor well informed.[206] Many creditors will not have the resources to carry out necessary monitoring, and if they do they might not have the sophistication to assess any details that are obtained from the company.[207] Again, if a creditor anticipates that it should monitor then it will have to build a cost factor in the price of its credit, because obtaining information and monitoring the affairs of a company are costly undertakings.[208] As Vanessa Finch has pointed out:

198 Petersen, M, and Rajan, R, 'Trade credit: theories and evidence' (1997) 10 *The Review of Financial Studies* 661 at 680.

199 Franks, J, and Sussman, O, 'An empirical study of financial distress of small bank-financed UK companies: a reassessment of english insolvency law' Part 3.2 (7 May 2000).

200 'The nature of the firm' (1937) 4 *Economica* 386 at 391–392.

201 *Op. cit.* fn 17 above at 28; Harvey, D, 'Bondholders' rights and the case for a fiduciary duty' (1991) 65 *St John's Law Review* 1023 at 1037; *op. cit.* fn 7 above at 28.

202 McDaniel, *op. cit.* fn 30 above at 236.   203 Schwarcz, *op. cit.* fn 41 above at 652.

204 Coffee Jr, J, 'Shareholders versus managers: the strain in the corporate web' (1985) 85 *Michigan Law Review* 1 at 84.

205 See Millon, *op. cit.* fn 49 above at 8.

206 See the comments of Professor Cheffins, *op. cit.* fn 109 above at 524.   207 *Ibid* at 523.

208 *Op. cit.* fn 36 above at 508.

Monitoring will be worthwhile if it costs less than the anticipated gain in risk reduction that it produces, where the latter is calculated by multiplying the diminution in the probability of non-payment and the size of the potential non-payment. It follows that small loans will justify only modest levels of monitoring.[209]

Monitoring is only useful if the one monitoring knows what to look for and what action should be taken when something untoward is found. Professional advice will be needed by many creditors, and this will, obviously, drive up the overall costs involved in the extension of credit.

While creditors always have to accept that the post-contractual actions of a company will increase the expected risk of default,[210] it is unfair that creditors are not able to be compensated for this occurrence, and not even usually able to renegotiate the contract when directors engage in action which clearly was not part of the *ex ante* bargain.

Diversifying the risk

If creditors diversify their interests then each debt is only a part of their exposure and will, if default occurs, only impact in a small way on their financial position.[211] The well-known economist lawyers, Judge Frank Easterbrook and Professor Daniel Fischel,[212] adopt such a position, yet implicitly accept that this is an unsustainable generalisation.[213] It is true that some creditors, such as banks, do diversify, but it is not the case for a significant number of creditors, such as many trade creditors, and it is totally inapplicable to other creditors, such as tort victims, employees and customers, as they have no opportunity to diversify.

Insurance

In a perfect capital market creditors could insure the risk that they take with a company. Trade credit insurance could be taken out to protect creditors against the risk of non-payment. But the fact of the matter is that in 2001 it was asserted by the Association of British Insurers that only five per cent of UK trade was credit insured.[214] This could be due to the fact that either creditors do not wish to insure, preferring to take the risk, or insurers might be reluctant to give cover. Many smaller creditors, who, ironically, are the

---

209 'Security, insolvency and risk: who pays the price?' (1999) 62 MLR 633 at 643.
210 Van der Weide, *op. cit.* fn 37 above at 44.   211 Cheffins, *op. cit.* fn 109 above at 502.
212 'Limited liability and the corporation' (1985) 52 *University of Chicago Law Review* 89 at 101.
213 *Ibid* at 107.
214 Posner, M, 'Credit insurance: an overview' *Credit Management*, April 2001, 18 at 19.

ones who need insurance the most as they can be severely harmed by the failure of one or two customers, provide credit in situations where they would not have the opportunity of obtaining insurance. Even if they did have, the cost of credit insurance is rising[215] and the cost element that they would have to build into their price for granting credit would, more often than not, price them out of the market. The stronger creditors, such as financial institutions, who might be able to get insurance, would usually prefer to self-insure.

Is protection from risky conduct really needed?

It has been asserted that creditors might not require protection as directors will not engage in risky conduct because when they return to the market for further credit their companies would be penalised as they would have to pay higher interest rates to obtain credit.[216] Yet this presupposes that the company will return to the market and, even if it does, that potential creditors will be aware of what the company has done and will, accordingly, build in an extra credit cost. It is questionable as to whether these are reasonable presumptions to make. We have already considered the fact that creditors often lack information on which to base their decision to extend credit. Certainly some creditors are likely to give credit in ignorance. Other creditors might, in spite of a company's previous defalcations, extend credit because of the tough competition that exists in the market. Moreover, if a company is in financial difficulty it might reason that if it does not engage in a high-risk strategy the company is doomed and consequently it will never be able to return to the market to get credit,[217] so the high-risk strategy is worth pursuing. In such cases the threat of the imposition of higher interest rates is otiose. Furthermore, directors might be motivated to continue to engage in high-risk dealings as they might receive bonuses and other benefits in the short term. The conclusion to be drawn is that protection of some sort against risky conduct engaged in by directors is required by many creditors.

Commentary

It has been said that 'creditors deal with a company as a matter of bargain, not as a matter of trust, and bargain involves risk'.[218] While this is true to a point, it does not take us far, as all transacting is about risk. But the assumption often made is that creditors are able to take whatever precautions are

---

215 Mandell, M, 'Money's costing more' (2002) 15(4) *Troy* 58 at 58.
216 Goddard, D, 'Corporate personality – limited recourse and its limits' in Rickett and Grantham, *op. cit.* fn 110 above at 27. But, see Fischel, D, 'The economics of lender liability' (1989) 99 Yale L J 131 at 139 where it is argued that reputation is more of a concern for lenders as they will return to the market time and time again.
217 Goddard, *ibid.*   218 Sealy, *op. cit.* fn 110 above at 176.

needed in order to protect their interests given the risk involved.[219] But are the protective measures feasible? The assumption is usually made in relation to banks[220] and other substantial institutions, but the fact of the matter is that a significant number of creditors are not sophisticated or powerful enough to demand terms that will compensate for risk. And there are some creditors, such as involuntary creditors, who do not intend to make a bargain and accept a risk, while others, like customers pre-paying for goods, may have no idea that they are entering into a bargain and taking on the role of creditor. Some creditors have little power and effectively are not engaged in bargaining – they have to extend credit or perish.[221] But many contractarians effectively assume that there is an 'unimpaired bargaining process',[222] when in fact this is not the situation in all or most cases.

There appear to be two main problems of a general nature for creditors. First, there are informational problems. It has been shown from empirical research that where trade creditors are supplying in the same industry, they will usually be able to obtain information, and more cheaply, *ex ante*, than banks.[223] But other trade creditors, not supplying in the same industry, will often be involved in dealings with companies where they will rarely have all the information that is needed to make a determination as to what price they should charge for credit. So, progressive scholars are like to argue that it seems fair that directors should be under a responsibility to consider creditor interests where financial difficulty exists,[224] in order to reduce 'information asymmetries between companies and their creditors'.[225] Even if a creditor is able to include in the contract with a company some restrictions, it might be difficult for the creditor to obtain the necessary information to allow him or her to determine whether the covenant is being adhered to, and unsecured creditors have been assessed as being relatively poor monitors.[226]

---

219 Nicholls, C, 'Liability of corporate officers and directors to third parties' (2001) 35 *Canadian Business Law Review* 1 at 23.

220 For instance, see Lin, *op. cit.* fn 37 above at 1502.

221 See the comments of Professor Lawrence Mitchell in 'Trust', *op. cit.* fn 49 above at 187.

222 Parkinson, J, 'The contractual theory of the company and the protection of non-shareholder interests' in Feldman, D, and Meisel, F (eds), *Corporate and Commercial Law: Modern Developments*, 1996, London: LLP, p 125.

223 See the study by Mian and Smith, 'Extending trade credit and financing receivables' (1994) 7 *Journal of Applied Corporate Finance* 75.

224 Because of this state of affairs Professor Cheffins accepts the need for some kind of regulation (*op. cit.* fn 109 above at 9).

225 *Op. cit.* fn 7 above at 28. Information asymmetries demonstrate market failures and social costs may result: Lipsey, R, 'Globalization and national government policies: an economist's view' in Dunning, J (ed), *Governments, Globalization and International Business*, 1999, Oxford: OUP, p 73 and referred to in Christensen, S, and Grinder, B, 'Justice and financial market allocation of the social costs of business' (2001) 29 *Journal of Business Ethics* 105 at 106.

226 Schwartz, A, 'Security interests and bankruptcy priorities: a review of current theories' (1981) 10 *Journal of Legal Studies* 1 at 11 fn 28.

Some empirical work has demonstrated that bank monitoring can reduce some information asymmetries,[227] although it has been asserted that bank monitoring is not always as beneficial as one might think.[228]

Second, there are several impracticalities facing creditors. When assessing what interest rates to set, it is impracticable and irrational for a creditor to research thoroughly a critical aspect of the risk that is being taken, such as things like the chances of the directors engaging in divergent behaviour post-contract,[229] a benevolent dividend policy, or a risky investment policy. Some things cannot be predicted and so it is impossible to compensate creditors for risks that are unpredictable.[230] Also, prescribing an appropriate rate of interest for the supply of credit depends[231] on obtaining an accurate view of the risk, but the cost of doing so is, for many creditors, such as trade creditors, often disproportionate to the value of the transaction.[232] A study on lending relationships by Petersen and Rajan in 1994 found that many trade creditors do not assess risk as they have standardised prices and terms of credit, and based on industry practice.[233] The learned researchers found from their study that where trade creditors are involved the terms on which they extend credit do not change to reflect the credit quality of the buyer/debtor. In a subsequent study Petersen and Rajan affirmed that 'credit terms are usually invariant to the creditor quality',[234] but indicated that the results of their study suggested that some trade creditors indulged in price discrimination. It has been suggested that those creditors who do assess risk rely on the debtor's past payment history and its tangible assets, but that leaves many components of risk that cannot be estimated,[235] and any information obtained can often be out of date.

A further problem is that, while creditors might take a raft of measures designed to protect themselves, the measures are unlikely to prevent some director improprieties, such as the expropriation of assets. Take the payment by the company of creditors who are not connected with the company. These payments usually cannot be recovered as preferences by an administrator or liquidator for a variety of reasons.[236] And there is often little that creditors can do *ex ante* to prevent this type of activity occurring. As it is not possible to predict the future, it is appropriate for there to be some kind of *ex post* adjustment.[237]

---

227 See, Low, S, Gorfeld, L, Hearth, D, and Rimbey, J, 'The link between bank monitoring and corporate dividend policy: the case of dividend omissions' (2001) 25 *Journal of Banking and Finance* 2069.

228 *Op. cit.* fn 191 above at 100.   229 Mannolini, *op. cit.* fn 110 above at 25.

230 Posner, *op. cit.* fn 36 above at 504–505.   231 *Ibid* at 508.

232 Landers, *op. cit.* fn 175 above at 529; Bebchuk and Fried, *op. cit.* fn 175 above at 885.

233 Petersen and Rajan, *op. cit.* fn 178 above at 23–25.

234 *Op. cit.* fn 198 above at 664.   235 Landers, *op. cit.* fn 175 above at 531.

236 See *Re M C Bacon Ltd* [1990] BCLC 324; also see *op. cit.* above fn 160.

237 Easterbrook, F, 'Two agency-cost explanations of dividends' (1984) 74 Am Econ Rev 650 at 655.

There are a number of reasons why a large percentage of creditors fail to protect themselves adequately. These are: ignorance of the ramifications of dealing with a company; concern that a competitor might be able to provide the supplies or the funds if a decision to supply or lend is not made speedily, and, consequently, there is a lack of time in which to undertake checks; taking action is costly; and the nature of risk changes over time. It is also clear that some creditors do not have the opportunity, given the circumstances in which they are extending credit, to avail themselves of protective measures. For instance, a supplier of building materials to a builder often does not have a chance to undertake a company search or a credit check because the goods have to be supplied forthwith. Any delay in providing supplies could see the company taking its business elsewhere.

It is sometimes suggested that creditors have the power to demand or even to influence directors to take a particular course of action, but this can be overstated. In some cases, directors are able, in effect, to hold creditors hostage to the threat of an insolvent administration,[238] such as liquidation, which might well see creditors receive little or nothing from the company. The ploy that directors might embrace is that they say to creditors, in effect, that if they are not given room to continue to proceed in the way that they have proposed to go, the directors will 'pull the plug' and take the company into liquidation, which will probably produce little or no return for unsecured creditors.

One of the fundamental problems for proponents of law and economics is that they hold to the view that in a perfect market, that is, where all creditors are apprised of all relevant information, there are no transaction costs and no uncertainty, creditors will be adequately compensated for the level of risk which they are bearing. But it is axiomatic that there is no such thing as a perfect market.[239]

Tort victims, customers and trade creditors are to be contrasted with the creditors who are largely the focus of the law-and-economics scholars, namely large institutional creditors, like banks.[240] Banks are able to demand guarantees from directors and can take the time, and go to the expense, of having a substantial contract drafted to protect their interests. Also, they have the necessary experience in their own organisation to advise on how to structure a particular transaction, something that is not available to most small-medium creditors. Little or no attention is paid by law and economics to different kinds of creditors.[241] Absent creditors that are in the strict sense 'involuntary', who are often addressed separately, law-and-economics analysis tends to lump all creditors together. But, there are different factors affecting different creditors.

---

238 *Op. cit.* fn 126 above at 72.   239 See Armour, *op. cit.* fn 24 at 357.

240 Contractarian theory has been criticised because it is said to obtain its view by 'reshaping the real world to fit the paradigm': Bratton, *op. cit.* fn 6 above at 456.

241 Implied in Freedman, *op. cit.* fn 64 above at 330.

Having referred to the fact that different kinds of creditors exist, something adverted to in Chapter 2, it is now appropriate to examine in brief the position of various kinds of creditors of companies in the context of the protective measures discussed earlier.

Types of creditor

Involuntary creditors

An Achilles' heel of the law-and-economics school is that its theory is unable to take into account involuntary creditors, such as those injured by the company's tortious acts, and even many voluntary creditors. Posner recognises the problem with involuntary creditors, but offers no solution.[242] Easterbrook and Fischel argue that directors have an incentive to insure against such claims as these creditors could cause serious damage to the company's financial position.[243] But, with respect, this does not deal with the issue. There is no compulsion to insure, except in some limited circumstances where the law requires it, and if directors do not insure, and the company is insolvent, the creditors are going to be, in most cases, left with a useless claim.

Involuntary creditors are particularly vulnerable because they have no chance to consider risk and to negotiate price or any forms of protection; they are not able, unlike voluntary creditors, to adjust their behaviour[244] and they unknowingly bear a disproportionately high risk.[245] While many victims of torts committed by companies in the UK are fully covered as a result of compulsory insurance requirements, for instance persons injured in road accidents and in the workplace, others such as persons affected by defective products or hazardous industries might not be.[246] It has been argued that companies ought to be required to obtain liability insurance against claims in tort to the extent that those claims cannot be satisfied from company assets.[247]

---

242 Posner, R, *Economic Analysis of Law*, 3rd edn, 1986, Boston: Little Brown, pp 368–372; *op. cit.* fn 36 above at 505.

243 *Op. cit.* fn 62 above at 52–54. The learned authors, Easterbrook and Fischel, in fact say elsewhere that voluntary creditors can protect themselves by seeking higher returns ('Limited liability and the corporation' (1985) 52 *University of Chicago Law Review* 89 at 105), but as already stated in this article of theirs, such creditors often do not know that they need to seek higher returns.

244 Leebron, D, 'Limited liability, tort victims and creditors' (1991) 91 Colum L R 1565 at 1602.

245 Byrne, M, 'An economic analysis of directors' duties in favour of creditors' (1994) 4 *Australian Journal of Corporate Law* 275 at 278.

246 If a company engages in hazardous activities and causes damage to the environment, it is not only individuals who might suffer loss, as councils, and of course ultimately the community, have to pay for the clean-up if companies end up hopelessly insolvent. See *Re Celtic Extraction Ltd (in liquidation)* [2000] 2 WLR 91; [1999] 4 All ER 684, CA.

247 Pettet, B, 'Limited liability – a principle for the 21st century?' in Freeman, M, and Halson, D R (eds), (1995) 48 *Current Legal Problems* 125.

While this suggestion would probably be criticised for being an inefficient resolution of the problem, as it would increase company costs, it has its attractions. But, one wonders if it is practically workable as insurers might be reluctant: to insure those companies that are the very ones (small and with high risks) that are most in need of insurance; to provide a reasonable amount of cover; and to grant insurance without strict exclusion clauses.[248]

Employees

Employees in a sense lend their human capital to their firms and to the extent that they are owed money for wages and other benefits, they are creditors of the company.[249] Little regard is given to these creditors who, apart from perhaps executives and the most senior managers: cannot diversify their risk like some creditors; rarely can undertake a risk assessment exercise before accepting employment; will not have the chance to demand a higher wage to compensate themselves for the risk of not being paid; and cannot (even if they were aware of any risks) include, in order to protect themselves, specialist terms in their employment contract. Halpern *et al* acknowledge this when they say that:

> Amongst corporate creditors, employees, as a class, probably face the most severe informational disabilities, have the least ability to diversify risk of business failure, and may have the strongest equity argument (in terms of relative capacity) to absorb losses.[250]

Trade creditors

The issue of trade creditors is a significant matter. In a US study, Elliehusen and Wolken found in 1993 that trade creditors made up 20 per cent of all non-bank, non-farm small businesses' liabilities, as well as the fact that 80 per cent of all companies used trade credit. Thus, trade credit represents a significant part of corporate liabilities[251] and the use of trade credit increases when companies are credit rationed.[252] In 2000 Franks and Sussman reported that trade credit in the UK is second only to credit obtained from the

---

248 *Op. cit.* fn 157 above at 654–655.   249 *Op. cit.* fn 103 above at 131.
250 *Ibid* at 149.
251 'An empirical investigation into motives for demand for trade credit' Federal Reserve Board Study, 1993, and referred to in Jain, N, 'Monitoring costs and trade credit' (2001) 41 *The Quarterly Review of Economics and Finance* 89 at 90 and Atanasova, C, and Wilson, N, 'Borrowing constraints and the demand for trade credit: evidence from UK panel data' July 2001, Leeds University Business School.
252 Biais, B, and Gollier, C, 'Trade credit and credit rationing' (1997) 10 *The Review of Financial Studies* 903 at 906.

company's main bank,[253] a finding that accords with the position in the US.[254] Trade creditors will normally be owed a large portion of a firm's unsecured debts.[255] As mentioned earlier, trade creditors often find it difficult to document transactions, for frequently they provide goods and services on 'open account' terms without entering into a formal written contract containing agreed terms.[256] Complicating things further is that the circumstances surrounding the order and supply of goods or services is often such that it is impracticable to draw up a complete specification of the rights of the parties.[257]

Of course, much of the discussion concerning involuntary creditors and employees is equally applicable to the majority of trade creditors. Absent the largest companies that are within this category, these creditors are likely to lack the technical knowledge required to assess risk effectively,[258] and are usually unable to insist on detailed contracts or other mechanisms to protect themselves. If trade creditors insist on more protection than the market will bear, such as charging high interest rates or setting tough terms for repayment, they risk losing customers to other traders who are willing to take more risks in extending credit to limited liability companies. Some trade creditors are major companies with a huge amount of turnover, and they might well be able to demand terms of trade and maybe supply subject to retention of title clauses. Notwithstanding this, they will still be limited by the market and might lose customers if they require terms that are perceived as being too tough. Trade creditors often lack the necessary bargaining power to obtain contractual concessions from companies because the market is competitive and a company will probably have little difficulty, in most lines of business, in finding another trading partner who will not demand concessions. Also, as Posner concedes,[259] because trade creditors are not extending the same amounts of credit as banks are, it is not so likely they will negotiate explicit terms of credit, and default is likely to have a greater impact on them compared with financiers.

Unlike banks and other lenders, who are able to diversify their operations and, therefore, their risk, by providing finance to creditors in different industries, many trade creditors have significant limitations in this regard. Yet some

253 *Op. cit.* fn 199 above.
254 Rajan, R, and Zingales, L, 'What do we know about capital structure: evidence from international data?' CRSP Working Paper, University of Chicago, 1993 and referred to by Petersen, M, and Rajan, R, 'Trade credit: theories and evidence' (1997) 10 *The Review of Financial Studies* 661 at 661.
255 This is certainly the case in the United States (US Department of Commerce, Quarterly Financial Report for Manufacturing, Mining and Trade Corporations, 1996, at 4) and referred to in de Barondes, R, 'Fiduciary duties of officers and directors of distressed corporations' (1998) 7 *George Mason Law Review* 45 at 97) and is likely to be the case in the UK.
256 Schwarcz, *op. cit.* fn 41 above at 652.   257 *Op. cit.* fn 204 above at 84.
258 *Op. cit.* fn 190 above at 316.   259 *Op. cit.* fn 36 above at 505.

commentators, it is respectfully submitted, completely miss the point and maintain that the only suppliers in need of assistance are 'those who are induced by vendee firms to make firm-specific investments; that is those suppliers who make investments in specialized capital assets that have little value except in producing particular goods for a particular purchaser'.[260] With respect, while suppliers who are so tied to a company that the company's financial demise could cause terminal harm to them are obvious examples of creditors who warrant protection, protection is needed by a much wider range of trade creditors. Take for example those tradespersons who work as subcontractors for one or two companies, particularly in the building industry. If the building companies collapse, then these tradespersons might well be unable to pay their own creditors as they are so reliant on the companies. Another example is where a supplier invests in new plant and equipment exclusively to supply one company.[261] Such a supplier can be placed in a very vulnerable position if its trading partner collapses.

It is said that creditors may investigate potential debtors by obtaining information, such as financial data and details of past credit history, in order to ascertain the probability of default and to determine on what terms, if any, credit should be extended.[262] This is undoubtedly correct in theoretical terms, but in practice this is rarely the case for many trade creditors, even the more sophisticated,[263] rely on being able to supply customers promptly.

It has been asserted by one commentator,[264] after acknowledging the difficulties that trade creditors have in extracting contractual concessions or assessing risk, that trade creditors would not be concerned whether directors were required to take their interests into account, as they are short-term creditors 'who can quickly respond to bad firm behaviour by taking their business elsewhere'.[265] Unfortunately, this is typical of the gross overstatements that pervade some works that have contributed to the law-and-economics literature. Some trade creditors will be in the position just adverted to, but, as mentioned earlier, many are owed such large sums by, and may be so dependent on trade with, certain companies that they are unable to do what is suggested, that is to cut their losses and run.

Customers

Customers who pay deposits or even pay in full for something that must be ordered from a company are creditors,[266] even though it would be a rare case where customers saw themselves in such a light, and would not, consequently,

---

260 Van der Weide, *op. cit.* fn 37 above at 52–53.
261 Kelly and Parkinson, *op. cit.* fn 42 above at 127–128.
262 Cheffins, *op. cit.* fn 109 above at 74.   263 *Op. cit.* fn 176 above at 56.
264 Van der Weide, *op. cit.* fn 37 above.   265 *Ibid*, 49.
266 Also included in this class are those who paid for airline tickets well before the flight date and the airline went into some form of insolvent administration and the ticket was not honoured.

consider taking any safeguards. They can be regarded in the same way as those who supply goods on credit to companies.[267] Yet customers are in an even weaker position, having little or no chance to protect their position.[268] Customers who pay for goods, either fully or partially are involuntary creditors. Unless they provide partial or full payment, they do not get the goods. The riposte to this will be that customer have a choice and can go elsewhere if they do not wish to pay. This is theoretically true, save for markets where there are virtual monopolies, but the fact of the matter is that the idea of choice is illusory, as virtually all retailers adopt the same strategy. In reality customers do not have a choice of whether they will or will not pay.

Summary

Clearly, there are significant differences in power among creditors, such that even if self-protection measures were feasible, disparities in bargaining power would prevent creditors from obtaining effective protection. These disparities lead to bargaining outcomes that are substantially unfair.[269] It might be argued that 'disparities in access to information and the ability to use it would appear to be central to the recognition of a duty'.[270] Frequently, in the finance and law-and-economics literature, protection is discussed with only banks and substantial institutions in mind.[271] These creditors are usually able to avail themselves of defensive strategies to limit their financial exposure should their corporate debtors default in repaying what is owed, but many creditors are simply unable to do so, and banks and others of their ilk are not typical of a large portion of the creditors of a company.

Creditors have no right to initiate proceedings

The existence of an obligation of directors to creditors has been criticised on the basis that it is a nonsense,[272] because 'a right without a remedy is

---

267 Insolvency Law Review Committee, *Insolvency Law & Practice* (commonly referred to as the 'Cork Report' after its chair, Sir Kenneth Cork) Cmnd 8558, 1982, para 1052.
268 *The Protection of Consumer Prepayments: A Discussion Paper* (OFT, 1984), at para 5.11 and referred to in Prentice, D, 'Corporate personality, limited liability and the protection of creditors' in Rickett and Grantham, *op. cit.* fn 110 above at 102.
269 Millon, *op. cit.* fn 49 above at 9.
270 Lipson, J, 'Directors' duties to creditors: volition, cognition, exit and the financially distressed corporation' (2003) 50 UCLA L Rev 1189 at 1238. Also, see *op. cit.* fn 99 above at 1619 fn 1.
271 For instance, see Cheffins, *op. cit.* fn 109 above at 501.
272 Sealy, *op. cit.* fn 110 above at 177. Sealy points to s 309 of the Companies Act 1985. Also, see Hartman, R, 'Situation-specific fiduciary duties for corporate directors: enforceable obligations or toothless ideals' (1993) 50 *Washington and Lee Law Review* 1761 at 1767 commenting in the wake of *Credit Lyonnaise Bank Nederlander NV v Pathe Communications Corp* 1991 Del Ch LEXIS 215; (1992) 17 *Delaware Journal of Corporate Law* 1099.

worthless'.[273] Provided that it cannot be argued that directors owe a direct duty to creditors, this is a fair point to a degree, and was considered in Chapter 15. While creditors cannot take legal proceedings against directors who fail to meet their obligation, the fact that the obligation exists might serve to cause directors to take fewer risks as they administer the affairs of their company. It has been argued that even where a duty is not directly enforceable it can influence managerial behaviour by affecting social norms.[274] Also, creditors might still benefit from liquidators or other office-holders taking proceedings for breach of duty as they have done on many occasions, so the argument that no remedy exists for creditors does not mean that imposing a responsibility on directors to creditors is otiose.

Commercial morality

There is a continual need for our law to strike a balance between two conflicting values, namely the need to develop commercial enterprise, on the one hand, and the need to ensure that there is commercial morality, on the other.[275] The former has been well served by the concept of limited liability. Imposing a responsibility on directors to creditors enhances commercial morality, something that, arguably, has been declining for many years. Too often the doctrine of limited liability, which shifts the risk of failure from the shareholders to the creditors,[276] is seen to be a tool of the unscrupulous entrepreneur, and this causes lack of confidence in the marketplace and amongst the public in general. The duty to take account of creditors' interests mitigates the shift to some extent. Limited liability still, in effect, rules but reliance on it is somewhat tempered by directors knowing that they might be held liable should they act improperly as far as creditor interests are concerned at a time when their company is in financial straits. Allied to this is the notion that a duty to creditors acts as a stick to get directors to raise their level of conduct and to encourage them to consider, more carefully perhaps, the effects of action that they are proposing to take when their company is in financial strife.[277] This will, in turn, promote corporate social responsibility, a major concern of many theorists, and particularly those in the progressive school.[278]

When a company is insolvent or near to that state, directors might find themselves subject to a conflict of interest, namely some feeling of responsibility to the creditors, on the one hand, and a desire to protect their

---

273 McDaniel, *op. cit.* fn 30 above at 309.
274 Chaver, and Fried, J, 'Managers' fiduciary duty upon the firm's insolvency: accounting for performance creditors' (2002) 55 *Vanderbilt Law Review* 1813 at 1814, fn 4.
275 See Rajani, S, 'Enterprise culture v stakeholder protection' (2001) 17 I L & P 121.
276 Posner, R, *Economic Analysis of Law*, 4th edn, 1992, Boston: Little Brown, p 394.
277 Just as s 214 of the Insolvency Act 1986 is intended to do: Mokal, *op. cit.* fn 41 above at 363.
278 For example, see Mitchell, 1990, *op. cit.* fn 44 above at 1168.

reputation (and possibly their financial investment) by seeking to pull the company out of the mire, on the other hand. Absent a duty to creditors, it is more than likely that the latter interest will hold sway. But the existence of a duty might well encourage a greater degree of morality in decision-making by directors, rather than focusing on self-interest.

Along the lines discussed in this section, are the comments of Cooke J *Permakraft* when he said (at 459) that:

> It [limited liability] is a privilege healthy as tending to the expansion of opportunities and commerce, but it is open to abuse. Irresponsible structural engineering – involving the creating, dissolving and transforming of incorporated companies to the prejudice of creditors – is a mischief to which the courts should be alive.

The creditors as residual claimants

As mentioned in Chapter 12, traditionally the shareholder is the sole residual risk-bearer of a company's failure. But this is not the case when a company is suffering financial stress. The predominant view in case law in all jurisdictions is that if a company is in various states of financial difficulty the creditors warrant some special consideration.[279] It has been said that if the company is insolvent, in the vicinity of solvency, or embarking on a venture which it cannot sustain without relying totally on creditor funds, the creditors are residual claimants. At this point, the creditors may be seen as the major stakeholders in the company,[280] as the company is effectively trading with the creditors' money, and as a result the directors have an obligation not to sacrifice creditor interests.[281] Certainly when one gets to the point where a company is in financial difficulty, it has been argued that duties should take into account both shareholders and creditors alike because 'there is no fundamental difference between debt and equity claims from an economic perspective'.[282]

As explained in Chapter 12,[283] directors will often favour actions which

---

279 For example, in *Standard Chartered Bank v Walker* [1992] BCLC 603, Vinelott J was willing to restrain the conduct of shareholders in a company that was sliding into insolvency because the conduct would destroy company property and that would prejudice creditors.

280 *Kinsela v Russell Kinsela Pty Ltd* (1986) 4 ACLC 215 at 221. See Goode, R, *Principles of Corporate Insolvency Law*, 2nd edn, 1997, London: Sweet & Maxwell, p 455; McDonnell, *op. cit.* fn 117 above at 185; de Barondes, *op. cit.* fn 255 above at 63; Sarra, *op. cit.* fn 123 above at 234–235.

281 Sarra, *ibid* at 235. See Moffat, M, 'Directors' dilemma – an economic evaluation of directors' liability for environmental damages and unpaid wages' (1996) 54 *University of Toronto Faculty of Law Review* 293 at 302.

282 Easterbrook, F, and Fischel, D, 'Close corporations and agency costs' (1986) 38 *Stanford Law Review* 271 at 274 fn 8.

283 See p 178.

involve more risk when companies are in difficulty, and consequently the position of creditors warrants some form of fiduciary protection, whereby the directors become accountable principally to the creditors (*Re Pantone 485 Ltd* [2002] 1 BCLC 266 at 285–286). And the closer a company gets to insolvent liquidation, the greater the incentive to engage in risky activity.[284] The shareholders have little or nothing to lose by such a gamble, and could well support it,[285] especially where the company is highly leveraged,[286] as they have already lost the money that they invested in the company and they cannot be pursued by creditors because of the concept of limited liability.[287] A venture, however risky, could conceivably turn the company around and provide the shareholders with some return in their capacity as the residual claimants, but such action, if it failed, would see the creditors suffer an even greater loss as they would be the ones to lose out if the company collapses.[288] Creditors will receive the same sum irrespective of how well the company performs, therefore they have the most to lose from risky actions being taken by directors.[289] This situation provides a 'heads I win, tails you lose'[290] situation for shareholders and managers of companies in relation to creditors.

The issue of gambling with company funds may, in some cases, be of greater significance in relation to closely held companies (the types of companies that are most frequently, according to the case law, the subject of actions for breach of duty to creditors), where the directors are usually also the major shareholders.[291] They are frequently so involved with the enterprise that they will seek to take every risk possible to extricate their company from its financial malaise. With some closely held firms, shareholder-managers are sentimentally attached to their firms and have often sunk their life savings into them as well as a lot of effort, such that they are ready to try anything to

---

284 Mokal, *op. cit.* fn 41 above at 347; Armour, *op. cit.* fn 24 above.

285 As opposed to when the company is clearly solvent. See Cheffins, *op. cit.* fn 109 above at 498.

286 McDaniel, *op. cit.* fn 187 above at 419.

287 While creditors always have to accept the risk that the post-contractual actions of a company will increase the expected risk of default (van der Weide, *op. cit.* fn 37 above at 43, 44), it is unfair that creditors are not able to be compensated when directors engage in action which clearly was not part of the *ex-ante* bargain, and may in some ways be regarded as improper activity. The fact of the matter is that creditors cannot be expected to foresee every action that directors take.

288 *Kinsela v Russell Kinsela Pty Ltd* (1986) 4 ACLC 215, 223. See Thomson, D, 'Directors, shareholders and insolvency: a fiduciary duty or a duty not to oppress?' (2000) 58 *University of Toronto Faculty of Law Review* 31 at 33.

289 McDonnell, *op. cit.* fn 117 above at 190.

290 Rose-Ackerman, *op. cit.* fn 108 above at 306.

291 In a study of the Savings and Loans industry in the United States, it was found that risk-taking is positively related to managers' interests in the company (Esty, B, 'Ownership concentration and risk-taking the S & L industry' (Working Paper, Harvard Business School, 1993) and referred to by Esty, B, 'Organizational form and risk-taking in the savings and loan industry' (1997) 22 *Journal of Financial Economics* 25 at 29).

keep their enterprise going.[292] Typically with closely held companies there will be a bank, as the major creditor, with not only charges over company property, but personal guarantees from the directors, and the holding of guarantees will often be sufficient to temper the incidence of gambling. However, this might not help other creditors as the case law, such as *Re Agriplant Services Ltd (in liq)* [1997] 2 BCLC 598; [1997] BCC 842, suggests that commonly directors will take steps to ensure that the creditor(s) holding guarantees are catered for, usually at the expense of the other creditors.

In larger companies, independent non-executive directors might be able to prevent the taking of excessive risks as their reputation might well be severely tarnished if the company collapses badly as a result of such risk-taking. The same could be said for executive directors in large companies whose chances of securing another post might be reduced if a collapse occurred.[293]

Conclusion

This chapter has evaluated the concept of a duty to creditors from the viewpoint of both law-and-economics and progressive theorists. It has accepted that efficiency is an important value to be considered in evaluating any law, but it has suggested that fairness is a value that also needs to be taken into account and that that value dictates that directors should consider creditor interests when their companies are in financial difficulty. An *ex post* adjustment, such as examining whether directors acted in the interests of creditor at a time when the company was in financial difficulty, is fairer in that it eliminates the risks endemic to *ex ante* action, and it is based upon what has actually occurred, not what everyone guesses might occur.[294]

The primary arguments that are often put in resisting the imposition of a duty to creditors, namely that it will reduce efficiency and it is not needed as creditors are able to protect themselves though other means, were discussed and while it was acknowledged that the imposition of a duty will cause some inefficiencies, namely that directors' risk-taking will probably have to be tempered when their companies are in difficulty, and there will be an increase in some transaction costs, it was suggested that these are worthwhile sacrifices to ensure that a fair outcome results for many creditors who are not able to negotiate sufficient protection in dealing with companies. Also, it has been

---

292 Mokal, *op. cit.* fn 41 above at 353–354.

293 Professor John Coffee Jr emphasises this point, but recognises that senior managers frequently have much of their personal wealth tied up in their companies: *op. cit.* fn 204 above at 17–18. Easterbrook and Fischel (*op. cit.* fn 4 above at 1441) acknowledge the same point and also note (at 1420) that in many cases managers are going to act in the interests of the shareholders because the former enjoy sizeable salaries and the benefits of office.

294 See McDaniel, *op. cit.* fn 30 above at 245. Professor Stephen Bainbridge concedes that with contractarianism, 'the best we can hope for is an educated guess about the rule most actors would choose if they could bargain' (*op. cit.* fn 27 above at 869).

suggested that the imposition of a duty does produce some efficiencies, such as the reduction of the costs involved in extending credit, drafting contracts and inquiring into the company's position *ex ante*, and ensuring that there is better monitoring of the financial health and other affairs of companies.

The chapter has suggested that while banks and other substantial creditors are able to protect themselves adequately, this is not the case for some creditors, such as employees, customers, involuntary creditors and many in the ranks of trade creditors whose future is left, in many cases, at the mercy of the competence and integrity of the directors of their corporate debtors. Without responsibility being visited on directors many creditors would be sacrificed on the altar of (unreasonable) risk-taking. It was concluded that many creditors are, whether because of time and costs, unable to undertake any or a proper risk assessment. Moreover, it is doubtful whether such creditors are able to demand the kinds of protection that would safeguard themselves against the risks to which they might be exposed.[295] But even if they are able to do so, directors can embark on very risky post-contractual activity, of which creditors will not be aware because they do not have the wherewithal to monitor the activities of companies, and, as a consequence, the price of the credit does not reflect the risk taken. As it is likely that there will be creditors involved in dealings with companies that will rarely have all the information that is needed to make a determination as to what price they should charge for credit, it seems fair that directors should be under a responsibility to consider creditor interests where financial difficulty exists,[296] in order to reduce 'information asymmetries between companies and their creditors'.[297]

Placing a responsibility on directors to creditors can provide *ex post* compensation for creditors where directors have not acted appropriately at a time when their company has experienced financial problems. In doing this it also fosters 'one of the social/political values which is thought to imbue the law', namely making individuals (directors in this case) responsible for their actions, thus producing the situation where the goal of efficiency and acceptability of the legal system is enhanced.[298]

It has been demonstrated that there are several arguments that support the existence of a responsibility to creditors, namely: protecting creditors; promoting distributive fairness; fostering commercial morality; and benefiting creditors in their role as residual claimants to the company's property. It has been stated that this provides a fairer state of affairs as it enables the reasonable and legitimate expectations of creditors, at the time of contracting, to be

---

295 See Prentice, *op. cit.* fn 268 above at 104.

296 Because of this state of affairs Professor Cheffins accepts the need for some kind of regulation (*op. cit.* fn 109 above at 9).

297 Whincop, M, 'Taking the corporate contract more seriously: the economic cases against, and a transaction cost rationale for, the insolvent trading provisions' (1996) 5 *Griffith Law Review* 1 at 28.

298 *Op. cit.* fn 39 above at 445.

fulfilled as well as protecting the many creditors who are the subject of unequal bargaining. Additionally, requiring directors to consider creditor interests could curb abuses of trust and compensate creditors of insolvent companies for whom liquidation is often 'an empty formality'.[299]

Imposing responsibilities on directors to take into account creditors' interests is not to be regarded as something totally novel, for there is nothing new about providing that directors are liable for harms done, and losses incurred, as a consequence of company activities,[300] and, in any event the responsibility is consistent with the approach advocated by many who have written on the subject of modern corporate governance, namely ensuring that directors have obligations to constituents other than the company as a whole or its shareholders when the company is in financial straits.[301] This follows from the fact that companies are a significant part of society and as a consequence society might properly require the businesses of companies to be carried on in a manner that protects the interests of those who deal with them.[302] Holding that directors are to take into account creditor interests provides an *ex post* settling up of the company's dealings with its creditors,[303] and provides protection.

There must be a balance between, on one side, the law not unduly hampering directors and placing unreasonable responsibilities on them, and, on the other side, the law must ensure that it does not permit directors to ignore completely the position of the creditors when financial strife exists. The imposition of the duty considered in this chapter and Chapters 11–17 goes part of the way to achieving a balance.

---

299 *Op. cit.* fn 156 above at 91.   300 *Op. cit.* fn 39 above at 421.
301 McDonnell, *op. cit.* fn 117 above at 191.   302 See Dodd, *op. cit.* fn 60 above at 1162.
303 McDaniel, *op. cit.* fn 117 above at 314.

20 A theoretical analysis of wrongful trading

Introduction

In Part C we considered the action available to liquidators under s 214 of the Insolvency Act 1986. This consideration involved a doctrinal study of the law and issues that flowed from that. The part also considered shortcomings with s 214. It was assumed in Part C that the existence of a provision outlawing wrongful trading is normative.

This chapter endeavours to consider whether this assumption is reasonable, and it examines, from a theoretical perspective, whether a wrongful trading-style provision is justified. First, the chapter rehearses and evaluates the arguments, mainly developed in Australia, that have been articulated for the abolition of provisions like s 214. Then the chapter investigates some of the reasons given for supporting the provision. Some of the arguments that were examined in the previous chapter in relation to the duty owed to creditors are relevant to this chapter. These arguments will be mentioned, although they will not be developed. Rather, readers are referred back to the previous chapter. In particular Chapter 19 discussed the views of the two main schools of thought in corporate law, namely the contractarians and the progressives, and the approaches of these schools to a wrongful trading-type provision are considered here.

At the outset we should acknowledge that wrongful trading-like provisions are forms of, in law-and-economics terminology, 'bonding' in that essentially the directors are providing bonds as to how they will manage the company.

Opposition to regulation

There has been little in the way of theoretical examination of the wrongful trading provision in the UK,[1] but there have been some significant

---

[1] A notable exception, in relation to aspects of the provision, is the work of Dr Rizwaan Mokal, 'An agency cost analysis of the wrongful trading provisions: redistribution, perverse incentives and the creditors' bargain' (2000) 59 CLJ 335; *Corporate Insolvency: Theory and Application*, 2005, Oxford: Oxford University Press, Chapter 8.

commentaries in Australia, discussing the Australian equivalent, ss 558G-Y of what is now the Corporations Act 2001. The commentators have been opposed to the existence of the provision. They have generally sought to adopt a law-and-economics approach to their studies. The main opponents of any provision like s 214 have been Justin Mannolini,[2] Professor Dale Oesterle[3] (providing some American views of the provisions) and Dr David Morrison.[4] While some of the points made by these commentators are section-specific, other points are equally applicable to any form of wrongful trading-type provision. In fact Oesterle offers his discussion as commentary on all wrongful trading-type regulations, and specifically those extant in Australia, the UK and New Zealand. It is helpful to discuss the objections voiced by the opponents thematically.

Discouraging people from becoming directors

The first argument that is mounted by Oesterle is that executives are less likely to take up positions on boards of directors because of the existence of a wrongful trading regulation.[5] This is not a new argument, for it has been asserted in other contexts when addressing the potential liability of directors. Professor Ron Daniels, for instance, states that the 'liability chill will deter talented individuals from accepting a nomination for board service'.[6]

First, it has been established in some studies[7] that directors are frequently not aware of their responsibilities when entering office and this state of

---

2   'Creditors' interest in the corporate contract: a case for the reform of our insolvent trading provisions' (1996) 6 *Australian Journal of Corporate Law* 14.

3   'Corporate directors' personal liability for "insolvent trading" in Australia, "reckless trading" in New Zealand and "wrongful trading" in England: a recipe for timid directors, hamstrung controlling shareholders and skittish lenders' in Ramsay, I M (ed), *Company Directors' Liability for Insolvent Trading*, 2000, Melbourne, Centre for Corporate Law and Securities Regulation and CCH Australia.

4   'The Australian insolvent trading prohibition – why does it exist?' (2002) 11 *International Insolvency Review* 153 and 'The economic necessity for the Australian insolvent trading prohibition' (2003) 12 *International Insolvency Review* 171.

5   *Op. cit.* fn 3 above at 29.

6   Daniels, R J, 'Must boards go overboard? An economic analysis of the effects of burgeoning statutory liability on the role of directors in corporate governance' in Ziegel, J S (ed), *Current Developments in International and Comparative Corporate Insolvency Law*, 1994, Oxford: Clarendon Press, p 569. Also, see Sealy, L S, 'Directors' wider responsibilities – problems conceptual practical and procedural' (1987) 13 *Monash University Law Review* 164 at 186; McDonnell, S R, '*Geyer v Ingersoll Publications Co*: insolvency shifts directors' burden from shareholders to creditors' (1994) 19 Del J Corp L 177 at 209; Nicholls, C C, 'Liability of corporate officers and directors to third parties' (2001) 35 Can Bus LJ 1 at 5.

7   For instance, see the government's White Paper, *Modernising Company Law*, Vol 1, Cm 5553-1, TSO, July 2002, at para 3.2; Tomasic, R, and Bottomley, S, 'Corporate governance and the impact of legal obligations on decision-making in corporate Australia' (1991) 1 *Australian Journal of Corporate Law* 55 at 83.

affairs, sadly, continues for many when they are in post. This causes one to ask why directors would resign or not accept a post because they are worried about possible liability under s 214, when many are obviously oblivious to the possibility of personal liability under this provision.

There has been some anecdotal evidence to the effect that people are now more wary about becoming directors,[8] but other evidence has been to the contrary, such as the following view: '[T]he truth is that there is no shortage of candidates for the board . . . It seems that people still want to belong to the club [FTSE 100 companies] that continues to exist at the top of British business.'[9] This is supported by Professor Harry Glasbeek when he states that:

> [S]ome well-informed people, with a great deal of worldly experience, whose reputation (as well as personal fortunes) ought to mean something to them, seem to be falling over themselves to sit on supposedly perilous boards of directors.[10]

Admittedly, in *Re Continental Assurance Co of London plc* [2001] BPIR 733 Park J recognised that if non-executive directors were liable in the kind of case before him (a wrongful trading case), many well-advised persons would refrain from taking up the office of director. But the fact of the matter is that the directors were not held to be liable, and as I explained in Chapters 8 and 10 in particular, only the most irresponsible of directors have been found liable for wrongful trading.

In fact those arguing that persons are being dissuaded from becoming members of boards seem to focus more on the liability of directors for breach of duty of care and skill rather than any mention of wrongful trading. Also, there does not appear to be any empirical study that has established that people are more wary of accepting directorial posts because of concerns over wrongful trading, and in any event there is no indication that directors or prospective directors are more concerned about wrongful trading liability, when compared with other heads of liability. Clearly, while there might have been more publicity concerning directorial liability in recent times, the imposition of responsibilities on directors is far from new.

It must not be forgotten that there are drawbacks with entering most professions, and liability attaches to many professionals. For example, there have been a significant number of actions taken against auditors over the past decade.[11] Despite this, there is no lack of talented individuals who are desirous

---

8 Gibb, F, 'Directors chilled by the fear of financial liability', *The Times*, September 23, 2003.

9 Wheatcroft, P, 'Let some others join the club', *The Times*, October 15, 2003.

10 Glasbeek, H J, 'More direct director responsibility: much ado about . . . what?' [1985] Can Bus L J 416 at 447.

11 In relatively recent days there has been a well-publicised investigation in the United States into the work of the auditors of Enron when it entered bankruptcy.

of entering the accounting profession, and even to act as auditors.[12] Further-more, there are all sorts of reasons why competent people do not enter a specific profession, even if they have the academic and personal qualities needed; it is too complex an issue involving personal choices to enable one to assert that people are not entering a particular vocation because of one issue. In any event, are we to determine what should be the appropriate legal position in a given area based on whether a particular post is attractive or not? If that were the case, and because many police services in the UK are experiencing difficulties in recruiting officers, we might consider legalising a number of activities so that we can make the job of police officers less demanding and more attractive.

It is probable that the resignations of directors are due to several issues. It is more likely that directors resign because they are worried by a whole raft of burdens placed upon them by a number of pieces of legislation and court decisions,[13] rather than fear over wrongful trading. The fact of the matter is that in most common law countries, legislatures and courts alike have got tougher with directors over the past 15 years, and it is not possible, short of a detailed empirical study, to ascertain if there is a single occurrence that causes directors to resign or deters qualified people from accepting posts as directors. Intuitively I would want to say that directors do not take up posts or resign because of a combination of factors, with one factor probably not making the difference.

Assuming that directors do feel more vulnerable, it is probable that they might be able to safeguard their position by obtaining director and officer (D&O) insurance. Section 309A of the Companies Act 1985 permits (as will the provisions in the Company Law Reform Bill 2005) companies to purchase insurance for their officers against liability, *inter alia*, for breach of duty. Such insurance appears to be available to companies, and, compared with the situation in the United States, it has been available in the UK at a reasonable cost, especially if purchased by the company itself.[14]

Directors will become more risk-averse

The argument has been made that even if people want to, and do, become, directors they will be effectively hamstrung in what they do. Oesterle has asserted that directors will be more cautious in taking risks; they will be more

---

12 It must be acknowledged that the auditing profession, most notably the big international accounting firms (known as 'the Big Four'), has lobbied for a cap to be placed on the liability of auditors, due to concerns over the size of damages awards against auditors.

13 This is indicated in Leibowitz, D, 'Cover charge', *The Lawyer*, November 10, 2003 at p 25.

14 Finch, V, 'Personal accountability and corporate control: the role of directors' and officers' liability insurance' (1994) 57 MLR 880, especially at 890 and 902. According to Finch, insurance for directors has not been placed under the same stress as insurance for auditors (at 905).

concerned about protecting their own positions, and this will lead to directors failing to maximise wealth for the benefit of shareholders as well as they could if they were freed from the fear of wrongful trading.[15] This is not necessarily so. Provided that directors are engaged in appropriate monitoring and reacting properly to the results of that monitoring, there is no reason for the directors to be overly risk-averse, unless and until those matters identified in s 214 come into play, that is when the directors know or ought to conclude that there is no reasonable prospect that the company would avoid going into insolvent liquidation. If such a point is reached it is expected that the directors would be more risk-averse. What Oesterle overlooks is that directors, particularly in private companies, are required by some creditors to guarantee personally the debts of their companies. If the possibility of liability for wrongful trading makes directors more risk-averse, then surely so must the giving of guarantees, for it is more likely that the directors will be called upon to pay the creditors under guarantees than be liable by way of a court order under s 214. Yet, notwithstanding this, Oesterle does not call for the abolition of guarantees. Rather, he states that the solution to dealing with companies that have problematical financial histories is to require a standard form personal guarantee and that this solution to the risk problem is elegant.[16]

The degree of risk permitted on the part of the directors of companies should always depend on the actual level of financial difficulty. The degree of financial instability and the degree of risk are interrelated[17] and the latter must be determined by the former. Hence, the more obvious it is that the creditors' interests are at risk, the less the degree of risk to which the directors should expose the company.[18] As mentioned earlier,[19] if the company is financially embarrassed the shareholders and directors might have nothing to lose by embracing a high-risk strategy; the taking of substantial risks could be highly profitable and might rescue the company from the financial mire. But if the gamble fails, the creditors will lose out.

Yet, undoubtedly, the point at which a director is subject to s 214 is not always precise. A director can reassess strategy when he or she knows that there is no reasonable prospect that the company would avoid going into insolvent liquidation, but concern that a court, at a later date, might hold that a director ought to have concluded that insolvent liquidation was a reasonable prospect, might lead to over-caution. This is an issue which is taken out of the hands of the director. Having accepted this point, there appears to be no evidence that since the introduction of s 214 there has been a reduction in

---

15 *Op. cit.* fn 3 above at 30.   16 *Ibid* at 33.

17 See *Kinsela v Russell Kinsela Pty Ltd* (1986) 4 ACLC 215 at 223; *Equiticorp Finance Ltd (in liq) v BNZ* (1993) 11 ACLC 952 at 1017.

18 *Ibid*. Also, see the view of Rao, R, Sokolow, D, and White, D, 'Fiduciary duty à la Lyonnais: an economic perspective on corporate governance in a financially distressed firm' (1996) 22 J Corp L 53 at 65.

19 Above at p 178.

the amount of risk-taking in UK markets. The same can be said about the New Zealand equivalent, s 135 of the Companies Act 1993. This provision outlaws reckless trading, and when it was first introduced it was widely criticised on the basis that it would suffocate enterprise.[20] This does not appear to have occurred. Furthermore, the fact is, as I discuss in the next section of the Chapter, the case law should not cause directors to feel that they must be unduly risk-averse.

The courts lack experience and ability

Oesterle is one among several commentators[21] that are sceptical when it comes to the suitability of the courts to assess the conduct of directors.[22] According to Oesterle: 'The forum for a decision . . . is stacked against the director.'[23] The learned commentator goes on to say that judges lack business experience and 'clever lawyers and paid experts will ably add to the confusion'.[24] This overlooks the fact that directors are able to hire clever lawyers to argue their case and to pay experts to substantiate their argument that they have acted properly. With directors we are not talking about naïve, vulnerable persons in society. But leaving that point aside, what about the argument that the courts are not the appropriate forum for considering whether directors have acted properly?

Oesterle argues that the sympathy of the judges will be with the trade creditors who have suffered losses and the judge will be against the directors who oversaw the company's demise.[25] The suggestion appears to be made, certainly by Oesterle, that the courts will hold directors liable as a matter of course. The claim is outlandish and, in any event, it simply does not accord with the only empirical evidence that we have in the UK, namely the reported decisions. There have not been many wrongful trading cases that have been reported since 1986, but in those that have been, directors have done pretty well. Courts, when reviewing what occurred to a company, often some years before the hearing of the action, have demonstrated a good deal of understanding of the positions in which directors found themselves at the relevant time. It is submitted that the judges have carefully analysed the situation confronting directors, and have generally come down on their side. For instance, in *Re Continental Assurance Co of London plc* [2001] BPIR 733,

---

20 Watson, S, 'New Zealand: company law – directors' liability' (1999) 10 ICCLR 34 at 35.
21 For example, Professor Brian Cheffins in *Company Law: Theory, Structure and Operation*, 1997, Oxford: Clarendon Press, p 543; Wishart, D, 'Models and theories of directors' duties to creditors' (1991) 14 NZULR 323 at 340–341.
22 *Op. cit.* fn 3 above at 38.
23 *Ibid.* A view apparently accepted by Varallo, G, and Finkelstein, J, 'Fiduciary obligations of directors of the financially troubled company' (1992) 48 Bus Law 239.
24 Oesterle, *ibid.*
25 *Ibid.* This is a view also held by Butler, H, and Ribstein, L, 'Opting out of fiduciary duties: a response to the anti-contractarians' (1990) 65 Wash L Rev 1 at 56.

Park J in a mammoth judgment considered what directors had done during the period in which they were alleged to have breached s 214. His Lordship was satisfied that the directors had available to them sufficient financial information, even though the systems employed were a little antiquated, and record-keeping systems were not particularly good (at 771). Surely if a judge was disposed to find for the creditors he could have at least attacked the directors for not having had a better financial system in place. But his Lordship did not. Even where the courts have been critical of a director, they have manifested a degree of generosity. For example, in *Re Purpoint Ltd* [1991] BCLC 491; [1991] BCC 121 Vinelott J said that he had some doubts as to whether a reasonable director would have permitted the company to have commenced trading at all because of critical factors such as a lack of a capital base and the only assets that the company had were purchased from borrowings or acquired on hire purchase. Yet his Lordship did not hold that the respondent director ought to have concluded that the company was doomed from the outset (at 498; 127). The conclusion that can be drawn from the case law is, as indicated above, that the judges have carefully assessed detailed and quite complex testimony, and the judgments demonstrate an appreciation of many of the business issues encountered by directors. For instance, the judgment in *Continental Assurance* is meticulous in detail and generous in result. The judges generally appear to realise that directors have to make tough decisions in often difficult circumstances. Furthermore, in *Re Brian D Pierson (Contractors) Ltd* [2001] 1 BCLC 275 the judge recognised (at 305) that what had to be taken into account in a wrongful trading case was the standard of the reasonable businessperson and that this sort of person would be 'less temperamentally cautious than lawyers and accountants'. The court was taking into account the position of a director and there was clear acceptance that the business approach of a director will involve some risk.

The favourite allegation that is asserted in relation to the courts is that they will base their decision on hindsight, and that will convict the director who always could have done more.[26] With respect, the courts appear to have been vigilant concerning this possibility. In *Re Sherborne Associates Ltd* [1995] BCC 40 the judge expressed the view that it is dangerous to assume that 'what has in fact happened was always bound to happen and was apparent' (at 54). The fact of the matter is that English courts have refused to second-guess directors in their commercial dealings.[27]

But is it the case that liquidators are threatening to issue, or even initiating, proceedings pursuant to s 214 and this has caused directors to feel pressured into making payments to avert or settle such proceedings because of the concern that the courts will find against them? Even Professor Brian Cheffins,

---

26 For example, *op. cit.* fn 3 above at 38,; Cheffins, *op. cit.* fn 21 above at 543.

27 Law Commission, *Company Directors: Regulating Conflicts of Interests and Formulating a Statement of Duties* (Law Commission Consultation Paper No 153, 1998), at para 15.30.

who is sceptical of the courts' suitability to deal with wrongful trading cases, thinks not, because s 214 does not provide a significant weapon in the liquidator's arsenal.[28] This is supported by more recent commentary.[29] One practitioner has stated that 'it is difficult to see, where the directors have conscientiously set about discharging their duties, given serious consideration to the matter and come to rational conclusions',[30] that the directors will be held liable.

The above statements quoted from judgments, together with the approach taken by the courts, do not suggest that judges fail to evaluate adequately the situation in which directors find themselves, and make decisions in favour of creditors because they feel sorry for creditors. The cases suggest that judges will only find directors liable where the latter have plainly acted irresponsibly, a point made in *Re Sherborne Associates Ltd* (at 56) and subsequently in *Continental Assurance*.[31]

In sum, while judges will, it is acknowledged, often have to wrestle with difficult questions flowing from differing views of what constitutes right action in the circumstances in which companies operated,[32] they are able to make a fair assessment of the actions of directors and are now able and better equipped to take practical and commercial decisions.[33] Judges have sought to achieve a balance between the protection of bona fide creditors, on the one hand, and ensuring that directors (on behalf of their companies) are not totally discouraged from taking appropriate business risks, on the other hand. The very paucity of cases where liquidators have succeeded contradicts the assertion that judges are going to be set against directors.

Creditors should protect themselves

A point that is often made in relation to many aspects of corporate law, and that was discussed at length in the last chapter, is that creditors do not need the benefit of regulation, for they are able to take care of themselves by means of 'an entire armoury of techniques'.[34] We now consider this issue in the context of wrongful trading. Oesterle brands wrongful trading as supporting paternalism, because it is based, wrongly in his view, on the idea that creditors warrant some form of protection.[35] Many contractarians are in the

---

28 Cheffins, *op. cit.* fn 21 above at 545.
29 Fidler, P, 'Wrongful trading after *Continental Assurance*' (2001) 17 IL & P 212; Spence, N, 'Personal liability for wrongful trading' (2004) 17 *Insolvency Intelligence* 11.
30 Fidler, *ibid* at 215.   31 See the quotation at pp 109–110.
32 Allen, W, 'Ambiguity in corporation law' (1997) 22 Del J Corp L 894 at 899.
33 A point accepted as far back as 1982 by the Insolvency Law Review Committee, *Insolvency Law and Practice* (generally referred to as 'the Cork Report') Cmnd 858, HMSO, 1982 at para 1800.
34 Goddard, D, 'Corporate personality – limited recourse and its limits' in Rickett, C, and Grantham, R, *Corporate Personality in the 20th Century*, 1998, Oxford: Hart Publishing, p 22.
35 *Op. cit.* above fn 3 at 41.

vanguard in espousing similar views to Oesterle. As we saw in the previous chapter, contractarians, while not being in agreement on all issues, generally take the view that the company is nothing more than a number of complex, private consensual contract-based relations,[36] either express or implied, and they consist of many different kinds of relations that are worked out by those voluntarily associating in a company.[37] The contractarian paradigm asserts freedom of contract, and hence creditors are entitled, in order to gain protection, to insist on what goes into their contract with companies, and if they do not like what the company wants to include in, or exclude from, the contract, the creditor can simply walk away.

Morrison asserts that besides contract-related protections, creditors can avail themselves of insurance.[38] In Chapter 19,[39] we noted that trade credit insurance can certainly be purchased so as to protect creditors against the risk of non-payment, but this is not a frequent occurrence, and in 2001 it was asserted by the Association of British Insurers that only five per cent of UK trade was credit-insured.[40] Earlier I concluded that this could be due to the fact that either creditors do not wish to insure, but prefer to take the risk of non-payment, or insurers might be reluctant to give cover. Even if creditors could insure, the cost of credit insurance is rising[41] and the cost element that they would have to build into their price for granting credit would, more often than not, price many of them out of the market.

Much is made by Mannolini of the fact that creditors can protect themselves by having a contract with the company that safeguards them. But, undoubtedly, *ex ante* contracts have their limitations in this regard.[42] One of the main drawbacks with this strategy is that it is impossible to draft a contract that deals effectively with all of the issues that the parties might want to address and which covers every possible contingency.[43] The issue was considered in detail the previous chapter.[44]

Finally, if a creditor is able to negotiate the inclusion in a contract of favourable terms, then this is only of any use, for the most part, if the creditor is willing to monitor the affairs of the company. The necessary monitoring

---

36 Referring to the relations as contracts is probably incorrect. Some authors refer to the relations as bargains as some of the relations do not constitute contracts in a technical sense. See, Klausner, M, 'Corporations, corporate law and networks of contracts' (1995) 81 *Virginia Law Review* 757 at 759.

37 Easterbrook, F H, and Fischel, D R, 'The corporate contract' (1989) 89 Colum L Rev 1416 at 1426. At p 1428 the learned commentators give examples of some of the arrangements.

38 *Op. cit.* fn 4 above (2002) at 170.   39 See at pp 320–321.

40 Posner, M, 'Credit insurance: an overview' *Credit Management*, April 2001, 18 at 19.

41 Mandell, M, 'Money's costing more' (2002) 15(4) Troy 58 at 58.

42 Whincop, M J, 'Painting the corporate cathedral: the protection of entitlements in corporate law' (1999) 19 OJLS 19 at 30–31. See above at pp 317–318.

43 See the comments of Riley, C A, 'Contracting out of company law: section 459 of the Companies Act 1985 and the role of the courts' (1992) 55 MLR 782 at 786 in this regard.

44 Above, pp 316–320.

can be time-consuming and costly, and even then it might not be sufficient to keep the creditor well informed.[45] Again, monitoring will increase transaction costs.[46]

Mannolini,[47] in a trenchant attack on the Australian equivalent of s 214, argues that creditors can protect themselves through three avenues. First, creditors can include in the credit contract, if they choose, a raft of debt covenants, providing, for instance, that the company will not take on any superior or equal-ranking debt.[48] A second defensive measure identified by Mannolini is the taking of personal guarantees from directors.[49] Finally, a creditor is entitled to require the creation in its favour of a charge to enable it to have some security over the debtor company's property.[50] If a creditor is able to negotiate successfully to have, for instance, restrictive covenants inserted in a contract, the taking of guarantees or security, then it is advisable that the creditor monitors the affairs of the company and, possibly, the directors. As stated above, this is time-consuming and costly, and even then it might not be sufficient to keep the creditor well informed.[51] Many creditors will not have the resources to carry out necessary monitoring, and if they do they might not have the sophistication to assess any details that are obtained from the company.[52]

Mannolini asserts that the contractual process is sufficient to ensure that creditors are adequately compensated.[53] He states that creditors are able to insist on a higher interest rate if they are dealing with a company that might fall into financial difficulty, and where the risk of repayment is not guaranteed.[54] If, so the argument goes, a creditor negotiates a contract and then at a later stage is able to recover any outstanding debt from the directors, the creditor is 'on a *risk-adjusted basis* . . . effectively overcompensated'.[55] But, when a contract is entered into, the parties decide on price depending on what they know at the time. A problem for parties to contracts, particularly some creditors, is the existence of informational asymmetries. Yet, one of the things that the parties are aware of at the time of the making of the contract is the existence of the wrongful trading provision. Just as the existence of security can affect the allocation of risk, so can the existence of the wrongful trading provision. As the late Dr Michael Whincop stated: 'If parties can price-protect in the absence of the rules, they are capable of price-protecting when they are present.'[56] Further to this, it is extremely difficult, if not impossible, to determine, in any given case, whether a creditor has been

---

45 See the comments of Cheffins, *op. cit.* fn 21 above at 524.
46 Posner, R, 'The rights of affiliated corporations' (1976) 43 U Chi L Rev 499 at 508.
47 *Op. cit.* fn 2 above.   48 *Ibid* at 23.   49 *Ibid* at 23–24.   50 *Ibid* at 24.
51 See the comments of Cheffins, *op. cit.* fn 21 above at 523–524.
52 *Ibid* at 523.   53 *Op. cit.* fn 3 above at 30.   54 *Ibid* at 31.   55 *Ibid.*
56 Whincop, M, 'The economic and strategic structure of insolvent trading' in Ramsay, I M (ed),
    Company Directors' Liability for Insolvent Trading, 2000, Melbourne: Centre for Corporate
    Law and Securities Regulation and CCH Australia, p 58.

overcompensated, an assertion made by Mannolini in relation to creditors obtaining benefits from a wrongful trading order. A number of factors have to be taken into account in determining overcompensation, namely: a model for pricing debt; information concerning the way in which interest rates are set in equilibrium; the information that the company had access to at the time of the credit being extended; and knowledge of the way that creditors trade off a provision for protection in the contract and price protection.[57]

Returning to the issue of information asymmetry for a moment, it is possible to say that directors have an incentive to encourage creditors to undervalue the risk that they are undertaking (so that the price of the credit will be lower), and so they may not disclose certain information. The existence of something like wrongful trading redresses the balance in some way so that creditors might get some benefit where directors have failed to make disclosure. Of course, wrongful trading will apply equally to all directors, whether they have acted openly or not.

Premature advent of insolvency regimes

It has been argued that the existence of a s 214-type provision is likely to cause directors, concerned about their personal liability, to take their companies into administration or liquidation prematurely.[58] But there is no evidence that directors are embracing liquidation or administration more often because of fear of s 214. The numbers of administrations have been very low over the years. The numbers in the past couple of years or so have increased, but this is probably because now companies can enter administration without the need for a court order, so it is less costly, quicker and more attractive. The only large increase in liquidation numbers since 1986 was during the early 1990s, in connection with the harsh recession of the late 1980s and early 1990s. Clearly, there were reasons other than fear of wrongful trading for the increase in numbers. This is borne out by the fact that after the effects of the recession died out, the liquidation numbers decreased.

This issue is linked in some ways with concern that directors will be more risk-averse as a result of s 214. We have already considered that issue. I might add to the earlier discussion that the only empirical evidence that seems to point to the fact that directors might be more risk-averse when their companies are struggling financially comes from the United States and relates to large listed companies.[59] This evidence is of little relevance to many

---

57 *Ibid.*
58 Above fn 3 at 30. Also, see Yeo, V C S, and Lin, J L S, 'Insolvent trading – a comparative and economic approach' (1999) 10 *Australian Journal of Corporate Law* 216 at 231–232; McDonnell, S, '*Geyer v Ingersoll Publications Co*: insolvency shifts directors' burden from shareholders to creditors' (1994) 19 Del J Corp L 177 at 207.
59 Lo Pucki, L, and Whitford, W, 'Corporate governance in the bankruptcy reorganization of large, publicly held companies' (1993) 141 U Pa L R 669.

companies, and particularly those that are closely held. The directors of closely held companies are usually also the major shareholders and often they are, naturally, so closely linked to the company's business that they will seek to take every risk possible to save their company. With many closely held firms, shareholder-managers are sentimentally attached to their firms and have often sunk their life savings into them as well as a lot of effort, and they are prepared to attempt almost any action that might turn around the company's fortunes.[60] In *Re Produce Marketing Consortium Ltd* (1989) 5 BCC 569, Knox J pointed to the fact that one of the two directors of the company was unable to see the realities of the company's trading position (at 598). In *The Liquidator of Marini Ltd v Dickensen* [2004] BCC 172; [2003] EWHC 334 (Ch) at [23] it was recorded that the directors of a small family company did not heed the advice of an insolvency practitioner that the company should enter liquidation, and decided to trade on. A survey of English case law suggests that it is the directors of closely held companies that are generally subjected to legal proceedings, and in the decisions that have gone against directors, closely held companies have been involved.[61] This is supported by a recent empirical study undertaken in Australia in relation to that country's insolvent trading provisions.[62] The study found that in 91 per cent of the cases brought against company directors, directors of private companies were involved. The study was only able to identify the number of shareholders in 16 of the 103 companies involved in the cases that were studied, and it found that the average number of shareholders in those companies was 1.81. There is evidence, certainly with respect to small companies, that directors fail to embrace an insolvency procedure early enough.[63] If companies initiated some insolvency procedure earlier, perhaps there might be more corporate rescue and less wrongful trading.

In suggesting that wrongful trading precipitates the premature embracing of insolvency regimes, the opponents of wrongful trading are assuming that the advent of an insolvency regime is tantamount to the end of the company's life. While this might be the case with liquidation, this is certainly not the case with administration. This is especially so since the introduction of the corporate insolvency provisions in the Enterprise Act 2002. These provisions are designed by the government to encourage the rescue of companies through the process of administration, which has been made more accessible.

---

60 *Op. cit.* fn 1 above, 'Agency' at 353–354.

61 For instance, *Re Produce Marketing Consortium Ltd* (1989) 5 BCC 569; *Re DKG Contractors Ltd* [1990] BCC 903; *Re Purpoint Ltd* [1991] BCLC 491; [1991] BCC 121; *Re Brian D Pierson (Contractors) Ltd* [2001] 1 BCLC 275.

62 James, P, Ramsay, I M, and Siva, P, 'Insolvent trading – an empirical study' (2004) 12 *Insolvency Law Journal* 210 and an earlier draft is available on the website of the Centre for Corporate Law and Securities Regulation, University of Melbourne www.cclsr.law.unimelb.edu.au/research-papers/monograph%20series/Insolvent%20Trading%20final.pdf.

63 *Op. cit.* fn 1 above, 'Agency' at 353–354.

Directors can now appoint an administrator extrajudicially (Sched B1, para 22(2) to the Insolvency Act 1986) and this will, *inter alia*, reduce time and costs. The appointment of an administrator could have two benefits, namely enabling directors to protect themselves and ensuring that their company's position will be assessed by a licensed insolvency practitioner in the shelter of a moratorium. The administrator's assessment might lead to a proposal for the company's rescue from its financial mire, thereby producing an optimal outcome for all stakeholders. In one reported case, *Re Chancery plc* [1991] BCC 171 at 172, the directors appear to have petitioned for an administration order so as to avoid wrongful trading occurring. In Australia it appears that the equivalent procedure to administration (voluntary administration) may have been used by directors to avoid engaging in insolvent trading.[64]

Directors are unfairly penalised

Mannolini, in arguing that placing liability on directors is unfair, has asserted that wrongful trading provisions can lead to directors being held liable for actions or inactions short of fraud or deliberate wrongdoing, such as a mere error of judgment.[65] Yet, Mannolini is ready to deny creditors any rights in relation to possible errors of judgment which they make, such as not assessing the commercial risks properly in extending credit to companies. There does not appear to be any reason why creditors should bear the burden of their errors, but directors are to be excused.[66] While Mannolini accepts that some creditors will not be sufficiently sophisticated to assess the risks pertaining to the extension of credit to some companies, he is not ready to accept that loss should fall on directors. His rationale for this view appears to be that directors of small closely held companies have, from a historical perspective, been the subject of most recovery actions initiated by creditors and liquidators.[67] This probably comes as news to lawyers acting on behalf of creditors and liquidators. To be sure, where guarantees have been given by directors this might be the case. But even then, why should directors be the objects of generosity and excused from liability? Mannolini's answer is that they are entrepreneurs involved in risk-taking that acts as the 'motor for the entrepreneurial economy'.[68] He asks rhetorically: 'Why should the law

---

64 Herzberg, A, 'Why are there so few insolvent trading cases?' (1998) 6 *Insolvency Law Journal* 177.

65 *Op. cit.* fn 2 above at 32.

66 It is to be noted that it has been held that directors are not able to be excused under s 727 of the Companies Act 1985 because relief is not compatible with s 214 (*Re Produce Marketing Consortium Ltd* (1989) 5 BCC 569; *Re Brian D Pierson (Contractors) Ltd* [2001] 1 BCLC 275). It is respectfully submitted that this is not necessarily the case. Both s 214 and s 727 involve subjective and objective tests, and so there should be no bar to the application of s 727 to s 214. See above at pp 118–120.

67 *Op. cit.* fn 2 above at 32.   68 *Ibid.*

constrain entrepreneurs to adopt conservative trading strategies when rational creditors and shareholders may well prefer risky strategies?' With respect, what Mannolini fails to tell us is why directors should be seen in this light and not creditors. Is it not the case that creditors are also entrepreneurs in the business of risk-taking?[69] In any given case, loss might fall on one group of entrepreneurs. Which one will it be? The fact of the matter is that when a company collapses, creditors will always lose out, but directors will not unless wrongful trading actions are initiated, and are successful.

While creditors will suffer if a company collapses, Morrison argues that directors also suffer in the sense that their reputation will be tarnished to the extent that they might find it hard to obtain work again.[70] The implication from the commentator's point is that the imposition of wrongful trading liability is just a further unreasonable injury that directors have to endure as a consequence of their company's collapse. But it is questionable whether loss of reputation is an issue for those directors who are involved in closely held companies. It is more likely that directors of these kinds of companies will start up afresh with another company which they control (unless they have been disqualified). Will their reputation with creditors, however, be tarnished so that if they do move to another company, or establish their own new company, they have difficulty in getting credit? It is not likely that potential creditors will be aware, save in the smallest of fields, of what the director has done in the past, for, as we have already considered, creditors often lack information on which to base their decision to extend credit. Certainly some creditors are likely to give credit in ignorance. Other creditors might, in spite of what a director has done previously, extend credit because of the tough competition that exists in the market.

It is likely, as indicated earlier, that wrongful trading is more relevant to directors of closely held companies for their monetary and human capital is tied up in these companies. In this regard, Cheffins points out that if a closely held company collapses, then the directors will have lost what they invested in the company, as well as possibly having to pay out on personal guarantees.[71] It certainly must be acknowledged that executive directors invest substantially in the company, in terms of their labour, and, unlike shareholders and creditors, they have no opportunity to diversify their risk; their fortunes do sink or swim with the company. After saying that, while directors' wealth will be affected, if they have not guaranteed company liabilities, they are able to walk away from a company without debts or capital losses.

Returning to the issue of reputation, if we assume that Morrison is correct in relation to medium to large companies and reputations of directors will

69 Whincop, M J, 'Taking the corporate contract more seriously: the economic cases against, and a transaction cost rationale for, the insolvent trading provisions' (1996) 5 *Griffith Law Review* 1 at 13. This is a point that Cheffins also makes, *op. cit.* fn 21 above at 523.

70 *Op. cit.* fn 4 above (2002) at 160.

71 Cheffins, *op. cit.* fn 21 above at 523.

suffer if their company collapses, it might be argued that the wrongful trading provision can be influential in directors ensuring that creditors' losses are minimised. As Professor Ron Daniels has stated:

> [I]n light of their imminent re-entry into the job market, managers may reason that the best strategy to adopt in a distress situation is one of honesty and integrity. Rather than using wrongdoing as a way of gambling the company back to success, the managers may decide to avoid unscrupulously any hint of wrongdoing out of a concern for inflict-ing irrevocable damage to their reputational capital in the managerial market.[72]

In any event, assuming Morrison to be correct, we might then ask whether a director's loss of reputation constitutes any reason for not making a director liable to creditors? The diminution in the level of the director's reputation does not compensate the creditors, who, while they might find some solace in the fact that the director has difficulty operating again, will be more concerned to recover some money.

Although a wrongful trading provision might lead to a director being held liable, it must be remembered that its existence is not so heavy a burden for directors as the imposition of a personal guarantee. Under most standard guarantees, the liability of directors is not limited and liability is automatic in relation to the company's liabilities to the creditor. In contrast, liability under s 214 only ensues if a court is satisfied that the directors knew or ought to have concluded that there was no reasonable prospect that the company would avoid going into insolvent liquidation, and the directors are unable to convince the court that they took every step with a view to minimising the potential loss to the company's creditors as they ought to have taken.

The changes made to the administration regime procedure by the Enterprise Act 2002 potentially lighten the burden of directors. Until the corporate insolvency provisions in the Enterprise Act became operative on 15 September 2003, if directors wished to place their company into administration, argu-ably one of the safest responses to concerns over the possibility of wrongful trading, they had to obtain a court order. Besides being costly, it took a significant amount of time to obtain such an order. Now directors are able to place their company into administration (Sched B1, para 22 to the Insolvency Act 1986) by simply giving notice to the holders of floating charges over the whole, or substantially the whole, of their company's property of an intention to appoint an administrator (para 26), as well as filing a copy of the notice of intention to appoint with the court (at para 27), and then, once an appointment has been made, the filing at court of a notice of appointment

---

72 Daniels, R, 'Must boards go overboard?' (1994–5) 24 Can Bus L J 229 at 241 and referred to in Mokal, *op. cit.* fn 1 above, 'Agency' at 352.

(para 29). It has been asserted that the easy access to voluntary administration in Australia, an extrajudicial form of insolvency process akin to administration in the UK, has reduced the number of insolvent trading actions.[73]

Increase in transaction costs

Although not specifically articulated by those attacking the wrongful trading provision, although implicit in a number of points made, it might be argued that in order to keep from falling foul of s 214, directors have to engage in more monitoring so as to minimise risk, and that, as a necessary concomitant, there is an increase in the company's costs, producing less-efficient use of company resources. This means that transaction costs will be higher and this is not favoured by many contractarians. They adhere to the view that higher transaction costs are likely to prevent resources being put to the most allocatively efficient use (the maximum productive use of resources). The concern is that any greater impositions on directors will make them less efficient in their role as agents of the shareholders of the company, because amongst other things, they will start to think of their own positions,[74] rather than maximising profits.

It appears that courts will take into account, when assessing the actions of directors, the costs that are associated with undertaking inquiries and realise that company funds cannot be used for every check possible and that directors must act quickly in some situations. As discussed above, the courts have tended, in coming to decisions concerning the conduct of directors, to view the position that confronts directors pragmatically. Whincop suggested that all that courts will require is that an adequate process of monitoring existed so that the directors would be informed, and that the directors took into account the information produced, and *Continental Assurance*, for instance, seems to support such an approach. Also, while the costs involved might be substantial, it is likely that the process implemented should be effected in order for the directors to fulfil management responsibilities, in general terms, and to enable them to be able to provide the required external reporting.[75] Hence, the marginal cost involved in taking steps to ensure that wrongful trading does not occur appears to be low.[76]

It could be pointed out that undertaking monitoring is an integral element of the normal duties of directors, something clearly indicated in *Re Barings plc (No 5)* [1999] 1 BCLC 433 at 489, and that the action that directors take to monitor their company's position also has potential for benefiting the company as a whole in that inefficiencies and problems in general could be identified. In effect, the monitoring is just practising good corporate governance.

---

73 *Op. cit.* fn 64 above.   74 *Op. cit.* fn 10 above at 421.
75 Whincop, *op. cit.* fn 69 above at 26.   76 A view to which Whincop subscribed: *ibid.*

Finally, it has been indicated in a significant amount of the recent law and economics literature in relation to companies that it is doubtful whether regulations that affect the terms of contracts in markets, have any allocative efficiency effects at all.[77]

Support for regulation

General

Generally speaking, little support for regulation has been articulated in the literature. Two academics, Dr Michael Whincop, in relation to the Australian insolvent trading provision, and Dr Rizwaan Mokal in relation to the British wrongful trading provision, have voiced support for regulation. The former was an avowed contractarian, and this is interesting as contractarians, certainly those embracing a law-and-economics approach to corporate law, are usually portrayed as being totally opposed to the provisions. Having said that, there are other contractarians who have not addressed wrongful trading-type provisions but who have favoured some kinds of mandatory provisions,[78] and who might support something akin to s 214.

It is likely that those scholars advocating a progressive approach to corporate law[79] would take the view that there should be regulation to proscribe wrongful trading. The progressive school as far as corporate law is concerned is centred in the United States and none of its adherents have addressed wrongful trading-style provisions, as there are no counterpart provisions in the United States, so some of the following discussion is based on what has been advocated in general progressive literature.

The view that been put in the progressive literature,[80] and referred to in Chapter 19, is that companies are public institutions with public obligations and it is necessary to have mandatory rules to control how they and their officers conduct themselves.[81] Rather than seeing the company as a nexus of contracts, as the contractarians do, they see the company as 'a community

---

77 *Op. cit.* above fn 56 at 45 and citing Black, B, 'Is corporate law trivial? A political and economic analysis' (1990) 84 *Northwestern University Law Review* 542; Butler, H, and Ribstein, L, 'Opting out of fiduciary duties: a response to the anti-contractarians' (1990) 65 Wash L Rev 1.

78 For example, Bebchuk, L, 'The debate on contractual freedom in corporate law' (1989) 89 Harv L R 1395.

79 The progressive school literature is voluminous and too extensive to cite in full. See fn 44 in Chapter 19 for some of the primary works.

80 Of course, just as with the law-and-economics school, not all progressives adhere to the same view on all matters.

81 For example, see Branson, D M, 'The death of contractariansim and the vindication of structure and authority in corporate governance and corporate law' in Mitchell, L (ed), *Progressive Corporate Law*, 1995, Boulder, Colorado: Westview Press, p 93.

of interdependence, mutual trust and reciprocal benefit'.[82] Progressives are concerned about the social effects of corporate activity, and not about the reduction of transaction costs.[83] They have rejected the concept that all of the parties who are involved in companies are able to protect themselves,[84] and even if self-protection measures were feasible, disparities in bargaining power would prevent creditors from obtaining effective protection. These disparities lead to bargaining outcomes that are substantially unfair. As a consequence, progressives have argued for mandatory rules in order to provide adequate protection.[85] Now let us to turn to some of the specific arguments that might support a wrongful trading provision.

Problems with protective measures

Earlier we noted that it has been argued that creditors are at liberty to take whatever precautions are needed in order to protect their interests given the risk involved.[86] Often banks[87] and other substantial institutions are in view when this is stated. Banks are able to demand guarantees from directors and can take the time, and go to the expense, of having a substantial contract drafted to protect their interests. Also, they have the necessary experience in their own organisations to advise on how to structure a particular transaction, something that is not available to most smaller creditors. A significant number of creditors are not sophisticated or powerful enough to demand terms that will compensate for risk. A study by Gilson and Vetsuypens[88] discovered that while banks were able to have covenants that influence corporate actions included in contracts, this was not the case with trade creditors.[89] Many of these creditors have little power and effectively are not

---

82 Millon, D, 'Communitarianism in corporate law: foundations and law reform strategies' in Mitchell, *ibid* at 10.

83 Millon, D, 'New directions in corporate law: communitarians, contractarians and crisis in corporate law' (1993) 50 *Washington and Lee Law Review* 1373 at 1379.

84 *Op. cit.* fn 82 above at 4.

85 *Ibid.*

86 See text relating to fnn 34–57. Also, see Nicholls, C C, 'Liability of corporate officers and directors to third parties' (2001) 35 Can Bus LJ 1 at 23.

87 For instance, see Lin, L, 'Shift of fiduciary duty upon corporate insolvency: proper scope of directors' duty to creditors' (1993) 46 *Vanderbilt Law Review* 1485 at 1502.

88 'Credit control in financially distressed firms: empirical evidence' (1994) Wash U LQ 1005 at 1010, 1011.

89 A US study undertaken in 1993 found that trade creditors made up 20 per cent of all non-bank, non-farm small businesses' liabilities, as well as that 80 per cent of all companies used trade credit, thus trade credit represents a significant part of corporate liabilities (Elliehusen and Wolken, 'An empirical investigation into motives for demand for trade credit' Federal Reserve Board study, 1993, and referred to in Jain, N, 'Monitoring costs and trade credit' (2001) 41 *The Quarterly Review of Economics and Finance* 89 at 90 and Atanasova, C V, and Wilson, N, 'Borrowing constraints and the demand for trade credit: evidence from UK panel data' July 2001, Leeds University Business School).

engaged in bargaining – they have to extend credit or perish.[90] While diversification of risk would be the most prudent option for trade creditors, thereby ensuring that any default would not impact so heavily on their financial position, this is not always viable, particularly for those involved in some industries.

Another option for creditors is to investigate potential debtors by obtaining information, such as financial data and details of past credit history, in order to ascertain the probability of default and to determine on what terms, if any, credit should be extended.[91] Yet this rarely occurs as far as many trade creditors are concerned, even those that could be regarded as the more sophisticated,[92] because like a number of the measures canvassed above, there is insufficient time, and creditors do not have the necessary staff to undertake this action, or cannot afford to employ professionals to act on their behalf.

There are multifarious reasons for the fact that a substantial portion of creditors fail to take measures that will provide adequate protection. These are: ignorance of the ramifications of dealing with a company; concern that a competitor might be able to provide the supplies or the funds if a decision to supply or lend is not made speedily, and, consequently, there is a lack of time in which either to undertake checks or to enter into negotiations on terms; taking action is costly; and the nature of risk changes over time.

In addition, while creditors might take measures to protect themselves, these will not, in all likelihood, stop some directors from acting improperly or irresponsibly. For instance, the payment by the company of creditors who are not connected with the company usually cannot be recovered, for a variety of reasons, as a preference by an administrator or liquidator.[93] As it is not possible either to predict the future or, for many creditors, to undertake monitoring of the affairs of companies, thus allowing creditors to protect themselves *ex ante*, it is appropriate for there to be some kind of *ex post* adjustment,[94] through the agency of s 214.

Absence of bargaining power

It would be argued by some commentators, and probably by progressive scholars in particular, that even if self-protection measures were feasible, disparities in bargaining power would prevent creditors from obtaining

---

90 See the comments of Professor Lawrence Mitchell in 'Trust. Contract. Process.' in Mitchell, *op. cit.* fn 81 above at 187.

91 *Op. cit.* fn 21 above at 74.

92 Hudson, J, 'The case against secured lending' (1995) 15 *International Review of Law and Economics* 47 at 56.

93 See *Re M C Bacon Ltd* [1990] BCLC 324; Keay, A, 'Preferences in liquidation law: a time for a change' (1998) 2 CfiLR 198.

94 Easterbrook, F, 'Two agency-cost explanations of dividends' (1984) 74 Am Econ Rev 650 at 655.

effective protection. These disparities lead to bargaining outcomes that are substantially unfair.[95] Many trade creditors[96] are almost 'involuntary' creditors, as they have little choice whether or not to deal with, and extend credit, to companies. Trade creditors often lack the necessary bargaining power to obtain contractual concessions from companies because the market is competitive and a company will probably have little difficulty, in most lines of business, in finding another trading partner who will not demand concessions. Also, because trade creditors are not extending the same amounts of credit as banks, and as the gains made by most trade creditors are relatively low, taking action to ascertain information about the company is regarded as inefficient and they are not so likely to negotiate explicit terms of credit. Of course, default is likely to have a greater impact on trade creditors compared with financiers.[97] Perhaps this answers the criticisms of some who say that too much responsibility has been placed on directors to be aware of the position of their companies and not enough has been placed on creditors to appraise risk and protect themselves;[98] simply many creditors are not lackadaisical, but are just unable to ascertain the necessary information that might assist their lending decisions. Wrongful trading provides compensation for the absence of true bargaining between the company and the creditors. Under progressive arguments, outlined in Chapter 19,[99] the provision makes life fairer for creditors.

Besides the issue of being able to negotiate fair terms, many creditors would not be able to anticipate the need to monitor the company directors, or they are simply not able to monitor the company. Even if they are, monitoring would be more expensive than bonding.[100]

Commercial morality

According to the Insolvency Law Review Committee, in its 1982 report, *Insolvency Law and Practice* ('the Cork Report'),[101] 'it is a basic objective of the law to support the maintenance of commercial morality',[102] and, according to the courts, to ensure high standards are maintained. Most would acknowledge that commercial morality must be fostered. The difficulty, of course, is finding agreement as to what commercial morality entails, and how far the courts and legislation should go in fostering it. While many would deny

---

95 *Op. cit.* fn 82 above at 9.
96 For a discussion of trade creditors and the difficulties they face, see above pp 326–328.
97 *Op. cit.* fn 46 above at 505.
98 Byrne, M, 'An economic analysis of directors' duties in favour of creditors' (1994) 4 *Australian Journal of Corporate Law* 275 at 281.
99 See above at pp 293–295.
100 Mokal, *op. cit.* fn 1 above, *Corporate Insolvency* at 279.
101 *Op. cit.* fn 33 above.   102 *Ibid* at para 191.

that company law carries out a public function generally, it would appear that some parts of company law have more than a private law impact.[103] Cheffins has noted that there is a public interest element connected with the regulation of directors and what they do.[104] Traditionally, the doctrine of limited liability, which shifts the risk of failure from the shareholders to the creditors,[105] has been viewed with great suspicion and has affected confidence in the market-place and amongst the public in general. Section 214, along with other rules, reduces the impact of the shift of the risk of failure.

Arguably, s 214 is one of those parts of company law to which Cheffins' comment in the previous paragraph refers. It is one of the elements of company law that indicates that, 'private law as well as public law has an important standard-setting role'.[106] Robert Walker J stated in *Re Oasis Merchandising Services Ltd* [1995] BCC 911 that an action under s 214 was not simply ordinary civil litigation, for it has a potential public aspect to it (at 918). More specifically, one can, as the law does, link s 214 with director disqualification. If there is a declaration under s 214, the courts may disqualify the respondent director(s) pursuant to s 10 of the Company Directors' Disqualification Act 1986; disqualification is a consequence of conduct amounting to a breach of commercial morality.[107] Section 214 obviously can be regarded, as discussed in Chapters 8 and 10, as potentially performing a public function, and a private person, the liquidator, indirectly carries it out.[108]

An option that is available to Parliament, and which signals to the community that the prohibition of wrongful trading is in the public interest, is to grant the Secretary of State for Trade and Industry the power to bring s 214 proceedings in certain cases, something that was argued for in Chapter 10. This is an approach that has been implemented in Australia in relation to its insolvent trading legislation, and it has been regarded as relatively success-ful.[109] An important aspect of the Australian legislation is that the regulator

---

103 For instance, Sugarman, D, 'Is company law founded on contract or public regulation? The Law Commission's paper on company directors' (1999) 20 Co Law 162 at 178.

104 *Op. cit.* fn 21 above at 548.

105 Posner, R, *Economic Analysis of Law*, 4th edn, 1992, Boston: Little Brown, p 394.

106 *Op. cit.* fn 103 above at 181.

107 See *Re Dawson Print Group Ltd* (1987) 3 BCC 322 at 326.

108 For a discussion of the use of private enforcement of public law-like provisions, see Yeung, K, 'Private enforcement of competition law' in McCrudden, C (ed), *Regulation and Deregu-lation*, 1999, Oxford: Clarendon Press, p 40.

109 For example, see two papers by Collier, B: 'ASIC and insolvency – current activities and future directions in enforcement and policy', a paper delivered to the Insolvency Practitioners' Association of Australia Conference, 28 May 2003 and available at www.asic.gov.au/asic/pdflib.nsf/LookupByFileName/IPAA_280503.pdf/$file/IPAA_280503.pdf, and 'The view from ASIC: a perspective on current activities and enforcement powers', a paper delivered to the Practical Insolvency and Practice Management Conference, 15 March 2004 and available at www.asic.gov.au/asic/pdflib.nsf/LookupByFileName/PIPM_speech_140304.pdf/$file/PIPM_speech_140304.pdf.

of companies, the Australian Securities and Investments Commission, is entitled to bring insolvent trading proceedings against directors.

Distributional fairness

As Mokal has demonstrated,[110] s 214 is redistributive for, *inter alia*, it provides claimants with rights to which they would not be entitled outside of insolvency law, and it is a cause of action that only comes into being on the insolvent liquidation of a company. Some may argue, particularly those who are part of the progressive school, that there must be distributional fairness, namely ensuring that the end effect of wealth distribution is fair. It might be argued that it would only be fair, so as not to lessen the amount paid to creditors from company funds, that the directors do not directly or indirectly transfer wealth from creditors to shareholders, either by the shifting of funds or causing an increase in risk when the company is heading for insolvent liquidation. To make sure that this does not occur, the law can threaten to impose some form of *ex post* liability on directors so as to redress unfairness. What do we mean by fairness in this context? It has been asserted[111] that in the context of company–creditor transactions, fairness requires an outcome that would be obtained where there is a bargain between unrelated parties with approximately equal bargaining power,[112] namely where there is fair dealing and a fair price.[113] Such a view is consistent with the general idea that fairness, throughout our legal system, involves balance and proportionality as far as the parties to transactions or proceedings are concerned, a view put forward in the previous chapter,[114] and provides support both for those who are vulnerable and the meeting of people's reasonable and legitimate expectations. We have already considered the fact that creditors are often the victims of an abuse of bargaining power. The idea of reasonable and legitimate expectations has its roots in contract law[115] and in this context it requires consideration of what the parties would have wanted where there are gaps in a contractual relationship,[116] namely: what the parties actually anticipated the

---

110 *Op. cit.* fn 1 above, *Corporate Insolvency*, at 269–273. The arguments against redistribution are discussed at pp 266–269.
111 See, Keay, A, 'A theoretical analysis of the director's duty to consider creditor interests: the progressive school's approach' (2004) 4 JCLS 307.
112 See, Anderson, A G, 'Conflicts of interest: efficiency, fairness and corporate structure' (1978) 25 UCLA L Rev 738 at 746.
113 Mitchell, L, 'Fairness and trust in corporate law' (1993) 43 Duke L J 425 at 446.
114 See above pp 298–300.
115 Hsieh, N, 'Moral desert, fairness and legitimate expectations in the market' (2000) 8 *Journal of Political Philosophy* 91 at 103. In *R v IRC* [1990] 1 WLR 1545 at 1569 Bingham LJ said that 'the doctrine of legitimate expectations is rooted in fairness.'
116 Bratton, W, 'The interpretation of contracts governing corporate debt relationships' (1984) 5 *Cardozo Law Review* 371 at 381–382.

contract would require in the situation that has in fact occurred.[117] Such a consideration allows taking into account such matters as the nature of the company's business and its future, and the circumstances of the creditor providing credit. Some, especially those from the progressive school, would, in assessing reasonable and legitimate expectations, submit that this assessment should include taking into account community values, such as fairness and decency.[118]

As discussed elsewhere,[119] it might be said that it is reasonable and legitimate for creditors to expect certain things of directors, such as ensuring that the entering into of fresh company liabilities is minimised, when there is no reasonable prospect of insolvent liquidation being avoided. If these expectations are not met then creditors can reasonably expect that directors would be held responsible, and make some contribution to the loss sustained by creditors.

Deterrent effect

The existence of a wrongful trading regulation might well act as a deterrent as far as the directors are concerned. First, and most obviously, the existence of a prohibition against wrongful trading might cause directors to be more prudent when there are financial problems for the company as they must consider that at some later time, if their company enters insolvent liquidation, they might be held to have been in a position where they ought to have concluded that their company could not avoid insolvent liquidation. Directors might be dissuaded from embracing risky courses of action in an attempt to turn around their companies. Mokal argues that the provision could have a broader deterrent effect, namely that as the provision applies throughout the life of a company and the provision is designed 'to encourage managers to do all they reasonably ought to, to minimise that loss [to creditors] in the first place',[120] it can apply to healthy companies as well.[121] Second, it might deter directors from passively acquiescing to risky actions proposed by other directors. Third, according to one practitioner's view the provision deters continuance of trading by insolvent companies.[122]

While there is significant doubt that the present wrongful trading provision has succeeded in deterring irresponsible trading,[123] a provision like s 214

---

117 Mitchell, L E, 'The fairness rights of bondholders' (1990) 65 NYULR 1165 at 1225.

118 Mitchell, C, 'Leading a life of its own? The roles of reasonable expectation in contract law' (2003) 23 OJLS 639 at 642.

119 Keay, A, 'A theoretical analysis of the director's duty to consider creditor interests: The progressive school's approach' (2004) 4 JCLS 307.

120 *Op. cit.* above fn 1, 'Agency' at 363.

121 *Ibid* at 368.

122 Spence, N, 'Personal liability for wrongful trading' (2004) 17 *Insolvency Intelligence* 11 at 11.

123 For instance, see Schulte, R, 'Enforcing wrongful trading as a standard of conduct for directors and a remedy for creditors: the special case of corporate insolvency' (1999) 20 Co Law 80. But see Mokal's comment: fn 1 above at 362.

which can attach substantial civil liability to a director, has the capability of having a strong deterrent effect.[124]

Achieving a balance

While the privilege of limited liability is well known and clearly enshrined in our law, there are occasions when this must in some way be the subject of interference. The law has to achieve a balance between the protection of bona fide creditors, on the one hand, and ensuring that directors (on behalf of their companies) are not totally discouraged from taking appropriate business risks, on the other hand.[125]

Judge Richard Posner asserts that specific doctrines of corporate law should not alter the balance of advantage between debtor and creditor,[126] yet, arguably, limited liability has altered the balance and, consequently, in some cases there is the need for a counterweight. Limited liability is still, in some ways, a privilege, notwithstanding the apparent demise of the concession theory,[127] and it must not be forgotten that it can work to the disadvantage of creditors.[128] It is, along with separate legal personality, 'easily manipulated and often is'.[129] The Cork Committee articulated similar thoughts (at [1805]) when proposing a wrongful trading provision (although its recommendation was subjected to significant change by the government of the day), as did Henry LJ in *Re Grayan Building Services Ltd (in liq)* [1995] Ch 241 at 255, stating that downright irresponsibility is discouraged and those able to avail themselves of protection under the limited liability concept, should be made personally liable when they abuse the concept.

Few people are arguing for the abolition of limited liability, but placing a responsibility on directors in times of a company's financial strife, would, at least, provide more of a balance between relevant interests.

Deepening insolvency

It is interesting to note that in the United States, which has no equivalent to wrongful trading, the courts have seen the need, in certain circumstances, to deter directors from prolonging the life of a company that is insolvent, by

---

124 *Op. cit.* fn 108 above at 41.
125 Schwarcz, S, 'Rethinking a corporation's obligations to creditors' (1996) 17 *Cardozo Law Review* 647 at 673.
126 *Op. cit.* above fn 46 at 505. The remit of the Company Law Review Steering Group when it was established in 1998, was to identify ways in which creation of wealth could occur but at the same as protecting the interests of others, such as creditors: *Company Law for a Competitive Economy*, Chapter 5.
127 Some still hold to the theory, but clearly the vast number of scholars do not accept it.
128 See Worthington, S, 'Shares and shareholders: property, power and entitlement' (2001) 22 Co Law 258 at 263 (Part 1).
129 *Op. cit.* fn 10 above at 422.

increasingly using the tort of deepening insolvency. The wrong involved here is the prolonging, improperly, of the life of an insolvent company so as to exacerbate the losses of creditors as the company becomes more insolvent (*Official Committee of Unsecured Creditors v R F Lafferty & Co* 267 F 3d 340 at 349 (2001); *Re Del-Met Corp* 322 BR 781 at 812 (2005) (TN).[130] It might be said that the courts have had to take this action to redress what they see as a void in the law.

Conclusion

This chapter has explored the theoretical arguments that have been mounted against the imposition of any wrongful trading-type liability on directors as well as considering the counter-arguments, and the points that might support such a liability. The arguments against wrongful trading can be summarised as follows: wrongful trading is unfair to directors, produces inefficiencies and potentially overcompensates creditors who could ably protect themselves without the need for regulation. Set against these are the arguments for the regulation which essentially involve producing a fair balance between the interests and rights of directors on the one hand and creditors, on the other, deterring irresponsible trading when companies are in financial straits and protecting creditors in certain circumstances. It has been submitted that while some aspects of the arguments that are opposed to wrongful trading have merit, overall they are not as compelling as those that support the continued existence of such a provision.

To be sure, arguments in favour of a proscription against wrongful trading should not be seen to be an argument in support of s 214 as it is drafted at the moment. The present provision is sadly lacking, as was mentioned in Part C. If there is to be a prohibition against wrongful trading, then the shortcomings that exist with s 214 must be remedied. Certainly, if we are to have a provision, then it must be as clear as possible so that directors know their responsibilities and liquidators can know when such proceedings might be worth bringing, given the fact that liquidators are risk-averse. Section 214 as it presently stands does not, arguably, 'fill the bill'. Clearly, if there is to be regulation, then it must be good regulation. At the moment the provision is frustrating, and Parliament needs to revisit the way that the provision is drafted. The provision is difficult to defend, but, as considered in this chapter, the concept has merit.

---

130 See, Heaton, J, 'Deepening insolvency', available on the Social Science Research Network at www.papers.ssrn.com/sol3/papers.cfm?abstract_id=622561; Ho, L C, 'On deepening insolvency and wrongful trading' (2005) 20 *Journal of International Banking Law* 426.

21 Directors' responsibilities and opting out

Introduction

For a number of years, and particularly over the past 15 or so years, there has been some reasonably hot debate in corporate law circles as to the kind of laws that should be applied to companies. Essentially there are two kinds. The first kind, mandatory laws, sometimes referred to as 'immutable rules',[1] are rules that cannot be varied by the parties; they are not subject to negotiation. The second kind are those which are usually known as 'enabling rules',[2] or default laws,[3] and are sometimes referred to as 'gap-filling', 'facilitative' 'standby', 'fallback' or 'backstop.'[4] This latter kind are rules that can be varied, permitting companies and others to modify or opt out of the application of those laws through contract.[5] Judge Frank Easterbrook and Professor Daniel Fischel even go so far as to describe the American corporate codes as enabling statutes.[6] It is notable that most discussions about opting out of rules in company law have been in relation to the shareholders of companies agreeing to the opting out of the application of fiduciary rules as far as directors are concerned. Of course, in this book we are concerned primarily with creditors.

---

1 Ayres, I, and Gertner, R, 'Filling gaps in incomplete contracts: an economic theory of default rules' 1989) 99 Yale L J 87 at 87.
2 Ramsay, I, 'Models of corporate regulation: the mandatory/enabling debate' in Rickett, C, and Grantham, R, *Corporate Personality in the 20th Century*, 1998, Oxford: Hart Publishing, p 221; Coffee, J, 'The mandatory/enabling balance in corporate law: an essay on the judicial role' (1989) 89 Colum L Rev 1618; Macey, J, 'Corporate law and corporate governance: a contractual perspective' (1993) 18 *Journal of Corporation Law* 185 at 186.
3 Eisenberg, M, 'The mandatory structure of corporation law' (1989) 89 Colum L Rev 1461; Coffee, *ibid*; *op. cit.* fn 1 above.
4 *Op. cit.* fn 1 above at 91.
5 See the discussion in Ramsay, *op. cit.* n 2 above; Coffee, *op. cit.* fn 2 above; Coffee, J, 'No exit? Opting out, the contractual theory of the corporation and the special case of remedies' (1988) 53 Brooklyn L Rev 919; Bebchuk, L, 'The debate on contractual freedom in corporate law' (1989) 89 Harv L R 1395; Gordon, J, 'The mandatory structure of corporate law' (1989) 89 Colum L Rev 1549.
6 'The corporate contract' (1989) 89 Colum L Rev 1416 at 1417.

This chapter seeks to answer the question: can the rules that provide for the responsibilities discussed in this book be seen as default rules from which parties can opt out? In other words: are these rules mandatory or enabling? The chapter concludes that the wrongful trading provision, the fraudulent trading provision and the duty to take into account creditors' interests are all mandatory. In each section of the Chapter, after assessing whether the rules are mandatory or not from a doctrinal perspective, I consider whether, from a normative perspective, the rules covering the responsibilities considered in this book should be mandatory, or whether there is a case for them being designated as default rules.

The most convenient way of dealing with this from an expositional perspective is, after providing a brief discussion of mandatory and enabling rules, to consider separately the three responsibilities that have been at the heart of the book. There will be some overlaps as common issues and principles will apply to all responsibilities discussed. I should add that I do not intend to discuss either the issue of mandatory and enabling rules in detail or many of the issues that are relevant to the concept of opting out, as that has been done ably by many scholarly pieces that are referred to throughout this chapter.

Mandatory and enabling (default) rules

Examples

There are many examples of mandatory rules in UK company law. One example, according to a recent case (*Exeter City AFC Ltd v Football Conference Ltd* [2004] BCC 498), is s 459 of the Companies Act 1985. The provision enables members of a company to petition for relief (under s 461) if the affairs of their company have been carried out in such a way that it is unfairly prejudicial to the interests of the members. What is interesting is that in *Exeter City* it was indicated specifically that the right under s 459 could not be removed by contract. Perhaps the classic example in UK company law of an enabling type of law is s 8(2) of the Companies Act 1985, which provides, in essence, that if a company does not modify or exclude the regulations of Table A in the Companies (Table A–F) Regulations 1985, they will automatically apply to the company.

Types of default and mandatory rule

Professors Ian Ayres and Robert Gerstner have stated that there are three sorts of default rule, namely penalty defaults, tailored defaults and strong defaults.[7] Penalty defaults involve forcing a party to disclose information that

---

7   *Op. cit.* fn 1 above.

he or she possesses to another party who does not. Tailored defaults seek to provide parties with that for which they would have contracted. Strong default rules are those that are difficult around which to contract, and they begin to appear to be like mandatory rules.

It has been asserted[8] that there are four kinds of mandatory rule, namely procedural, power-allocating, economic-transformative, and fiduciary standards-setting. The following are UK examples of these various kinds of rule: procedural – the requirement that a certain majority of votes be obtained before resolutions are passed at a general meeting of members; power-allocating – shareholder voting rights in the election of directors; economic-transformative – the company's dissolution; fiduciary standards-setting – the rule that directors are to act bona fide in the best interests of their company.

The issue: should rules be mandatory or enabling?

The essential issue in considering whether rules should be mandatory or enabling is: are those involved in and with companies in a better position than government to decide what should govern the relationships between a company and others? Regulation involves the use of a system where government endeavours to direct or encourage the subject to behave in a way that would not occur save for the making of a mandatory rule.[9] In contrast, the making of enabling rules presupposes that government envisages that those affected by certain rules should be permitted to adopt or disapply them by agreement with the participating parties, depending on the respective needs and positions of the parties.[10]

The debate that has developed centres on the issue of contractual freedom, with many contractarians calling for fewer, and some no, mandatory rules.[11] Compared with many corporate law statutes in the United States, such as the one applying in the State of Delaware, there is relatively little provision in UK company law for opting out.[12] While the issue of opting out has received the most attention in the United States, ironically it might be seen as more critical in the UK than the United States, because in the United States a company can, if it is disenchanted with the regulations of its home jurisdiction, choose to reincorporate in another state that might be seen as a 'friendly

---

8 *Op. cit.* Gordon, fn 5 above.
9 Ogus, A, *Regulation: Legal Form and Economic Theory*, 1994, Oxford: Clarendon Press, pp 1–2.
10 *Ibid.*
11 Although some contractarians such as Professor Lucian Bebchuk (*op. cit.* fn 5 above) and Dr Michael Whincop ('Taking the corporate contract more seriously: the economic cases against, and a transaction cost rationale for, the insolvent trading provisions' (1996) 5 *Griffith Law Review* 1) have supported the existence of a number of mandatory rules.
12 Essentially, the law across the UK is the same.

jurisdiction' (as Delaware is often perceived[13]). So, unless every state in the United States adopted the same rules it would be impossible to have a preponderance of mandatory provisions.[14] But UK companies cannot move to another jurisdiction if they wish to remain domiciled in the UK, because the law applies across the whole country. And although reincorporation in another European Union jurisdiction might be initially thought of as an option, especially given the greater efforts at corporate harmonisation in the EU, the fact of the matter is that other EU jurisdictions are perceived as providing more heavily regulated systems than that operating in the UK.

Why mandatory or enabling rules?

This issue has been subject to voluminous commentary and I only want to pick out the main points relevant to the Chapter's focus. The reason for the use of mandatory rules is often that the market is unable to protect the relevant parties, who are not able to bargain effectively,[15] because of a number of factors, including informational asymmetry, whereas in relation to enabling rules, the government adopts the view that the market is able to protect adequately. Probably there are other reasons besides acknowledgment that the market is unable to protect relevant parties adequately for laying down mandatory rules, such as the needs: to reduce risk; for reasons of fairness; to define boundaries; and to maintain equilibrium (for financial issues this means maintaining a stable commercial environment to enhance confidence).[16] Professor Jack Coffee[17] identifies three reasons for mandatory laws: people can only anticipate a certain number of contingencies;[18] 'the process of contracting about a long-term business relationship in which one party must place trust and confidence in another makes it difficult to explore the "downside" possibilities that such party will be defrauded'; and the process of opting out can impose costs on parties (externalities) that will affect others in society. Certainly all of these reasons for having mandatory rules have been considered in depth or in passing in one form or another in Chapters 19 and 20, and we will not consider them here, although in the rest of this chapter I will use them to evaluate whether mandatory rules should apply to

---

13 Delaware courts have been willing in recent times to uphold novel departures from prior law: Coffee, *op. cit.* fn 2 above at 1633.

14 A point made by Professor Roberta Romano in 'Answering the wrong question: the tenuous case for mandatory corporate laws' (1989) 89 Colum L Rev 1599 at 1599.

15 Coffee, *op. cit.* fn 2 above at 1618.

16 For a discussion of these other reasons, see Francis, J, *The Politics of Regulation: A Comparative Perspective*, 1993, Oxford: Clarendon Press.

17 Coffee, *op. cit.* fn 2 above at 1676–1678.

18 Professor Jeffrey Gordon makes a similar point when he says that an advantage of mandatory rules is that it reduces uncertainty: *op. cit.* fn 5 above at 1564–1565. This was discussed in Chapters 19 and 20.

the responsibilities under discussion and, consequently, whether opting out should be permitted?

The argument is often put, primarily by contractarians, that imposing mandatory laws increases transaction costs, and hence there is a diminution of efficiency, whereas the use of enabling rules can 'operate to reduce the transaction costs which would otherwise be incurred in continually negotiating new contracts.'[19] Other scholars and practitioners will argue that mandatory rules can actually reduce transaction costs provided that they encapsulate what the parties would always agree to include in the arrangement, for in imposing uniformity there is no need to obtain and study the company's memorandum and articles of association before contracting with the company,[20] and there is no need to engage in negotiating about the issues that are covered by regulation. The riposte to this latter point might be that it is not easy to apply mandatory rules to a wide range of cases because of the different preferences and aims of those involved in and with companies.[21] Of course, many will argue, taking the contractarian line, that parties should be given the freedom to devise the terms that will govern their transactions with others. Some will argue that a mix of mandatory and optional rules provides for a better commercial environment.[22] We saw in Chapter 19 that certain parties, such as particular kinds of creditors, are unable to protect themselves by contractual means, so mandatory rules are introduced to protect them, and this produces a fairer and more balanced state of affairs. Professor Ian Ramsay has submitted that there are four factors in determining the appropriate balance between mandatory and enabling rules. The three primary ones (that apply transnationally) are: the strength or bargaining power of the ones to be subjected to the rule; the view of the effectiveness of market forces in safeguarding the constituents' interests; and the expertise of the regulating body initiating the rule.[23]

The primary argument in providing enabling laws is that it allows the parties to make the bargain that they think is best for them. Overly relying on mandatory rules in formulating corporate law is seen by some as practising paternalism. In deciding to enact enabling laws the government or regulating body obviously has to consider what form the laws will take. One of the prime standards for determining what form a particular law should take is known as the hypothetical contracting standard. Under this approach the government or regulatory authority should ask what arrangement the parties would have agreed to if they were apprised of all the relevant information.[24]

We should note that it is not always easy to determine into which classification an existing law actually falls: mandatory or enabling. As Ramsay has pointed out, some enabling rules are so difficult to opt out of that they almost

19 Ramsay, *op. cit.* fn 2 above at 221.   20 *Op. cit.* fn 14 above at 1605.
21 Ramsay, *op. cit.* fn 2 above at 227.   22 Gordon, *op. cit.* fn 5 above at 1554.
23 *Op. cit.* fn 2 above at 229.   24 Bebchuk, *op. cit.* fn 5 above at 1410.

become mandatory in application.[25] Professor Bernard Black has argued[26] that other rules that appear to be mandatory are in fact trivial. He states that this might be because of the following: the rule ('market mimicking') would have been adopted by the parties in any event if they had considered it; the rule can be avoided; some rules may appear to be important in the short term, but in the long term they are susceptible to amendment by the courts or the legislature; they relate to circumstances that are very rare or can be adhered to at nominal cost.

Fraudulent trading

Generally speaking we can say that the government in enacting the first fraudulent trading provision in 1929 took the view that the market had failed to protect creditors, so regulation was needed. As far as the issue of criminal liability is concerned, under s 458 of the Companies Act, it is not possible for the company to agree with its creditors that there be an opt-out of this provision. Simply contracting out of penalty provisions is not possible. Any provision that involves criminal liability is concerned with protecting the public and is not concerned with providing for some civil relief for one or more private parties. The community is nominally affected when the directors of a company commit the offence of fraudulent trading and it will not be a liquidator acting on the part of the creditors who will be taking action, but the Crown on behalf of the community.

Prima facie, one might think that the situation with the civil right to proceed under s 213 could be the subject of opt-out. However, the provision also plays a public role, as was discussed in Chapter 6, in that the section is linked to directors' disqualification; under s 10(1) of the Company Directors' Disqualification Act 1986 a court is able to disqualify a director if he or she has been in breach of s 213. While proceedings under the Company Directors' Disqualification Act are not criminal, but rather are categorised as regulatory and civil in nature (*Re Westminster Property Management Ltd* [2000] 2 BCLC 396), the disqualification process is intended to protect the public from reckless and/or dishonest directors (*Re Lo-Line Electric Motors Ltd* [1988] Ch 577; *R v Evans* [2000] BCC 901; *Official Receiver v Wadge Rapps & Hunt* [2003] UKHL 49; [2004] 1 AC 158; [2003] 3 WLR 796, HL). As the issue of fraudulent trading is not purely a matter between the company, the directors and the creditors, it is doubtful whether opting out should be permissible.

If one were to apply the concept of hypothetical bargaining as some commentators do, then (and to adapt what Romano says in relation to the

---

25 Ramsay, *op. cit.* fn 2 above at 228.
26 'Is corporate law trivial? A political and economic analysis' (1990) 84 *Northwestern University Law Review* 542 at 544.

director's duty of loyalty[27]), eliminating the fraudulent trading prohibition is too incredible to be seriously considered, for what sane creditor would agree to license unscrupulous conduct like fraudulent trading? The average creditor would be highly suspicious of directors who wanted any agreement to include an opt-out of the fraudulent trading provision.

Wrongful trading

Directors might be keen to have a prospective creditor agree to an opt-out where they fear that a court might consider, at some later date, that they ought to have concluded that there was no reasonable prospect of the company avoiding going into insolvent liquidation. As with the advent of the first fraudulent trading provision, it could be said that the Government took the view, with its lead coming from the Cork Report, that the market (and the existing fraudulent trading provision) had failed to protect creditors, so regulation was needed. Like s 213, s 214 contains a public element. But, while the public element is similar to s 213, in that wrongful trading can constitute the grounds for a court making a disqualification order against directors, the fact is that the conduct that is regarded as fraudulent trading involves more morally reprehensible activity than that covered under s 214. This follows from the fact that fraudulent trading can constitute the basis for a criminal prosecution, while wrongful trading cannot. As argued in this book, wrongful trading does not involve blameworthy conduct, but something akin to negligence. Having said that, the public is concerned if directors are not acting responsibly.

Would s 309A of the Companies Act 1985 prohibit opting out?[28] This provision prevents contracting out in relation to a director's actions that constitute 'negligence, default, breach of duty or breach of trust'. While it has been asserted justifiably, it is respectfully submitted, with some support coming from Knox J in *Halls v David* [1989] 1 WLR 745 at 751, that s 214 provides a sanction in relation to a duty that exists, namely that they should not incur liabilities with no reasonable prospect of paying them,[29] it is contended that s 309A is designed to prevent the opting out of fiduciary responsibilities; opting out in relation to s 214 liability involves something that is different, namely something that is merely adversarial and a matter of contract.[30]

How does s 214 line up with the reasons, identified earlier, for having mandatory rules? Certainly the provision might be regarded as providing for

---

27 *Op. cit.* fn 14 above at 1601.
28 Section 309A will be replaced by cll 210 and 211 of the Company Law Reform Bill, but the effect is the same.
29 Oditah, F, 'Wrongful trading' [1990] LMCLQ 205 at 220.
30 Whincop, *op. cit.* fn 11 above at 19.

fairness. In Chapter 19 it was submitted that an obligation to take into account creditor interests is fair as it compensates for things like informational asymmetry, failure to meet legitimate expectations and the vulnerable position in which creditors often find themselves *ex ante*. The existence of s 214 might be thought to reduce risk as directors, if aware of the provision, will be encouraged to take more care in carrying on business if their company is in financial difficulty, lest they be found liable for wrongful trading at some later date. In the same way it might be thought that the provision will contribute to enhancing a stable commercial environment, as unreasonable risk-taking might be reduced. The provision defines boundaries in that it indicates to directors that if insolvent liquidation is unavoidable then they must take certain steps. Of course, it might be argued, with some degree of adroitness, that s 214 does not set the boundaries of conduct very precisely.[31]

Besides the fact that s 214 is a provision that has a distinct public element to it, as discussed above, it is also notable that the provision[32] is one that does not provide a remedy to individual creditors, but to all creditors as a group.[33] It gives a power to the liquidator in his or her capacity as liquidator, and not a power to creditors individually, to take action, so creditors cannot agree to the provision being made inapplicable.[34] All of the foregoing leads one to the conclusion that it would appear that as it stands at the moment, it is not possible to opt out of s 214. Accepting that fact, we must ask the normative question of whether opting out should be permitted?

While a mandatory rule against wrongful trading reduces transaction costs in that there can be no negotiation and contracting out in relation to the actions of directors, it does inhibit the parties from making whatever deal that they want to make. In effect it limits contractual power, and might, arguably, lead to an inefficient result. It might, however, be countered that even if the rule were an enabling rule there would be added cost if the parties wanted to opt out.

The benefit of regarding s 214 as a default rule is that it might encourage directors, in order to get a creditor to opt out, to disclose information that they would not ordinarily disclose. The creditor would then reassess the risk involved in extending credit. The danger for creditors is that the directors might fail to disclose all of the information that creditors might need to factor into the decision whether to give credit or not. This is something that might have to be the subject of court adjudication at a later date and particularly consideration as to whether the directors engaged in misrepresentation

---

31 See Chapter 10.

32 A provision that is clearly not trivial, given the definition of Black, B, *op. cit.* fn 15 above.

33 Mokal, R, *Corporate Insolvency: Theory and Application*, 2005, Oxford: Oxford University Press, p 270.

34 It has been asserted by Professor Jack Coffee (*op. cit.* fn 2 above at 1631) that the courts are probably more likely to uphold an opt-out arrangement when it relates to a common law rule, rather than one found in a statute.

or other misconduct. But if there is full disclosure, then the risk is priced accurately and the benefit for directors is that they are kept safe from any possible liability under s 214. Disclosure will mean that some transactions will not proceed, as creditors will pull out, but that is always going to happen sometimes in the course of doing business.[35]

If opt-out were allowed, then creditors might expect some benefit in a contract with the company for giving up any rights (indirect) under s 214, and if this occurred then it would cost the company something if the transaction were to proceed. The potential beneficiaries would be the directors, at the expense of the company. The only benefit for companies from an opt-out could be that their directors might be less risk-averse if their company suffered some financial difficulty, in that if the directors see a potentially lucrative, but risky, project they might be inclined to pursue it, knowing that they cannot be held liable for wrongful trading. Of course, directors would still have to be concerned that they were not breaching the fraudulent trading provisions. Another possible benefit of opt-out for the company might be that the directors, whom the company wishes to retain, will feel less vulnerable and might agree to put aside any ideas of leaving the company.

Of course, if an opt-out provision was allowed and the directors, in the course of negotiations with creditors, sought to favour opt-out, it might be seen as a signal to the creditors to be wary, and to consider whether the directors had a hidden agenda. Creditors might not be willing to trust directors. However, if the creditors were to be granted some benefit in exchange for permitting opt-out, then they might see it as worthwhile and cost-effective.

Perhaps the biggest hurdle for any opting out is the fact that under the provision as it now stands, the unanimous consent of all unsecured creditors to an opt-out would have to be obtained, because all are entitled to share in the proceeds from a wrongful trading action initiated by a liquidator. The transaction costs of obtaining such consent would be high,[36] even if it were practically possible. Dr Michael Whincop identified two major problems in relation to the Australian equivalent of wrongful trading. First, if unanimous consent is required, and the creditors know this, there is the possibility of individual creditors refusing to consent unless they are given some benefit. Second, it would not be easy to identify, at any one time, all of the creditors who need to agree to an opt-out.[37] As contracts are made a company could agree with each creditor to an opt-out, but the company might not be aware of some creditors, such as tort creditors, who, not being consensual creditors, have no opportunity to negotiate with the company. Also, the larger the

---

35 Whincop, *op. cit.* fn 11 above at 29.
36 Whincop, M, 'The economic and strategic structure of insolvent trading' in Ramsay, I M (ed), *Company Directors' Liability for Insolvent Trading*, 2000, Melbourne: Centre for Corporate Law and Securities Regulation and CCH Australia, p 66.
37 *Ibid.*

number of creditors, the more difficult it is to come to an arrangement that will bind all creditors.

The only possible way, practically speaking, that one could have an opt-out regime is if creditors were able to bring proceedings personally, and at present they cannot do so. Naturally, if creditors could do so, they could then decide to surrender their right to litigate. For creditors to be given the right to bring proceedings, in the first place, one has to deal with the argument that to do so would be tantamount to queue-jumping and would offend against the principle of *pari passu*. Of course, there is always the argument that *pari passu* has little bearing on the outcome of liquidated estates today in any event,[38] because of the large number of exceptions to the principle.[39] An allied point against opt-out is that s 214 supports the insolvency goal of collectivisation,[40] and permitting opt-out would inhibit that. Besides having normative benefits, collective action has a significant advantage when it comes to efficiency in that it 'reduces strategic costs, increases the pool of available assets and generates administrative efficiencies'.[41] If one were to permit individual creditor action then that is likely to increase costs. Also, s 214 would have to be amended so that courts are not empowered to order that directors make a contribution to the assets of the company, but are required to pay compensation to the creditor taking proceedings. One assumes that this would consist of the debt owed and any interest accrued. Having stated the problem of individual creditor action, it is worth noting that there are a number of points that favour creditor action over action taken on behalf of all creditors leading to equal sharing. First, not all creditors are equal. There are creditors like banks and other institutional creditors who are able to take adequate protective measures, and, arguably, should not benefit from a wrongful trading claim. Some creditors are able to build into the price for extending credit provision for the possibility of loss, others are not. Second, arguably not all creditors warrant protection from a wrongful trading provision. Some creditors have extended credit when they were fully aware that the company had a good chance of ending up in liquidation,[42] and it might be thought that they should not be entitled to compensation; they took a risk and have lost out.

It might be argued that there should be no opt-out allowed as that would attenuate the public function of s 214. That is, if wrongful trading is seen as a

---

38 See Mokal, R, 'Priority as pathology: the *pari passu* myth' [2001] CLJ 581.

39 See Keay, A, *McPherson's Law of Company Liquidation*, 2001, London: Sweet & Maxwell, pp 710–723.

40 Mokal, R, 'An agency cost analysis of the wrongful trading provisions: redistribution, perverse incentives and the creditors' bargain' (2000) 59 CLJ 335.

41 Dabner, J, 'Trading whilst insolvent – a case for individual creditor rights against directors' (1994) 17 UNSWLJ 546 at 569 and referring to Jackson, T, 'Bankruptcy, non-bankruptcy entitlements and creditors' bargain' (1982) 91 Yale LJ 857 at 860–868.

42 The Insolvency Law Review Committee's *Insolvency Law & Practice* (the 'Cork Report') Cmnd 8558, 1982, adverted to this, at para 1797.

trigger for the disqualification of directors, then it should not be possible for the creditors, acting in self-interest, to permit the directors to 'escape' the provision. A way around this problem, and discussed in Chapter 10, might be to grant the Secretary of State for Trade and Industry the power to bring s 214 proceedings in certain cases. But if that were implemented directors might be rather hesitant about entering into an opt-out arrangement, on the basis that while it might reduce the chance of litigation it would not rule it out totally. Furthermore, if any monetary award could be made on the application of the Secretary of State, and one was made, to whom would the money be paid (after the payment of liquidation expenses), if all of the creditors opted out of the wrongful trading provision? Any order might just have to be declaratory and able to form the basis for an application for a disqualification order.

It might be argued that if even if the rule were enabling, then it would be unlikely that there would be opt-out in most transactions involving vulnerable creditors, such as suppliers because, in most cases, the goods or services have to be supplied quickly. In relation to transactions where time is not so short, and negotiations can take place, the prospective creditor might well be in a stronger bargaining position and be able to consider a deal which included opt-out.

Duty to consider the interests of creditors

Opting out in relation to this issue is not complicated by the fact that there is the same public element to the responsibility as with fraudulent trading and wrongful trading. Although having said that, there is a community factor relating to the non-payment of creditors. In the short term the creditors of the company's creditors might not get paid, causing a ripple effect in the market. In the long term it might lead to an increase in the cost of credit for future debtors of the creditors who lost out. Therefore, there could be a reduction in social wealth. However, the principal concern of the duty is that creditors are safeguarded in situations where it is warranted, such as where a company is in financial difficulty. The issue here is whether parties should be entitled to opt out of principles laid down by the courts to achieve a number of aims. One aim clearly is the protection of creditors when the debtor company is in some form of financial difficulty. I think that it is fair to say that most law and economics scholars take the view that economic efficiency is not compatible with imposing a duty on directors in the way that the courts have. This issue has been discussed in detail in Chapter 19, and I came to the conclusion that the duty is justifiable.

While I have called for, in Chapters 13 and 14 in particular, greater precision to ensure both fairness for directors in knowing when they are subject to the duty and how they should act when subject to it, and guides for liquidators and administrators in knowing when they should hold directors responsible, I recognise that the rules are not so strict that a judge is not able to refrain from imposing the duty if he or she feels that it is appropriate, given both the law and the circumstances of each case. This is something that Coffee has noted should be the case,[43] and he has argued that in relation to the whole process of opt-out, the courts should be given the role of judging whether a particular opt-out is valid.[44] Coffee has submitted that given the principle of legislative supremacy, courts have been less constricted in upholding an opting-out provision where the rule is founded on the common law compared with a statutory rule.[45] So, prima facie, courts might be more prepared to allow opting out here, rather than in relation to wrongful trading.

But, the duty under discussion here, whether it is regarded as direct or indirect, is a duty that has been established by common law and equitable principles and involves directors acting bona fide in the best interests of the company.[46] It could be argued that opting out is prohibited by s 309A of the Companies Act 1985 as that provides that it is not possible to contract out of (*inter alia*) a breach of duty, and clearly failing to take into account the interests of creditors in certain circumstances is a breach of duty. Section 309A is protecting fiduciary rights from being contracted away, and the duty that we are talking about is a fiduciary duty. In this regard the mandatory element is set by the judiciary, for it has expanded the law on breach of duty to situations where creditors are hurt. So, it is concluded that there can be no opting out in relation to the duty.

From a normative perspective should there be room for opting out? Much of what was discussed in relation to wrongful trading is apposite. If we say that the duty is indirect, then many of the practical problems identified in the wrongful trading section of the Chapter are pertinent. At present any breach of the duty could, as with a wrongful trading claim, only be enforced by the liquidator (or an administrator) of the company as the duty is owed to the company. If the duty were owed to creditors directly the practical problem just mentioned would largely disappear, although it would create other problems, of the type discussed in Chapter 15.

Conclusion

This chapter has considered whether the responsibilities imposed on directors, and discussed in this book, could be the subject of an opt-out arrangement. It has concluded that under the present law there cannot be such an arrangement as the responsibilities are established by mandatory rules. The legislative provisions that apply to directors' conduct that constitutes fraudulent and wrongful trading are clearly mandatory, primarily

---

43 *Op. cit.* Coffee, fn 2 above at 1621.   44 *Op. cit.* Coffee, fn 5 above at 970–974.
45 *Op. cit.* Coffee, fn 2 above at 1631.
46 It is to be codified in the companies legislation if cl 156 of the Company Law Reform Bill (as introduced into the House of Commons) becomes law.

because of the public element that exists with these provisions. As far as the duty to take into account creditors' interests is concerned, while the responsibility is based on common law development, it has been concluded that it is a mandatory rule because of s 309A of the Companies Act 1985, which does not permit the opting out of a breach of duty. In any event, it was concluded that even if the rules regulating the responsibilities were not mandatory, there would be significant practical problems associated with opt-out. Even putting aside these practical problems, it might be argued that it would be difficult to permit opt-out in relation to these obligations as the right to take legal proceedings is given to the liquidator and not the creditors. If creditors were granted the right to bring proceedings, then opt-out is a possibility, although fraught with its own practical problems.

22 Conclusions and reflections

In this book we have focused on three major responsibilities that the law has visited upon directors: to avoid fraudulent trading; not to engage in wrongful trading; and to take into account the interests of creditors when their company is in financial difficulty. These three responsibilities are the ones which, of the many responsibilities that directors owe, directly or indirectly, to creditors, are the most subject to argument. Wrongful and fraudulent trading are more settled obligations when compared to the duty to creditors, in that they are the subject of statute, while the principles concerning the duty to creditors are evolving. While there are several issues that still need to be worked out by the courts in relation to the duty to creditors, there remain a number of issues in respect of both wrongful and fraudulent trading that are not clear. This book has discussed the main ones. The book has sought to try and clarify many of the unclear aspects of the law that covers the responsibilities owed to creditors, and discussed here, as well as offering suggestions for reform, particularly in relation to wrongful trading.

It has been argued in this book that the responsibilities of directors discussed here are justifiable from a normative perspective. In particular the view has been put that the market is not able to protect certain parties who are deserving of protection. However, it has been submitted that problems lie in the manner that s 214 has been drafted and the fact that many of the decisions delivered in relation to both s 213 and s 214 as well as in relation to directors' duty to creditors, do not provide clarity. The case law on s 213 has failed to clarify the meaning of intent to defraud and, until recently, a number of questions were left unanswered in relation to what 'knowingly' meant in s 213(2). As far as wrongful trading goes there is lack of precision concerning the meaning of parts of s 214, and in particular in terms of knowing what directors are to do in order to avoid wrongful trading. The duty to take into account the interests of creditors is solely based on common law and equitable principles and is not, unlike most of the law pertaining to directors' duties, subject to codification by the Company Law Reform Bill. The law in this area has not evolved in an orderly way and lacks precision in respect of several issues, principally the time when the duty arises and how directors are to fulfil the duty, or to put it another way: how do they avoid failing to take into account creditor interests?

The present law precipitates problems for directors on the one hand, and creditors, liquidators and administrators on the other. Directors, primarily in relation to wrongful trading and duty to creditors, are not provided with sufficient guidance as to what they should do and when they should do it. The most significant problems for liquidators and administrators lie in enforcing the obligations against directors. This latter concern led me to consider in the book whether it might be appropriate for the law to consider reforming the law so as to give creditors the right, along with shareholders, to be entitled to commence proceedings under s 459 of the Companies Act 1985 if they can establish that the affairs of the company have been carried on in an unfairly prejudicial way as far as the interests of creditors are concerned. I suggested that provided that provision was made requiring creditors to obtain leave before being able to proceed, as is the case in Canada, the idea had merit. I also considered whether creditors should, along with members, be given the right to apply for leave to take derivative proceedings against recalcitrant directors for breach of duty, and, again, felt that there was a case in favour of such a provision.

On the subject of the duty to take into account the interests of creditors, the book has considered whether the duty is one that is independently owed to the creditors or is one that is owed to the company, and the creditors benefit from it indirectly. It has been contended that the latter is consistent with the positive law. It has been concluded from a normative perspective that the duty to the company should include consideration of the interests of creditors when a company is in financial difficulties and that during this time, absent when the company is insolvent, the directors should seek to maximise the wealth of the corporate entity. When the company is insolvent the directors should run the company for the benefit of the creditors. It seems from what is contained in the Company Law Reform Bill that while the government felt that it was inappropriate to codify the responsibility of directors to their company's creditors in times of financial strife, it is going to permit the judiciary to develop this obligation of directors.

In relation to fraudulent trading, recent case law, such as *Bank of India v Morris* [2005] EWCA Civ 693; [2005] 2 BCLC 328; [2005] BPIR 1067, has taken the provision forward, and this, and the fact that courts have found directors and others liable, has probably given liquidators some hope. However, there are two issues that remain to be resolved before we can be too optimistic. First, many of the most recent s 213 cases have involved the liquidation of Bank of Commerce and Credit International and it remains to be seen whether liquidators in less high-profile liquidations will be so ready to initiate proceedings. Second, the courts must be consistent in defining the meaning of intent to defraud. In Chapter 5, I sought to synthesise the case law, and it is critical that courts in subsequent cases come to grips with some of the issues that have been raised in the judgments.

Wrongful trading started life with much promise, but arguably it has been little used and had little impact. This is due to a number of factors. I identified the problems with the provision and how it has been interpreted. I advocated certain changes to the provision. But I also submitted that it was preferable to undertake a radical overhaul of the provision. I advocated that directors should be liable if they failed to prevent the incurring of debts at a time when they knew that their company was insolvent or there were reasonable grounds for suspecting that the company was insolvent or would become insolvent as a consequence of incurring a debt or a reasonable person in a like position in the company in similar circumstances would have been aware, or ought to have been aware, of the company's financial position.

The final thing to say is that, with any principles and rules that regulate directors' obligations to creditors, there must be a balance. Directors must take their responsibilities seriously and, where their company is in potential financial danger, they must act prudently. However, it must be remembered that directors can only obtain so much information and advice and even if they do this, they might make wrong, but honest, decisions. Consequently, any obligations imposed on them must be realistic. In this book I have sought to do this. I believe, with respect, that Justice Michael Kirby, a judge of the Australian High Court, captured it well when he said, extrajudicially:

> [T]he need for effective checks upon, and appropriate standards for, company directors is obvious. The challenge before law-makers is to establish a regime which will provide these checks and uphold such standards without unduly reducing the capacity of the company and its officers to perform the economic functions for which the corporation was established.[1]

It is submitted that our law must do what his Honour suggests so that we achieve a fair balance.

---

1 An address to the Australian Institute of Company Directors, Tasmanian Division, 31 March 1998 and quoted in Pascoe, J, and Anderson, H, 'Personal recovery actions by creditors against company directors' (2002) 10 *Insolvency Law Journal* 205 at 228.

Index